THE INVENTION OF WORLD RELIGIONS

The Invention of World Religions

*Or, How European
Universalism
Was Preserved
in the Language
of Pluralism*

TOMOKO MASUZAWA

The University of Chicago Press
Chicago and London

The University of Chicago Press, Chicago 60637
The University of Chicago Press, Ltd., London
© 2005 by the University of Chicago
All rights reserved. Published 2005.
Printed in the United States of America

21 20 19 18 17 16 15 14 13 12   5 6 7 8 9

ISBN-13: 978-0-226-50988-4 (cloth)
ISBN-13: 978-0-226-50989-1 (paper)
ISBN-10: 0-226-50988-5 (cloth)
ISBN-10: 0-226-50989-3 (paper)

Library of Congress Cataloging-in-Publication Data

Masuzawa, Tomoko
    The invention of world religions, or, How European universalism
was preserved in the language of pluralism / Tomoko Masuzawa
        p.   cm.
    Includes bibliographical references and index.
    ISBN 0-226-50988-5 (hardcover: alk. paper)—ISBN: 0-226-50989-3
(pbk.: alk. paper)
        1. Religions.   2. Religion.   3. Europe—Religion—History.
4. Universalism.   I. Title: Invention of world religions.   II. Title:
How European universalism was preserved in the language of
pluralism.   III. Title.

BL80.3.M27   2005
200'.7'04—dc22

                                        2004021998

To the memory of Walter H. Capps (1934–1997)

Contents

Preface   ix

Introduction   1
   1 World Religions in the Academy Today   2
   2 The Discourse on Religion as a Discourse of Othering   14
   3 A Synoptic Overview   21
   4 Writing History in the Age of Theory:
     A Brief Discourse on Method   29

PART 1

Chapter 1   *"The Religions of the World" before "World Religions"*   37
   1 "World Religions" in the Age of World Wars   37
   2 Early Modern Taxonomy, or the Order of Nations   46
   3 Before the Birth of Science   64

Chapter 2   *The Legacy of Comparative Theology*   72
   1 Two Pioneers: Frederick Denison Maurice and
     James Freeman Clarke   75
   2 Strategies for Representation   79
   3 A Critic: Charles Hardwick   86
   4 The Variety of Parascientific Comparativism   95

PART 2

Chapter 3   *The Birth Trauma of World Religions*   107

Chapter 4   *Buddhism, a World Religion*   121
   1 Before Buddhism   122
   2 Europe Discovers Buddhism   125
   3 Buddhism and the Future of Europe   138

Chapter 5   *Philology and the Discovery of a Fissure in the European Past*   147
   1 The Discovery of the Indo-European Past   149
   2 The Birth of Comparative Grammar   156
   3 The Supremacy of Inflection   163
   4 The Essential Nature of the Semitic: Ernest Renan   171

Chapter 6 Islam, a Semitic Religion 179
          1 The Problem of Islam for Premodern and
             Early Modern Europe 180
          2 The Problem of Semitism and Aryanism for
             Nineteenth-Century Europe 186
          3 Islam, the Arab Religion: Abraham Kuenen 192
          4 Sufism, an Aryan Islam: Otto Pfleiderer 197

Chapter 7 Philologist Out of Season: F. Max Müller on
          the Classification of Language and Religion 207

          1 The Aristocracy of Book Religions 210
          2 On the Possibility of the Common Origin
             of Languages 221
          3 The Trouble with the Turanian 228
          4 The Real Trouble with the Turanian 234
          5 A Tale of Two Burnoufs 244

          PART 3

Chapter 8 Interregnum: Omnibus Guide for Looking toward
          the Twentieth Century 259

          1 Bequest of the Nineteenth Century: The Sacred
             Books of the East, 1879–1910 259
          2 The World's Parliament of Religions, 1893 265
          3 Amateur Interests Have Their Say:
             Private Foundations and Endowed Lectureships 274
          4 Colonial Self-Articulation 282
          5 Transitional Systems 291

Chapter 9 The Question of Hegemony: Ernst Troeltsch and
          the Reconstituted European Universalism 309

          Unconcluding Scientific Postscript 324

          Bibliography 329

          Index 351

Preface

A few steps around the corner from the Pantheon, in the heart of Rome, one comes upon a small square, typically crowded with parked cars during the day. At the center of Piazza Minerva stands a curious monument, a charming stone statue of a smiling elephant carrying an obelisk on its back, tilting its head to the side and playfully lifting its trunk, as if in greeting. As with all the pagan relics of conspicuous size erected in the city, the obelisk—not a very tall one by comparison—is crowned with a cross, and in this fashion the monument graces the approach to the church of Santa Maria Sopra Minerva, or as one local guidebook translates it, Our Lady on Top of Minerva. The church, indeed, was originally built in the eighth century on the ruins of a temple of Minerva, and the obelisk, which was discovered in 1665 in the garden of the Dominican monastery attached to the church, is said to have belonged to a temple of Isis that once stood nearby. The elephant, a somewhat diminutive creature with demure aspect, smaller ears, and stubby tusks, suggests that it could be of an Asian variety, and its ornate saddle reminds one of a royal howdah from India. To be sure, what the image of an elephant conveyed or what "India" meant to the contemporary observer when the monument was erected in 1667 could not have been quite the same as what such things signify to us today. Nor is it likely—given that this was nearly two centuries before Champollion deciphered the Egyptian hieroglyphics—that either the artist, Gian Lorenzo Bernini, or Pope Alexander VII, who commissioned the work, knew what the inscription on the obelisk had to relate, namely, certain exploits of Apries (known in the Hebrew Bible as Hophrah), a pharaoh in the sixth century BCE and an ally of Zedekiah, king of Judah, against Nebuchadnezzar. Today, all this intelligence is readily available to anyone who consults the Blue Guide, the vade mecum of post-Victorian British travelers, and still the tour book of choice for the learned. For this, we owe much to the scholars of the nineteenth century,[1] as well as to their contemporaries' sudden passion for travel and sightseeing,

---

1. The culmination of this scholarship may be observed in William S. Heckscher's learned article published in the mid-twentieth century, "Bernini's Elephant and Obelisk" (1947).

Gian Lorenzo Bernini and Ercole Ferrata,
Elephant Obelisk in Piazza della Minerva (1667).
S. Maria sopra Minerva, Rome, Italy.
Author's photograph.

a relative novelty among the middle classes that has since become a general habit. Today, the best view of the piazza can be obtained from the front rooms of the Grand Hotel Minerva, now owned and operated by an American concern, InterContinental Hotel Group, the parent company of Holiday Inn.

Not exactly a panorama of world cultures, the small Roman square thus turns out to be a miniature theater nonetheless, upon which the historically minded observer can find traces of high drama, of what might be billed as the struggle for modern European identity, or the making of the "West" —a complex negotiation straddling the past few centuries, involving all the typical processes: acquisitive incorporation of the ancient and venerable, the imprint of some unknown catastrophe, fragmentation, transference of objects and meaning, oblivion, erasure, and the partial, symptomatic recovery of what was once lost. Neither a mere anachronistic aggregation nor a parliamentary assembly of representative religions, this monument and its precinct together seem to symbolize an accomplishment of sorts, if only, in the end, to signal to the casual observer just who is on top.

This book concerns a particular aspect of the formation of modern European identity, a fairly recent history of how Europe came to self-consciousness: Europe as a harbinger of universal history, as a prototype of unity amid plurality.

The book finds its central question in the following historical fact. For many centuries Europeans had a well-established convention for categorizing the peoples of the world into four parts, rather unequal in size and uneven in specificity, namely, Christians, Jews, Mohammedans (as Muslims were commonly called then), and the rest. The last part, the rest, comprised those variously known as heathens, pagans, idolaters, or sometimes polytheists. This conventional ordering began to lose its ruling authority in the first half of the nineteenth century, and in the early decades of the twentieth, there suddenly appeared an entirely new system, namely, a list of roughly ten to a dozen "world religions"; the list was often accompanied by an indeterminate number of other, minor traditions. This new system of counting the religions of the world replaced the old hierarchy of nations—that is, "nations" in the archaic sense of the term, not yet construed as nation-states—and the new system has since turned into a convention, which is still regnant today. The list has not been significantly altered or seriously challenged in the past hundred years. This book is an investigation into what happened in the nineteenth century to produce this change.

Without a critical investigation, the change from the old four-part classification to today's world religions list might appear to be simply a matter of revision and refinement, that is, a matter of subdivision of the fourth category of the old system (the pagans/heathens/idolaters) into more specific, individual religions, hence a matter of more precise differentiation supposedly made possible by the increasingly more exact and accurate state of empirical knowledge. Such a speculative train of thought celebrating the achievements of modern knowledge may also give license to the presumption that the prevalence and stability of the world religions list today—and of the standard description of each religion—is but a consequence of better science. If there is a convention to list ten, eleven, twelve, or so world religions, may it not be simply because there really are just so many major religions in the world, together with numerous other minor traditions that may be roundly called "others"?

This study suggests that the actual historical process that resulted in the current epistemic regime was different from what this "just-so" story would lead us to believe. What went on in the course of reshuffling the old categories—seemingly a purely conceptual exercise—was in fact part of a much broader, fundamental transformation of European identity. In the last analysis, this transformation undoubtedly was reflecting a sea change in the European relation to the rest of the world, a change that had been under way for several centuries by then; but most immediately it was facilitated by an influential new science of comparative philology, an enterprise whose significance went far beyond the technical examination of language. With the discovery of language families or language groups—which was an empirical as well as speculative construction of the genealogical relation among the languages spoken by various peoples past and present—new possibilities opened for European scholars to reconstruct their ancestral roots, realigning their present more directly with pre-Christian antiquity. This new thought about a specifically European ancestry located its genealogical origin above all in the imagined glory—and allegedly "timeless" modernity—of ancient Greece, but also found a root of even greater antiquity, the hitherto unknown past of the so-called Proto-Indo-European progenitors.

One of the weightiest implications of this new mode of thought, initiated and supported by philological scholarship, was that among the entire spiritual and cultural legacy of Europe (reconstituted as "the West"), Christianity alone now appeared to be of Semitic origin, unlike all the other constituents, which were supposedly thoroughly Greco-Aryan. This suddenly rendered the traditional religion of Europe potentially at odds with the rest of its heritage—unless, of course, Christianity itself could be shown to be somehow more Hellenic than biblical. The idea of Aryan Christianity was apparently intriguing to many, so much so that there appeared a number of sensationally successful treatises in the latter half of the nineteenth century advocating that the true origin of Christianity, qua religion of Europe, should be sought not in the Hebrew Bible, but in some late Hellenic, possibly Indo-Persian, or even Buddhist traditions. This strong drive to hellenize and aryanize Christianity paralleled another tendency that originated around that time: to semitize Islam. Thenceforward, to the modern European eye, the religion of Mohammed was to be rigidly stereotyped as the religion of the Arabs, as an intolerant religion determined and constrained by the Arabs' national, ethnic, and racial particularities. This semitization of Islam came about in spite of a fact well known to the Europeans, namely, that the vast majority of the Muslims, then as now, were not Arabs. Notwithstanding the long-established internationality and multiculturality of this religion, then, Islam came to stand as the epitome of the racially and ethnically determined, nonuniversal religions.

Concurrently with the conundrum of the possibly "mixed" heritage of Europe, there arose another intriguing question hitherto unimaginable: whether monotheism—the doctrine of one universal god—should continue to be assumed as the basis of universality. Some writers seemed to suggest, at this historical juncture, that it was no longer the absolute authority of some irascible creator-judge deity ruling in the desert, but rather something more mellifluously philosophical and abstract, that genuinely embodied the principle of unity and universality. After all, was it not reason—that faculty fully realized for the first time, purportedly, by the Greeks—that allowed the ancients to discern the true unity of myriad phenomena amid the multiplicity and diversity of a marvelously prolific nature? And, as some of the nineteenth-century hellenizing enthusiasts went on to suggest, was it not this discernment that became the foundation of science, the best system of governance, and art—in effect, the bona fide universals of the True, the Good, and the Beautiful? In contrast, monotheism, which was increasingly portrayed as a Semitic tendency, came to represent exclusivity (rejection of multiplicity) rather than universality (orderly embrace of multitudinous totality). It is not surprising that the old alliance of Abrahamic monotheisms began to crack under the mounting pressure of these new thoughts, and out of the ruins of this old structure suddenly soared a new conception of Christian Europe—or of European modernity with or without

Christianity, as the case might be—and in this commotion the rest of the world was reshuffled and recast, eventually to settle into a new map.

It is a contention of this book that the thoughts animating these novel ideas were instrumental in the collapse of the old four-part ordering of nations, and also in the eventual consolidation of the new conceptual order, which on the surface appears as no more than a quiescent pluralism of "world religions."

The principal focus of this study is therefore what went on before, what led up to, the installation of the world religions discourse, rather than the moment of the birth of that discourse. This being the case, it might have been more literally accurate to entitle this book something like *Toward the Invention of World Religions*, or even *Behind the Invention of World Religions*, in order to signal some sense of anteriority. I should emphasize, in any event, that I do not claim to reveal in this work a conclusive explanation for the origination of the world religions list or of the customary characterization of each religion that accompanies this list. Rather, what I hope to bring to the foreground is a certain logic, or certain ideological persuasions that are covered over by and at the same time still operative in our present-day discourse, that is, in the now familiar, routinized strategy for mapping the world religiously. It will be suggested, in effect, that the new discourse of pluralism and diversity of religions, when it finally broke out into the open and became an established practice in the first half of the twentieth century, neither displaced nor disabled the logic of European hegemony—formerly couched in the language of the universality of Christianity—but, in a way, gave it a new lease.

This book is about European history, about how scholarly works of some prominent nineteenth-century savants and intellectuals exemplified the way Europeans reimagined themselves as "the West" and reconceptualized their relation to the rest. On the other hand, the reality of world religions today—that is, the stubborn facticity of these categories and the actual world that seems to conform to them in many ways—is obviously not of the European academy's making, no matter how decisive its role. Nor is it to be presumed that the role played by factors other than the European academy was always reactive. Accordingly, a comprehensive understanding of the formation, the foundation, and the function of the world religions discourse as a viable and compelling frame of reference for us today must take into account all of these factors. It goes without saying that such an overall accounting is a task far greater than any single volume could reasonably contain. In fact, such a holistic view—if there is to be one—would likely emerge only as an after-effect, that is, as an image conjured up by some efficacious assembling of so many particular, historically and regionally specific, comparative studies. Useful studies of the kind have already appeared, and others no doubt are under way. In the meantime, I write this book with a conviction that we would only be placing our understanding at risk if we were to remain imprecise in our knowledge of what went on in the European academy.

Introduction

Poor grammar, fuzzy semantics, or uncertain orthography can never stop a phrase from gaining currency if there is enough practical demand for it in the spirit of the times. In our times, the term "world religions" testifies to this general truth. This imperfectly wrought, decidedly ambiguous phrase—sometimes hyphenated, most often not, sometimes as a possessive ("world's religions"), other times not—is as commonplace as any subject heading in the usual docket of things to be learned in school. College students with no previous instruction on the subject seem to understand what it is when they decide to enroll in a course by that name. Any bookstore clerk can direct the customer to the appropriate shelves when inquired about a title in that category. Everybody, in effect, seems to know what "world religions" means, more or less, that is to say, generally, vaguely.

What this familiarity belies, however, is a rather monumental assumption that is as pervasive as it is unexamined, namely, that religion is a universal, or at least ubiquitous, phenomenon to be found anywhere in the world at any time in history, albeit in a wide variety of forms and with different degrees of prevalence and importance. We seem to imagine ourselves living in a world mapped—though not very neatly—in terms of so many varieties of religion, which sometimes overlap, converge, and syncretize and often conflict with one another. It is presumed, moreover, that religion is one of the most significant— possibly the most significant—factor characterizing each individual society, and that this is particularly true in "premodern" or otherwise non-Western societies. Broadly speaking, the more "traditional" the society, the greater the role religion plays within it—or so we presume, regardless of how much or how little we happen to know about the society in question or about its supposed tradition.

To be sure, these are mostly precritical, unreflected assumptions on the order of street-corner opinions, but when it comes to the subject of religion, it appears that the scholarly world is situated hardly above street level. In the social sciences and humanities alike, "religion" as a category has been left largely unhistoricized, essentialized, and tacitly presumed immune or inherently resistant to critical analysis. The reasons for this failing on the part of the academy, this general lack of analytic interest, and the obstinate opacity of the subject of religion, are no doubt many and complex. But the complexity may begin to yield to critical pressure if we are to subject this discursive formation as a whole to a different kind of scrutiny, a sustained and somewhat sinuous historical analysis.

The central focus of the present study is the period in which the protean notion of "religion"—which had not been, until the eighteenth century, a particularly serviceable idea, at least for the purposes we employ it today—came to acquire the kind of overwhelming sense of objective reality, concrete facticity, and utter self-evidence that now holds us in its sway. As a result of this development, it has come to seem to us entirely gratuitous, if not to say quixotic, to challenge the reality of religion or to question those familiar truisms that are freely circulated about this reality.

1. World Religions in the Academy Today

A casual glance at numerous textbooks designed for classroom use today readily testifies to the following general consensus. "World religions," or major religions of the world, almost invariably include Christianity, Buddhism, Islam, Hinduism, and Judaism, and also typically count among their number Confucianism, Taoism, and Shinto (though these may be variously grouped together or conflated as Chinese, Japanese, or East Asian religions). Somewhat less typically but still very frequently included are Zoroastrianism (Parsee or Parsiism), Jainism, and Sikhism.[1]

These so-called great religions of the world—though what makes them "great" remains unclear—are often arranged by means of one or the other of various systems of classification, with binary, tripartite, or even more multifarious divisions. What these systems do, regardless of the variation, is to distinguish the West from the rest, even though the distinction is usually effected in more complicated ways than the still frequently used, easy language of "East

---

1. Very broadly speaking, if we compare the more recent versions of world religions books with the older versions in the early decades of the twentieth century, it appears that Sikhism is nowadays more frequently included, whereas Taoism and Confucianism are occasionally included, Shinto and Jainism less frequently itemized and treated on their own, and Zoroastrianism, even less. The addition of Baha'i is not uncommon. With regard to the inclusion of various tribal-scale religions (African, Native American, etc.), see below.

and West" suggests.[2] The demarcation, in any event, is articulated from the point of view of the European West, which is in all known cases historically aligned or conflated, though not without some ambiguity, with Christendom. These inherently asymmetrical, unilaterally conceived systems of classification exude a pretense of symmetry that appears to balance "East" and "West."[3] This binary may be put in terms of biblical religions versus all others, or in another classic version, prophetic religions versus wisdom religions.[4] The tripartite system, on the other hand, at first glance appears to correspond to certain geographical locations. Under this system, each of the above named great religions of the world falls into one of the three categories, depending on the location of its origin: those originating in the ancient Near East (Judaism, Christianity, Islam), in South Asia (Hinduism, Buddhism, Zoroastrianism, Jainism), or in the Far East (Confucianism, Taoism, Shinto). This system has been closely associated with, and given its justification by, a racialized notion of ethnic difference. The three locations correspond to what the nineteenth-century science of comparative philology came to identify as three distinct groups of languages: Semitic (or Hamito-Semitic), Aryan (or Indo-European), and Turanian (roughly, Oriental). This originally philological and later racial demarcation complicates the constitution of the West, while the rest of the world seems to turn into an ever-receding region of the premodern lurking at the edge of the world historical stage.

In addition to these sets of great "Western" and "Eastern" religions, many world religions texts, some dating back to the early twentieth century, mention yet another category of religions that are perhaps not so great, or what are sometimes termed "little traditions," which tend to go by certain generic, lower-case names (such as shamanism and animism), often with a particular

2. As we shall see, the tripartite demarcation was more often favored by those writers who were informed by philology, with a result that the West-and-rest distinction was palpably more complicated. Yet even those expert taxonomists at times freely availed themselves of the language of the East and West binary, despite the apparent incongruity.

3. By explicitly rendering the foundational dichotomy as "the West and the rest," Johannes Fabian, in his *Time and Other* (1983), exposes the inherent asymmetry and unilateralism of the construction of the West's relation to the non-West.

4. See categories in R. C. Zaehner, ed., *The Concise Encyclopedia of Living Faiths* (1959). In this binary scheme of things, the position of Islam (and sometimes Zoroastrianism) has been somewhat ambiguous. Nonetheless, the differential logic itself, which allows the demarcation of the Western domain from the rest, has proven remarkably persistent and impervious to any complication by factual details.

place marker attached (e.g., Native American, Siberian, Aboriginal Australian). This category in its entirety used to be uniformly called "primitive religions" in the earlier days, but more recently it has been variously termed "primal," "pre-literate," "tribal," or even "basic religions."[5] The restless shifting of appellations may be a measure of the discomfort felt by contemporary scholars of religion in their effort not to appear condescending to those peoples who used to be referred to as savages.

Despite these incessant circumlocutions and the fine nuancing of the classificatory systems, there seems to be some underlying logic silently at work in all variations, and the intent of differentiation probably has not changed appreciably. At its simplest and most transparent, this logic implies that the great civilizations of the past and present divide into two: venerable East on the one hand and progressive West on the other. They both have been called "historical," but implicitly in different senses. In a word, the East preserves history, the West creates history. In contradistinction from both East and West, the tertiary group of minor religions has been considered lacking in history, or at least lacking in written history, hence its designation as preliterate. A corollary assumption is that the peoples of small-scale tribal societies may likely possess an unusually tenacious historical memory, but no historical consciousness.[6] On the strength of this assumption, these societies are relegated to a position in some sense before history or at the very beginning of history, hence, primal. This loose but deep association of the primitive and the prehistoric further complicates the tertiary category. The ancient and extinct traditions are conflated with the contemporary savage or tribal traditions, often treated at the outset under a single rubric signifying "beginning," "incipient," or "elemen-

---

5. "Basic religions" is a designation employed by Lewis M. Hopfe in *Religions of the World* (1976). He subdivides the category into "Native American religions" and "African religions." Throughout the many revised editions of his work over the course of two decades or more, this category, its designation, and its subdivisions have remained constant. The latest edition, the seventh, was posthumously revised and edited by Mark R. Woodward and published in 1998.

6. It is often assumed—most famously by Mircea Eliade—that it is only by relinquishing the traditional kind of sheer memory (active re-presencing of significant past moments) that a people enter the domain of history proper. More specifically, in *Zakhor: Jewish History, Jewish Memory* (1982), Yosef Hayim Yerushalmi narrates the advent of Jewish historiography in the nineteenth century as taking place in the wake of the collapse of the traditional Jewish religious imperative to remember. The ideological tow of this privileging of "historical consciousness" will be discussed in chapter 9.

tary"; or else they are discussed in tandem, in any case separately from the great religions of the East and the West.[7]

With these foundational categories more or less assumed in the table of contents, a typical world religions textbook opens to an actual map of the world showing an oddly irregular, often illegible, and frankly uninterpretable picture of the distribution of these religions, sometimes accompanied by a list of figures indicating the respective size of the "adherents" or "believers" that each religion supposedly claims. As a rule, both the map and the list admit to situations of "significant overlap," that is, the situations of coexistence or intermixture of traditions that are in principle—so it is implied—distinct. This overlap inevitably compromises the clarity of representation considerably and, despite the palpable intentions of the mapmakers, no comprehensive view-at-a-glance of the religious condition of the world is to be obtained from such graphics. In this respect, East Asia traditionally, and North America increasingly, present especially challenging situations for visual representation.[8] These are regions known for a greater degree of coexistence, admixture, and even syncretism.

---

7. We can observe the transmutation and repeated reappellation of the category in the case of some texts that have gone through multiple revised editions. A particularly instructive case is Ninian Smart's *The Religious Experience of Mankind*. The first edition of 1969 contains a chapter, early in the book, entitled "Primitive Religions," which is divided into a section on "prehistoric religions" and "primitive religions." In the third edition published in 1984, the content of the original chapter was greatly expanded and came to constitute three separate chapters, respectively entitled: "Primal Religions," "Religions of Africa," and "Religions of the Americas and the Pacific." In the fifth edition of 1996, the title of the volume was modified and now reads, *The Religious Experience*, and the erstwhile chapter on "primitive" or "primal" religions was renamed "Small-Scale Religions," which contains the following sections: "The Small-Scale World," "Mana," "The Australian Aboriginal Experience," "The High God," "Tabu," "Totemism," "Ancestor Veneration," "Shamans," "Patterns of Myth," "Prehistoric Beliefs," and "Theories about the Genesis of Religion."

Two years before the third edition, Smart also published an anthology, *Sacred Texts of the World* (1982), with Richard D. Hecht. Its first chapter is entitled "The Powerful Dead," by which is meant, the editors explain, "a representative selection of religious documents from the great urban civilizations of ancient Egypt, Mesopotamia, Greece and Rome, and the Maya and Aztec of Mesoamerica" (1). The chapter also includes texts representing Zoroastrianism. After ten chapters representing the usual list of world religions from Judaism to Sikhism, we encounter a chapter called "Small-Scale Traditional Religions," by which is meant those religions that are "usually described as 'primitive' religions or the religions of 'non-literate' peoples" (337).

8. This fact may in part account for the recent appearance of books and projects on "world religions in America." See, for example, Jacob Neusner, ed., *World Religions in America* (2000),

Yet the difficulty of representation may be more than a matter of mixed population or multiple affiliations. For, in some localities, being religious—or, to
put it more concretely, practicing or engaging in what has been deemed "religious"—may be related to the question of personal and group identity in a way
altogether different from the one usually assumed (i.e., assumed on the basis
of the western European denominational history of recent centuries). In some
cases, for that matter, religion and identity may not relate at all.

For the moment, then, let us note that a map of this sort, with a demographic
chart and a table of contents that name a dozen or so "major religions of the
world," sets the stage and determines the outlook of "world religions." Such
maps, tables, and lists lend immediate facticity to the subject matter through
sheer repetition and proliferation, and thus implicitly endorse as empirical and
true what is in reality a particular way of conceptualizing the world, or, one
might say, an idiosyncratic system of demarcating certain supposed contents
of the world.

Here, then, lies a question as obvious as it is seldom asked: Whence comes
this geospatial mapping of the world in religions? At its advent, did the classificatory system of world religions replace another framework for representing
the relation between Christianity and all other known forms of religious belief
and practice? What is the logic of "world religions" that has become so prevalent, so naturalized in our discourse that it seems as though it were no logic, no
ideology at all, but a mere reflection of the way things are?

One might expect scholars of religion to have done more to guide and direct our
critical attention to these pervasive assumptions about religion and religions,
but in fact, this is hardly the case.[9] There may be more than one reason for this

Diana Eck, *A New Religious America* (2001), and Eck's CD-ROM with the Pluralism Project of
Harvard University, *On Common Ground* (2000). Also the collection of essays on religious pluralism in the city of Atlanta edited by Gary Laderman, *Religions of Atlanta* (1996).

9. Lately, there have been exceptions to this state of inattention, but they are exceptions that
highlight the overwhelming obtuseness of the subject matter all the more. The most long-
standing and celebrated of all such critical endeavors is Jonathan Z. Smith's scholarly production, now spanning four decades, beginning with the influential collections of essays *Map Is Not
Territory* (1978) and *Imagining Religion* (1982), and more recently "A Matter of Class" (1996) and
"Religion, Religions, Religious" (1998). Also long-standing is Michel Despland's study, from
his early work, *La Religion en Occident* (1979), and continuing to his most recent monograph,
L'Émergence des sciences de la religion (1999). In addition, Talal Asad, *Genealogies of Religion* (1993),
Bruce Lincoln, *Theorizing Myth* (1999), Russell McCutcheon, *Manufacturing Religion* (1997), and

general inattention. To begin, as some adamantly secularist scholars—who constitute a sizeable and vocal minority in the field—have observed with some displeasure, there is a higher concentration of unreconstituted religious essentialists in this department of knowledge than anywhere else in the academy.[10] This should not come as a surprise, it is often said, given that the field is populated, and by sheer number dominated, by the representatives, partisans, and sympathizers of various religions or, more recently, by those who may be best described as advocates and sympathizers of "religion" in general. For many of these religion-friendly scholars and teachers, the line between asserting the reality of religion(s) and asserting the legitimacy of religion(s) as a proper subject for study is at best ambiguous. Understandably, those who stand on the side of religion(s), in whatever sense of that phrase, are not likely to feel an immediate need to interrogate the category that names, for them, a reality sui generis. Second, even for those academicians who are generally wary of such naive or ambiguous religious essentialism, it appears that certain institutional circumstances of "religious studies" impart some disincentive to proceeding with critical reflection. The institutional situation of this department of knowledge may be roughly described as follows.

Daniel Dubuisson, The Western Construction of Religion (2003), variously address this matter. Especially valuable for their historically specific investigations are Peter Harrison, "Religion" and the Religions in the English Enlightenment (1990), and David Chidester, Savage Systems (1996). With regard to the history of the study of religion more generally, J. Jacques Waardenburg's two-volume publication—one volume an annotated anthology and the other a comprehensive bibliography—entitled Classical Approaches to the Study of Religion (1973–74) made available a bird's-eye-view of the science of religion in the early period. See also a recent important monograph by Hans G. Kippenberg, Discovering Religious History in the Modern Age (1997).

10. One of the most conspicuous assemblies of such a minority may be the North American Association for the Study of Religion (NAASR), a member organization of the International Association for the History of Religions (IAHR), and also affiliate of the American Academy of Religion (AAR) and of the Society for the Scientific Study of Religion (SSSR). NAASR began as a gathering of scholars generally disaffected by what they perceived as unduly religious (as opposed to scientific) and essentialist tenor of the AAR membership (this latter being by far the largest association of religion scholars in the world). Some representative members of NAASR have been advocates for secular and naturalistic explanations of religion (especially in the model of cognitive science), but more recently it has also become a forum for younger generations of scholars variously interested in critically examining the discursive practice about "religion," including the scholarly discourse of Religionswissenschaft. This interest is also represented by some subgroups within the AAR—most obviously the Critical Theory and Discourses on Religion Group—and also by the Ideological Criticism Section of the Society for Biblical Literature (SBL), another important professional organization.

"World religions" has become a standard designation for an introductory survey course commonly found in the religious studies curricula of many North American and British universities, colleges, and, increasingly, secondary schools.[11] As a rule, world religions courses in American institutions of higher education—especially in the institutions where the teaching faculty of religious studies consists of a significant number of research scholars who represent a variety of geographical areas—have been taught by those members of the faculty whose area of specialty is described as "history of religions," which in turn has been a virtual code word for any specialty other than Christianity or Judaism.[12] Today's historian of religions is therefore typically a scholar in an Asian or some other non-Western religion, and he or she seems inclined to take this teaching assignment in stride, taking the state of affairs more as a matter of convention and practical necessity than as a matter of principle.[13] These non-Western specialists turned teachers of "world religions" not infrequently complain that such a comprehensive treatment of the subject in one course, or

11. The concept of "world religions" may be represented in a single course, usually of that name, or by a series of introductory or midlevel courses designed to acquaint students with what are deemed as major (and sometimes including minor) religions of the world, often grouped together regionally or semi-chronologically, such as "American religious history," "Buddhist traditions," "Biblical religions," etc.

We find in the United Kingdom the most systematic and long-standing effort to date of implementing "world religions" in secondary and primary school curricula. See, for instance, various publications by the Shap Working Party on World Religions in Education (c/o the National Society's Racial Equality Centre, London). It is noteworthy that the enterprise of this educational charity organization (registered address at the Chichester Institute of Higher Education) has been supported by the Commission for Racial Equality (commission set up by the Race Relation Act of 1976, reporting to the home secretary).

12. This is supposedly more a matter of convention than principle. In categorizing the specialties for job advertisements, for example, no one in the profession would mistake this designation. There are, however, notable scholars, such as Jonathan Z. Smith, who would be described as historians of religion for a very good reason, but whose specialty does not fit this stereotype.

13. It is a presumption among many in the field of religious studies that, in comparison to specialists in Judaism or Christianity, specialists in any of the so-called non-Western religions are better equipped or at least better disposed to handle other non-Western religions as well. The unspoken but obvious assumption here is that scholars of religion are Western, which means, in the language of this same ideology, either Christian or Jew by birth and upbringing. Therefore, specialists in Christianity or Judaism study their own religion, in contrast with non-Western specialists, who in effect must be cognizant of at least two religions, one of their own, and the other of their specialty. This further belies another unspoken and unexamined assumption that

even two courses, is impossibly ambitious or inexcusably simplistic, as it is bound to be too broad a survey, too flattening an analysis. It would be an unmanageable survey indeed, unless, perhaps, one begins with the scholastically untenable assumption that all religions are everywhere the same in essence, divergent and particular only in their ethnic, national, or racial expressions. Of course, this is an assumption alarmingly prevalent among the world religions books now available on the market. And it cannot be denied that this well-meaning yet uncritical assumption is what brings a large number of people into our classrooms year after year.

Today, colleges and universities in the United States, be they private or public, are inclined to regard themselves as at bottom business enterprises; they admit to being institutions that are market driven in some fundamental way. Transcribed at the level of curricular units—that is, departments and programs with their own budget allocation—market driven means first and foremost enrollment driven. This is particularly true in the humanities and many social science departments, where the percentage of outside funding in relation to the total operational cost of the unit is much smaller than most natural science departments and professional schools. Units that do not generate sufficient total student enrollment numbers in their courses in proportion to the number of faculty positions are liable to be marked as not carrying their weight and, by implication, as less fiscally responsible. In the unapologetic free market and entrepreneurial climate pervading universities and colleges in the nation, it is clear that the consistently large enrollment figure in world religions courses— as well as in derivative courses, such as courses in "Asian religions," "biblical traditions," and "religious diversity in America," to name a few—has been the single most powerful argument and justification for maintaining the steady budget line and faculty positions in the religious studies departments and programs.

Given this institutional reality, the absence of any systematic critical investigation into the discursive formation of "world religions" seems at once predictable and inexcusable. At the outset of the present investigation therefore lies this basic recognition: if a scholar of religion, of whatever kind and of what-

---

non-Western specialists are automatically *comparativists*, since they already have the "knowledge" of two religions. In recent years, as more people who are neither Christian nor Jew have come to populate the scholarly field, the new condition presents challenges to these assumptions, but the profession at large apparently has yet to be adjusted accordingly.

ever persuasion, is in fact making a living in this lately prominent domain of world religions discourse and capitalizing on its impressive market value, one cannot assume that this line of work is intellectually responsible just because it is economically viable. The present study is a proverbial small step in the direction of a critical investigation.

The principal motive force of the study, however, is neither moral outrage against professional mendacity nor an impulse to set the institutional history of the study of religion aright. Nor do I imagine myself, at the conclusion of this book, to be in the position to advocate a particular programmatic scheme or a change of course in the way the study of religion is to be done. To be sure, it is always more difficult to name what one's objective is than to make a list of what it is not. While I acknowledge the truth of this generally, with regard to the present study more specifically, it may be marginally clarifying to note that I have been always more inquisitive about the marvelously loquacious discourse on religions—which, to my mind, is one of the most curious and conspicuous features of Western modernity—than about what this modern Western discourse insists on calling "religion itself." I have hitherto made this discourse the primary object of my research. But if, accordingly, my own aims and strategies here seem rather deviant from the usual scholarly mission of the study of religion, I certainly cannot claim that this line of investigation is anything unique, let alone original. For, in recent decades, discourse analysis has become a regular component of any discipline in the human sciences, and the field awkwardly known as religious studies is no exception in this regard.[14]

Today, we understand the term "world religions" to be more or less equivalent to "religions of the world," which is to say major religions, that is, those conspicuous-enough religions distinctly and properly identified as now existing in the world. But the history of its usage in this general sense, in any typographic variation—"world religions," "world-religions," or "world's religions"—is vexingly obscure. It is not immediately obvious when the term came into use, or in what sense. If one looks into instances of what appears to be early use of

14. In a sense, I am taking rather literally the programmatic statement famously issued by Jonathan Z. Smith—though possibly with somewhat different motives and errant consequences than originally intended—at the beginning of the introduction to his *Imagining Religion*. In any event I am by no means the first one to follow the lead. For further discussion on the topic, see Masuzawa, "The Production of 'Religion' and the Task of the Scholar" (2000).

the term roughly consistent with our contemporary meaning, which seems to have occurred in the early decades of the twentieth century, there is nothing to suggest that the phrase was patently new or expected to be unfamiliar to the reader. Rather, "world religions" makes its appearance without ceremony, without explanation, and seemingly without a history. Typically, in those early texts purporting to treat all the major forms of religion to be found in the world, the author either has no use for the term or else takes it completely for granted. In either case, no one bothers to index the term, let alone define it.

The situation may suggest that the history of the idea of world religions as we understand it today, on the one hand, and the history of the term itself, on the other, have had separate lines of descent. To be sure, there is nothing to warrant an outright presumption that the relevant history of the term/concept is conveniently separable into two such neat halves, the halves that in due course came to meet and intertwine. The actual history in fact seems to be considerably more disorderly, confluent, and multifarious. This more complicated history explains the particular mode of presentation employed in this book, namely, why the investigation does not proceed in an orderly chronological fashion. In short, after preliminary research into the matter, it seemed to me plausible that the discursive formation of "world religions" has been a rhizomatic growth. According to this hypothesis, much of the logic of this discourse had already taken shape underground before its appearance. Owing to the complex, highly charged prehistory, moreover, once above ground, the discourse of world religions continued to be sustained and ruled by an occult network of significance not immediately transparent. Or, to resort to another metaphor, if this discourse can be said to have developed at all, it does not seem to have been in the manner of an organic growth like the development of an oak tree from an acorn, but rather more like that other type of development that occurs in the processing lab, in which a photographic image finally appears.

All this is to suggest that the genealogy of the world religions discourse is not amenable to a linear, developmental, cumulative, or incremental narration. The relatively sudden appearance of the phrase "world religions" in its familiar sense indicates that this was an outbreak of sorts, not a gradual culmination or fruition. The advent of the discourse on world religions therefore may be finally described in analogy with the onset of a certain serious illness, an illness that is deeply systemic and already metastasized at the time of its first full manifestation. The outbreak of the discourse—that is, the actual appearance of the phrase, which brought forth a sense of utter familiarity and self-evidence—effectively marked the moment when all of its "prehistory" was suddenly overwhelmed, covered over in an avalanche of a new reality and thenceforth rendered unrecognizable.

If our time, that is, the era beginning in the early decades of the twentieth century, has been preponderantly characterized by the discourse of world religions and the concomitant ideology of religious pluralism, in the nineteenth century a rather different paradigm was at work. The eighteenth- and nineteenth-century discourse on religion is reputedly dominated by an array of abstract speculative theories about the origin of religion and the subsequent stages of its development. By common accord, scholars today opine that these bygone theories of religious evolution were concocted largely on the basis of the unwarranted assumption of European hegemony, that is, on the basis of a monolithic universalist notion of history as a singular civilizing process, of which modern Europe was the triumphant vanguard and all other civilizations and non-European societies merely markers of various interim phases already surpassed by the people of European descent. It may be reasonably suggested that it was the European interest in the future of religion—or the future beyond religion, as the case may be—that motivated much of the nineteenth-century search for the origin of religion and, by the same token, the search for the most primitive forms of religion, which were presumed to be equivalent, more or less, to the ones observable in the lives of contemporary savages, lives on the brink of disappearance.

The narrative of world historical development, as envisioned by the eighteenth- and nineteenth-century European writers, may be simply linear, that is, the story of a gradual but steady progress from the lowest, the crudest, and the most primitive to the highest, the finest, and the most complex. Or it could be lapsarian/redemptive, starting with a state of primordial innocence, then a fall into corruption and degeneration, followed by a precarious process of recovery and maturation, eventually culminating in the fulfillment of providential destiny. If we survey comparatively Hume's *Natural History of Religion* (1756), Lessing's *Education of the Human Race* (1780), Hegel's oddly majestic *Philosophy of History* (1830–31), as well as works by Auguste Comte, Herbert Spencer, E. B. Tylor, James Frazer, and numerous other accounts of the nineteenth century, it is evident that their developmental schemata forecast the impending moment of apotheosis in varying ways. One version of the account projects rational Protestant Christianity transcending its own historically particular origins, its own cultural limitations and finitude; consequently, triumphant modern Christianity will become something else altogether than "mere" religion. Or, alternatively, a new, transcultural, objective world consciousness of science will override and vanquish the magical, religious, and metaphysical world-views hitherto dogmatically upheld by hidebound traditions; consequently, religion—and certainly any particular religion—will be obsolete and irrelevant. In either scenario, the universal principle that guarantees the unity of the world, or the world as totality, ultimately comes to prevail as a direct extension of European Christianity, or Europe as (erstwhile) Christendom. The question for us, then, amounts to this: What happened to this providential forecast and its robust universalism when the new discourse of world religions and its official doctrine of pluralism supervened?

The advent of "world religions" as a dominant discourse is generally understood to mark an explicit turn away from the nineteenth-century obsession with the primitive and the original. An implicit assumption here, often made explicit nowadays, is that it was also a turn away from the Eurocentric and Eurohegemonic conception of the world, toward a more egalitarian and lateral delineation. By converting from the evolutionary, pseudotemporal, hierarchical order to a geographic, pseudospatial, decentralized order of representation, the emergent world religions discourse appears to have liberated itself from Eurocentrism of a certain kind, since it acknowledges the actual plurality of cultures and of civilizing processes. But how does the discourse of world religions achieve this liberation? Or does it achieve it at all?

Today, the pluralist doctrine, albeit usually in a tepidly imprecise rendering, seems to have become the ruling ethos of our discourse on religion, scholarly and nonscholarly. Consequently, it takes some contrivance to stake out a position from which to regard and to question this ethos with due seriousness: On what moral or ideological grounds is the pluralist doctrine, as exemplified by the world religions discourse, predicated? What interests and concerns animate this doctrine and keep it viable? Are there elements of contradiction or even false consciousness in the way in which we are naturally led to subscribe to this doctrine? Instead of philosophically arguing for such a critical position, however, this book takes recourse in history and initiates an investigation with a set of fairly uncomplicated empirical questions posed on relatively uncontroversial grounds, namely, when, and how, this particular mode of counting and mapping religions came about.

2. The Discourse on Religion as a Discourse of Othering

Let us now consider briefly the broader historical contexts in which the plural-ist discourse on religion emerged. The purpose of this section is to paint a backdrop, as it were, against which to stage the nineteenth-century episode, the main subject of the book. As with any stage setting, the backdrop presented here may seem unnaturally flat, ultimately incidental and inessential to the drama, and therefore arbitrary; yet the scenery chosen has the virtue of provid-ing a perspective that allows us to focus on the academic context of nineteenth-century Europe.

In 1996, the Gulbenkian Commission on the Restructuring of the Social Sci-ences, a team of ten international scholars headed by Immanuel Wallerstein, published its report under the title *Open the Social Sciences*.[15] The first chapter of the report describes the emergence, mostly in the course of the nineteenth century, of several new branches of knowledge, all pertaining to the nature of collective human life, that is, what we today refer to as the social sciences or, alternatively, the human sciences. The report begins by describing the intellec-tual outlook at the end of the eighteenth century. Learned Europeans of that time understood or assumed the broad-stroke division of the realm of knowl-edge into two domains: natural science on the one hand, and what we have been accustomed to calling "arts and letters" on the other. We are also re-minded that there was a generally shared sentiment among the educated that the newfangled, recently productive science—the quintessential embodiment of the spirit of modernity and progress—was clearly surging ahead of the more classical, genteel sort of learning based on arts and literature, insofar as the empirical spirit of science had incontrovertibly triumphed over speculative philosophy.

As the report further informs us, several new sciences of human social phe-nomena arose, more or less concertedly, representing a tertiary domain of knowledge, located between, yet distinct from, the two preexisting domains. From the beginning, these novel disciplines of the social sciences clearly leaned toward and emulated the already well-established and well-regarded natural sciences, with the difference that the objects of study were matters human and

15. In addition to the chairperson, Immanuel Wallerstein, the following individuals are listed as members of the commission established by the Calouste Gulbenkian Foundation of Lisbon: Calestous Juma, Evelyn Fox Keller, Jürgen Kocka, Dominique Lecourt, V. Y. Mudimbe, Kinhide Mushakoji, Ilya Prigogine, Peter J. Taylor, and Michel-Rolph Trouillot.

social, rather than natural phenomena.[16] In the atmosphere of this general predilection for the scientific, history—a time-honored ideographic, as opposed to nomothetic, study of human past activities—was transformed into a scientific discipline. No longer a narration of morally and spiritually edifying tales about bygone eras, history became for the first time essentially a work of research, whose cardinal objective now was to establish certain facts about the past. Following this reconstitution and disciplinarization of history, then, the nineteenth-century soon saw the rise of three new social scientific disciplines.

In this report and elsewhere, Wallerstein has suggested that the triangulation of these nomothetic social sciences reflected nineteenth-century liberal ideology, which envisioned the workings of human society in terms of three distinct though intertwined spheres.[17] There is political science, which studies the realm of power and the state; economics, which studies the market; and sociology, which studies what is left, that is, civil society. Because nineteenth-century intellectuals saw their own society as consisting of these spheres, this set of three sciences seemed to them entirely adequate to achieve a comprehensive understanding of modern European society. It was quite another matter, however, when it came to the study of non-European societies. As Wallerstein points out, along with these nomothetic social sciences that were proper to the West, there developed two additional disciplines specifically to study nonmodern, non-European societies. If the society in question was small and "tribal" in its scale and lacked the technology of writing, it would be an object of study for anthropology. If on the other hand, the society happened to be a large-scale, regionally dominant kingdom or empire and had a long and illustrious written tradition, it would fall under the aegis of Orientalism. In sum, in addition to the refurbished discipline of history being made more scientific, the nineteenth century saw the formation of three nomothetic disciplines to understand the West, and two more new sciences to investigate the rest.

Here, we may note that, in this picture of nineteenth-century intellectual development and disciplinary formation, what some scholars of the time had

16. Immanuel Wallerstein et al., *Open the Social Sciences* (1996), 9–14.

17. Because the publication is in the name of the commission, it would not be proper to equate the observation made here as that of Wallerstein alone. A few years before the publication of the Gulbenkian report, however, I heard him speak at the University of North Carolina at Chapel Hill, and on that occasion he rehearsed the same argument contained in the report, and he delivered his lecture without particular reference to the commission. Owing to these circumstances, I have taken—for the sake of convenience—the liberty of letting Wallerstein stand for the views expressed in the book.

already begun to call the "science of religion," or *Religionswissenschaft*, is no-where to be found by name. This fact, rather than discrediting or diminishing the value of Wallerstein's schema for our purposes, actually illuminates it from behind, for, once we probe into the logic of objectification and the principle of differentiation that must have been at work in the formation of these five new disciplines just named, it becomes evident that religion was indeed an exceed-ingly important factor.

To examine the side of the three sciences for the West first, it stands to rea-son that political science, economics, and sociology should come into exis-tence just at this time, just as politics, economy, and the social life of citizens were seemingly coming into their own, in short, just as this society was becom-ing secularized. According to the narrative of secularization now eminently fa-miliar, these spheres were emerging from the control of church authority and becoming increasingly liberated from the sphere of religion. In effect, the logic here seems to be that these new sciences became viable and effective as ways of understanding European society because this society had finally reached ma-turity, that is, had sufficiently developed in accordance with rational principles and established itself on the basis of the rule of law, instead of on some real or imagined supernatural authority.

In contrast, every region of the nonmodern non-West was presumed to be thoroughly in the grip of religion, as all aspects of life were supposedly deter-mined and dictated by an archaic metaphysics of the magical and the super-natural. In the case of preliterate tribal society, it was assumed that the dom-inant metaphysics would be a form of natural religion, that is, a moral universe saturated by supernatural and autochthonous powers, a cosmology deeply in-grained in the landscape, the cycle of seasons, and the natural rhythms of life. As we know, this type of assumption concerning tribal-scale society induced many anthropologists of the nineteenth and early twentieth centuries to concentrate their attention on what they were inclined to identify as "religion," in order to find therein some obscure logic or arcane "prelogical" system of thought presumably governing all aspects of tribal life. For this reason, in contrast to their more recent counterparts, Victorian anthropologists were ex-tremely keen on the subject of what they called "religious beliefs and prac-tices." They eagerly collected, cataloged, compared, and attempted to system-atize myths, rituals, and other noteworthy customs and habits that seemed to make a given tribal society unique and peculiar and, at the same time and in an-other sense, very much like tribal societies found elsewhere. The presence, or rather the supposed predominance, of religious and supernatural elements was believed to mark tribal society as decisively different from modern European society.

Orientalist scholarship, in the meantime, had been discovering, editing, and translating the literary treasures of some of the most powerful nations known in history. Following the pioneering work of eminent savants and intrepid discoverers of the eighteenth century such as Thomas Hyde, Anquetil-Duperron, N. B. Halhed, and William Jones, the study of the Orient emerged as a fashionable and respectable science, or *Wissenschaft*, in the nineteenth century. The Orient, "the land of origin," had been so named by the Europeans long before, rather more symbolically than precisely, and it came to encompass an enormous spread of regions, peoples, and languages ranging from North Africa to the Pacific East. As more and more archaic literary languages of the legendary nations of the East became known to the scholars of the West, and more and more of the venerable texts of these nations were amassed and cataloged in the libraries of European metropoles, this scholarship acquired a burgeoning authority over the indigenous institutions of knowledge. In the face of this formidable learning, the non-European nations—which by the end of the nineteenth century had largely come under direct European colonial control (in the case of India and Egypt) or under its overwhelming influence and intervention (as was the case in China and Japan)—no longer seemed to possess the power and the prerogative to represent their own legacy apart from this scholarship.

Like anthropology, the "science of the East" was preoccupied by the subject of religion. For Orientalists, however, the religions in question did not amount to generic supernaturalism or varieties of natural religion but instead were presumed as specific, historically unique traditions. According to nineteenth-century opinion, countless examples of primitive tribal religions might be just so many expressions of some basic and natural human propensities and behaviors in the face of the mysterious and the superhuman, whether in the form of worship, propitiation, or other observances. In contrast, each of the so-called Oriental religions was deemed singular and irreducible to a common genre. Many of these ancient Oriental religions died out, supposedly, together with the peoples and civilizations to which they respectively and uniquely belonged. But others apparently survived in altered forms and came to be recognized as "living religions," or today's world religions. These great religions of the past and present, unlike the tribal religions, are deemed not generic but unique and proper to themselves because, presumably, they have developed as culturally and historically particular delineations, and because they were predicated on specific defining events or acts, usually associated with certain historical personages—founders, teachers, prophets, reformers. Furthermore, nineteenth-century Europe was generally of the opinion that, upon encountering and confronting any of these world religions, an indigenous tribal religion would eventually and inevitably dissipate or disappear, through the process of assimilation, atrophy, or banishment.

As the science of religion began the task of identifying and classifying Oriental religions in the latter decades of the nineteenth century, each of these great, historically unique religions came to be recognized as a vast and powerful metaphysical system deeply ingrained in the social fabric of a particular nation, and in the psychical predilections of its individual citizens and subjects. As such, these religions offered European scholars a powerful, far-reaching, and comprehensive categorial framework by virtue of which they could hope to explain the characteristic features of a given non-European society. In effect, according to the essential logic of this scholarship, a non-European nation of any stature was presumed to have one (or sometimes more than one) of these world religions in lieu of Christianity. Just as Christianity had shaped and disciplined the European nations for centuries, in a non-European nation, a world religion of one kind or another had been functioning as the veritable backbone of its ethos.

The difference between Christianity and other "great religions" of the world, of course, has been told in myriad ways by Europeans and by others for nearly two centuries. Some of these articulations will be examined closely in the following chapters. What may be usefully recognized provisionally at this point is that, throughout the nineteenth century, endless speculation on the differences and similarities between religions continually provided opportunities for modern Europeans to work out the problem of their own identity and to develop various conceptions of the relation between the legacy of Christianity on the one hand and modernity and rationality on the other. As we shall see in more detail presently, there was by no means a consensus as to what place Christianity was to have in the future destiny of what was then beginning to be called the European "race." Nor was there clear agreement over the question of whether Christianity, which had been an incontrovertibly dominant institution in Europe since late Roman times, was indeed an essential and permanent component of this destiny. Closely tied to these weighty concerns was the question of the historical (or possibly congenital) relation between Christianity and Judaism, and the question of whether Jews and Judaism had a role in the future of Europe. In proximity to these concerns were issues arising from the lately prevalent notion that most of the prized institutions of the modern West (science, art, rationality, democracy, etc.) were of Greek origin; this rendered religion (Christianity) a conspicuous anomaly amid the Hellenic pedigree of the European heritage. There were also questions stemming from the newly discovered affinity and apparent fraternity between "India" and Europe.

These matters are taken up for further deliberation in later chapters. Suffice it to observe for the time being that the subject of religion and religions began to seep into visibility under these interesting circumstances: When religion came to be identified as such—that is, more or less in the same sense that we think of it today—it came to be recognized above all as something that, in the opinions of many self-consciously modern Europeans, was in the process of disappearing from their midst, or if not altogether disappearing, becoming circumscribed in such a way that it was finally discernible as a distinct, and limited, phenomenon.[18] Meanwhile, the two new sciences pertaining to non-European worlds, anthropology and Orientalism, promoted and bolstered the presumption that this thing called "religion" still held sway over all those who were unlike them: non-Europeans, Europeans of the premodern past, and among their own contemporary neighbors, the uncivilized and uneducated bucolic populace as well as the superstitious urban poor, all of whom were something of "savages within." For, as those enlightened moderns of the nineteenth century—as represented by those who wrote and those who read the ever-growing number of books on the subject of religion, magic, and superstitions—observed with an admixture of horror and fascination, the oppressive supernaturalism of hidebound traditions and umbrageous priestcraft continued to control and command those hapless others' thoughts and acts in myriad idiosyncratic ways.[19]

These general observations may in turn suggest some broad theses of the

18. This does not mean that all or even most of those nineteenth-century writers and participants in the emerging discourse on religion were expecting to relinquish Christianity altogether. Yet it is significant that, at least among the scholars of religion, the predominant tendency was a willingness to retain or to reappropriate, out of their own religious heritage, something other than Christianity as it had been passed down to them (or what they construed as such). To the extent that they believed Christianity offered something of essential truth and permanent value, they would reclaim it anew on their own recognizance, largely free and independent of any ecclesiastical authority.

19. For a well-documented analysis of the European interests in the occult and the exotic of the period, see Randall Styers, *Making Magic* (2003).

following sort. The modern discourse on religion and religions was from the very beginning—that is to say, inherently, if also ironically—a discourse of secularization; at the same time, it was clearly a discourse of othering. My suspicion, naturally, is that some deep symmetry and affinity obtain between these two wings of the religion discourse; that they conjointly enable this discourse to do the vital work of churning the stuff of Europe's ever-expanding epistemic domain, and of forging from that ferment an enormous apparition: the essential identity of the West.

This book does not seek to prove the above-mentioned theses conclusively. Yet it is my sense that these statements adequately summarize the overriding theme that the materials covered in the book, and the readings performed therein, continually and recurrently present.

༄

I come now to the point of professing the nature of the present project more specifically. The principal objective is a genealogy of a particular discursive practice, namely, "world religions" as a category and as a conceptual framework initially developed in the European academy, which quickly became an effective means of differentiating, variegating, consolidating, and totalizing a large portion of the social, cultural, and political practices observable among the inhabitants of regions elsewhere in the world. This pluralist discourse is made all the more powerful, I believe, by a corollary presumption that any broadly value-orienting, ethically inflected viewpoint must derive from a religious heritage. One of the most consequential effects of this discourse is that it spiritualizes what are material practices and turns them into expressions of something timeless and suprahistorical, which is to say, it depoliticizes them.

To put this phenomenon in a somewhat broader context, various works categorized under the rubric of colonial and postcolonial studies have made us aware of the sacralizing character of Orientalism.[20] On this point Nicholas Dirks usefully explains:

> When Said used the term Orientalism, he meant it in a number of interdependent senses. These senses included the general tendency of thought, found throughout colonial establishments, in which the Orient was made

20. Among relevant works of colonial and postcolonial studies I cite selectively the following: Talal Asad, *Genealogies of Religion* (1993); Nicholas B. Dirks, *The Hollow Crown* (1987); Vicente Rafael, *Contracting Colonialism* (1988); Gauri Viswanathan, *Outside the Fold* (1998).

to be Europe's other, a land of exotic beings and exploitable riches that could service the economy and the imagination of the West. Orientalism also refers to a much more sophisticated body of scholarship, embodied in such practices as philology, archaeology, history, and anthropology, all glorifying the classical civilizations of the East (at the same time they glorify even more the scholarly endeavors of the West that made possible their recuperation) but suggesting that all history since the classical age was characterized by decline, degeneration, and decadence. Orientalism, whether in the guise of colonial cultures of belief or of more specialized subcultures of scholarship, shared fundamental premises about the East, serving to denigrate the present, deny history, and repress any sensibility regarding contemporary political, social, or cultural autonomy and potential in the colonized world.[21]

In view of this insight, it has become exigent that the discourse on religion(s) be viewed as an essential component, that is, as a vital operating system within the colonial discourse of Orientalism. Moreover, as the statement by Dirks cogently reminds us, there is from the beginning a symbiotic, or perhaps better, congenital relation between Orientalism in the narrow sense (scholastic subculture) and Orientalism in the more general sense (culture of colonialism). To reiterate a key point that has been proclaimed by numerous proponents of colonial and postcolonial criticism: the problem of Orientalist science is not a matter of would-be pure knowledge contaminated by ulterior political interests, or science compromised by colonialism. Our task, then, is not to cleanse and purify the science we have inherited—such efforts, in any case, always seem to end up whitewashing our own situation rather than rectifying the past—but rather it is a matter of being historical *differently*.

3. A Synoptic Overview

The present project is therefore an attempt to excavate, albeit in a piecemeal fashion, some of the nineteenth-century discursive practices that may be plausibly said to constitute the prehistory of the present-day world religions discourse, and to recover the half-forgotten worries, hopes, and controversies that animated these practices, which became instrumental in generating the new classificatory regime that is now ours.

21. Nicholas B. Dirks, "Introduction: Colonialism and Culture," in *Colonialism and Culture* (1992), 9.

The primary excavation site—which, in chronological terms, falls roughly in the purview of the "long" nineteenth century[22]—refers to the ever-expanding discursive domain within which the new sciences of comparative philology and comparative religion emerged. It may be fairly supposed that the comparative science of religion laid grounds for academic legitimatization of the pluralist discourse of world religions. In the first chapter, this domain will be circumscribed by brief sketches of its outer limits. The first section of the chapter identifies the moment when the new discourse of world religions suddenly erupted full-fledged, namely, the early decades of the twentieth century. The second section moves back in time to an earlier period and gives an account of the long reign of a premodern to early-modern system of classifying religions—or more precisely, system of ordering nations—the system that began to lose ground but survived into the first half of the nineteenth century. The final section of the chapter considers several texts published in the first half of the nineteenth century that represent the transitional or metamorphic phase, as they testify to the decline of the old taxonomic regime, and a slide into something else that was tentative, uncertain, and as yet unnamed.

The second chapter further defines the contour of the nineteenth-century comparative science of religion by examining a discursive domain that is adjacent to, but customarily excluded from, that science. This adjacent realm is known by the name "comparative theology"—in contradistinction to "comparative religion," which is roughly synonymous with "history of religions," "science of religion," or *Religionswissenschaft*. Comparative theology, in contrast, is generally understood to be a religiously motivated discourse. In its heyday in the latter half of the nineteenth century, comparative theology was a very popular, highly regarded, and respectable intellectual-spiritual pursuit. The proponents of the science of religion in the twentieth century and thereafter, however, have been careful to keep their own practice at a distance from this once prolific enterprise, while reserving the privileged term "science" for studies based on objective appraisal of empirical data, supposedly unmixed with pious sentiments or partisan denominational interests. To this day, the disciplinary history of the science of religion has been intent on distinguishing comparative religion from comparative theology. When we examine these two nineteenth-century schools, however, it would be difficult to deny that comparative theology actually has much in common with today's discursive prac-

---

22. This, in accordance with historians' convention, refers to the years 1789–1914. But in the context of the present study, the dates are approximate and somewhat coincidental.

tice of world religions. In fact, it may be credibly suggested that the popularity of world religions was more a legacy of the religious-evangelical enterprise of comparative theology than of the arcane technical and scholarly tradition of the nineteenth-century science of religion. If this should be the case, the present-day suppression of—or, at least, what appears to be a willful ignorance about—comparative theology may be an intriguing historical conundrum in its own right.

The project of comparative theology has been deemed not scientific on the grounds that it either presupposed or invariably drew the self-same conclusion as Christian theology, that Christianity was fundamentally different from all other religions, thus, in the last analysis, beyond compare. This singularity of Christianity was often expressed in a vaguely oxymoronic phrase: "uniquely universal." In the opinion of the theological comparativists, Christianity alone was truly transhistorical and transnational in its import, hence universally valid and viable at any place anytime, whereas all other religions were particular, bound and shaped by geographical, ethnic, and other local contingencies. The comparative theologians admitted that Christianity did have a temporal beginning just like any other religion, yet it alone was said not to have been determined or constrained by the accidents of its historical origin. The earliest known manifestation of the term "world religion," albeit in German, was in this sense of the "uniquely universal" religion of Christ—in other words, the religion of the world—as distinct from all other homegrown, indigenous religions particular to the land: Landesreligionen, or "national religions," as the latter term was commonly translated. This Christian-monopolistic use of the term "world religion" persisted concurrently with the development of the scientific/taxonomic sense, as we see, for example, in the title Christianity the World-Religion (1897), a book by John Henry Barrows, the president of the World's Parliament of Religions and the Haskell Lecturer on Comparative Religion at the University of Chicago.

It might be surmised, therefore, that something like a watershed for the more objective-scientific, classificatory use of the term "world religions" was reached just when the term came to appear in the plural, that is, when more than one religion was recognized as belonging to this category. This turning point, which occurred in the 1880s, is the subject of chapter 3, which also marks the entry into part 2, the principal locus of the book. As we shall see, the first non-Christian religion to be included in the category "world religion" had only recently been recognized as a distinct tradition and identified with a single name—Buddhism, a neologism. Chapter 4 examines the European discovery of Buddhism and how this suddenly visible "great religion" was conceptually constructed as a world religion from the beginning. It is almost as though, had it not been for Buddhism, science would not have had an immediate need for the term "world religion." Meanwhile, there was a controversy among those same first-generation scientists of religion as to whether Islam should be counted as a world religion. Given that Islam had long been known to Europeans as a de facto transregional religion and, moreover, as a formidable, imperious domain of non-Christianity and a constant threat to it, the eruption of this controversy at this time is highly peculiar. It is significant, in any event, that the first scholarly debate about world religions had as much to do with the problematic status of Islam, as with the possible relation—morphological or genealogical—of Buddhism, a newly discovered religion of Aryan origin, to European Christianity.

It is hardly a coincidence that Friedrich Max Müller, renowned Sanskritist and perhaps the most conspicuous philologist of the second half of the nineteenth century, has been regarded as preeminent among the founders of the science of religion. As it appeared, this new science owed its comparative logic to the science of language, also known as comparative philology, which had been flourishing ever since the European discovery of Sanskrit literature in the latter half of the eighteenth century. The transference of the scientific method from the field of language to that of religion was carried out explicitly for the first time by Müller, on the occasion of his historic lecture series delivered in 1870, appropriately entitled "Introduction to the Science of Religion." To the extent that this founding narrative is true, certain incipient components of the world religions discourse may be traced in the history of comparative philology. With this in mind, chapter 5 sketches the nineteenth-century development of philological scholarship, which yields the following observation:

Whatever fascination and promise the science of language might have held for the pioneering scholars of Oriental languages, one driving passion of comparative philology was in the exaltation of a particular grammatical apparatus: inflection. Metaphysically and abstractly imagined rather than historically documented, inflection was construed as a syntactical structure resulting naturally and directly from the innermost spiritual urge of a people (Volk), and as such it was said to attest to the creativity and the spirit of freedom intrinsic to the disposition of those who originated this linguistic form. Not surprisingly, these attributes, together with the grammatical form itself, were touted as the defining characteristics of the family of Indo-European (Aryan) languages, the family comprising Sanskrit as its "eldest daughter" in the East, Persian as her close kin, but also with the Western siblings Greek, Latin, Teutonic, Slavonic, and so forth, of which most modern European languages were unmistakable descendants. The ancient, broad band of the Indo-European language family, stretched across from east to west, had been intersected, in both space and time, by another linguistic family. This other group, the Semitic languages, included Arabic and Hebrew, which were well known to Europeans because they were the language of the Qur'an and of the Old Testament respectively. The great majority of nineteenth-century philologists maintained that, in comparison to the first family, this second tribe of languages was decidedly imperfect and inchoate in inflectional capability, and with this imperfection came all the limitations that characterized their native speakers as a race. Müller's contemporary and longtime correspondent, Ernest Renan, is among the most celebrated exponents of this view.

Much of world history—as nineteenth-century scholars understood the matter—had been the work of interaction between these two "families" or "races," Aryan and Semitic. Extending beyond this huge crossroads of world historical powers lay an almost indefinite domain of a third estate, consisting of innumerable languages whose genealogical relation was less certain, except for some obvious local clustering here and there. Comparative philology suggested that these languages had syntactical structures even further removed from inflection than the Semitic tongues; in fact, their mode of signification was believed to have developed in reverse order to that of the Aryan languages. The syntax of these languages, it was speculated, had begun as the concatenation of root words and was formed through gradual coalescing of the roots and the attendant atrophy of what had been distinct, originally independent word roots. This process of agglutination was exactly the opposite of the development of "pure" inflection, in which each word ending grew naturally and spontaneously out of the word root, as it were, from within. According to this theory widely embraced by philologists of the nineteenth century, the inflectional structure of Semitic languages was fated to remain imperfect and constrained, and therefore impure, because the process of development was already compromised by incipient agglutination.

It is in light of this devaluation of the Semitic in relation to the Aryan (or Indo-European) that we may begin to understand the new logic and the renewed momentum behind the particularly harsh condemnation of Islam (chapter 6). With the emergence of the science of comparative philology, it is as though the age-old European anti-Semitism—or more precisely, negative sentiments against the Jews—took a new turn and found a novel deployment.

In short, this scientifically based anti-Semitism facilitated a new expression of Europe's age-old animosity toward the Islamic powers, insofar as this science categorized Jews and Arabs as being "of the same stock," conjointly epitomizing the character of the Semitic "race."

It is difficult to ascertain the full implications of this powerful notion, and to appreciate its utility for reconceptualizing the self-understanding of Christian Europe. Chief among the new challenges posed by this idea was its deployment in the semitization of Islam. Thenceforward, the zealously monotheistic, materially poor, mentally rigid, and socially illiberal desert Arab—already frequently described by nineteenth-century writers as "fanatic"—has come to stand as the quintessential Muslim, thus displacing the earlier image of the "Mohammedan" as an indolent Turk wallowing in opulent infidelity. At the same time, in obvious correlation to the vilifying and condescending image of Semitic Islam, there surged among European scholars a renewed interest in so-called Islamic mysticism. Sufism was particularly valorized as a higher form of Islam, Persian (or possibly Indian or neo-Platonic) in origin, therefore essentially Aryan in nature, hence exterior to what was deemed Islam proper.

Chapter 7 considers the position of F. Max Müller with respect to these philological innovations and the subsequent development of the science of religion and of the world religions discourse. As a reputed patriarch of modern comparative study of religion and advocate of the genealogical classification of religion modeled after the science of language, it might be expected that his role was above all to authorize the tripartite division of the human race and to advance the comprehensive mapping of the world religions. While these outcomes indeed appear to have followed in the wake of his scholarly endeavors and they are often personally attributed to him by posterity, a closer examination of Müller's work suggests that much of this result was, in an important sense, despite his own theoretical standpoint and against his wishes and opinions. As is evident especially from his early work—most significantly, "Last Results of the Turanian Researches," also known as "On the Turanian Language" (1853) and *The Languages of the Seat of War in the East* (1854; 2d ed., 1855), two lengthy essays written with great energy and in haste, but little read ever since—his outlook on the origin and development of language and of language groups diverged markedly from those of comparative philologists up to his time, as well as of scholars who came thereafter. Not surprisingly, his idea of scientific classification of religions, too, was considerably at odds with the various taxonomies advanced by his peers, the latter being beholden to the logic of philological classification. The divergence of Müller's views from the mainstream was generally understood by his contemporaries as attributable to his religious (rather than scholarly) orientation. It was thought that his old-fashioned attachment to the biblical doctrine of the unitary origin of human-kind, or monogenesis, did not allow him to entertain fairly the possibility of multiple and separate origins of races; hence much of what was distinctive in his own theorizing was roundly dismissed as mere idiosyncrasy, something stemming from his prescientific sentiments, and thus of little scholarly im-port. Müller in turn protested against this dismissal precisely on philological scientific grounds, but apparently to no avail.

The analysis in chapter 7 thus provides occasion to reflect critically not only on the position of Müller in the legacy of the science of religion, of which he is reputedly a key founding figure, but also on the relation—and distance—between the logic of scientific comparativism and the doctrine of religious pluralism.

What transpired between the closing decades of the nineteenth century and the 1920s—that is, the efficient causes, so to speak, that finally brought about the new discourse of world religions—will not be comprehensively studied in this book. It does not seem likely, in fact, that this transition could be ade-quately described or credibly explained by examining academic trends and reli-gious movements alone. Instead of attempting such a speculative global expla-nation, then, the last portion of the book, part 3, offers a series of open-ended, that is to say, inconclusive and rather more projective, observations. In effect, the individual sections comprising chapter 8 identify various events and do-mains that might warrant further investigation in the future: (1) the historical significance and influence of preeminent publication projects, most impor-tantly, the *Sacred Books of the East*; (2) the preconditions and the aftermath of the World's Parliament of Religions, held in Chicago in 1893; (3) the role played by various private individuals and foundations in promoting the new scholar-ship on religion, or what was more likely called "natural theology" in the nine-teenth century and "history of religion(s)" in the twentieth. Section 4 acknowl-edges what this book, out of practical necessity, leaves out: the participation of the non-West in the production of the world religions categories. The final sec-tion (5) considers another possible strategy for tracing the transformation of the world religions discourse from the older, more restrictive notion (as uni-versalistic religions) to the later, more inclusive one (as all of the major reli-gions of the world). This metamorphic process may be illumined by a broad survey and comprehensive analysis of world religions texts published in the early decades of the twentieth century—a task beyond the scope of this book.

Here, an example or two must suffice. An expressly pedagogic volume called *Religions of the World*, edited by Carl Clemen, for example, clearly distinguishes between the categories of "world religions" and "national religions"; yet, in addition to Christianity, Buddhism, and Islam, the category of world religions now includes a religion hitherto considered a quintessential national religion, namely, Judaism—though with another name, "religion of the Hebrews." Although Clemen's is but one example and not necessarily typical, the inclusion of Judaism in the league of world religions at this point may prove significant also in that it roughly coincided with the inception of a new concept of the West defined as Judeo-Christian. This hyphenated identity of the West—which gained momentum almost exclusively in the United States in the 1930s—appears to have eclipsed the significance of the older idea of Europe defined as Christendom.

Chapter 8 concludes with a brief reflection on the significance of Max Weber in this moment of transition. In his massive unfinished work *Economic Ethic of the World Religions* (*Wirtschaftsethik der Weltreligionen*)—of which the disproportionately famous *Protestant Ethic and the Spirit of Capitalism* was a harbinger—Weber effectively undermined the erstwhile distinction between world religions and national religions, much debated by the nineteenth-century scientists of religion. Weber accomplished this not by means of any theoretical deliberations but seemingly by default: he had no use for the term "national religions." More specifically, Weber was interested in the subject of so-called world religions—which now included not only Christianity, Buddhism, and Islam but also Hinduism, Confucianism, and with some qualifications, ancient Judaism—because, in his opinion, each of these religions without exception was determined by particular characteristics of the society in which it had been a long-standing tradition. From his adamantly secularist sociological standpoint, it was axiomatic that all religions were particular, no matter how universalistic their cosmologies and their evangelical aspirations. For Weber, in effect, all of what he called "world religions" were what the nineteenth-century scholars called "national religions."

It still remains to be inquired in earnest, however, whether the transformation of the concept of world religions from the highly selective, discriminatory sense of the nineteenth century to the seemingly more inclusive sense of the twentieth can be considered a triumph of the pluralist ethos, whether the expansion of the list is something to be celebrated as democratization of the science of religion and decentralization of Eurohegemonic perspective more generally, or for that matter, whether the intent and import of Weber's unfinished project had anything whatsoever to do with such a "pluralist" agenda. The discourse of world religions, in any event, finally came of age when the potent and dangerous challenges and opportunities for world-hegemonic power and glory presented themselves, for the first time, to the naked eye of the European. Chapter 9 casts a glance in the direction of this question by considering one of the leading theologians of the time, Ernst Troeltsch. We will attend to the conceptual and rhetorical maneuvers observable in the last lecture he wrote, but never delivered, owing to his untimely death in 1923. The lecture, tellingly entitled "The Place of Christianity among the World Religions," was a plea for a united front of the coalition of all religions—or what he termed "religion as such"—against the surging tide of secularism. At the same time, his clarion call amounted to a fresh declaration of the universal relevance of Christianity, which Troeltsch called unambiguously and without irony the religion of Europe. This last chapter, then, entertains the possibility that the discourse of world religions, whose rhizomatic growth in the nineteenth century I trace, when it finally erupted in the early twentieth century, facilitated the conversion of the Eurohegemonic claim from one context to another—that is, from the older discourse of Christian supremacy (now considered bankrupt by many liberal Christians) to the new discourse of world religions, couched in the language of pluralism and diversity.

4. Writing History in the Age of Theory: A Brief Discourse on Method

Everything Kraus wrote is like that: a silence turned inside out, a silence that catches the storm of events in its black folds, billows, its livid lining turned outward.

WALTER BENJAMIN, "Karl Kraus"

It may be said that the academy as an institution in modern times has been a relatively sequestered place, self-consciously detached from the surrounding world, thus somewhat more amenable to the centripetal forces of close analysis. The alleged isolationism of the academy, of course, is not to be taken at face value. Yet, habitual proclamations of autonomy and relentless pursuits of self-fashioning are characteristic of this institution, and these habits often cause academicians to leave a considerable trail of paper in their wake.

Despite the abundance of self-commentary, it nonetheless remains very difficult to ascertain why or how some changes in ideas or changes in scholarly conventions occur. To be sure, such events as scholarly debates and controversies can be fertile ground for historical excavation. But it is essential that we begin by recognizing, with utmost seriousness, that these events are, first and foremost, rhetorical events. Be they disputes, supplications, intellectual courtships, or apologia, these dealings are carried out over language and by means of language, in a fairly ordinary sense of that term. To overlook this utterly obvious fact, and to trivialize such a discursive event by declaring that it is merely about language, is at once to short-circuit any possible path for a critique of ideology and to be duped by the crypto-idealist ruse of the academy's own self-fashioning. What matters is the practice of language that is never, in the long run, merely about language.

To put this more graphically, when a headstrong intellectual actively attempts to inflect someone else's prose or to outwit the rhetorical force of a predecessor's (or an adversary's) statement by giving it further momentum or a novel spin, the attempt often ends up dragging out, pulling up, and thereby revealing certain forces and discursive tectonics that are not reducible to anything so local and insular-sounding as the "personal motives" of the interlocutors concerned. Such general geotectonic factors are, in a word, historical. They remain viable for the most part invisibly, but on occasion they flare up. Particularly in moments of conceptual difficulty or ideational "fix," these factors often burst into visibility, and this happens not only in dialogues and debates among several interlocutors, but also in the contemplative monologue of a single individual, where the solitary author may be trying to write herself out of a certain prescripted problem, trying to outmaneuver the logical constraints and rhetorical compulsion of that script, in order to reshuffle the hand she has been dealt by the historical moment. It is these gestures and maneuvers—conformist, reactionary, or revolutionary—that we shall attend to and seek to understand.

But what does a turn of phrase reveal? How could something so minute and seemingly so incidental as a gesture of language indicate anything beyond what has its provenance in the author's person and his immediate circumstance, that is, anything over and above his conscious intentions, unconscious motives, habits, dispositions, social milieu, and the like? Above all, could forms of language employed by this or that author, rhetorical moves made at this or that moment, disclose to us anything of significance about history, and if so, how? Or, perhaps more to the point, could an analysis of such forms and moves be enlisted and incorporated for the purpose of producing historical knowledge, or even historical narrative?

These questions are difficult to answer. Even though I know the answers to be generally in the affirmative, the reasoning that could be articulated to support them might seem too intricate to be fully credible; it could appear either suspiciously obscure or improbably clever, and in the end, devious and inscrutable. This impression may be unavoidable, particularly in the eyes of some historians schooled in another method, who may see their own professional practice precisely as a powerful antidote against pseudohistorical pronouncements, including those proffered by the overly literary, language-obsessed, rhetorical analysts who are predisposed to the kind of intellectual activities described as "close reading," the kind of neoformalist interpretation carried out, so it is charged, hermetically sealed off from everything outside "the text." All too often, it is said, such an empirically undisciplined approach ends up taking the anecdotal for the historical.

I acknowledge the legitimacy of these concerns, though not of a blanket dismissal of the rhetorical analytic strategy itself. At the same time, I am moved to point out—though I am certainly not the first to do so—that what often underlies the historical-realist suspicion is a particular assumption about the nature of language, or what is often referred to as the representational theory of language, an assumption not generally shared by the contemporary partisans of rhetorical analysis. According to the least subtle version of this theory, language at its best reflects what it is not, that is, reality; language mirrors reality, ideally, with minimum refraction. This theory presupposes a particular ontology and thereby precludes other ways of construing and configuring the relation between language and reality, or between language and history. It would not hear of what Walter Benjamin describes in the passage quoted above, a negative revelation of language, the possibility of the seamy underside of a quiescent language billowing out in the ferocious passing of a "storm of events" that are too real, too wild, too volatile for representation.

Given divergences in professional orientation, it seems doubtful that there should be definitive answers that would satisfy all readers once and for all. For one thing, it must be conceded that the degree of clarity and transparency attainable while various parties are separately encamped is not great. It seems unlikely, moreover, that an abstract methodological exposition alone would cause people to reconsider their own position or to switch camps merely out of, say, curiosity or sympathy. Under the circumstances, then, since what can be persuasively said theoretically about the method is limited, I will instead briefly describe, in a prosaic and practical manner, the procedures that I have actually followed in producing this work.

Above all, I have sought to compose a work of critical history fundamentally driven and animated by the logic and the rhetorical forces of the primary sources. The general argument of the book is constructed as a series of readings performed upon the body of some prominent, exemplary, exceptional, or otherwise significant texts, in particular, those written in the vernacular for lay audiences, published between the early seventeenth and the early twentieth century, whose subject matter can be broadly described as "religions of the world." Although the texts and passages privileged for close scrutiny are necessarily selective, I have intended that this reading project as a whole be supported by a comprehensive survey of the genre, amounting to roughly two- to three-hundred titles in all, depending on how narrowly or broadly one defines the genre. In practical terms, my strategic aspirations entailed, on the one hand, speed-reading a large quantity of fairly old, voluminous texts (often under conditions of limited access because of their rarity and antiquity) and on the other hand, detailed, slow reading of selected texts with heightened rhetorical sensitivity. Expending more time and effort on the primary sources in this fashion, rather than following the lead of existing scholarship that might be partially or tangentially related to my own concern, was a choice I made early in the project.[23]

Needless to say, speed-reading and rhetorical analysis both require a relatively high degree of linguistic competence, the ability I may claim to possess adequately in English, my second language, but decidedly less in German, French, or Italian, and none or close to none in some other European languages that would or might have been of relevance (Dutch, to be sure, and possibly Spanish, Danish, and Swedish, for example). This, admittedly, contributed to the focus on the texts written in or translated into English analyzed here; but there is also another, more structural reason for the predominance of the Anglophone literature. For, as already adumbrated in the previous section and as will be demonstrated extensively in what follows, the actual manifestation of the world religions discourse in the form familiar to us today was very much an American phenomenon; twentieth-century America was a final destination

---

23. This may explain, if not excuse, the relative paucity of reference to secondary literature. This is not to say that I have not learned much from the existing scholarship on related areas and topics. These topics include the history of the study of religion as a modern scientific discipline and, to some extent, recent debates on the so-called Western construction of religion as a concept or as a category. Some of the relevant literature has been mentioned in note 9 above. But I did not choose to commence the argument by entering into direct conversation with any of the existing critical literature.

of the migration of a European concept (*Weltreligion* or *Wereldgodsdienst*).[24] This concept was first transposed upon the nineteenth-century (mostly British) schemata for classifying and mapping "other religions," and eventually it became instrumental in the ascendancy of the discourse of religious pluralism and diversity, the discourse that has since been viewed as a signature attribute of a specifically American ethos. In this course of transmigration and mutation, moreover, certain ideological underpinnings of the older hierarchical discourse did not so much diminish and disappear as become unrecognizable under the new outlook of the pluralist ideology—or supposed democracy—of world religions.

Such, then, are the procedures, constraints, parameters, and the emergent scenario of the present work. This brief statement may not amount to a theoretical justification of a methodology, but for reasons I have rehearsed above, it seems injudicious for an author to attempt to convert the readers before the first chapter begins. Instead, I merely wish to earn from my readers as much benefit of the doubt as is reasonable. Hence my best hope for this introduction, as I see it, is to impart a certain illumination in advance, and—to shift the metaphor slightly—to help conjure an atmosphere for felicitous reading.

24. I should add, however, that in recent years, there is evidence that this notion of world religion has been successfully exported to various other linguistic and cultural domains.

PART I

1

"The Religions of the World" before "World Religions"

The historical domain that is the principal concern of this book, in chronological terms, roughly coincides with the "long" nineteenth century, or the period spanning the late eighteenth and early twentieth centuries, up to the outbreak of the First World War. As noted in the introduction, this time in European history is characterized—among very many other things, to be sure—by pronounced uncertainty, volatility, and multiplicity in the ways in which religions were identified and categorized. The task at hand is to demarcate this domain provisionally by marking its outer limits, as it were, and this task will be approached from several directions. The chapter begins in section 1 with a snapshot of what came immediately after this period, then moves back in time in section 2 to offer a rough sketch of what preceded it, and concludes in section 3 with a brief look at a few examples dating from the first half of the nineteenth century that testify to the erosion—thus adumbrating the eventual collapse—of the previous, long regnant system of classification.

1. "World Religions" in the Age of World Wars

We begin with a glance at the moment when the term "world religions" in the English language came to be commonly used in more or less the same sense—and for more or less the same purpose—that we employ it today. Because there was a visible increase in the publication of books on this general topic, one might make a preliminary judgment that the 1920s and early 1930s mark something of a watershed. As we shall see, this is also the period when something closely resembling today's world religions courses began to appear in college curricula in North America.

Considering that the period in question came in the wake of one devastating world war and coincided with an uneasy calm before another, it may seem unsurprising that the literature from those years on any topic should be fraught with a heightened sense of crisis. Yet why should the study of religion and the topic of "the religions of the world" be particularly tied to this period of crisis? Arguably, the earliest instance in which the first global war was rendered in print specifically as a *religious* crisis may be Stanley A. Cook's *The Study of Religions*. In the preface, dated September 1914, the author states:

This book was prepared and written in the conviction that there was an impending crisis in religious thought. The finishing touches to the last proofs were given at the beginning of a war which will mark an epoch in history. While it had not been doubtful that a very distinctive stage in the development of thought was at hand, this war will have a significance, which one can hardly conceive, for ideas and ideals, for conceptions of humanity, righteousness, culture, and progress, and for religious, ethical, and related problems of life and thought.[1]

Whether his pronouncement should be judged as truly prescient or merely as an early appearance of a cliché, the intuition expressed by this author seems to have endured for decades thereafter. In the meantime, the sentiment only gained strength that the study of religions (in the plural) was an especial exigency of modernity, that is, modernity as an experience fraught with novelty and violence. Two of the earliest books bearing "world religions" in their titles—with "religions" again in the plural[2]—share this sentiment, as the nearly identical titles themselves make obvious: one is called *Modern Tendencies in World Religions* (1933), and the other, *Modern Trends in World-Religions* (1934). The prevailing mood of these books is that the whole world is undergoing a profound transformation utterly unlike any other in history. At the same time, it is also implied that an adequate appreciation and comprehension of this transformation is possible only from a widely panoramic, indeed imperially global, perspective. The opening paragraph of the first volume announces:

> One who is awake to what is happening in the big world outside his own limited section of it finds tangible evidence every day in his newspaper that humanity everywhere is amove. Here political revolution, there economic upheaval, yonder an intellectual awakening! Something interesting seems to be happening anywhere he turns his attention. "How fares religion amid all this change?" is a question that must occur many times to one who is interested in the faiths of mankind.[3]

1. Stanley A. Cook, preface to *The Study of Religions* (1914). Despite what the title might suggest, this text does not take the typical world religions survey form but rather discusses the multiplicity of religions comprehensively, without running down the list one by one.

2. As will be discussed later, "world religion," or "world-religion," in the singular had appeared earlier in book titles, but significantly in a different sense, meaning only Christianity.

3. Charles Samuel Braden, preface to *Modern Tendencies in World Religions* (1933), vii.

As the author goes on to qualify, his point here is not that religion had never changed in earlier times but rather that the nature and the magnitude of change occurring in the present era is unprecedented.[4] This sentiment is echoed exactly by the opening paragraph of the other volume:

Change has always been characteristic of living religions. For religion is not an abstraction. It has vital significance only as it is deeply rooted in the moving processes of folk life. . . . But in all past ages the drift of religions into new forms has been relatively slow and dignified. It was a process of modernizing a traditional heritage rather than a radical reorientation. Today the great historic religions are compelled to come to terms with revolutionary forces unknown to any earlier era. . . . It may be that religions of the world are in this generation passing through the greatest transformation of all time. The age-old search of men for a satisfying life-fulfillment . . . is now assuming a new embodiment so strikingly different from the old as to appear to the shocked eyes of the orthodox, if not an abandonment of religion, at least a betrayal of the fundamentals. However religion may be defined it could not now remain static and still continue to be a vital phase of culture. Only dead religions, safely remote from the turbulent stream of human living, could escape change in this age of altered thought-forms, enlarged desires, new hopes, and novel problems.[5]

The prose of both these texts is vibrant with the pulse of the present. There is a feeling of great urgency as religions everywhere are said to face unprecedented radical challenges from without. We witness here the great religions of the world precipitously rising to the field of common discourse as something eminently alive, that is, as "living" religions, very much present among us, if not in our own immediate neighborhood then elsewhere in the very same

---

4. "[T]he fact that religion does actually change is undeniable. It is necessary only to look at the religion of any given people as it was one thousand years ago and as it is today, to see that a religion does not remain static. Indeed the whole history of religion reveals a continuous process of change in the world's religions whether in the more primitive or in the more advanced stages. . . . Religion has always changed. Must it always continue to change or have we arrived finally at a stage beyond which religious progress may not go? . . . Far from being settled and static and incapable of variation it is probable that no single age has witnessed more profound movements in the direction of change in religion than our own twentieth century" (ibid., 1-2).

5. A. Eustace Haydon, introduction to Modern Trends in World-Religions (1934), vii.

world we live in.⁶ And if the living religious traditions are thus multiple, what ushers them all to the common moment of great crisis is one and the same: modernity. In short, what makes "world religions" imaginable and palpable as an objective reality is something like a new sensibility of global awareness, a sense of immediacy of the far and wide world.

What gave particular urgency to this new perception of the increasingly global reality was that the news coming from afar was on balance not very good; certainly by the 1930s there was a growing sense of an impending, or perhaps already unfolding catastrophe. Indeed, a few years earlier, in 1929, a book entitled *Christianity and Some Living Religions of the East* was issued, which opened with an even more pronounced tone of alarm:

> It has become a platitude to say that the earth is now a very small place. Secure and speedy means of communication, the cable and the wireless, have taken from distance much of its meaning. Our newspapers bring to our breakfast table the news of the whole world. Not only are we at once informed of the events of other lands; we are ourselves dependent on them. A failure of the monsoon in India reacts on the prosperity of Lancashire. A crime committed in Sarajevo involved in the miseries of a world-war peoples who before had not even heard of that remote Bosnian town. The success of the young Turks brought Europe once again to the brink of conflict, whilst the civil strife in China has been watched with anxiety by many in Europe who rightly saw in it the possibilities of fresh international disaster. Without peace there can be no security, and peace de-

---

6. This focus on the present and the "living" becomes a prominent feature in publications beginning in the 1920s, as reflected in book titles and subtitles. For example: Sydney Cave, *An Introduction to the Study of Some Living Religions of the East* (1921), Victor Branford, *Living Religions: A Plea for the Larger Modernism* (1924), Robert Ernest Hume, *The World's Living Religions* (1924), William Loftus, ed., *Religions of the Empire: A Conference on Some Living Religions within the Empire* (1925), Lewis Brown, *This Believing World: A Simple Account of the Great Religions of Mankind* (1926), John Clark Archer, *Faiths Men Live By* (1934), Alban G. Widgery, *Living Religions and Modern Thought* (1936), William Ernest Hocking, *Living Religions and a World Faith* (1940), Joseph Gaer, *The Wisdom of the Living Religions* (1956), R. C. Zaehner, ed., *The Concise Encyclopedia of Living Faiths* (1959). This tendency continues to hold in today's publications on the subject of world religions, as we see, among other things, in examples such as Father John T. Catoir, *World Religions: Beliefs behind Today's Headlines* (1985; revised edition of *The Way People Pray*, 1974), or Richard Kirby and Earl Brewer, *The Temples of Tomorrow: World Religions and the Future* (1993), and one of the latest scholarly compendia, John R. Hinnells, ed., *A New Handbook of Living Religions* (1997).

pends not on one nation but on all. We cannot, if we would, restrict our interests to our own country for the events of any country are the concern of all.[7]

Here, again, a precipitous plunge into uncanny awareness of the global is the opening move of a world religions text. In fact, all three of these books seem to persuade their readers at the outset that one should want to acquire, and acquire quickly, a sweeping knowledge of the multiplicity of religions in the world because a new techno-geopolitics was unfolding dramatically before one's eyes, and it was vitally necessary to come to terms with this strangely brave new world, indeed with a brand new sense of the world itself. The new vision of the world was a necessary consequence of violent globalization in the form of colonialism and the explosive expansion of so-called free trade, as these were the principal means through which the West had become connected, inextricably linked with the whole world. At the same time, in this novel state of global connectedness, the West suddenly found itself to be not so much in masterly control as perilously vulnerable, as it found its own state of well-being inexorably dependent on unseen and unknown realities as remote as a village halfway across the planet. In order to avert real dangers that lurked everywhere, far-reaching attention was urgent, gathering of global intelligence essential.[8]

It may be said, therefore, that in the decades following the First World War, world religions discourse unseated an earlier obsession with primitive, prehistoric, or rudimentary religions. Not only did the surging interest in the immediate present supplant the search for the distant, possibly irrecoverable, moment of the origin of religion, there also was a new, or renewed, appreciation of the fact that the time-honored great religions of the world had already gone through many processes of radical transformation, even if the past transformations had been "relatively slow and dignified" by comparison. Of utmost interest now were each tradition's resiliency, adaptability, and sheer vitality for

7. Sydney Cave, Christianity and Some Living Religions of the East (1929), 7. This is a companion volume to the title by Cave cited in note 6 above, An Introduction to the Study of Some Living Religions of the East.

8. For an intriguing analysis of the relation between the technology of global intelligence gathering, the operation of the British Empire as a virtual reality, and the emerging aviation technology, see Thomas Richards, The Imperial Archive (1993).

survival and growth in the face of the rising tide of modernization and increasing global competition.

∾

In contrast to the great world religions, each with its own history, primitive religions lacked interest at this time because, supposedly, primitive religions had experienced little historical transformation. The following statement from the introduction to Hegel's *Philosophy of History* may be cited as a prototype of this line of thought. After a brief discussion concerning the total absence of political constitution, the presence of cannibalism, and other curious features of the African continent, Hegel concludes:

> At this point we leave Africa, not to mention it again. For it is no historical part of the World; it has no movement or development to exhibit. Historical movements in it—that is in its northern part—belong to the Asiatic or European World. Carthage displayed there an important transitionary phase of civilization; but, as a Phoenician colony, it belongs to Asia. Egypt will be considered in reference to the passage of the human mind from its Eastern to its Western phase, but it does not belong to the African Spirit. What we properly understand by Africa, is the Unhistorical, Undeveloped Spirit, still involved in the conditions of mere nature, and which had to be presented here only as on the threshold of the World's History.[9]

Clearly, a tacit understanding among those who felt themselves to be riding the crest of the historical wave was that primitive peoples of Africa and elsewhere—brittle and unmalleable remnants of the past as they were, hitherto untouched and untested by time—were doomed to extinction in the near future, whether this process was to be through actual obliteration of the population or through irreversible assimilation into another, more developed mode of existence, whether this anticipated outcome was to be celebrated or lamented.[10] Primitive religions thus abdicated their place of prominence in the study of re-

9. G. W. F. Hegel, *The Philosophy of History* (1956), 99.

10. Although it is not regarded as an exceptionally prominent text, the organization of *Man Seeks the Divine* (1957), by Edwin A. Burtt, who is identified as being on the faculty of the Sage School of Philosophy, Cornell University, exemplifies this conceptual framework well. The book is divided into four parts. Part 1, "How Religion Outgrows Its Primitive Forms," contains the chapters "Primitive Religion," "From Primitive to Civilized Religion," and finally "Great Religions of Civilized Man." Parts 2 and 3 are entitled "Religions of the East" and "Religions of the

ligion and gave way to the great historical religions of the world.[11] Henceforth cultic practices that were not part of the world historical movement came to be treated primarily in a cognate field specializing in the study of the prehistoric and the primitive called "anthropology of religion."[12]

This new arrangement notwithstanding, "primitive religion," though somewhat demoted, did not disappear entirely from the new mapping. To the extent that the world religions discourse aspired to embody the impartial principle of global coverage, many historians of religion were reluctant to endorse a summary dismissal of the minor and the inchoate, and hence they sought and found a way to accommodate the little traditions of tribal societies in the new epistemic regime. When these minority traditions came to be included in the scope of world religions, it was under a generic rubric, now named "primal," "tribal," "indigenous," or "preliterate" religions, distinguished from, but still kept adjacent to, ancient and prehistoric religions. We see this arrangement succinctly expressed by Jack Finegan in *The Archaeology of World Religions* (1952):

> There are many living religions in the world today. In addition to the more prominent systems of belief and practice cherished by groups which have long recorded histories of political or numerical importance, there are the numerous forms of faith found among preliterate peoples in various parts of the earth. If the latter may be dealt with collectively under the heading of "primitivism" the major religions of the present world are at least twelve.[13]

One may reasonably ask why, in the case of preliterate peoples alone, their "faith" can be "dealt with collectively" as a generic type, whereas all other "forms of faith" are treated individually as historically unique and specific

---

West" respectively, and part 4 contemplates the present and the future: "Religion in the Present and the Future: Summary, Comparison, and Forecast."

11. George Foot Moore's statement regarding his own important work on world religions may be regarded as authoritative: "The plan of this work embraces only the religions of civilized peoples. What are miscalled 'primitive' religions are a subject for themselves, demanding another method, and much too extensive to be incidentally dispatched in the prolegomena to a History of Religions. Nor is an investigation of them necessary to our purpose; the phenomena which occur in the higher religions as survivals are just as intelligible in Babylonia or in Greece as in Africa or Australia" (*History of Religions* [1913-19], 1:v).

12. This refers, of course, to the classical formulation of the anthropological enterprise, which has been much criticized and altered in recent decades by anthropologists themselves.

13. Jack Finegan, preface to *The Archaeology of World Religions* (1952), vii.

traditions.[14] The convention of summarily treating "primitivism," under whatever name, is now more or less routine, such that an explicit justification for this peculiar arrangement is not to be found unless one looks into some early-twentieth-century texts. In a book published in 1904, John Arnott MacCulloch (1868-1950), for instance, blithely opines that "the aspects of savage religion do not vary greatly wherever it is found," and on that ground, he suggests, a general treatment of them as a type would "ensure a better acquaintance with religion at a low level than a separate account of each savage race would do."[15] As we shall see, this handling of "primitivism" is analogous to the way an older system of classifying religions dealt with the myriad varieties of paganism or idolatry.

Setting aside for the moment the peculiar problem of "primitivism," the twelve living religions of the world enumerated by Finegan are Judaism, Christianity, Islam, Zoroastrianism, Hinduism, Buddhism, Jainism, Sikhism, Confucianism, Taoism, Shinto, and primitivism. While Finegan's text is from a later decade (1950s), the formation of the list itself seems more or less contemporaneous with the three titles discussed above. Indeed, the list is virtually identical to the one in Robert Ernest Hume's trend-setting volume, *The World's Living Religions* (1924).[16] It is in fact exactly the same as the one in John Clark Archer's *Faiths Men Live By* (1934).[17] The latter volume may be the first world religions

14. This question is generally not addressed, even though the problem is implicitly acknowledged and often partially averted by making provisions for more geographically specific locations—that is, if "African," "North American," and the like could be considered "specific"—and allocating to each of them an individual section or subsection.

15. John A. MacCulloch, *Religion, Its Origin and Forms* (1904), 9.

16. This book treats only eleven, leaving out "primitivism," for the reason that "the scope of this volume includes only those movements in mankind's religious life which have maintained continuous social organization, art and literature, as well as worship, through a succession of centuries" (Hume, *The World's Living Religions*, v).

17. According to Archer, "Twelve great faiths are living still: Primitivism, Taoism (pronounced as *dowism*), Confucianism, Shinto, Hinduism (including Brahmanism), Jainism, Buddhism, Parsiism (or Zoroastrianism), Sikhism, Judaism, Islam, and Christianity. They claim the total population of the globe, some seventeen hundred million souls, but we may properly suppose that the sum of the really 'faithful' falls far short of such a figure. However, if their total is a billion only, as someone has reminded us, we still find substantial evidence that religion is a vital factor in the human world" (Archer, *Faiths Men Live By*, 1).

textbook specifically designed for a liberal arts college course.[18] Archer, who was Hoober Professor of Comparative Religion at Yale University, notes that the book was "written primarily to provide the author's students with a coherent, comprehensive guide to their study of the living faiths," designed to serve "college upper classmen, theological students and general students of religion," and "intended for a full year's course, three hours weekly."[19] The volume comes complete with "A Students' Manual" (or what would be called today "study questions") and "Collateral Readings," an indication that by the 1930s, if not earlier, a curriculum in comparative religion had been duly established in some of the leading American universities.[20] Just as significant is the indication

18. It may be prudent to qualify this statement by acknowledging that there are several earlier texts explicitly designed as textbooks for classroom use, but they were meant primarily for the education of seminarians and future missionaries. Among the latter, perhaps the earliest was written by William Fairfield Warren (1833-1929), then the president of Boston University and the inaugural occupant of what was reputedly the first chair in comparative religion in North America. In the preface he elaborates: "In the year 1873, in Boston University, was established the first chair ever instituted in an American university for instruction in religions and religion in the widest possible sense." But he also makes clear that his orientation is at variance with the usual rationale for later world religions texts intended for the liberal arts curriculum: "The standpoint of the present work is frankly that of Christian theism. The author can conceive of none higher, deeper, or more scientific. This being the case, it would be an unworthy affectation were he to profess to write without personal prepossessions or personal convictions" (*The Religions of the World and the World-Religion* [1911], ix, xii-xiii).

A better contender to the rank of the earliest world religions textbook, then, may be *The Religions of the World* (1917; 2nd ed., 1919) by George Aaron Barton (1859-1942). Barton, professor of Semitic languages at the University of Pennsylvania, explains the organization of the book as that which he "has found most advantageous in his own classroom," namely, topics in the following order (reflecting, understandably, his own specialty interest in Semitic traditions): (1) an outline of primitive religions; (2) religions of Babylonia and Egypt, which approach most closely to the primitive type; (3) the other religions which have sprung from the Hamito-Semitic stock, the religion of the Hebrews, Judaism, and Mohammedanism; (4) passing eastward to Persia, the study of Zoroastrianism; (5) religions of India, China, and Japan; (6) religions of Greece and Rome; (7) Christianity.

In addition, among the early "textbooks" in world religions, one of the most intriguing was apparently designed for what is probably the first correspondence course in world religions, a twelve-volume series of lessons edited by Edmund Buckley, docent of comparative religion at the University of Chicago, entitled *Universal Religion* (1897).

19. Archer, *Faiths Men Live By*, vii, 471.

20. Louis Henry Jordan informs us that a professorial chair with at least partial responsibility to lecture on comparative religion was established first at Boston University in 1873 (see note 18 above), at Princeton Theological Seminary in 1887, and at the University of the City of New

that, concurrently, something like a standard list of "living religions" had come into existence with this curricular development.[21]

What is notable about this list of eleven religions—or twelve, if we include "primitivism"—is that, on the one hand, it remains essentially unchanged today, more than seven decades later,[22] and on the other hand, it bears little resemblance to the many and sundry examples we find in the nineteenth century. In fact, there does not seem to have existed anything like a typical list of religions before the early decades of the twentieth century. Other than the well-marked tradition of the infidels who had abutted and threatened Christendom for centuries, namely, Islam (which was more likely called "Mahometanism," "Mohammedanism," or some other variations thereof) and the lately prominent "Buddhism" (which was increasingly captivating the European imagination as an embodiment of "the Light of Asia"), the nineteenth century was rather vague as to what other religions there were, or which ones among them were still living.

2. Early Modern Taxonomy, or the Order of Nations

For the purpose of determining, more or less, the other chronological limit of the period of concern, our exposition now moves back in time. The conceptual

---

York (today's New York University) in 1887. The first chair at an American University devoted entirely to comparative religion was at Cornell (1891), and this was followed by University of Chicago (1892), which also established a department of comparative religion. Meanwhile, the Dutch government created a chair of the science of religion in each of the four universities in the Netherlands (Amsterdam, Groningen, Leiden, and Utrecht), and the French did likewise at Collége de France, Paris. See Jordan, *Comparative Religion* (1905), 377-85.

Eric Sharpe, by contrast, locates the origin of the professorial chair in comparative religion in the establishment of the position called general history of religion (*Allgemeine Religionsgeschichte*) at the University of Geneva and the University of Basel, "where from 1834 to 1875, J. G. Müller lectured on 'The History of Polytheistic Religions' in the Faculty of Theology" (Sharpe, *Comparative Religion* [1986], 120).

21. The significance and the utility of Archer's text may be surmised from the following fact. In the preface to the second edition posthumously published in 1958, Carl E. Purinton (professor of religion at Boston University), who revised the volume, reports that this title had been continuously in print since the original publication.

22. To take a major recent work, *A New Handbook of Living Religions*, edited by John R. Hinnells (1997), lists under "religions" Judaism, Christianity, Islam, Zoroastrianism, Hinduism, Sikhism, Jainism, Buddhism, Chinese religions, Japanese religions, followed by what might be considered diversification of "the other": Native North American religions, religions of the Pacific, African religions, new religious movements in primal societies, modern alternative religions in the west, and Baha'ism.

order of religions and nations that prevailed in European discourse until the early decades of the nineteenth century was a well-established, yet also greatly elastic taxonomy. This older system divided the nations of the world into four categories rather unequal in size, value, and stature. There were Christians, Jews, Mohammedans, and the rest.[23] This last, the rest, were variously termed pagans, heathens, idolaters, or, occasionally, polytheists—terms that could be used more or less interchangeably.[24]

Reflecting this archaic taxonomy long after its heyday was a book by Vincent Milner that first appeared around 1860, entitled *Religious Denominations of the World* and bearing a typically long-winded, yet eminently revealing subtitle: *Comprising a General View of the Origin, History and Condition of the Various Sects of Christians, the Jews, and Mahometans, as well as the Pagan Forms of Religion Existing in the Different Countries of the Earth.* Milner helpfully explains the meaning of some of the nearly synonymous terms:

> Pagans are the worshippers of many gods, the heathen who were so-called by the Christians, because, when Constantine and his successors forbade the worship of the heathen deities in the cities, its adherents retired to the villages (*pagi,* hence *pagani,* countrymen), where they could practise their ceremonies in secrecy and safety. In the middle ages, this name was given to all who were not Jews or Christians, theirs being considered the only true religion and divine revelations; but, in more modern times, Mohammedans, who worship the one supreme God of the Jews and Christians, are not called *pagans.* . . . The distinction between pagans and non-pagans, so far as claims to a revelation are concerned, is very slight, since

23. Until fairly recently, Europeans customarily called Muslims "Mohammedans" (or several variations thereof), and their religion "Mohammedanism" instead of "Islam." Since that was the common practice during the period in question, I will adhere to it in much of this book.

24. In his informative study "Polytheisms: Degeneration or Progress?" (1987), Francis Schmidt shows that the term "polytheism," coined by Philo of Alexandria and "rediscovered" in the sixteenth century by Jean Bodin, came to be used in place of "idolatry," which had been hitherto firmly tied to a biblical context. Schmidt describes how Gerardus Joannes Vossius (1577-1649) and some English Deists beginning with Herbert of Cherbury (1583-1648) were instrumental in shifting the grounds of debates concerning idolatry, from the problem of graven images to that of any homage paid to false gods, and how the Deists came to favor the term "polytheism" to "idolatry" in the course of this transition. The term "idolatry," however, did not entirely disappear thenceforth but remained casually interchangeable with "paganism" or "heathenism" and "polytheism," as we see, for example, in David Hume's usage of both terms in *The Natural History of Religion* (1757).

there are many heathenish peoples who have traditions of revelations made to them. We also find in some religions of paganism (for example, with Zoroaster, Plato, and Socrates) pure and elevated notions, and precepts of morality, which would not disgrace even Christianity. Paganism has likewise her moral heroes, as well as Judaism and Christianity. And although St. Augustine declared that the virtues of the heathens were but splendid vices, yet this assertion is by no means born out by facts. The true point of distinction is therefore to be placed in the recognition or denial of one universal, perfect Being.[25]

This seemingly sympathetic account—at least the author is willing to contradict the formidable Christian saint's less charitable view—is predicated on a notion broadly accepted until the early nineteenth century, namely, that the most significant chasm among nations was between those who had knowledge of the one supreme deity and those who did not. The latter, whether they were those who had lamentably fled to the hills and to the "heath," clinging to their old bucolic ways at the advent of Christianity,[26] or those who simply had the misfortune of having lived before the time of Christ, or those now inhabiting hinterlands still remote from the saving grace of the church, were all spiritual rustics, as yet untouched by the civilizing knowledge of Christianity. They did

25. Vincent L. Milner, *Religious Denominations of the World* (1872), 517-18.

26. Earlier, taking exception to this line of argument, which probably was felt to accord too much willfulness to those who resisted Christian evangelism, Daniel Defoe gave a somewhat different explanation of the word's etymology in his *Dictionarium Sacrum seu Religiosum* (1704): "PAGANS, From *Pagus*, a Village, were so denominated, not because they retired into the Country, but that when the Christians began first to Preach in Cities, the Inhabitants of them were converted, before that those of the Country could have the means dispensed to them."

Also diverging from Milner's view on paganism was an early nineteenth-century "Hebraist," John Bellamy, who proposed an alternative, and questionable, etymology in his *History of All Religions* (1812), 160-61: "The word PAGAN is derived from the Hebrew *Phagang*, which means to *approach, to intercede*. But when the descendents of the ancient Pagans became an ignorant people, ignorant with regard to true worship of God, it was used by the Rabbis to mean a rustic, a barbarian, or one uncultivated, or untaught in things appertaining to religion, and was written *Pagan*, with *nun*, instead of *oin*, or *ng*, as it is now written PAGAN." Behind Bellamy's reasoning was the notion that, originally, all humankind had the knowledge of true religion. So he continues: "From the original meaning of the word, we are naturally led to conclude, that the first Pagans were not worshippers of idols, but of the true God. . . . But in process of time, the images of these things [in outward nature] were placed in their temples; the original understanding and application was first neglected, then lost, and they worshipped God through the images, which were originally representative only; hence began idolatry."

not have religion in the proper sense of the term, but in its place they had some-thing that resembled it, a compensatory or consolatory substitute in the form of idolatry. As an adage quoted in an early-nineteenth-century text put it: "Na-tions ignorant of God, contrive a wooden one."[27]

In contrast, other non-Christians, those presumably with knowledge of the Supreme Being in some way, did possess religion, but obviously they did not have it quite right. They either failed to recognize Jesus of Nazareth as Christ the Savior, or worse, they chose to follow a false prophet, Mohammed the Im-poster. Nevertheless, the Jews and the Mohammedans were kindred to Chris-tians, despite their status as renegade relations who willfully made themselves outcasts.[28] Liberally interpreted, the logic seems to run like this: insofar as Jews and Mohammedans know God, they have religion, in the proper sense of the word, and insofar as they have religion, they are, as it were, almost Christian, or at least would-be Christians, but at the moment remain in rebellion against religion's salvific Truth.

It was in recognition of this affinity and kinship among the three nations that John Toland (1670-1722) named one of his famed treatises by an otherwise non-sensical title: *Nazarenus, or Jewish, Gentile, and Mahometan Christianity* (1718). In a similarly ecumenical spirit, Gotthold Ephraim Lessing (1729-81), a towering figure in the late-eighteenth-century German Enlightenment, admonished fellow Christians to acknowledge the true brotherhood, and thus the legit-imacy, of all three branches of the Abrahamic family. The last of his great dra-matic works, *Nathan the Wise* (1779), was a fictional vehicle for this theologi-cal view, which the playwright certainly would have expressed explicitly and

27. In Charles A. Goodrich, *Religious Ceremonies and Customs* (1834), 14. It should be noted here that most seventeenth-century and early eighteenth-century Deists differed from this opinion (for example, John Bellamy quoted in the previous footnote), in that, for them, all nations, no matter how depraved their current state of spiritual knowledge, were originally true theists, that is, believers in one true God. For them there was no essential difference between the Abrahamic monotheists and the rest. In this respect, then, Hume and Lessing—both often called "deistic" in their tendency—represent a significant departure from the earlier Deists.

28. A succinct expression of this view can be found in the irregularly paginated introduction to Robert Adam's treatise *The Religious World Displayed* (1808), vol. 3: "The Religious world is divided into four grand Systems, viz., Judaism,—Paganism,—Christianity,—and Mahommedism. *Judaism* comprehends under it, all those who still expect and look for a promised Messiah. *Pa-ganism*, all those who have not the knowledge of the true God, but worship idols. *Christianity*, all those who believe that the promised Messiah is already come, that Jesus Christ is the Messiah, and the Saviour of the World;—and, *Mohammedism*, all those who acknowledge Mohammed to have been a Prophet."

didactically, one would assume, had he not been censored and prohibited from writing theological tracts by church authority.

From the standpoint of Deists and freethinking Christians such as Toland and Lessing, the brotherhood of Abrahamic monotheisms may be roundly celebrated in spite of their obvious differences. But from another, more orthodox and churchly standpoint, the non-Christianity of Jews and Mohammedans is all the more grievous and condemnable—far more so than that of the hapless heathens—because theirs is not a matter of ignorance or inadvertence but a deliberate act of rejection and willful infidelity. Therefore, while the heathen souls may be ministered to and saved from perdition, the infidels' infirmity must be fought against until their will is broken. Implicit in this logic was the familiar double imperative for Christians: to evangelize the faraway heathens and to crusade against the infidels nearby.

There was, however, another perspective on the problem of idolatry, a view concurrent with, and ultimately complementary to the one just discussed. Augustin Calmet's *Dictionnaire historique . . . de la Bible* (1712)—first translated in 1732 and known in later editions as *Calmet's Great Dictionary of the Holy Bible*—was evidently an immensely popular reference manual, whose numerous editions, translations, and printings continued to be issued well into the early decades of the nineteenth century. It explains the origin of "idolatry" in this fashion:

> If we inquire into the true causes of idolatry . . . we seek them in the depravity of man's heart, in his ignorance, vanity, pride, love of pleasure, his fondness of sensible things, his libertinism, his brutal passions; the irregular and excessive affection of lovers; the mistaken tenderness of a father for his child; or a wife for her husband; extravagant respect of subject for a prince, or of children for their father; excessive gratitude for benefits and services received from certain persons; admiration of the great qualities of creatures, or of persons who had rendered themselves illustrious; one of the many of these causes, joined with the indelible idea conceived by man of a divinity, induced him to pay superstitious respect, worship and adoration to what he loved, esteemed, or honored to excess.[29]

29. The entry for "idolatry" quoted here is from the first English translation (1732) of the *Dictionnaire historique.*

Idolatry is thus defined as any wrongful ascription of supreme value to anything other than the Perfect Being specified by Christian authority. This broad, philosophical conception of idolatry implies that the danger of religious deviance and infidelity is everywhere, not just in heathendom. Following this understanding, then, we may begin to suspect that the elastic nature of the four-part classification system might be such that, just as the category of "Christians" in certain instances—such as with Toland—could be stretched to include Jews and Muslims, the category of "idolaters" could be likewise extended, from the opposite direction, to encompass all those who are not Christians or, indeed, those who are not Christians in the correct manner. On this point, David Benedict (1779-1874) opines that paganism or idolatry is but a name for the general depravity of the soul; as such, "this class of mankind [idolaters] are found in almost all parts of the world," though he does add significantly: "the great body of them reside in Hindostan, China, Tartary, Japan and the neighbouring regions of the east."[30]

It may be useful to note that it was this generalized conception of idolatry—rather than the liberally inclusive notion of "Christianity" entertained by the Deists—that gave a new incentive and justification for examining the most alien forms of un-Christianity. For, as many authors were to argue, there was a lesson to be learned in all these countless ways of deviating from the true faith.

To view one of the early examples articulating this standpoint, we do well to choose a celebrated tome published in 1613, known as *Purchas His Pilgrimage, or Relations of the World and the Religions Observed in All Ages and Places Discovered, from the Creation unto This Present*. With this publication, Samuel Purchas (1577?–1626) became the author of one of the earliest and most successful treatises written in the vernacular for a general audience, that surveyed extensively the plurality and diversity of religions well beyond the European horizon. The endeavor appears to have been something of a novelty then; such an extravagant indulgence of interest in matters so outlandish and so far removed from true faith called for an explanation. For this purpose, cleverly enough, Purchas appealed to the venerable authorities not only of the church fathers but also of the Bible itself. Thus he proclaims confidently in the preface:

> Now if any man thinke, that it were better these rotten bones of the passed, and stinking bodies of the Present superstitions were buried, then [than] thus raked out of their graves . . . I answere, That I have sufficient example

---

30. David Benedict, *A History of All Religions* (1824), 6.

in the Scriptures, *Which were written for our learning to the ends of the World*, and yet depaint unto us the ugly face of Idolatry in so many Countries of the Heathens, with the Apostasies, Sects, and Heresies of the Jewes, as in our first and second booke is shewed: and the Ancient Fathers also, Justin, Tertullian, Clemens, Ireneus, Origen, and more fully, Eusebius, Epiphanius, and Augustine, have gone before us in their large Catalogues of Heresies and false Opinions.[31]

In effect, Purchas persuades the reader that, if no less authority than the Bible and the "Ancient Fathers" could display various apostasies, sects, heresies, and false opinions—all forms of divisiveness and deviation from God—expressly for the educational benefit of the pious, then he, for the same edifying purpose, can discuss a whole range of un-Christian religions, past and present.

In his articulations, we may also begin to detect a chain of association linking divergent forms of plurality, from the matter of subtle domestic deviance within Christendom to the problem of prolific foreign devilry, all of which could be seen as just so many ways of straying from the true faith. This lateral association among different types of plurality, apparently, was as irresistibly suggestive as it was dangerous, for, this train of thought seems to imply, plurality in religion is necessarily a matter of divergence from the unity and singularity of God, whether it is the plurality of gods among the idolaters, the plurality of religions in the present state of the world, or the sectarian plurality within Christianity itself. The problem of heresy, too, could be recognized as an aspect of this last type of plurality.

The cause of all these manifestations of fallacy, moreover, is said to be the same. In the preface to his *Dictionarium Sacrum Seu Religiosum* (1704), commonly known as *A Dictionary of All Religions*, Daniel Defoe (1661?–1731) observed frankly: "There has yet been no Religion (that I know of) upon Earth, though never so pure, which hath not been subjected to alterations, Division, Sects and Heresies." He attributes this tendency for proliferation of sects, denominations, and heresies to human frailty. As he puts it, "the Corruption of Humane Nature having found out so many false Deities of both Sexes, Idols, Images, and vain Representations," this condition is due to vanity. While, in principle, this state of affairs also obtains within Protestant Christianity, Defoe is careful to note how he would present the latter case with a certain conceptual

---

31. The quotation is from Samuel Purchas's unpaginated preface to the third edition: "To the Reader," *Purchas His Pilgrimage* (1617); emphasis is in the original.

discipline: "The several Denominations of Christians of the *Reformed Churches*, are here fairly represented, without using the Opprobrious Names of *Schismaticks* or *Sectaries*, and the like Appellations, which serve to rend them asunder, instead of cementing them together against the *Common Enemy*."[32] Defoe, in effect, knew which divisions and divergences were to be overlooked and which ones were to be indicted, and this distinction was maintained, it seems, to his own satisfaction.

The same mental discipline—distinguishing the problem of foreign religions from the problem of Christian schisms and heresies while acknowledging their common cause—is applied with equal vigor by certain authors as late as a century after Defoe. Charles A. Goodrich (1790-1862), for example, in his 1834 publication *Religious Ceremonies and Customs*, begins by explaining the diversity and multiplicity of religions in terms of what he calls "the radical depravity of the human heart." In short, the author maintains, idolatry, or religious deviance in whatever form, whenever and wherever it occurs, is a natural result of the inherent propensity of humankind. As he ominously puts it:

> Mankind having apostatized from God, have, in every nation, and in every period of time, been successively brought under the dominion of Satan. . . . We may form some idea of the extent and power of Satan's empire, from the fact, that all the nations of antiquity, except the Israelites, were idolaters by profession, and even the latter were practically idolaters, at times. That system of religion was called Polytheism, as acknowledging a plurality of gods.[33]

This being the sorry state of humankind in general, it should not be surprising that bona fide nonpolytheists are few, even among those who outwardly profess their faith in one single supreme deity. Idolatry lurks everywhere.

But if a state of division and deviation is the condition of the world, what

---

32. Defoe's preface continues: "A Pretence of Holiness and supposed Degrees of Purity in some above their Neighbours, were the Principal Causes of Separations in all Religions: Hence arose the Jewish Sects of *Pharisees, Sadducees*, etc. the many Singularities of this Kind among the *Pagan Idolaters*; the almost innumerable Orders and Communities under the *Papal Hierarchy*, as well as the *Patriarchates of the East*, the Sects of *Moatazali, Kalenderi, Jabari*, etc. among the Mahometans."

33. Goodrich, *Religious Ceremonies and Customs*, 16.

could possibly set Christendom apart from anywhere else? The distinction is difficult to maintain, it would seem, from any humanly attainable vantage point. Goodrich's answer in fact is that God's grace alone can save humankind from the state of "continual propensity to depart from God and his institutions—to lose sight of religious truth, and become involved in gross darkness and superstition." In the natural state of perdition, according to Goodrich, "the mind is prepared for every absurdity."[34] In the last analysis, then, the difference in the forms of deviation is immaterial and insignificant; the only important distinction to be maintained is between all those myriad forms of idolatry on the one hand and, on the other, the blessed realm of Christianity, or to put it more precisely, "where the Bible is strictly received as the rule of life."

But of course even this Bible-clad holy community of evangelical Christians is not entirely free from the propensity for divergence and deviation. As Goodrich admits:

> So obvious is it that the depravity of the heart has dictated the various false religions that prevail in the world, that even the infirmities remaining in pious persons have given rise to *minor differences* among the evangelical sects of Christians. Every wrong and perverted feeling of the heart is likely to engender a degree of deviation from the truth. Hence *those unhappy, though not fatal separations* which take place among persons who, on the whole, adhere to the same great fundamental principles.

The state of internal division within Protestant Christianity is of course lamentable, but fortunately, Goodrich stresses, the differences "among the evangelical sects of Christians" are "minor"; besides, he concludes rhetorically, "Christian integrity secures a substantial, though not literal, agreement in the truth and observances of religion. If that integrity were perfect in this world, or more

---

34. Some of the "absurdities" itemized are familiar ones depicted in the Bible. As Goodrich continues: "Hence arose the alt[a]rs and demons of heathen antiquity, their extravagant fictions, and abominable orgies. Hence we find among the Babylonians and Arabians, the adoration of the heavenly bodies, the earliest form of idolatry; among the Canaanites and Syrians, the worship of Baal, Tammuz, Magog, and Astarte . . . among the Persians, religious reverence offered to fire; and among the polished Greeks, the recognition in their system of faith, of thirty thousand gods. Hence, moreover, we find at the present time among most pagan tribes, the deadliest superstitions, the most cruel and bloody rites, and the most shocking licentiousness and vice practiced under the name of religion" (ibid., 14-15).

nearly perfect than it now is, there might literally be but one creed, and one mode of worship."[35]

In this self-serving argument, then, the deviation and division within Christianity, too, are the results of the imperfection of the world, yet Christianity itself cannot be held responsible for this errant condition; nor does this sorry state of the world diminish the uniquely universal truth of Christian doctrine but on the contrary amplifies it. Conservatively and charitably read, the argument seems to suggest that there is more unity among the Christians than it appears; in any case, it would be but fuelling the deviant tendency of the sinful world to call these "minor" differences by "the Opprobrious Names of *Schismaticks* or *Sectaries*, and the like Appellations," as Defoe warned earlier.[36]

Yet Goodrich, for one, seems to want to claim more. Not only does an examination of religious plurality not endanger Christian unity, but according to his logic, a display of the state of divisiveness could in fact enhance the unitary truth of Christianity. To expound on this point, the author enumerates no less than six benefits his treatise has to offer to the pious.

[First, a] view of these religions, will present to us a melancholy account of the apostasy of the human species. . . . [Second,] a view of these religions, so far as they are departures from the truth, will furnish a sad detail of the extent and power of Satan's empire in the world. . . . [Third,] a view of the absurd religions which mankind have embraced, shows the necessity of a divine revelation. . . . [Fourth,] a knowledge of the opposing religious systems among mankind, will evince the necessity not only of a divine revelation, but also of the direct influence of the Supreme Agent, in causing mankind to harmonize in their views. . . . [Fifth,] an account of the clashing and absurd religions that have controlled such numbers of mankind, will impart an exalted idea of the mercy of God, in promulgation of Christianity. As the only true religion—the great centre of divine communications—the point where all the rays of revelations meet, (the Jewish system being only preparatory to it, though very important in that

35. Ibid., emphasis added.

36. Similarly, the advertisement prefacing Hannah Adams's *Alphabetical Compendium of the Various Sects* (1784) announces that "the reader will please to observe" that the author throughout the book has carefully avoided "giving the least preference of one [Christian] denomination above another," and "making use of any such appellations as *Hereticks, Schismaticks, Enthusiasts, Fanaticks*, etc."

view,) it will manifest God's benevolent desire to guide and influence mankind aright. . . . [Sixth and finally, the book] will furnish Christians with a powerful incentive to unite in diffusing a knowledge of Christianity.[37]

Interestingly, then, the very existence and the considerable prosperity of false religions—or what amounts to a vast reign of "Satan's empire"—turns out to be proof of the absolute truth, necessity, and mercy of the Christian God. In short, in this formulaic calculation, the more numerous and powerful those benighted un-Christians are, the more is it certain that Christians have it right, for, ultimately, all the misfortunes of the world—including the current state of apparent powerlessness and failure of Christendom to reign universally—are attributable to original sin and the consequent universal perdition; and this truth about the human condition, it seems, Christians understand more profoundly than any other members of the human race. At least as far as official creeds are concerned, it may be said that Christians have always prized their own clear knowledge and conviction of the universal damnation of humankind. As evidenced by Goodrich's readiness to resort to this argument, the doctrine of the original sin—and, concomitantly, the doctrine of the impossibility of salvation except through the grace of God as precisely understood by Christians, that is, through Jesus Christ—obviously had considerable utility.

Goodrich, however, did not invent this acrobatic, tortuous, and inescapably tyrannical logic of sin and damnation, which he offers as an explanation for the menacing existence of un-Christians in the world. We see the same line of argument articulated by Samuel Purchas's 1613 treatise mentioned above. In his preface, "To the Reader," Purchas identifies the most important benefit his work has to offer to the reader, and especially to the religious professional:

The Divine . . . may here contemplate the workes of God, not in Creation alone, but in his Justice and Providence, pursuing sinne everywhere with such dreadfull plagues; both bodily, in rooting up and pulling downe the mightiest Empires; and especially in spirituall Judgements giving up so great a part of the World unto *the efficacie of Errour in strong delusions, that having forsaken the fountaine of living waters, they should digge unto themselves these broken Pits that can hold no water*; devout in their superstitions, and superstitious in their devotions; agreeing all in this, that there should bee a Religion, disagreeing from each other, and the TRUTH, in the practice thereof.

37. Goodrich, *Religious Ceremonies and Customs*, 15-18.

Nor was Purchas alone in resorting to this view. His contemporary Edward Brerewood (1565?–1613) proclaimed that one of the causes of the great and mighty spread of Islam—what he called Mahumetanism—was none other than "the justice of almighty God." For, according to him, God in effect "is punishing by that violent and wicked sect, the sins of Christians (for wee see that by the conquests of the Arabians, and Turkes, it hath chiefly seased [seized] on those regions, where Christianity in ancient time most flourished, both in Afrique and Asia, and partly in Europe)."[38]

These Christian authors, however nominal or earnest they might have been in their faith, could acknowledge the fact of religious plurality as the way of the world, and this was duly accounted for by the official teaching of their religion. As treatises on the subject of the religions of the world, their arguments had to accomplish two things at the same time. First, they had to display a broad range of alien religions such that their exposition would bear witness to the doctrine of sinful plurality as a universal condition. Second, they had to treat the subject in such a way as to circumvent too much affinity, or too easy slippage between, on the one hand, the perditious multiplicity of creeds and opinions outside the bounds of Christendom, and on the other, the regrettable plurality of churches and sects within Christianity. Both kinds of plurality stemmed from the same human sin and frailty, yet the distinction had to be maintained.

The difficulty of separating these two domains points to a more fundamental question: Where is the line of demarcation between Christianity and other religions? In other words, what groups and nations are denominations within Christianity, and which ones are religions external to it? While this question seems to us today altogether elemental and obvious, none of the texts written before the early nineteenth century seems to exhibit any particular inclination to address it.[39]

Consistent with this noteworthy indifference to the task of distinguishing Christianity from non-Christianity is the fact that there was a general tendency

---

38. Edward Brerewood, *Enquiries Touching the Diversity of Languages* (1614), 85.

39. For example, the treatise by William Turner (1653-1701), *The History of All Religions in the World* (1695)—not to be confused with William Burder's 1848 work with an almost identical title—treat individual topics (or "heads," as he calls them) under "Jewish," "Christian," "Mahometan," "Ancient Heathen," and "Modern Heathen," but he also regularly adds to the list "Muscovite," "Diabolical," "Armenian," and other such sects or groups.

among these early modern authors[40] to regard all matters of religious diversity and plurality of opinions in the vocabulary of "denominations" and "sects," regardless of how securely within or how far beyond the pale of "the correct religion" they might lie. Meanwhile, the correct religion, or religion proper, was always presumed identical to whatever variety of Christianity a given author endorsed. (Needless to say, in a familiar rhetorical gesture of any such treatise, the author immediately co-opts the reader into his own position as a matter of course.) It was only gradually over the course of the nineteenth century that the language of sect and denomination receded and became confined to the matters pertaining to the internal divisions of a single religion. It was only then that certain of the groups and nations gained independence, as it were, and attained autonomous status as separate *religions*.

This monumental transition—a critical step in the future development of the pluralist discourse on the religions of the world—is perceptible in how the titles of some of the publications changed in the course of the nineteenth century. *An Alphabetical Compendium of the Various Sects Which Have Appeared in the World from the Beginning of the Christian Era to the Present Day* (1784) by Hannah Adams (1755-1831) became, at least as of the fourth edition of 1817, *A Dictionary of All Religions and Religious Denominations*.[41] Similarly, Vincent Milner's aforementioned *Religious Denominations of the World*, published in 1859 or 1860, was renamed *Religions of the World* in the later editions beginning in 1870s.

Despite, or perhaps because of the mutability and instability of the categories, the four-way classificatory system endured and remained useful for centuries. Its authority is well attested by the simple fact that numerous monographs, which purported to survey all the nations of the world, ancient and modern, clearly assumed this taxonomy. One such text is *Enquiries Touching the Diversity of Languages, and Religions through the Chiefe Parts of the World* (1614), the work by Edward Brerewood already mentioned, in which he organizes religious diversity

40. I realize that the application of the term "early modern" to anything so late as the early nineteenth century violates historians' convention. I use this term merely as a shorthand, to serve my particular purpose here, for the lack of a better alternative.

41. It may be suggested, however, that in the case of Hannah Adams's treatise the demarcation between the Christian denominations and other religions was clearly implied from the beginning in that, in the first edition, "other religions" were actually treated in a lengthy appendix (83 pages), rather than as a part of the main text. The change of the title itself, nonetheless, seems significant, especially in view of the general shift in the terminology of "denomination."

in these terms: "There are foure sorts or sects of Religion, observed in the sundrie regions of the World. Namely, Idolatrie, Mahumetanisme, Iudaisme, and Christianity."[42] Analogously, Samuel Purchas termed the three non-Christian groups as "heathenish, Jewish, and Saracenicall."

In the eighteenth century there appeared several exemplary texts whose titles themselves reveal the adaptation of this taxonomy. For instance, Daniel Defoe's *Dictionarium Sacrum Seu Religiosum* has the better-known vernacular title mentioned above: *A Dictionary of All Religions, Ancient and Modern, Whether Jewish, Pagan, Christian, or Mahometan* (1704). Likewise, a few decades later, Thomas Broughton (1704-74) entitled his monograph *Bibliotheca Historico-Sacra, or An Historical Library of the Principal Matters Relating to Religion, Antient and Modern; Pagan, Jewish, Christian, and Mohammedan* (1737). The popular American compendium by Hannah Adams is called *A Dictionary of All Religions and Religious Denominations, Jewish, Heathen, Mahometan and Christian, Ancient and Modern*. This formula for categorizing remained dominant until the early decades of the nineteenth century, from which period we can draw further examples, such as Robert Adam's *The Religious World Displayed, or A View of the Four Grand Systems of Religion, Judaism, Paganism, Christianity and Mohammedanism* (1808) and David Benedict's *A History of All Religions, as Divided into Paganism, Mahometanism, Judaism and Christianity* (1824).

Thus four seemingly well-marked categories—Christianity, Judaism, Mohammedanism, idolatry (or heathenism, paganism, or polytheism)—recur in book after book with little variation from at least the early seventeenth century up to the first half of the nineteenth century.[43] But it is also clear that this taxonomy was not functioning as an apparatus to answer the simple question of how many religions there were in the world. Any answer forthcoming from this conceptual device, in any case, would be more confounding than clarifying.

To take but one example, touting the comprehensive scope of his *Dictionary of All Religions*, Defoe proclaims unambiguously as soon as the book begins: "The Four Grand Religions of the World are those Known by the Name of Judaism, Paganism, Christianity, and Mahometanism," only to add, three paragraphs later: "As Religion consists principally in *Worship*, or at least naturally

---

42. Brerewood, *Enquiries Touching the Diversity of Languages*, 79.

43. No doubt the origin of this four-part taxonomy is older than the seventeenth century and probably traceable to the medieval period. In this context, however, I am not directly concerned with the question of its origin, in part because of the practical limitation of the this project, in part because I believe, for the present purpose, the sudden proliferation of these texts in the vernacular in the seventeenth century is more significant than the source of this taxonomy itself.

implies it, and that *Worship* unavoidably requires some object or other; the *True Object* can be but one, *viz.* the Creator of Heaven and Earth; but the Corruption of Humane Nature having found out so many false Deities of both Sexes, Idols, Images, and vain Representation, it requires some Pains and Judgment to Collect and Digest them." Thus recognizing the necessarily ambiguous nature of the answer to the question "Is religion one, or many?" he strikes a practical compromise in the entry named "Religion," which begins with this sentence: "RELIGION is properly the Worship given to God, but 'tis also applied to the Worship of Idols and false Deities."

Defoe's contemporary, Augustin Calmet, is more exacting in his *Great Dictionary* with regard to the varying meanings of the term "religion," and he traces divergent and inconsistent uses of the term back to the Bible itself. Hence we read under the entry "Religion" the following helpful notes: "This Latin Word *Religio*, is taken in three Senses in Holy Scripture. First, for the external and ceremonial Worship of the *Jewish* Religion. . . . Secondly, *Religio* is put for the true *Religion*, the best manner of serving and honouring God. . . . Thirdly, and lastly, the Word *Religion* in Scripture, as well as in profane Authors, is often put for *Superstition.*" Depending on the context, then, "religion" could be several, one and only, or countless.

On one hand, we might say that according to the early modern system, there were four clear categories—that is, three individually distinct religions and one generic type, under which all the rest were subsumed. It evidently mattered little to the earlier writers just how many individual variations there were within the last category, for, whatever the count, the matter of significance was that they were numerous.[44] On the other hand, it can be reasonably suggested that, in the last analysis, only one religion—the true one—was recognized; alongside it were two forms of deviance; and, as for the rest, they were nations bereft of religion altogether. In effect, the last category comprised those who adhered to myriad substitutions for want of religion; lacking the knowledge of the Deity, they venerated pseudodeities, or idols. In sum, either there were countless religions or there was only one, yet, somehow, both assertions were true. The elasticity of the taxonomic system variously and flexibly enabled the demar-

---

44. As William Turner puts it in his chapter "Schisms and Sects" in *The History of All Religions in the World*: "Heathens, in respect of Religion, were as diverse as the Countries which they inhabited: Every Nation having peculiar Deities, and Rites of worship. . . . Modern Heathens, are likewise diversified, according to the number of countries, where they inhabit, Tribes or Castes, and sometimes Families and Persons" (192-96).

cation of "our" sanctified domain from "their" state of perdition, but it enabled little else.

It is useful to remember, also, that the early modern taxonomic system does not identify *religions* as such—that is, its aim apparently is not to sort out the plurality of "belief systems" as we understand the term today; instead, it recognizes and categorizes different "nations," or in our terms, different "peoples." That is to say, this system does not name Christianity *in addition to* so many alternative "religions" just like it, only different; rather, it classifies peoples according to the kinds of homage they pay, the ceremonies and customs they observe for that purpose, as well as according to the specific objects and beings to which they perform these acts. In other words, it recognizes "Christians," "Jews," "Mohammedans," and "heathens," rather than different "isms" that supposedly prescribe distinct spiritual cosmologies and so-called worldviews particular to each of these different peoples. It is not surprising, then, that the early modern accounts seem far more interested in collecting and enumerating empirical particularities and material details than in discovering any organizational principle that might help systematize these particulars and details.

The early modern texts are indeed punctilious—if also often grievously or amusingly wrong—in recording the habits and customs of particular peoples and their dealings with their gods, demons, and spirits. Moreover, the items thus noted are generally represented as a somewhat incidental (and never complete) assembly of oddities and curiosities, rather than as a set of practices emanating from a particular spiritual doctrine or a cosmology. As such, they are often mixed up with a great many other "customs and ceremonies" which we today do not consider necessarily or obviously religious. This apparently bothered neither the authors nor the readers. The titles of some of the texts betray this peculiar conceptual disposition, which seems to us strangely haphazard and disorderly, and certainly not very scientific.

One of the illustrative examples of this was an American publication commonly known as *Fessenden's Encyclopedia.* Edited by J. Newton Brown (1803-68), this reference work was officially entitled *Encyclopedia of Religious Knowledge, or Dictionary . . . Containing Definitions of All Religious Terms; An Impartial Account of the Principal Christian Denominations That Have Existed in the World from the Birth of Christ to the Present Day with Their Doctrines, Religious Rites and Ceremonies, as well as Those of the Jews, Mohammedans, and Heathen Nations, together with the Manners and Customs of the East* (1837). If we attend to the long explanatory subtitles of these texts, we can appreciate the integral relation in which "religions" were identified, intermeshed with various natural and cultural features of different localities.[45] The 1613 treatise by Purchas mentioned earlier—whose all-encompassing subtitle, we recall, reads *Relations of the World and the Religions Observed in Al[l] Ages and Places Discovered, from the Creation unto This Present*—includes, as that first edition announced: "briefe descriptions of the countries, nations, states, discoveries, private and publick customes, and the most remarkable rarities of nature, or humane industrie, in the same." Similarly, *Calmet's Great Dictionary* brings his sundry and indiscriminate interests into the Bible itself. Thus the subtitle of its 1827 edition reads *Historical, Critical, Geographical, and Etymological; Wherein Are Explained the Proper Names in the Old and New Testaments; the Natural Productions, Animals, Vegetables, Minerals, Stones, Gems, &c.; the Antiquities, Habits, Buildings, and Other Curiosities of the Jews; With a Chronological History of the Bible, the Jewish Calendar, Tables of the Hebrew Coins, Weights, Measures, &c. But perhaps most revealing of all is the jubilantly polymorphous and vaguely perverse title of a two-volume compendium published by John Hartley in 1703: *An Universal, Historical, Geographical and Poetical Dictionary: Containing Likewise the Lives of Eminent Persons, also the History of the Pagan Gods, of the Several Sects among the Jews, Christians, Heathens and Mahometans, of General Councils and Synods, of the Establishment and Progress of Religious and Military orders; and of the Genealogies of the Most Illustrious Families.* Its encyclopedic ambition notwithstanding, we may safely surmise, this is not a work of an aspiring *Religionswissenschaftler* seeking to present a systematic survey of all the religions of the world.

We might conclude that the foremost objective of the authors and publishers of these books was neither to contribute to a science that was yet to come into existence, nor, for that matter, to offer practical intelligence considered efficacious for the vocational training of future missionaries. We might reasonably conjecture, indeed, that the prospective readers of these books—who were necessarily of comfortable circumstances to be able to afford such leisure—

45. In this connection, there is at least one text from a much later period that is very much akin to these earlier publications, so that it may be considered an atavism of sorts. Its author is identified simply as "Frank S. Dobbins, of Yokohama, Japan." The title has a distinctly archaic character: *Error's Chains: How Forged and Broken—Complete, Graphic, and Comparative History of the Many Strange Beliefs, Superstitious Practices, Domestic Peculiarities, Sacred Writings, Systems of Philosophy, Legends and Traditions, Customs and Habits of Mankind throughout the World, Ancient and Modern* (1883). This 777-page book, palpably a costly production, also contains numerous engravings, most of which, at least, are as amusing as they are factually inaccurate.

expected above all else to be amused and diverted by the narratives of exotic lore, travels, and adventures abroad, and to be charmed and transported by the exquisite plates and engravings that often lavishly accompanied such accounts.[46] In fact, what is arguably the most widely disseminated early-eighteenth-century book on the subject of "religious ceremonies and customs" was known by the name of the engraver, Bernard Picart (1673-1733), rather than by the authors of the text—although the abbé Banier and the abbé Le Mascrier are mentioned in the title of the original edition, *Ceremonie et coutumes religieuses de tous les peoples du monde*, published by Jean Frédéric Bernard of Amsterdam in 1723. The book was extensively reprinted, excerpted, copied, and published in several languages throughout the eighteenth and the nineteenth centuries. The first of many English editions began to appear only ten years after the original, in seven volumes, under the title *The Ceremonies and Religious Customs of the Various Nations of the Known World: Together with Historical Annotations, and Several Curious Discourses Equally Instructive and Entertaining, . . . Written Originally in French, and Illustrated . . . by Mr. Bernard Picart, . . . Translated into English, by a Gentleman* (1733-39).[47]

It was through such texts that Europe began to learn about religions observed elsewhere, and ever since, "religions of the world" has been a steady growth industry of the literate world. The prescientific and nonvocational interest of a purely consumptive sort—"curiosity" seems to capture only part of the indeterminate yet pervasive interest—was what initially supported the publishing ventures of the kind we find in the earlier modern period. Needless to say, neither the advent of *Religionswissenschaft* and the concomitant boosting of scientific interests nor the surge of active and concerted efforts on the part

---

46. An early example of such observations on curious and exotic religions in the context of travelogue and adventure stories is *The True Travels, Adventures, and Observations of Captaine John Smith* (1630). Amid the tales of battles, captivity, and escape is inserted "his description of the Tartars, their strange manners and customes of religions, diets, buildings, warres, feasts, ceremonies, and living."

47. Another French edition that appeared in the early nineteenth century under a different title provided the source for Charles Goodrich's *Religious Ceremonies and Customs* (1834), cited earlier. In addition, several works by David Herrliberger (1697-1777) of Zürich published between 1746 and 1751 appear to be based on Picart's work, for example, *Gottesdienstliche Ceremonien . . . der Christen* (1746). William Burder's *A History of All Religions* (1848) is also apparently an abridgement of Picart's work. There are numerous American editions and reprints of this work in the nineteenth century.

of Christian missionary organizations to appropriate the knowledge of the world's religions as an instrument of their evangelizing work—both of these trends can be traced back to the middle of the nineteenth century—ever undermined or overshadowed this diversionary interest. Today this interest continues to be served by a veritable flood of material generated by various departments of the culture industry, from numerous glossy coffee-table books to highly touted television documentaries, videotaped lectures for rent and for sale, luxury tours and cruises led by media-friendly academics—all claiming to be "equally instructive and entertaining" in manners utterly unimaginable by M. Picart's contemporaries, and yet perhaps quite similar in appeal.

3. Before the Birth of Science

Nothing about this continuity of basic interest, however, diminishes the significance of the changes that did occur in the European classificatory system: the older, four-way system of demarcating religions (or nations) visibly declined during the first half of the nineteenth century. Consequently, the middle to the latter half of the century was a period of general uncertainty and taxonomic indeterminacy, or rather, a period of proliferation of new systems of naming and grouping religions, so much so that none could be said to be predominant. In a sense, this was a period of transition, marking the passage between the demise of the old taxonomy and the establishment of the new one in the early twentieth century, at which time, as we have already seen in an earlier section of this chapter, the taxonomy came to be organized definitively as a pattern of coexistence—correlation, affiliation, and even alliance—of a dozen or so "world religions." Not coincidentally, it is precisely in this interim period of taxonomic volatility that the scientific study of religion—or what was to become the very backbone and legitimating authority of the modern discourse on religion—took root. The collapse of the old taxonomy was not, however, simply a matter of one framework losing ground and eventually being replaced by another. What changed was not so much the method of how to count and categorize religions, but the very manner in which—in an important sense, for the first time— a "religion" was to be recognized, to be identified as such, so that it might be *compared* with another.

This change, to be sure, should be counted as a gain for the fledgling science of religion. It would seem highly improbable that such a science could have been initiated in the absence of this foundational presupposition, in other words, without the seemingly axiomatic notion that both "religion" as a genus and "religions" as particular species are objectively discernible, identifiable, and at least in principle, isolable.[48] This conceptual framework as a whole, appropriately enough, was heralded by the very first of F. Max Müller's lectures on the science of religion (1870).[49] On this occasion, he famously proclaimed, paraphrasing Goethe, "[H]e who knows one, knows none," thereby promoting the comparative method as the basis of all truly scientific endeavors. Such a science would not have been possible—so it would seem, if we are to follow this train of thought—so long as "religious ceremonies and customs" had remained commingled with the sundry acts, habits, and mores of tribal/national forms of life, as had been the case for many earlier writers.

Before the advent of this science, however, there appeared a few notable texts in the middle of the nineteenth century, which may be considered as marking the watershed, separating the reign of the older system of classification at the moment of its demise and its yielding to the new state of proliferation and volatility.

By profession, Josiah Conder (1789-1855) belonged to the old school, if we take into account that the most celebrated of his achievements was a thirty-volume compilation, with ample plates and maps, called *Modern Traveller: A Description of the Various Countries of the Globe* (1824-30). But his book on religion, or rather, on religions, appears to express a novel sort of design, if its title can be taken at its face value: *An Analytical and Comparative View of All Religions Now Extant among Mankind: With their Internal Diversities of Creed and Profession* (1838). The intentions proclaimed in the title were to be both "comparative" and "analytical" by means of representing the diversity of "creed and profession"—or something we might call "beliefs"—instead of parading, as had been routine, myriad strange and colorful ceremonies and customs. This aspiration seems conspicuously novel, adumbrating as it does the ambition of the science to come.

As for the actual content of Conder's study, his organization is an intriguing admixture of the old and the new. Of the twelve chapters, nine are devoted to Christianity. The last two chapters are given respectively to "monotheistic

48. This, however, is probably more a matter of logical order, rather than a chronological sequence. In fact, there may be something fallacious in thinking that *before* comparison there must be *already* a recognition of multiple, discrete religions. In his illuminating study *Savage Systems* (1996), David Chidester has argued with respect to pioneering European observers in seventeenth- and eighteenth-century southern Africa that the act of comparison was constitutive of the very first recognition—identification, invention—of the native religions.

49. This lecture series was published three years later as *Introduction to the Science of Religion* (1873) and will be discussed in greater detail in chapter 7 below.

religions" and "polytheism and pantheism." Specifically, monotheistic religions include Judaism and Mohammedanism, as might be expected, but also Magianism (what would be today identified as pre-Islamic Iranian religion). In addition, Conder also mentions in this chapter what he calls "ambiguous sects," which he specifies by way of a rather unfamiliar list: "the Druses," "the Anzairies" (Anzanites?), "the Yezidees" (Yezidi), "the Zabians." In the final chapter, under the rubric of "polytheism and pantheism," he covers the following topics:

early religion of India allied to Magianism / Brahminical idolatry / Buddhism and Jainism / discussion on the characteristics of polytheism and pantheism / Vedas, Pooranas, Tantras, Reformed sects [of Hindustan] / Sikhs / Lamaism / religion of China and Japan / Birma and Siam / illiterate superstitions.

In effect, the separate, disproportionate, and privileged place the book accords to Christianity, along with the grouping of Judaism and Mohammedanism (albeit with a few additions) separately from the large group of other religions comprised by "polytheism and pantheism," seems to indicate the basic acceptance of the older four-part classification system standard up to that time. What is new is in the details. The specification of the last chapter, "polytheism and pantheism," in particular resembles those of many later books, in that his list is about as idiosyncratic as "typical" late-nineteenth-century texts and, at the same time, includes many topics and groupings favored by the later writers. But perhaps even more significant may be that, in Conder, there is not only a clear recognition of "polytheism" (or what has been otherwise called "idolatry," "heathen," or "pagan worship") as a type, but also the recognition of "monotheistic religion" as a type, even though Christianity is still treated as something that exceeds this type, insofar as it is discussed separately. In this manner, the organization of the topics becomes more a classification of religions, and less a hierarchy of nations, even if Christianity is still placed in a position clearly above them all.

Our second example from this period is William Burder's abridgment of Bernard Picart's famous work of engravings, published under his own name and specifically for an American audience. In the title page to the 1848 edition, the publisher (if not the author) claimed that the volume was "greatly improved, as a book of reference, by the insertion of a full account, historical, doctrinal, and statistical, of the principal religious denominations in the United States, by Joel Parker." Some of Picart's very fine, and oftentimes very amusing engravings are duly included in this volume, as were some of the textual descriptions of "religious customs and ceremonies." This Burder rendition first appeared in 1841, and it was followed by very many later printings and revised editions with varying titles, published throughout the rest of the nineteenth century. *A History of All Religions: With Accounts of the Ceremonies and Customs, or the Forms of Worship Practiced by the Several Nations of the Known World, from the Earliest Records to the Present Time*—as the 1848 and subsequent volumes were called—was indeed something of an improvement "as a book of reference." The material was now organized differently from the original multivolume work, which covered the nations of the world simply geographically, without any concern for typology or taxonomic principle of any kind. Burder's version, in contrast, presents "all religions" in accordance with the following organizational framework:

history and religious ceremonies of the Jews
history and religious ceremonies of the Mohammedans
religious tenets, ceremonies and customs of the Greek and Roman
    Catholic Churches
religious customs and ceremonies of the Protestant Communities
brief account of religious denominations in the United States
religious ceremonies and customs of Pagan nations and tribes

As in the case of Conder's work, Burder's last section, on "pagan nations," covers many particulars, whose assembly likewise resembles the cacophonous listing of "other religions" of the later-nineteenth-century texts. Burder's roster of "pagan nations" runs as follows:

ancient Egyptians / Carthaginians and Tyrians / Assyrians / Babylonians / Medes and Persians / Scythians, Scandinavians, Celts or Druids / ancient Greek and Romans / Chinese / Japanese / Thibetans and Tartars / Hindoos / Laplanders / Indian tribes / Malagasy / Polynesians

The same proliferation of the "pagan nations" is also exemplified by a third example, Vincent L. Milner's book mentioned earlier, whose full title reads: *Religious Denominations of the World: Comprising a General View of the Origin, History and Condition of the Various Sects of Christians, the Jews, and Mahometans, as well as the Pagan Forms of Religion Existing in the Different Countries of the Earth; With Sketches of the Founders of Various Sects; From the Best Authorities.* As the subtitle indicates, this work likewise assumes the older four-part division of nations. As does Conder, Milner discusses many Christian sects, but he includes sections not only on "Jews" and "Mahometanism," but also on "Bramins," "Buddhists," "Atheists," and "Pantheists," as well as several independent sections on "pagans" of various sorts—pagans of Africa, of China, of Japan, of Lapland, of Madagascar, of Mexico, of North America, of Peru, and of Polynesia. His special note on the "founders" is also noteworthy, as this resonates with the lately commonplace idea that each of the world religions—with Hinduism and Shinto being notable exceptions—have a historical founder figure to which the authority of the whole tradition may be traced.

As a counterweight to this forward-looking outlook, what is also conspicuous in Milner's volume is that the author offers a series of detailed, item-by-item descriptions of paganism in a great many varieties, ultimately for the purpose of exposing all possible forms of religious deviation, as measured from the standpoint of the spiritually chaste and temperate Protestantism that he happened to endorse. The forms of deviance, in fact, could range from the most naive and primitive heathenism to the most urbane and sophistic pantheism, the latter of which Milner describes as "a philosophical species of idolatry, leading to atheism, in which the universe was considered as the Supreme God," and which he finally pronounces an "absurd system."[50] In the end, it may be claimed that, despite the signs of innovation, an account such as this is more

---

50. Milner, *Religious Denominations of the World,* 413. Perhaps not entirely irrelevant to this wholesale attack on all forms of idolatry is another publication by Milner, which is an explicit polemic against Roman Catholicism, as the title makes evident: *Paganism, Popery, and Christianity, or The Blessing of an Open Bible: As Shown in the History of Christianity, from the Time of Our Savior to the Present Day* (1855). This latter work also includes an essay by Joseph F. Berg (1812-71): "A View of the Latest Developments of Rome's Hostility to the Bible . . . and an Expose of the Absurdities of the Immaculate Conception and the Idolatrous Veneration of the Virgin Mary."

Apparently, deists and atheists presented intriguing taxonomic challenges to some other authors as well. Robert Adam—who is described as "Minister of the Episcopal Congregations, Blackfriar's Wynd, Edinburgh; and Chaplain to the Right Honourable the Earl of Kellie"—comments: "The only people who may not be classed under one or other of these four divisions, are, the *Deists,* and the *Atheists;*—the latter differing from them all, in owning *no religion;* and the *former,* in owning no *revelation* as the foundation of their religion." And when it comes to counting their number, it proves impossible. Having tabulated the major subdivisions among Christians,

dogmatic than analytic, more parochial than objective, more theological than scientific.

It is of course one of our contemporary habits of thought to deem such religiously compliant—and, in fact, denominationally particular—interests as prescientific, which is also our way of saying unscientific. To regard such a narrowly confessional orientation as a throwback, therefore, presumes a certain self-understanding of the position of science, or what has been baldly called the ideology of scientific progress. This scientistic ideology is predicated, or so it seems, on a certain form of anticlericalism, or, as some religious advocates would argue, antireligionism. In any event, it may not be prudent for us today to swallow whole either the scenario of progress or any version of scientific triumphalism if we hope to claim evenhandedness and analytic equilibrium. What should be noted here, then, is not the backwardness of these texts, but rather the complex and multifaceted appeal they were making to their prospective readers, who must have included clerical and state authorities. What is thus particularly interesting in that transitional moment is the texts' articulation of the rationale—an excuse?—for bringing into broad daylight and making a public display of what was likely to have been called, only a few generations earlier, a heap of "rotten bones of the passed, and stinking bodies of the present superstitions."

In present academic practice, the question of whether a given author was theologically motivated or free of all such parochial interests continues to be asked, explicitly or implicitly, whenever any writing on religion is evaluated. We seem to have developed a nearly automatic, hardly conscious habit of administering a low-grade litmus test on this particular register, presumably in order to help us assess the credibility of the sources or the cogency of the argument. But even if such a measurement should prove reliable, it can reveal the nature of the writing only in one register. And it is doubtful that such monochromatic information in and of itself could be interesting or valuable to anyone not personally or professionally invested in matters of doctrinal fidelity, either on the side of religious orthodoxy or on the side of some self-circumscribed scientific correctness. Perhaps more seriously, our insistence on

---

the author appends a note: "In the former table, Deists and Atheists are comprehended, but not specified, as they are no where distinct, and as it is not possible to ascertain their numbers." The quotations are from the author's preface to *The Religious World Displayed* (1808).

a compulsory interrogation into authors' religious/scientific compliance could constrain our own analytic strategy. Indeed, as a result of such a compulsory testing, the outlook, the posture, and the attitude, the sense and the nuances of the gestures exhibited in those earlier texts (whose authors obviously had not anticipated the sort of interrogation we routinely put them through) become somehow muted or altogether invisible. In order to avoid such an outcome, then, we would be well advised to note at the outset the following truism. These "prescientific" authors were, just as purposefully as authors of any other time, striking rhetorical poses, articulating rationales and apologia, issuing challenges, taking chances or taking liberties, perhaps even defending a cause; and all these gestures were in the anticipation of one reaction or another from their prospective readers, the readers imagined by them, who were not us.

It may be profitable, then, to dwell for a moment on the imagined audience intrinsic to these "prescientific" texts, and to learn to discern (rather than morally judge) the function of their shared "ethnocentrism" in their progressively and aggressively expanding mapping of the world. For, as it is most assuredly a cliché to say, the assumption of Euro-Christian supremacy over all others—an assumption commonly held, presumably, by those writers and their readers alike—played a decisive role in the emergent sense of "the world" as a totality. Why should Christians of Europe concern themselves with those residing elsewhere, or those bygone nations long past? Who, in the total scheme of the universe, were those others, creatures of God just as much as anything else in the universe yet who did not know or honor him? What moral or spiritual lessons for the Euro-Christians were contained in the state of ignorance and perdition of those others elsewhere?

It is not altogether clear to me whether these were in fact the burning questions that fueled the production of texts such as the ones we have been examining. What is amply evident, however, is that these texts concertedly aspired, or at the very least alleged or pretended to address, these religiously fervent concerns above all else. These concerns were prominently foregrounded, announced at the beginning as part of the justification for the whole enterprise; and such an announcement served as a premise for claiming that the book was to be more than just entertaining or satisfying to idle curiosity. The loftier purposes thus espoused in the prefaces and the introductions to these books were, first and foremost, patently theological questions. In our own time, we seem to have learned to consider it most prudent to forgive their presence by ignoring them. Indeed, these theologically grounded, publicly confessional considerations were soon to be pushed to the background, attenuated, submerged, and sometimes loudly denounced and banished from later generations of books on the subject of world religions. But if our overall objective is to understand the vicissitudes of European discourse on the religions of the world, it is precisely such processes of diminution, submersion, or transmutation of interests that should engage our critical attention.

2

The Legacy of Comparative Theology

In chapter 1, the discursive domain of nineteenth-century ferment most relevant to the formation and authorization of the world religions discourse, which
is to be the topic of part 2, was demarcated and its temporal limits defined by a
rough sketch each of the period "after" and the period "before." The present
chapter will further define the contours of this discursive domain. Specifically,
we will look at another concurrent and adjacent domain of discourse pertaining to religion—a domain that is generally excluded from the "history of the
science of religion." One might say that it is precisely against the backdrop of
this alternative domain of religion discourse that the project of the scientific
study of religion, especially as this history is viewed from the twentieth century
and beyond, came to define itself and came to its own self-consciousness. This
adjoining realm of religion discourse can be instrumental in circumscribing
the principal object of our concern in yet another way.

Despite the lack of consensus as to how many or exactly what types of religions
there were in the world, the educated classes of the latter half of the nineteenth
century evidently had a penchant for the subject of what they often referred to
as "great religious systems," or sometimes "ancient religions," and other times
"Oriental religions," meaning, roughly, religions other than their own. The
heartiness of their interest is attested by the steady increase in publications on
this general topic, although the term commonly encountered then was not
"world religions" but "comparative theology."[1] Today, more than a century
later, this voluminous literature, which once filled the libraries of Europe and
North America, is rarely read, and its very existence hardly recognized.

To be sure, upon glancing at the texts, it is not difficult to imagine what
contemporary scholars might say in explaining and justifying this wholesale

---

1. Just after the turn of the last century, Louis Henry Jordan could compile an impressive list
of publications and lectures on this general topic. See Jordan's *Comparative Religion: Its Genesis and
Growth* (1905), especially 415–80, 562–72.

neglect of comparative theology. One might point out, for instance, that nineteenth-century treatises on non-Christian religions were generally based on poor empirical knowledge, hampered as they were by woefully insufficient and often faulty data, and that they are therefore altogether useless today. Even more seriously, it might be further charged that the underlying interests of the majority of the authors of these works were, in the end, to provide opportunities to reflect favorably on Christianity, to justify the presumption of its superiority over all other religions, and finally to infuse new energy, vitality, and legitimacy to its missionary expansion. This outright Christian favoritism was due, presumably, to the practical reality that Christianity, in whatever variety or whatever degree of seriousness, was the religion to which the authors themselves subscribed, and which they also presumed on the part of their readers. All this, from the viewpoint of the contemporary scholarly guild, seems at odds with scientific principles and interests, whose allegiance should be to empirical facts alone, not to be swayed by personal religious commitments or preferences. The seemingly benign silence that reigns over the legacy of comparative theology, justified or not, does not easily provide an occasion to ponder whether it should be examined at all in relation to the formation of the academic discipline of the science of religion.[2]

The nineteenth-century literature of comparative theology is clearly less valued as a disciplinary heritage of the science of religion than the now

---

2. In the early stage of research for this project, I was surprised by the large quantity of the material on this subject dating back to midcentury. Apparently any university library that was in business during the nineteenth century, as well as many of the public libraries, had an ample stock of these texts. For instance, the Davis Library of the University of North Carolina where I began my research, not only housed a great variety of books in this category but also very many editions of some of the titles, and even multiple copies of the same edition, signaling considerable readership in the university community. Of course, the existence of multiple copies at the university library does not imply that the institution actually purchased them in order to meet the readership demand; this more probably was an indication that several different individuals affiliated with the university (or their executors) chose to donate a personal library to the university upon their retirement or death. This probable scenario, however, does not detract from the overall popularity of these books at the time.

The general neglect of this literature today, on the other hand, is illustrated by the following fact. In some research libraries whose physical holding capacity is limited, such as the Hatcher Library at the University of Michigan, almost all of these books are kept in a storage facility rather than on the open-stack shelves. This, in the case of Michigan, means that no library patron has asked for the titles for decades. In most cases, those books in storage had not been charged out since the 1950s or, not infrequently, the 1930s.

likewise discredited but still widely acknowledged legacy of the armchair-anthropological, pseudoevolutionary "theories" of religion that were advanced at about the same time.[3] This state of affairs is rather peculiar, given that, even at a cursory glance, it is amply obvious that there is great affinity and commonality of interest between the present practice of world religions (as the mainstay of the business of "religious studies" curricula) and nineteenth-century comparative theology, whereas there is little continuity between the assumptions governing the scholarly practice of religious studies today and that of Victorian anthropology.[4] As we shall see, the resemblance—or, possibly, unconscious or atavistic continuity—between nineteenth-century comparative theology and the contemporary world religions enterprise is not superficial. Nor could it be claimed that nineteenth-century exponents of comparative theology have been ignored because of their lack of erudition or academic prestige. For, however one might judge the value of their works now, most of them were without a doubt men (and women) of considerable stature in their own times, well-educated and greatly esteemed, as well as highly positioned.[5]

3. To take but two examples, Frederick Denison Maurice and James Freeman Clarke—authors of two of the most prominent books of this genre, which will be discussed below—receive only passing mentions in Eric Sharpe's *Comparative Religion* (2nd ed., 1986), primarily as an influence on the next generation of scholars. Sharpe does indicate in a footnote, however, the immense popularity of Clarke's volume, which passed through thirty editions between 1871 and 1893, and he opines as follows in the main text: "Clarke's work was genuinely comparative, and written as it was within a year of the programmatic statement of Max Müller concerning the possible scope of the science of religion, must be reckoned to be one of the early milestones of the subject" (137).

4. There may be, of course, a facile way of making this observation less interesting and less surprising: to draw a distinction between scientific research/theorizing and popular interest, and to claim that there is no need to assume a parallel development in the course of scholarly progress and the relatively slow pace of progress in the general public's understanding. Yet such a separation of scholarly practice from popular practice, professional interests from lay interests, has its limitations; in fact it is rather myopic, not only with respect to the contemporary situation but also in the context of the nineteenth century. There was nothing unprofessional or amateur about the works and the credentials of those authors who became famous by writing books on comparative theology, as measured against better remembered figures like Max Müller, Robertson Smith, Tylor, Frazer, Durkheim, or Freud, whose works, after all, were immensely popular as well as scholarly.

5. I have come across only a few women among the writers on the topic of comparative theology in the nineteenth century or early twentieth century. There are, to be sure, a larger number of women writing on certain topics or aspects of religion and other related subjects—Harriet Martineau (1802–76), Jane Harrison (1850–1928), and Evelyn Underhill (1875–1941) among

1. Two Pioneers: Frederick Denison Maurice and James Freeman Clarke

Frederick Denison Maurice (1805–72) was a prominent Christian Socialist and founder of the Working Men's College, also professor of divinity at King's College, London, and later professor of moral philosophy at Cambridge University. Although something of a political radical, he was a well-respected figure in the most illustrious of the literary, philanthropic, and scientific societies in Britain of his time. His most famous work, *The Religions of the World and Their Relations to Christianity* (1847), comprised eight lectures he delivered in 1846. The lectureship itself was a celebrated one established in 1691, pursuant to the will of the renowned natural philosopher and son of a wealthy colonist of Ireland, Robert Boyle. The terms of Boyle's bequest specifically stated "that eight Sermons should be preached each year in London for proving the Christian Religion against notorious Infidels, to wit, Atheists, Theists, Pagans, Jews and Mahometans; not descending lower to any controversies that are among Christians themselves."[6] The list is a familiar one, assuming, as one may reasonably do in this context, that Boyle was using the term "Theists" to mean, more or less, "Deists." Also noteworthy is the last provision, warning not to "descend lower" to the sectarian divisiveness within Christianity, which, in effect would confuse the matter of the condemnable dissension and plurality of the Infidels with the matter of pardonable internal variety and multiplicity of sects and opinions within the Christian community.[7]

As the 1846 appointee of the lectureship, Maurice managed to transcribe and

---

them. But when we limit the consideration to comparative religion/theology more specifically, the list is limited. The scholarship of Julia Wedgwood (1833–1913), whose work *The Moral Ideal* (1888) covers various religious traditions (Egypt, India, Persia, Greece, and Rome), is on the whole not of a quality comparable to that of others discussed in this chapter. Annie Besant (1847–1933) gave two series of lectures on the topic of "great religions" in 1897 and 1901 and is on that account a notable figure. Her treatises, however, are written from an expressly Theosophical point of view, which make them rather atypical. See *Seven Great Religions* (1966).

6. Boyle's will quoted in Frederick Denison Maurice, *The Religions of the World and Their Relations to Christianity* (1847), 1. Hereafter references to Maurice's work will be cited in the text by page number.

7. Here, then, is the same concern as the one we heard Defoe express in his *Dictionarium Sacrum Seu Religiosum* (1704), when he proposed to treat the matter of differences and plurality of opinions within the Christian world "without using the Opprobrious Names of *Schismaticks* or *Sectaries*, and the like Appellations, which serve to rend them asunder, instead of cementing them together against the *Common Enemy*."

update the spirit of Boyle's will to suit the conditions of the nineteenth century. "In compliance with the directions of Boyle," Maurice identified what he took to be "the most prevailing form of unbelief in [his] day," and found in it "the tendency to look upon all theology as having its origin in the spiritual nature and faculties of man" (252), that is to say, not in divine sources. In order to challenge this tendency to naturalize, humanize, and equalize all religions without exception, his intention was "to examine the great Religious Systems which present themselves to us in the history of the world . . . enquiring what was their main characteristical principle" (10) and eventually to contrast them with that of Christianity. His list of "great religious systems" notably differs from Boyle's list of Infidels, as well as from the world religions list of the twentieth century. In his lectures, Maurice gives considerations to "Mahometanism," "Hindooism," "Buddhism," and finally what he calls "the defunct Religions," which are specified further as the Persian, the Egyptian, the Greek, the Roman, and the Gothic. After a preliminary round of investigation, he reaches the following conclusion, which is generally resonant with most of the early modern texts examined above, but his reasoning is different:

> Look at each of these religions, and you see that there is a witness of oneness in all places and times. Look at them again, and you see there is something which divides them from each other. They feel that if they are to unite, it must be in something above themselves; they cannot unite for things beneath themselves, the accidents of their life, the climate, the soil of the lands in which they dwell, seem to determine what it is that is above them. They feel that if they are to unite, it must be in something above themselves; but their habits, tempers, tastes of their own minds, determine what it is which is above them. (129–30)

In other words, all religions, insofar as they are bona fide religions, aspire to what is transcendent and universal; yet this aspiration remains unfulfilled in each religion examined because of some ineradicable human factors, historical particularities, and local limitations. In each of these religions, the understanding of the universal and transcendent remains inevitably particular and limited, determined as it is by the idiosyncrasy of the region and the people in question. Yet if bearing witness to unitary transcendence is the very nature of religion, as Maurice assumes, any limitation, any partiality, is more than a mere flaw; it signals a fatal contradiction in its own constitution as a religion. The question, for Maurice, is whether Christianity, too, is fraught with the same limitation, partiality, and self-contradiction.

With this problem in mind, Maurice proceeds to consider in the second half of the lecture series non-Christian religions expressly in contrast with Christianity. Not surprisingly, at the end of these deliberations, he comes to this observation:

> Do not *all* [religions] demand another ground than the human one? Is not Christianity the consistent asserter of that higher ground? Does it not distinctly and consistently refer every human feeling and consciousness to that ground? Is it not *for this reason* able to interpret and reconcile the other religions of the earth? Does it not in this way prove itself to be not a human system, but the Revelation, which human beings require? (252)

In effect, for Maurice, a comparison of the "religions of the world" yields an essential *religious* truth—rather than *scientific* facts—namely, that Christianity is the only true religion among the multitude of what turn out to be, in the last analysis, pseudoreligions.

Maurice's lecture series was, as numerous later references to it attest, undoubtedly one of the most celebrated and among the earliest examples of the new rationale and the new direction for the comparative examination of religions. Two decades later, in 1868, nearly the same argument was reiterated on the other side of the Atlantic, in the widely read and oft reprinted essays of the distinguished Unitarian minister and Bostonian savant, James Freeman Clarke (1810–88), originally serialized in the *Atlantic Monthly* and in 1871 published as a single volume entitled *Ten Great Religions: An Essay in Comparative Theology.*[8] As was a regular practice among many of his contemporaries, Clarke employs the pair of terms "catholic" and "ethnic" to signify the difference between the intrinsically universal religion (Christianity) and the intrinsically limited, race-specific religions (all the rest). As for his list of what count as "great religions," from the standpoint of contemporary conventions, it may seem as odd as Maurice's, yet at the same time also vaguely familiar: Confucianism, Brahmanism, Buddhism, Zoroastrianism, the religion of Egypt, of Greece, of Rome, Teutonic and Scandinavian religion, Judaism, and Islam.[9]

---

8. Its original publisher, Houghton, Mifflin, produced numerous editions between 1871 and 1883. I refer to the 1881 edition, hereafter cited in the text by page number.

9. More accurately, they are designated in the chapter headings thus: "Confucius and the Chinese: The Prose of Asia," "Brahmanism," "Buddhism: The Protestantism of the East,"

This being the general lay of the land, it appears that the lack of symmetry or balance among the "ethnic religions" ultimately mattered little to Clarke for, his underlying assumption is that, though religions may be many, only one among them is founded on a genuinely universal principle, hence that religion alone has universal appeal and unifying power. It is not surprising, therefore, that Clarke goes on to announce, early in his introduction, that the study of the different religious systems of the world, or comparative theology, is a new area of thought as yet largely unexplored in which "to establish the truth of Christianity":

> For if we can make it appear, by a fair survey of the principal religions of the world, that, while they are ethnic or local, Christianity is catholic or universal; that, while they are defective, possessing some truths and wanting others, Christianity possesses all; and that, while they are stationary, Christianity is progressive; it will not then be necessary to discuss in what sense it is a supernatural religion. Such a survey will show that it is adapted to the nature of man. When we see adaptation we naturally infer design. If Christianity appears, after a full comparison with other religions, to be the one and the only religion which is perfectly adapted to man, it will be impossible to doubt that it was designed by God to be the religion of our race; that it is the providential religion sent by God to man, its truth God's truth, its way the way to God and to heaven. (14)

Clarke's "ifs" drop off soon thereafter, as this announcement is followed by what amounts to a detailed synopsis of the entire volume, displayed in the form of a series of "findings" the reader should anticipate. The section headings of the nineteen-page synopsis at the end of the introduction tell all:

> §6. It [comparative theology] will show that, while most of the Religions of the World are Ethnic, or the Religions of Races, Christianity is Catholic, or adapted to become the Religion of all Races. (15)

> §7. Comparative Theology will probably show that the Ethnic Religions are one-sided, each containing a Truth of its own, but being defective, wanting some corresponding Truth. Christianity, or the Catholic Religion, is complete on every Side. (21)

"Zoroaster and the Zend Avesta," "The Gods of Egypt," "The Gods of Greece," "The Religion of Rome," "The Teutonic and Scandinavian Religion," "The Jewish Religion," and "Mohammed and Islam."

§8. Comparative Theology will probably show that Ethnic Religions are arrested, or degenerate, and will come to an End, while the Catholic Religion is capable of a progressive Development. (29)

For both Maurice and Clarke, then, the most important and at the same time most edifying consequence of a "fair survey" of the great religions of the world is that it testifies to the truth and universality of Christianity, alone among all others. This judgment, to be sure, seems fundamentally consistent with that of the earlier generation of writers. Yet the logic and the rhetoric have changed significantly. Heathendom broadly conceived—that is to say, all of non-Christianity, or what Boyle roundly called "Infidels"—is no longer Satan's empire testifying, by its own state of perdition, to the absolute truth of the Bible and to the doctrine of original sin. In this new literature of comparative theology, non-Christendom comes to be represented as the domain of so many incomplete religions, which are at best preparatory phenomena, and whose transcendent aspirations have been from the beginning—insofar as they are humanly and thus capriciously contrived—doomed to fail. The myriad forms of their inadequacies are but woeful testimonies to the absolute necessity of the real thing. Christianity is thus the consummate religion yearned for and aspired to by all others, but in vain. In this, Christianity is utterly unlike them; it is the fulfillment of all others' futile yearning.

2. Strategies for Representation

The sentiment that construes Christianity as the final answer to the spiritual demands embodied by other religions is typically expressed in the idea that all non-Christian religions are somehow "older" religions. What is implied here is that they are archaic traditions already effectively superseded by the coming of Christ, yet lingering still, because the Gospel truth has not yet reached everyone, while some others who have heard the good news, stubbornly continue to resist its salvific tidings. These religions are essentially antiquated remnants of the past, residual primitivism surviving to this day, as analogous to the "Stone Age" savages found living in the nineteenth century. The "old religions" are but chance assemblages of shards from so many flawed vessels; they may never become part of the New Risen Truth; yet the broken fragments still may reflect, in a melancholy fashion, the splendor of the Complete.

Sharing this outlook, among many others, was George Matheson (1842–1906), a parish minister of Edinburgh, who published a book entitled *The Distinctive Messages of the Old Religions* (1892), in which he wrote that the non-

Christian religions "have their origin in a much remoter past" and they are all "long passed away, and Christianity is still Green."[10] A very similar opinion was expressed by a fellow Scottish divine, John Caird (1820–98), then the principal of the University of Glasgow, and apparently something of an amateur specialist on Buddhism and Brahmanism. In the opening essay of a volume entitled *The Faiths of the World* (1882)—a publication based on the St. Giles Lectures, consisting of twelve essays authored by various Scottish clergymen, some of whom were also professors at Edinburgh, Glasgow, or Aberdeen—Caird underscores the value of learning about what he calls "the earlier and imperfect forms of faith":

> The study of the pre-Christian religions possesses both a practical and a speculative interest for the Christian mind. As he who would teach a child must himself, in a sense, become a child—throw himself back into the childish attitude of mind, and adapt his instructions to its immature conceptions, and even to its vagaries and illusion; so there is a sense in which it may be said that he who seeks to convert a heathen must himself become a heathen—must, by a kind of intellectual self-abnegation, endeavour to throw himself into the point of view of the minds he would elevate, and attain to some measure of sympathy with them. Catholic missionaries have, justly or unjustly, been sometimes accused of gaining a too easy victory for Christianity by assimilating its doctrines to heathen superstitions. But whilst that is only a nominal conversion which reclaims from heathenism to a Christianity which has itself become heathenish, it may yet be averred that a true conversion can be achieved only by a process of which this is the travesty—not, that is, by tampering with Christian truth, but by discerning and exhibiting its affinities to the unconscious longings and aspirations of the human spirit at all stages of its development.[11]

10. George Matheson, *The Distinctive Messages of the Old Religions* (1892), 327; hereafter cited in the text by page number.

11. John Caird, "Religions of India" (1882), 1–2. The titles of the individual essays compiled in *The Faiths of the World* closely resemble Freeman Clarke's list: "Religions of India: Vedic Period, Brahmanism," "Religions of India: Buddhism," "Religion of China: Confucianism," "Religion of Persia: Zoroaster and the Zend-Avesta"; "Religion of Ancient Egypt"; "Religion of Ancient Greece," "Religion of Ancient Rome," "Teutonic and Scandinavian Religion," "Ancient Religions of Central America," "Judaism," "Mahommedanism," and finally, "Christianity in Relation to Other Religions."

Adequate knowledge of heathenism and even a degree of sympathy—as long as it does not go to the extent of those Catholic missionaries who went half-way native—offers practical benefits to missionary work, as it allows the Gospel-bearing Christian to find an optimal meeting place in the heart of the prospective convert. But the benefits of the comparative study, Caird goes on to say, extend beyond such practical matters, as it touches on a more fundamental question about the nature of the relation between Christianity and other religions.

At this juncture, we may begin to detect a complex set of problems that the acceptance of the anteriority of non-Christian religions is liable to raise. First, and perhaps most broadly and seriously, if Christianity was something of a late-comer, at least in a simple chronological sense, is it possible, or even likely, that it is in some ways derivative of, and thus indebted to, some of its predecessors? After all, Christianity avowedly presupposes the ancient authority of Mosaic tradition, insofar as it has accepted the Hebrew Bible as the Old Testament. To claim Christianity as the perfection and fulfillment of the older, imperfect religions—is this not to acknowledge the fundamental continuity between the old and the new, and by implication, the dependency of the latter on the former? Is Christianity, then, absolutely original? Is it, for that matter, all that unique? Is it possibly the case, instead, that the superiority of Christianity is tantamount to its being merely the latest and the best?

It was amid these deeply unsettling questions, saturated with worries the earlier catalogs of customs and ceremonies did not share, that the comparative endeavors of the sort we have been surveying were launched. One way or another, any given author seems to have felt called upon to address, or else to table dexterously, these troublesome issues. On balance, most authors seem to have been sufficiently mindful not to delegitimatize the comparative endeavor itself by letting it be inferred that the act of comparison equalizes and homogenizes all religions; they insisted that comparative theology would not compromise the unique and exclusive authority of Christianity. At the same time, the benefits of the comparative representation of religions had to be articulated more positively and persuasively. How, then, could the comparison of religions be made not only safe but also beneficial for Christianity? Reverend Caird, for one, put the matter this way:

Even those who shrink from any such notion as that the religious history of the world is the expression of a natural process of development, are not thereby precluded from recognizing in the earlier stages of that history a preparation and propaedeutic for the more advanced. It is possible to hold that Christianity is no mere combined result of Jewish and heathen elements, and yet to discern in the characteristic ideas of the pre-Christian religions the germs at least of conceptions of God and of His relations to the world, which find at once their unity and their explanation in our Christian faith.

Whilst . . . we may hold that Christianity is neither a reproduction nor a natural development of the imperfect notions of God in which the religious aspirations of the world embodied themselves, it is possible at the same time to maintain that the study of the old religions sheds new light on the Christian religion, and gives to us a new and deeper sense of its spiritual significance and power.[12]

In short, far from exerting a detrimental effect on the authority of Christianity, Caird insists—here, he is essentially in agreement with Maurice and Clarke—comparative theology felicitously strengthens Christian religion by deepening its self-understanding.

The anteriority of the non-Christian religions, however, raised another conundrum that must have been as obvious to these comparativists as it was irritating, namely, the question of Islam. Once singularly dominant and still powerful, this religion of the seventh-century prophet Mohammed could not be said to be old, anterior, or preparatory to Christianity in the chronological sense. George Matheson, in *The Distinctive Messages of the Old Religions*, chose to eschew the problem by leaving out Islam entirely, as if it had never existed. Nor did the Reverend James Cameron Lees, the author of "Mahommedanism," the eleventh lecture of the St. Giles series, address this issue squarely. Instead, he reasserted the opposition between the chronologically older yet eternally youthful, vigorous, and resilient Christianity on the one hand and the wizened, inert, and unyielding latecomer on the other, with an argument that was countlessly repeated during the nineteenth century, and whose echo can be heard to this day:

Christianity is a living spiritual religion, adapting itself to all forms of human life, and thought, and action. In Mahommedanism there is no

12. Caird, "Religions of India," 2–3.

regenerative power; it is "of the letter, which killeth,"—unelastic, sterile, barren.[13]

Lees then reiterates this judgment with a quotation from a certain Lord Houghton:

Mahommed's truth lay in a holy book,
    Christ's in a sacred life.

So, while the world rolls on from change to change,
    And realms of thought expand,
The letter stands without expanse or range,
    Stiff as a dead man's hand.

Latecomer though it was, then, this "newer" religion was as good as dead at the time of its origin. Islam, in effect, was stillborn, a religion that happened to come late; and it came precisely to the most barbarous—that is to say, least advanced—peoples of the desert and had considerable success among them for a time, owing to their extreme "backwardness."[14] It was, strange as it might sound, a *belated* "old religion."

This, as we shall see in later chapters, is not the last time the case of Islam made its appearance as a uniquely thorny problem for the comparativists of the nineteenth century. But among the comparative theologians under review here, the problem tended to be ignored or improbably resolved and dismissed. As it appears, then, the comparative theologians did not perceive it as a particularly pressing issue. There was, however, another more exigent problem. As alluded to earlier in connection with Caird's essay, this problem had to do with the disturbing implications that seemed to follow from the new understanding of the connection between Christianity and other religions, characteristically delineated as a relation between posterity and anteriority, between the perfect and the deficient, between the paradigm and the imitators, or between fulfillment and longing. Now, once the question of Islam had been put to the side, non-Christian religions were repeatedly and consistently represented as "old" or "ancient" and, in fact, effectively dead. No doubt, some religions in comparison to others were more legitimately and incontrovertibly called "defunct,"

13. James Cameron Lees, "Mahommedanism" (1882), 331.
14. To be sure, this is far from historically accurate, and, moreover, Europeans of earlier times would not or could not have represented the prosperous domain of Islam this way.

for example, the Egyptian, Greek, Roman, Babylonian, Aztec, or religions. Others were categorized as de facto "extant" but only to the extent that they were "living fossils," which is to say, but ancient survivals from bygone eras; they did not properly belong to the present, and even less to the future.

This emphasis on the ancientness and the dead or moribund character of the non-Christian religions of the world contrasts rather strikingly with the representation of world religions as "living faiths," which became common in the early twentieth century, as observed in chapter 1. In nineteenth-century discourse, the fossilization of "old religions" was so pervasive that to presume any sign of life in them seemed an unnatural act. To breathe life into the desiccated remnants of past religions—this required a heroic measure, so to say, a mental contortion that was as counterintuitive as it was precisely aimed.

In this regard, when the American academic J. N. Fradenburgh (1843–1914) published a book with a title utterly uncharacteristic for the nineteenth century, *Living Religions, or The Great Religions of the Orient* (1888),[15] he seems to have been well aware that what he was intending would not be readily accepted. He proposed to go back to the ancient source of each religion, the sacred texts, in order to comprehend present-day practices and even latter-day alterations and degeneracy in the light of unique ancient roots.[16] Admittedly, to examine a scripture in order to understand a religion is nothing new. What is conspicuous about Fradenburgh's outlook is that consulting the sacred text is tantamount to going back to the time when, presumably, the religion was a living voice, before it had been transcribed into "lifeless" letters, before its calcification into customs and traditions. "To really appreciate an Oriental religion," he says, "we

15. As far as I know, Fradenburgh's is the earliest work to bear the phrase "living religions" in the title. In his 1885 publication *Witnesses from the Dust*, he is identified as "Member of the American Oriental Society, the Society of Biblical Archaeology of London, etc." According to another publication dated 1891, he was "the president of the North Dakota University."

16. This way of thinking about "living" religions is therefore in marked contrast with the notion of "living faiths" typical since the 1920s. The later notion, which is also the sense in which we today understand the phrase, emphasizes the *current* viability and vitality of a given religion, as seen, for instance, in the following statement by Sydney Cave, the author of two books on the subject: "The Living Religions of the East have changed much since the time of the beginning of the modern missionary enterprise. In their transformation many influences have been at work. The translation by Western scholars of *The Sacred Books of the East* revealed to the East the rich heritage of the past, and brought to light treasures which had been forgotten. In consequence, many Orientals gained a new pride in their religion and learned to pass from its baser to its nobler elements" (*Christianity and Some Living Religions of the East* [1929], 20). See also by the same author, *An Introduction to the Study of Some Living Religions of the East* (1921).

must resort to its own sacred books, endeavor to get at its heart, and feel its life-currents. We must place ourselves in sympathy with the people, listen to their hymns and prayers, and witness their rites and ceremonies. We must know their religious ideals, as well as their corruptions in practice."[17]

All this, of course, is a truism today, and Fradenburgh's vaguely moralizing rhetoric so familiar that it is easy for us to overlook its novelty and its relative strangeness. For one thing, as he recognizes clearly, this approach may have the effect of shedding a considerably more favorable light on Oriental religions than European Christians of his time were accustomed to, more favorable, in their view, than the subject deserved. But this, argues Fradenburgh, is for good purpose: "This volume may, perhaps, fairly represent the bright side of each of these religions. . . . When we have seen the brightest side of an ancient religion, and then compared it with Christianity, we shall begin to appreciate the supreme excellence of the latter. The truth discovered in heathen faiths is the hope of the missionary. He finds the common ground upon which he may stand with those whom he would save, and the sure foundation upon which he may build." Again, the justification of his strategy concludes with the assurance that it is entirely harmless and positively gainful to Christian religion.[18]

This was also the argument used by George Matheson to explain his intention to extract "messages" from desiccated religions of the past. His title *The Distinctive Messages of the Old Religions* may seem diametrically opposed to *Living*

---

17. Fradenburgh, *Living Religions*, 2.

18. Ibid., 2–3. *Living Religions* was the first of the trilogy Fradenburgh published in the course of three years, whose overall purpose he explained in the preface to the last volume as follows: "The present work is a concluding volume of a series in which are treated in a popular way, and yet with a fair degree of thoroughness, the great religions of the world, both living and extinct. 'Living Religions' possesses peculiar interest in that it discusses the faiths of the present heathen world in fields now mapped out and occupied for Christian missionary conquest. 'Fire from Strange Altars' [1891] is not less important in that it attempts to place in systematic array many of the ascertained facts concerning the archaic literatures and old cults of Israel's neighbors, from the earliest period which history has reached to that when these mighty empires, which shook the world while it was yet but young, dropped in pieces with the advent of more advanced political and religious ideas, more efficient engines of war, and wiser military organizations and plans for defense or conquest. The present volume, it is believed, will command an equally generous welcome, both because of its connection with the classic nations, and much more because it treats of the religions of our own fathers before the light of Christianity shot its mild and beneficent rays into the world's first gloom" (J. N. Fradenburgh, *Departed Gods* [1891], 3–4). Here then, the meaning of the phrase "living religions" begins to bleed into the more recent usage.

Religions, yet Matheson's project, too, was intended as a resuscitation of dead or moribund religions, in the sense that he sought to detect and decipher the living voice of each of them. He resolved to take this extraordinary measure because, he says, it was precisely Christianity that recognized them as alive, preserved them in its own infinite wisdom. He was swayed by the conviction that, unlike all other religions, the "distinctive message" of Christianity and its particular mission to the world was "one of *reconciliation*. No religion has ever before claimed to be the bearer of such a message." He asks rhetorically: "Is it possible that the religions of the past may themselves be included in this message of reconciliation? Is it conceivable that Christianity has furnished a ground for peace not only within but without its own fold?" (327–28). Given the vital relation that obtains between past religions and ever-current Christianity, he concludes:

> The religion of Christ ought to have peculiar interest in the faiths of the past. They are not, to her, dead faiths; they are not even modernised. They are preserved inviolable as parts of herself—more inviolable than they would have been if she had never come. Christianity has claimed to be "the manifold wisdom of God." In this ascription she has been candid to the past. She has not denied its wisdom; she has only aspired to enfold it. She has not sought to derogate from the doctrines of antiquity; she has only sought to diminish their antagonism. China may keep her materialism, and India may retain her mysticism; Rome may grasp her strength, and Greece may nurse her beauty; Persia may tell of the opposition of God's power, and Egypt may sing of His preeminence even amid the tombs; but for each and all there is a seat in the Christian Pantheon, and a justification in the light of the manifold wisdom of God. (341–42)

3. A Critic: Charles Hardwick

Although these comparative theologians may seem, by today's standard, Christian triumphalists of the first order, it should not come as a surprise that, in the nineteenth century, we also find others who were more conservatively Christian, and on that account profoundly irritated by the easygoing ecumenicism of the kind espoused by Fradenburgh and Matheson. For their part, those stalwart churchmen exhibited no inclination to rush to a universal embrace of all religions. This notwithstanding, and much as they objected to the too sympathetic, too conciliatory attitude toward non-Christian religions, these critics were themselves not always opposed to the comparative study of religions as such. In their opinion generally, it was not the study itself that was censurable, but the inferences and conclusions the more feebleminded and softhearted were prone to draw from such study. These critical voices had begun to be raised, in fact, well before comparative theology became a widely popular enterprise.

One of the most eminent, well-informed, and sharply articulate conservative critics was Charles Hardwick (1821–59), archdeacon and "Christian Advocate" at Cambridge University. In the mid-nineteenth century—that is, a few decades earlier than most of the works in comparative theology that we have been discussing thus far in this chapter—he published a highly acclaimed two-volume treatise entitled *Christ and Other Masters: An Historical Inquiry into Some of the Chief Parallelisms and Contrasts between Christianity and the Religious Systems of the Ancient World* (1855–59).[19] Early in the first volume, Hardwick identifies, and discusses individually and extensively, what he calls three types of modern thought.

> One class . . . of educated Englishmen have never drifted far from the position of the previous generation. They continue to look down unmoved on all the tossings of their neighbors. Nor can theirs be termed the silence of misgiving or the self-possession of indifference; it is rather the tranquility of deep and living faith. For in their ranks are many of the brightest luminaries both of scholarship and science. (10)

Tacitly but unmistakably, this is the class with which the author presumed to identify himself. "On men like these," he continues approvingly, "the effect of modern progress and discovery is to strengthen their belief in the announcements of the Bible" (11).

This, to be sure, is what virtually every historical author we have examined thus far, from Purchas to Matheson and Fradenburgh, also claimed. Nothing, we have heard them insist, about the result of the comparative study of religions could challenge the authority of Christianity; on the contrary, it could only fortify Christian faith and stoke its missionary fervor. This, however, was not how Archdeacon Hardwick saw the actual effects on some of his contemporaries. For, as he observed,

---

19. I refer throughout this discussion to volume 1 of the second edition of 1863, posthumously edited but, according to its preface, a reprint of the first edition, with "a few notes from the author's manuscript" added; hereafter cited in the text by page number.

there is a powerful class of minds in England as in other parts of Europe, who are differently affected in their estimate of sacred topics by the fluctuations of the present day. The widening of their field of vision and the light that has been thrown on many of their favourite studies, so far from adding vigour to the principle of faith, has rather tended to disturb their intellectual balance, and induced a state of feeling which approaches, here and there at least, to very serious misbelief. . . . [A]ll whom I include in this division are alike dissatisfied with what they style "the popular religion," or the views of Christianity now current in different branches of the Church. (12)

It cannot be denied that there were many in England and elsewhere in Hardwick's time who were "dissatisfied" with churchly Christianity, with what we today might more likely call established religion or institutional religion. Such anticlerical dissent had been a long-standing tradition in Europe for centuries. What was new in the nineteenth century was that the domains of "favorite studies" seem to have expanded and multiplied, and the resultant volatility of the atmosphere led to a certain mental and spiritual instability in some among the educated flock, the condition that the archdeacon diagnoses, with a measure of professional authority, as "very serious misbelief." Hardwick apparently felt that this tendency had to be recognized clearly, because what might have begun as a slight easing of traditional Christian discipline was liable to deteriorate further and to bleed into what he would soon describe as the third type of minds. But at this juncture he simply withholds his judgment as to whether the authors and readers representing the second, intermediary class of minds should be considered un-Christian: To be sure, they are often exposed to "the charge of striving to disparage the supremacy of Christianity, by placing it in the same line with philosophical systems of the heathen world, and recognising also in such systems a prophetic office and a genuine revelation," but, he adds, with equanimity and detachment:

It is not my purpose to determine how far the charge has been substantiated. I notice it in order to bring out more clearly the supposed connexion of these modes of thought with others that will be discussed hereafter. But candour, in the meantime, urges me to add that wild as may have been the intellectual aberrations of the former [second] class, they are not consciously opposed to Christianity itself. Their reverence for the Person of our blessed Lord is warm and constant; their devotion to His service is indisputable. (14)

It was quite another matter, however, with the third class of minds. According to Hardwick's classification, this third group consisted of those who, drawing "bolder inferences" from the ideas shared by the second group, resolved "to free themselves entirely from the irksome fetters of tradition." In a sense, their position was a natural extension of the second group's. Hardwick's erudition allowed him to recognize that both positions represented the endpoint of a "very short and slippery" path from Gnostic tendencies already present in the primitive church, though the lapse had certainly been facilitated by recent intellectual trends—in this regard, he singles out Samuel Taylor Coleridge—undermining the authority of the Bible. This derogation of biblical authority, he argues, manifests most clearly in these thinkers' assumptions about and attitude toward non-Christian religions:

> If it be . . . contended, that all branches of the human family possess the same kind of inspirations, owing to the universal presence of the Word of God within them; if the Holy Ghost be rather sent to waken up a slumbering consciousness of Christianity already planted in the soul than to infuse the elements of supernatural life, and bring the fallen spirit back to fellowship with Christ, a door is opened for the broad and specious theory, that the Gospel is at best a higher stage of natural religion, or, it may be, one of numerous forms, in which the spiritual instincts of humanity have found an utterance for themselves. (19)

Hardwick's appellation for people of this third type is at once idiosyncratic and instructive. He identifies them most generally as "spiritualists,"[20] on the grounds that, in their opinion, "religions generally, and the Gospel as one member of the class, are . . . mere expressions of the fundamental beliefs inherent in our spiritual nature"; for them, then, the many points of affinity between Christianity and other religions are ultimately unremarkable, since they all naturally result from "the unaided operation of the religious sentiment in man, awakened and directed by peculiar circumstances" (21).

It may be said that, in a way, Hardwick happened upon an early stage of a powerful predilection, just emerging then—an all-encompassing, broadly progressivist, well-meaning but incorrigibly monocentric universalism. It is a

---

20. It should be remembered that this was before the rise of "Spiritualism" in the nineteenth century as a particular "modern sect," as a dubious form of supernaturalism associated with the supposed possession of a medium by the spirits of the dead, a phenomenon suddenly fashionable in Victorian England as well as North America.

strong undercurrent both in the discourse of world religions and in the discourse of "spirituality" today. Hardwick claims to have found this same tendency, however, not only among some of his contemporaries but also in various long-standing theological and metaphysical—and heretical—traditions of Europe. It is of course a matter of debate whether one should concur with his historical judgment here and assume that this nineteenth-century "spiritualism" had such a deep-rooted genealogy. Yet his descriptive language is interesting. While it echoes, or rather anticipates, the later comparative world religionists' own language of self-description (which is usually earnest and without irony), Hardwick's articulation—for example, in the passage quoted below—clearly signals disapproval and imparts a measure of sarcasm. At the same time, he does not fail to expose what often remains a tacit claim of contemporary "spiritualists," namely, their implicit assumption that they occupy a privileged position "above them all," that is, above and beyond all "old" religions that they "impartially" survey and compare, including Christianity. This attitude receives an inhospitably precise rendering by Hardwick:

[Spiritualists] affirm that something higher, deeper, heavenlier, is reserved for us; that growth must be expected and promoted not only in our apprehension of religious truth, but in the orb of truth itself; that their peculiar mission is to hasten this result by shewing man his real dignity and destiny, by sounding all the depths of human consciousness, and calling to their aid the newest facts of history and the last discoveries of science. They do not, indeed, con[d]emn the worthies of antiquity. The statues of Confucius, Moses, and Pythagoras; of Socrates and Zoroaster; of Buddha, Christ, and Apollonius; of Máni and Muhammad, are all elevated side by side in the Walhalla of spiritualism. These all in different measures are applauded as the saints, the prophets, the apostles of their age; yet, notwithstanding the enormous latitude of his belief, the spiritualist is not content with any of the forms in which religion has hitherto appeared on earth. However well adapted to peculiar countries or to transitory phases of the human mind, they are unequal to the wants and the capacities of the present century. He would not himself have worshipped either with his "swarthy Indian who bowed down to wood and stone," or with his "grim-faced Calmuck," or his "Grecian peasant,'" or his "savage," whose hands were "smeared all over with human sacrifice"; but rather aims, by analysing the principles of heathenism and cultivating a deeper sympathy with what is termed "great pagan world," to organise a new system which he calls the Absolute Religion, the Religion of Humanity, the Religion of the Future. (22–23)

Hardwick's description of this futuristic religion of the spiritualist resembles, to an uncanny degree, the sentiments expressed by today's consumers (if not the producers) of world religions treatises.[21] Indeed, not altogether coincidentally, many of our contemporaries prefer to call their disposition "spiritual" rather than "religious," thereby signaling their desire not to be fettered by what they often term "conventional religions" (more or less equivalent to what was derisively called "popular theology" in Hardwick's time), which they say feels not genuinely theirs, not true to their "heart." Again, what is different about Hardwick's language here is the acerbic tone of unforgiving criticism. In such a freewheeling religion of personal spirituality, he remarks pointedly,

all special dogmas are to be eliminated; sentiments which every one may clothe according to his fancy, are to occupy the place of facts; the light of a spontaneous Gospel is to supersede the clumsy artifice of teaching by the aid of a historical revelation. Thus, while the promoters of this scheme affect the greatest reverence for the wisdom and the so-called "inspirations" of the past, they aim to soar indefinitely above it. Nearly all the doctrines of ancient systems are abandoned or explained away, as things which really have no stronger claim upon us than the cycle of luxuriant mythes that captivated Greek imaginations in the pre-historical period. The Christ and Christianity of the Bible are thus virtually denied. (23)

Who, then, were the futuristic "spiritualists" among Hardwick's contemporaries? If we were to devise a short answer on his behalf, "certain Unitarians

---

21. We may not have paid enough attention to the fact that scholars of religions have had significant share in this popular trend. That is, despite their avowed fidelity to the historical facts available in the form of traditions, some historians effectively recast or re-created the tradition by positing an idea or principle over and above the particularity of the historical tradition itself. Relevant in this connection is Steven Wasserstrom's *Religion after Religion* (1999), which examines the significance of Henry Corbin, Gershom Scholem, and Mircea Eliade—all prominent historians of religion of the mid-twentieth century—in the field of Islamic studies, Jewish studies, and history of religions, respectively. Wasserstrom argues that each of them privileged what was supposedly the higher mystical essence of the religion in question over and above the exoteric tradition.

and Transcendentalists" might do as well as any. "Mr. Theodore Parker," says Hardwick, singling out an ultra-liberal representative of New England Unitarianism, is "one of their chief oracles"; Parker is also called "if not their most cultivated, certainly their most intelligible exponent" (23, 157).[22] After his three introductory chapters, Hardwick appends a special section expressly to represent in some detail the viewpoint of the advocates of what he calls, following Parker's own appellation, "Absolute Religion." In that context, in addition to Parker, he also mentions William Johnson Fox (1786–1864) and Robert William Mackay (1803–82), whose relevant publications had appeared several years before—a good decade before the first appearance of *Ten Great Religions* by James Freeman Clarke, another prominent Unitarian from Boston.[23]

Hardwick augments his remarks on his contemporaries with a typically astute (if also always controversial) historical observation: "It is instructive to place in contrast with these views of Christianity the main position of one of its more learned assailants before the birth of Spiritualism and the discovery of the Absolute Religion" (160) and proceeds to conclude the section with a long quotation from Charles François Dupuis's (1742–1809) celebrated treatise, *Origine de tous les cultes, ou Religion universelle* (1795). This last turn indicates clearly that, like many other concerned Christians before him, Hardwick saw a direct correlation between Dupuis's thesis—which reduced all religions (including Christianity) to one single essence or principle hitherto unsuspected, namely, sun worship—and outright atheism.[24] In his estimation, the work of both Dupuis and his "spiritualist" heirs amounted to the denial of the absolute truth of Christianity. A very serious misbelief, indeed.

According to Hardwick, the legacy of this "spiritualist" denial of a personal God—or, as he puts it in another way, this tradition of objections to the absolute validity of the Gospel—is deep-rooted and pervades history. In fact, he expends a dozen or so pages, supported by numerous footnoted references, in order to trace this legacy of rebellion, beginning with early Gnostics, Neoplatonists, and Manicheans, through similar heretics of later centuries, and up to various English and French Deists and the German contemporaries influenced

22. Theodore Parker (1810–60) was a prominent and controversial Unitarian minister in Boston. He published a number of works, including *A Discourse of Matters Pertaining to Religion* (1842) and *Theism, Atheism, and the Popular Theology* (1853).

23. Fox was the author of *The Religious Ideas* (1849) as well as a pamphlet entitled *The Apostle John, an Unitarian* (1823). Mackay wrote the two-volume work *The Progress of the Intellect, as Exemplified in the Religious Development of the Greeks and Hebrews* (1850).

24. The historical significance of Dupuis's treatise will be discussed further in chapter 8.

by the latter (27–39). In fact, Hardwick seems especially keen on impressing upon his readers that, despite the appearance of novelty and the spiritualists' insistence on progress, "all the tendencies of this belief . . . are absolutely *retrogressive; it is carrying men afresh to paganism*" (24). It will become evident in the course of his treatise, he announces, that the "denial of the Personality of God pervaded nearly all the heathen systems of the ancient world, and everywhere produced the same results in ethics and theology" (27). The contention is a familiar one, if we recall the line of reasoning typical of the early modern texts we surveyed in chapter 1. Like his predecessors in earlier centuries, Hardwick finds direct correspondence between the heathens in distant regions of the world (who tend to be polytheists) and the religious deviants within the civilized world (who are likely pantheists, deists, or atheists). There is little surprise, then, that modern spiritualists should foster excessive sympathy toward heathenism.

Presently we arrive at this militant paragraph—perhaps the most memorable, the most strident in Hardwick's entire treatise:

Impelled by the necessity of coping with these wild and retrogressive tendencies, the Christian advocate has never shrunk from the encounter, and has seldom found his labours altogether unsuccessful. He may not indeed be always guided by a sound discretion; he may fail to understand the nature of the malady in certain cases, and in others may suggest an antidote that does not work its cure; but still his consciousness of the profound importance of the issue has been ever visible. He feels that to reduce our blessed Lord into the category of human seers is practically to dethrone Him. Christianity will tolerate no rival. They who wish to raise a tabernacle for some other master, be it even for the greatest worthies of the old oeconomy,—a Moses or Elias,—must be warned that Christ, and Christ alone, is to be worshipped: they must hear Him. (39)

A person less sanguine about such Christian absolutism might be moved to ask why someone of Hardwick's conviction—whose main preoccupation, after all, seems to have been more with the malady of contemporaries in his own nation than with the spiritual welfare of faraway heathens—would want to expend such intellectual effort engaging in the survey of non-Christian religions. But his answer most probably is no different from the one suggested by his predecessors for centuries, sometimes meant as a real objective, and other times issued as a convenient excuse for engaging in an enterprise that might otherwise be thought dubious.[25] The exposure of heathen errors and perdition could only increase the glory of the true faith; and for this purpose, the more truthful the accounts and more accurate the information, the better.[26]

Before this general conclusion is reached, however, an earlier chapter entitled "Unity of Human Race" rehearses the gist of the well-worn argument with notable thoroughness and economy of prose. The first premise is, as it appears, the one shared by virtually every writer on comparative religions past and present, so much so that it is taken to be axiomatic and, as such, never really demonstrated inductively or deductively. In Hardwick's words the axiom reads: "Man is a religious being. The ideas of God, of sacrifice, of prayer, have been inwoven with his spiritual constitution, and have, therefore, always struggled for expression in his personal and social life." This is followed by a second premise recognizing the empirical fact of diversity, which is also taken for granted by the majority of modern comparativists: "The effect of individual character, of isolation, of climate, the phenomena of nature, and a host of adventitious agencies would soon be visible in the altered aspects of traditions; while a corresponding modification of the forms of social life would gradually affect the tone and sensibility of the human spirit." When it comes to the question of the root cause for this diversity, however, Hardwick is clearly aligned with the early modern authors, who by and large strove to remain (or to appear to remain) theologically correct and doctrinally compliant. For, like them, he attributes the fact of plurality to the sinfulness of man: "In beings ever liable to fall, and

25. Another, equally feasible explanation may be that Hardwick was simply an insatiable researcher and pedant, given to upholding the most rigorous standard of scholarship. Indeed, for someone who died in his thirty-ninth year, Hardwick left an impressive scholarly output. In addition to two capacious volumes of church history (one on the Middle Ages and another on the Reformation), he published such highly scholastic works as *A History of the Articles of Religion: To Which Is Added a Series of Documents, from A.D. 1536 to A.D. 1615; together with Illustrations from Contemporary Sources* (1851), as well as several shorter works of like nature. He also edited the first three volumes of *A Catalogue of the Manuscripts Preserved in the Library of the University of Cambridge* (1856–67).

26. "If it be found hereafter on a strict examination of their sacred books and other ancient documents that nearly all the heathen systems were defective in those very points which form the leading characteristics of Revealed Religion; if the general tendency of pagan thought was in philosophers to pantheism, or the worship of nature as a whole, and in the many to polytheism, or the deification of particular energies of nature; . . . we may thence derive not only a fresh stock of motives for disseminating truths that we possess, but special reasons for abstaining from all heathenish speculations, and for listening with more docile spirit to 'the oracles of GOD'" (154–55).

ever prone to substitute their speculations for the holy will of God, this great substratum of religion might in course of time be overgrown and buried" (76). As a consequence of the partial erasure of the real core of faith, "the cycle of religious mythes would be indefinitely enlarged," as each locality would spontaneously produce "the drapery of imagination with which they clothe their gods" (77).

The fact of diversity, then, is for him, as it was for most early modern writers, a reality that was at once rueful and a matter of course. It is against the backdrop of this infelicitous disunity that the light of true faith shines forth:

> In spite of every wayward tendency of human nature, disuniting men from God, and substituting for the steadier light of old traditions, the capricious glimmerings of their own imagination; there was ever on the earth one ark of refuge, and one beacon planted on a hill. The Church of God, the keeper and the witness of the true religion, rested on a sure and stable basis, so that while the heathen were abandoned to themselves to test the systems of their own devising, and were "given over to a reprobate mind"; its inmates had continual access to the oracles of God,—the children of Israel had light in their dwellings. (78–79)

4. The Variety of Parascientific Comparativism

It is probably resolute creedal assertions of the kind expressed here—orthodox to the point of sounding archaic, staunchly church-abiding and dogmatically partisan —that have caused today's historians of comparative religion to judge Hardwick's accomplishments more negatively than his enormous erudition and undeniable sagacity warrant. For instance, Eric Sharpe—one of the leading historians of the discipline, whose comprehensive survey Comparative Religion has been widely read by students of religion since its first publication in 1975—compares and contrasts Hardwick and Frederick Denison Maurice with regard to their respective roles in the formation of comparative religion as a scholarly enterprise. Sharpe unequivocally champions Maurice, noting with approval that the latter's Boyle Lectures "exhibit a breadth of sympathy, together with a desire for accurate and up-to-date information, which were unusual at the time." Then Sharpe goes on to remark:

> The qualities of this influential book stand out clearly if we contrast it with another Anglican product, Charles Hardwick's Christ and Other Masters. Hardwick knew far more than Maurice, who could on occasion be dreadfully

inaccurate, and yet it was Maurice who succeeded in presenting the non-Christian religions, not merely as tissues of falsehood, but as evidence of an unalienable aspect of human nature—the desire to worship. The *fulfilment* of the desire Maurice believed was to be found ultimately only in the Church; nevertheless he could speak of a "wonderful testimony... borne from the ends of the earth" and of Christians as "debtors" to Buddhism, Hinduism, and Islam.[27]

In this instance, then, Maurice's "desire for accurate and up-to-date information" seems to be valued as much as, in fact more than, the accuracy actually achieved by Hardwick. In Sharpe's view, what justifies the higher estimation of Maurice's work is its success in "representing the non-Christian religions" in a manner that did not judge them "false." Sharpe's principle of evaluation here seems to boil down to a matter of greater "sympathy," that is to say, a certain "attitude." In fact, setting aside this sympathy factor, it must be observed that Maurice's treatise closely resembles those written by any number of writers of his time, including Hardwick, in the sense that his work, too, is firmly predetermined by a settled conviction concerning the unparalleled superiority of Christianity.[28] Maurice's delineation of the relation between Christianity and other religions differs little from those of his contemporaries; it typifies the mode of representation adopted by a great majority of the nineteenth-century divines turned amateur comparativists. Moreover, as we have seen, he was by no means unique in exercising "sympathy" or in touting its virtue.

None of this seems to matter much to the historian Sharpe. He presumes to rank Maurice higher than Hardwick primarily, if not solely, on account of the appropriateness of the general outlook and attitude, rather than on the (perceived) accuracy of their accounts or the nature of their conclusions. Does this imply that, for this particular historian at least, good intentions (i.e., the *desire* to achieve accuracy) is more important than the actual result? Needless to say, the difference in attitude and manners is not the same thing as the difference in the degree or the quality of their personal religious conviction. This said, an intriguing question still remains: Is a historical evaluation of this sort—for example, Sharpe's comparative evaluation of Hardwick versus Maurice—in the end, a religious judgment? A scientific judgment? Or neither?

27. Sharpe, *Comparative Religion*, 147.

28. This is a point duly acknowledged by Sharpe in the previously quoted passage: "The *fulfilment* of the desire Maurice believed was to be found ultimately only in the Church" (ibid.).

This question is seldom raised in earnest, it seems, because modern practitioners of comparative religion (usually called "historians of religion") overwhelmingly, if not to say automatically, concur with the view expressed by Sharpe. As long as the cardinal importance of the "sympathetic attitude" as a desideratum for comparing religions is unanimously agreed upon, there is no need to stare in consternation at the aporia hidden beneath this professional credo. This seemingly sacrosanct, golden rule of conduct—or attitude—for comparativists is itself predicated on no prior justification. Nor does it seem necessary to spell out what measure of sympathy is appropriate for "presenting non-Christian religions." Is it possible that the lack of deliberations on these issues might be an indication, moreover, that certain sentiments, dispositions, and other difficult-to-specify but historically specific cultural ethos are being taken for granted and thus *passing* as the bottom line, as virtually axiomatic, as good as a universal and inviolable principle, though they may never be publicly spoken of in this manner?

While Sharpe may serve as a prominent example today, the equivocation underlying his judgment on various comparative endeavors of the nineteenth century is not unique; nor is it particularly new. A much earlier example is provided by Louis Henry Jordan (1855–1923), an early-twentieth-century Canadian scholar whose *Comparative Religion: Its Genesis and Growth* (1905) was one of the first and most thorough histories written on the subject. While Jordan as a rule was never reticent to classify, rank, or otherwise pass judgments on works by various scholars, major and minor, concerning Hardwick, he issued only a few laconic lines, an assessment remarkable for its ambivalence and lack of precision: "This author also was by preference a student of history; but he wrote at least one book which no student of Comparative Religion should overlook. In various respects, this treatise has been superseded; yet it contains much that is suggestive, and it will repay examination."[29] This set of vaguely contradictory statements issuing from an otherwise consummate documentary historian may signal a notable circumspection already at work. Apparently, the pall of piety enveloping the appropriately sympathetic attitude of the forerunners had already descended, and the sanctity of the pluralist-ecumenical discourse was thus assured, well before Sharpe's time.

In sum, we might observe in retrospect, it was not in Hardwick's favor that,

29. Jordan, *Comparative Religion*, 418. In addition to this famous volume, Jordan also authored the following titles: *The Study of Religion in the Italian Universities* (1909), *Comparative Religion: A Survey of Its Recent Literature* (1910), *Comparative Religion: Its Adjuncts and Allies* (1915).

with all the prodigious expenditure of scholarly labor that went into his treatise, he wrote expressly as a "Christian Advocate" and never as a pioneer of some upstart science. (It is of course quite another matter if Hardwick would ever have wished to be evaluated in such a light.) By the same token, his "consciousness of the profound importance of the issue" was less preoccupied with matters such as "breadth of sympathy" in representing the basic human "desire to worship" in all its varieties than Maurice supposedly was; Hardwick was palpably more concerned about the matter of discipline, rectification, and safeguarding of what was to him the true faith. That this faith was resolutely and unapologetically Anglican (rather than something else) should surprise no one, given this author's chosen vocation. What is remarkable about his case, therefore, is the fact of his exclusion itself—that is, the elimination of works such as his *Christ and Other Masters* from the proper lineage of the science of religion, and even from the tradition of world religions discourse. Rather than being a contributor to the scientific development, he is seen as a counterforce. Despite his avowedly different purpose, and despite the negative judgment against him because of it, he was incontrovertibly engaged in the business of representing and comparing religions. It is equally beyond doubt that, to this end, he managed to draw upon the best and the latest in numerous branches of the scholarship of his time. His exclusion, therefore, may be fairly accounted for more as a consequence of his outspoken noncompliance with the prevailing ethic and disposition of the world religions discourse generally and its ideology of pluralism in particular than as a matter of his deviation from the twentieth-century standards of scholarship.

Hardwick may have been the most learned and sharp-minded of the conservative religionists of his time engaged in comparative theology, so much so that his treatise—especially as a milestone achieved so early in his career, cut short by his death at an early age—was bound to be a challenge to historians such as Jordan and Sharpe, and an irritating problem particularly for those intent on policing the border between scientific objectivity and theological dogmatism, between scholarly impartiality and religious partisanship. But Hardwick was by no means the only one to take this seemingly problematic stance. Indeed, as the nineteenth century wore on, some religionists of like mind came to feel that the need to take such a stance was exigent.

In 1881, John Wordsworth, bishop of Salisbury, delivered at Oxford University eight lectures in the prestigious series established in 1779 by the will of

John Bampton, canon of Salisbury. Wordsworth describes his Bampton Lectures specifically as "a contribution to the comparative study of religion from a Christian point of view." As he readily acknowledges, this is "a subject that has been ably treated by Mr. F. D. Maurice, Archdeacon Hardwick, and others. But," he adds pointedly, "it has long been evident that some fresh discussion of it was needed, owing to the new light which has fallen upon it from so many quarters; and Christians have of late been constantly reminded of the misconceptions to which a partial study of the history of religion is liable."[30] The danger he sees here is essentially the same as what Maurice called the "most prevailing form of unbelief." In Wordsworth's opinion, no one was more susceptible to this grievous error than a certain kind of historian of religion:

> It is at present far too common a habit of mind to be satisfied with tracing out the conditions and circumstances under which a belief or a religious custom arises in the world. Some men exhaust themselves in classifying the phenomena of religion under this or that heading of myth or symbol. . . . But, when they have done all this useful work . . . they are in danger, and leave their readers in danger, of tacitly assuming that the subject is closed, and that religion is a natural development, out of which the positive action of God, as a real existing Being, is excluded. Their mouths are full of the various ways in which other men have thought of God, but He Himself is far from their own thoughts. (78–79)

It appears that, like Eric Sharpe, Bishop Wordsworth here is also raising a certain "attitude" question, albeit from another angle and against another party. He charges that some historians of religion—namely, those comparativists who stop short in their investigation and fail to grasp the essential nature of religion—are precluding, either deliberately or inadvertently, religion's true basis.

Against such a foreclosure of the Divine, against all the pluralist nonsense, and in order to drive his point home directly and absolutely, Wordsworth titled his treatise *The One Religion: Truth, Holiness and Peace desired by the Nations, and Revealed by Jesus Christ*. The bishop surged forth in this work not only in defense of Christianity against other religions but more specifically—in a manner reminiscent of Matthew Arnold's polemic in *Culture and Anarchy* (1868)—he championed the Church of England as the exemplary church of Christian unity and

---

30. John Wordsworth, *The One Religion: Truth, Holiness and Peace Desired by the Nations, and Revealed by Jesus Christ* (2nd ed., 1893), xi; hereafter cited in the text by page number.

universality, over against both the sectarian pluralism of Nonconformist churches and the rival universalism of the Roman Catholic Church (305–11).[31] His is an extreme partisan polemic, one might say, carried out in the name of universality.

In contrast to Hardwick's high scholasticism, Wordsworth was decidedly more clerical in his orientation, more pragmatic in his purpose. As he announces at the outset, his lectures were meant above all to serve the end of Christian missions:[32]

> I have written this book especially for candidates for ordination, and for those recently ordained, some of whom it may help to realize not only that their message is superior to that of other religious teachers, but how and why it is unique and universal. I offer it also more particularly to those who have an interest or a share in foreign missions, from association with whom I have derived constant help and encouragement, for which I should wish in some degree to make a return. (xii-xiii)

In effect, what today's historians might consider an illicit collusion of interests—between the scientific and the evangelical—was unapologetically championed by numerous nineteenth-century comparativists. Wordsworth saw, perhaps more frankly and naively than any other writer we have examined so far, the complete consistency and identity of purpose between the comparative study of "old" religions and the theological justification of Christianity as "uniquely and universally" true:

31. This opinion, incidentally, echoes almost exactly sentiments expressed at the beginning of the seventeenth century by Samuel Purchas in Purchas His Pilgrimage (1613), book 1, chapter 4: "This . . . is the effect of sinne and irreligion, that the name and practise of Religion is thus diversified, else had there bin, as one God, so one religion and one language, wherein to give it with just reason, a proper name." Furthermore, according to Nicholas Lash, "in case his readers were in doubt as to the chief cause of religious corruption and complexity, he told the Archbishop of Canterbury in his dedicatory Preface, that he wrote the book so that others might learn 'two lessons fitting the times, the unnaturalness of faction and atheism . . . And if I live to finish the rest, I hope to show the paganism of anti-Christian popery'" (quoted in Nicholas Lash, The Beginning and the End of "Religion" [1996], 13).

32. By so doing, Wordsworth was fulfilling the mandate of Canon Bampton's will, which stipulated that "eight Divinity Lecture Sermons shall be preached on either of the following Subjects—to confirm and establish the Christian Faith, and to confute all heretics and schismatics—upon divine authority of the holy Scriptures—upon the authority of the writings of the primitive Fathers" (v-vi).

The object, then, of the present Lecture is, in the first place, to put before our eyes a faithful picture of the way in which the nations of the world—whose times God has allotted, and whose bounds He has set—have experienced this mysterious drawing towards Him, and have felt, as it were, with their hands, after Him, and not all in vain have sought to find Him. Yet if we listen attentively, we shall hear a sad epilogue to all these strivings, a confession wrung with tears from many noble souls, that what they found did not satisfy the tests which truth should satisfy, that the living rock was not reached, that God was not clearly known. (77)

Meanwhile, across the Atlantic, an analogous opinion was presented by Frank Field Ellinwood (1826–?), secretary of the Board of Foreign Missions of the Presbyterian Church (U.S.), and also lecturer on comparative religion at the University of the City of New York (later known as New York University). Although Ellinwood held an academic position in comparative religion—in fact he was one of the earliest occupants of such positions in the United States—the venue for his most memorable pronouncements was the Union Theological Seminary, on the occasion of the Elias P. Ely Lectures on the Evidence of Christianity, which he delivered in 1891. His lectures were published the following year under the innocuous and familiar title *Oriental Religions and Christianity*. In the preface, he observes:

I have labored under a profound conviction that . . . the general class of subjects treated is destined to receive increased attention in the near future; that the Christian Church will not long be content to miscalculate the great conquest which she is attempting against the heathen systems of the East and their many alliances with the infidelity of the West. And I am cheered with a belief that, in proportion to the intelligent discrimination which shall be exercised in judging of the non-Christian religions, and the skill which shall be shown in presenting the immensely superior truths of the Christian faith, will the success of the great work of Missions be increased.[33]

33. Frank Field Ellinwood, *Oriental Religions and Christianity* (3rd ed., 1906), vi–vii. The lectures had been established by Zebulon Stiles Ely, with the following stipulation: "The course of lectures given on this foundation is to comprise any topics that serve to establish the proposition that Christianity is a religion from God, or that it is the perfect and final form of religion for man."

Ellinwood goes on to caution that the study of "comparative religion" hitherto has been too much in the hands of "non-evangelical writers" such as James Freeman Clark and Moncure Conway.[34] At the same time, he admonishes his fellow evangelicals for not having taken seriously hitherto "the need of understanding the false religions."

It remains to be mentioned that there were still others who went even further than Ellinwood or Bishop Wordsworth in claiming explicitly the compatibility of aims of "comparative religion" and religious mission. Some argued that Christian absolutism went hand in hand with what they termed "fair comparison" of other religions. For example, the Reverend Robert Flint, professor of divinity at the University of Edinburgh, whose St. Giles lecture appeared as the concluding chapter of *Faiths of the World*, contends that it is Christianity—and its uncontestable superiority above all others—that makes possible an impartial overview of (other) religions in the first place.

> Christianity is the only religion from which, and in relation to which, all other religions may be viewed in an impartial and truthful manner. It alone raises us to a height from which all the religions of the earth may be seen as they really are. Towering above them all, it is easy to perceive from it how far they fall short of it in elevation, magnitude, and beauty, while yet from no other point can their actual grandeur be so clearly seen, their relations to one another so distinctly traced, and the significance of each of them as a revelation of God and of men so readily and fully understood. No other positive religion thus affords us a point of view from which all other religions may be surveyed, and from which their bad and their good features, their defects and their merits, are equally visible.[35]

The argument appears to be that one must first be fully convinced of the unique and universal truth of Christianity before one can even begin to view other religions with equanimity. In effect, this author seems to proclaim, Christianity is the sole foundation of all comparative endeavors.

Such a value-laden panoramic survey of "old," "inferior," and "false" religions, with its evangelizing and missionizing agenda so unequivocally pronounced,

34. Ibid., 2.
35. Robert Flint, "Christianity in Relation to Other Religions" (1882), 336.

would likely not only embarrass contemporary scholars but also offend the pluralist doctrine of today's world religions discourse more generally. It has become a prevailing ethic and custom to edit out from both academic and public discourses on religion any sign of hierarchical valuation, any overt expression of self-serving and self-elevating motives lurking behind the work of comparison—that is, motives other than those in the interest of science or of the ecumenical harmony of the world. At the same time, scholars today are aware that in former times a large number of biased treatises dismissive of religions other than the author's own were written in the name of "fair surveys" and "comparative religion." As we learn from the ever-resourceful Louis Henry Jordan, the explicitly partisan, apologetically motivated comparativism has long thrived side by side with, and often in collusion with, the new science of "comparative religion" or "history of religions." Further examples of this type of comparativism, which Jordan calls "revelation school," include James Clement Moffat's *A Comparative History of Religions* (1871–73),[36] Samuel Henry Kellogg's *The Genesis and Growth of Religion* (1892) and *A Handbook of Comparative Religion* (1899), John Arnott Macculloch's *Comparative Theology* (1902), James Haughton Woods's *Practice and Science of Religion* (1906), and William St. Clair Tisdall's *Comparative Religion* (1909). These are all instances of "comparison" done expressly in the interest of Christian apologetics, though one may never discern this fact from the titles alone.[37]

It seems to us today rather remarkable that so many nineteenth-century authors of varying attitudes toward non-Christian religions claimed—or, for the most part, assumed—that their enterprise of comparing religions without bias was not only compatible with but in fact perfectly complementary to their own proudly unshakable conviction in the supremacy of Christianity. Nowadays, we generally discredit this claim as naive at best, disingenuous at worst. We behold in disbelief the seriousness with which some of those comparativists with strong dogmatic views pronounced that their surveys of other religions

36. Jordan, *Comparative Religion*, 221. Moffat was professor of church history at Princeton Theological Seminary.

37. An earlier example of this type of Christian apologist is Thomas Broughton (1704–74), who wrote his *Christianity Distinct from the Religion of Nature* (1732) in response to Matthew Tindal's famous treatise, *Christianity as Old as the Creation* (1730). Broughton also published *An Historical Dictionary of All Religions: From the Creation of the World to the Present Time* (1742). Volumes with somewhat more revealing titles include Joseph E. Riddle's Bampton Lectures, *Natural History of Infidelity and Superstition in Contrast with Christian Faith* (1852), and Samuel H. Kellogg, *The Light of Asia and the Light of the World* (1885).

were—not just in principle, but in actuality—"fair," "sympathetic," and "impartial."[38] And since we find ourselves incapable of taking these pronouncements seriously, there is little incentive today to reexamine the nineteenth-century reasoning that might have made it feasible for these authors to advance such an argument in earnest. But this may be our loss. Surely, our thorough lack of interest in their logic is ultimately to the detriment of our own historical understanding.

38. I should note that to draw such a sharp contrast between their credulity and complacency and our self-critical vigilance is to speak from the point of view of today. In a sense, this is one-sided. For, from a tertiary point of view, the difference between them then and us today might seem less a matter of greater or lesser scientific sophistication or divergent analytic principles; rather, it may have to do more with whether one feels entitled to hold a certain stance—such as regarding the compatibility between Christian universalism and comparative religion—and to announce it in public.

PART 2

3

The Birth Trauma of World Religions

We now turn to the matter of the origins of the term "world religion"—or "world religions" or "world-religion(s)," as the case may be, or, also possibly, "world's religions." The question at hand is how this somewhat slipshod, weirdly composite term came to be associated with, and subsequently made more or less equivalent to, the topic that had been typically called by phrases like "all the religions of the known world," or "religious denominations of the world," or simply, "religions of the world."

As the uncertainty of the appellation itself may signal, there is not much that can be called clear and distinct about the term, the idea, or its history. There is little available information concerning its etymology; nor is there any definitive record of its early deployment. It appears that the phrase suddenly emerged as a commonplace. Although it is thus difficult to trace its usage precisely or to identify the exact generative network, a promising suspicion arises at this point, namely, that the very indeterminacy of typography, with all the awkward variations, could be telling something about its compromised heritage. The phrase's origin is likely nonunitary and disconcerted; it is most probably a foreign import, only imperfectly assimilated into English.

The 1870s are often regarded as the beginning of *Religionswissenschaft*, or the modern science of religion. This convention—which is shared by Louis Henry Jordan and Eric Sharpe, among other historians of the discipline—stems from several notable events, particularly those surrounding two figures often named as principals in the founding of the new science: Friedrich Max Müller (1823–1900) and Cornelis Petrus Tiele (1830–1902).[1] As Eric Sharpe tells us, in Oc-

---

1. Analogous to these developments in Britain and Holland, the 1870s and 1880s also marked the origin of the *science des religions* in France. See Bertrand Pulman, "Aux 'origines' de la science des religions." It is not entirely clear why, at least in the English-speaking world, British and Dutch scholars are given prominence as "founder" figures of *Religionswissenschaft*, over the French. The journal, *Revue de l'histoire des religions* was founded and inaugurated in 1880 by Albert Réville and Maurice Vernes (who also translated Tiele's and Kuenen's works into French).

tober 1877, the Dutch government did something remarkable and unprecedented when it passed the Dutch Universities Act, which

> separated the theological faculties at the four state universities (Amsterdam, Groningen, Leiden, Utrecht) from the Dutch Reformed Church; the original draft of the Bill had referred to the establishment of "faculties of Religious Sciences," but in the event, the title "Faculties of Theology" was retained. However, dogmatics and practical theology were removed from the curricula (though the subjects were taught elsewhere by church-appointed professors), their place being taken by the history of religions, which was assumed to be neutral and scientific. Tiele [who had been teaching the history of religions at Leiden since 1873] became professor at Leiden, P. D. Chantepie de la Saussaye at Amsterdam.[2]

Concurrent with these institutional developments, the pioneering Dutch scholars of religion—including Tiele, Chantepie de la Saussaye, Abraham Kuenen (Leiden), Lodewijk Willem Ernst Rauwenhoff (the Hague), and some other regular contributors to the prominent periodical *Theologisch Tijdschrift* (Leiden)—as well as Otto Pfleiderer, the German theologian and early exponent of the so-called history of religions school (*Religionsgeschichteschule*) at Göttingen, were involved in a controversy of sorts, over a topic that was to have a significance beyond this original context. The point of disagreement among them had to do with a broad-stroke distinction they were apt to draw among the so-called higher religions, namely, the distinction between the ethnically or

---

Vernes's monograph on the discipline was one of the earliest to appear in any language. Cf. Maurice Vernes, *L'Histoire des religions* (1887).

2. Eric J. Sharpe, *Comparative Religion* (2nd ed., 1986), 121. Jonathan Z. Smith also cites this event in the Dutch universities as a significant moment in the formation of the modern science of religion. See *Imagining Religion* (1982), 102–3. For a discussion of this occurrence in relation to the history of the Dutch universities and of the Dutch Reformed Church, see Simon John De Vries, *Bible and Theology in the Netherlands* (1968).

The earliest reference to this event in the Netherlands seems to be M. van Hamel's essay published in the inaugural issue of *Revue de l'histoire des religions* (Paris), which appeared in 1880: "L'Enseignment de l'histoire des religions," reprinted as an appendix to Vernes, *L'Histoire des religions*, 217–29.

Concerning the development of *Religionswissenschaft* in the Netherlands more generally, see also Julien Ries, "Postface: Quelques aspects de la science des religions à la fin du XIXe siècle" (1982), 147–72.

geographically specific "national religions" (in Dutch, *Volksgodsdiensten*; in German, *Landesreligionen*), on the one hand, and the religions that transcend such ethnic and national boundaries, or "world religions" (Dutch *Wereldgodsdiensten*; German *Weltreligionen*), on the other. In Tiele's work, for example, these two categories constituted part of a larger morphological system of classification, as opposed to a genealogical or purely historical system.

In the opinions of those scholars just named, that Buddhism as well as Christianity belonged to the category of world religions was not in dispute. There was a question, however, as to whether Islam belonged to the same class or not, and ultimately, whether the division into these categories itself was legitimate and efficacious or, on the contrary, tendentious and unscientific.

This classificatory system and the naming of the two categories almost immediately found their way into the English-speaking world. Tiele's monograph *Geschiedenis van den Godsdienst tot aan de Heerschappij der Wereldgodsdiensten* (1876) was translated into English only a year after the publication of the original; Kuenen presented his *Volksgodsdienst en Wereldgodsdienst* in English as the Hibbert Lectures of 1882; in 1885, Tiele reiterated his position, in English, in the "Religions" entry to the ninth edition of the *Encyclopaedia Britannica*; and Chantepie de la Saussaye's *Lehrbuch der Religionsgeschichte* (1887–89)—in which the author summarized Tiele's and others' classification systems—was translated by Max Müller's daughter, Beatrice S. Colyer-Fergusson, and published in 1891 as *Manual of the Science of Religion*.

Whatever the precise definition and value individual scholars ascribed to the category, those who rendered these texts into English understood the sense of the term well enough that, almost in all instances, *Wereldgodsdiensten*, as well as *Weltreligionen*, was translated as "universal religions," or what Tiele preferred, "universalistic religions." Accordingly, Tiele's aforementioned monograph was translated into English as *Outlines of the History of Religion to the Spread of the Universal Religions* (1877), and Kuenen's as *National Religions and Universal Religions* (1882). Only Tiele, writing in English for the *Encyclopaedia Britannica*, explicitly specifies "world religions" as a synonym for "universalistic religious communities," and he dwells on the problem of the category itself at some length.[3] Tiele's morphological classification in its entirety—one of the most elaborate of such systems—is as follows:

3. I owe this crucial suggestion—that Tiele's article in the *Encyclopaedia Britannica* was probably the first time the term "world religions" was mentioned in English—to Jonathan Z. Smith (personal communication, November 1996).

I. Nature Religions

a. *Polydaemonistic Magical Religions under the control of Animism*
Religions of the so-called savages or uncivilized peoples, but they are degraded remnants of what they once must have been

b. *Purified or organized Magical Religions. Therianthropic Polytheism*

1. UNORGANIZED:

Japanese Kami-no-[michi]; The non-Aryan (Dravidian) religions of India, principally in the Deccan; Religion of the Finns and Ehsts; Old Pelasgic religion; Etruscan religion before its admixture with Greek elements (?); The old Slavonic religions

2. ORGANIZED:

The semi-civilized religions of America: Maya, Natchez, Toltecs-Aztecs, Muyscas, Incas in Peru; The ancient religion of the Chinese empire; Ancient Babylonian (Chaldaean) religion; Religion of Egypt

c. *Worship of manlike but superhuman and semi-ethical beings.*
Anthropomorphic Polytheism
The ancient Vaidic religion (India); The pre-Zarathustrian Iranic religion (Bactria, Media, Persia); The younger Babylonian and Assyrian religion; The religions of the other civilized Semites (Phoenicia, Canaan, Aramaea, Sabaeans in South Arabia); The Celtic, Germanic, Hellenic, and Graeco-Roman religions

II. Ethical Religions

a. *National Nomistic (Nomothetic) religious communities*
Taoism and Confucianism in China; Brahmanism, with its various ancient and modern sects; Jainism and primitive Buddhism; Mazdaism (Zarathustrianism), with its sects; Mosaism; Judaism

b. *Universalistic religious communities*

The last category, "Universalistic religious communities," is the translation of what Tiele has been calling *Wereldgodsdiensten*, or "world religions." As we learn from this and other contemporary sources, the debate was above all about this category:

> With regard to the ethical religions the question has been mooted—and a rather puzzling question it is—What right have we to divide them into

4. As will be apparent throughout the texts I quote, nineteenth-century transcriptions of Arabic, Sanskrit, and other foreign words can be idiosyncratic.

nomistic or nomothetic communities, founded on a law or Holy Scripture, and universal or world religions, which start from principles and maxims, the latter being only three—Buddhism, Christianity, and Mohammedanism? The division has been adopted, among others by Prof. Kuenen, in his Hibbert Lectures, though with the important restriction that Islâm, as being essentially particularistic, ought to be excluded from the class of universalistic religions. In an interesting paper. . . Prof. Rauwenhoff rejects the whole class and particularly disapproves of the term "world religions," for which he substitutes that of "world churches."[5]

No sooner had the term been introduced, it seems, than these Dutch scholars were ready to take back the category altogether. As Tiele continues: "We now think that the term 'world religions' must be sacrificed, though indeed 'world churches' would do no better, perhaps even worse." This, of course, by no means put an end to the controversy because, as all the principals surely must have been aware, the issue was not about the choice of nomenclature, but about the rationale for the demarcation between national and universal(istic) religions.

Kuenen, who wrote a whole book devoted to the subject, begins by observing this apparent fact: "The *universal religions* are, with fair unanimity, placed in one group, and opposed to the *national religions*. Nothing is more natural. The difference on which this division rests is sufficiently striking, and seems, moreover, to have its roots in the nature of the religions themselves." Pitted against national and particularistic religions, world religions are understood above all as those religions which are "born of the nation and rising above it."[6] As natural and self-evident as it may seem, however, this distinction is hardly a simple matter. How is the universality—or even more problematic, the *degree* of universality—of a given religion to be ascertained? Is the raw number of adherents or the mere historical fact of having spread beyond the border of a particular nation or ethnic group a sufficient reason to call it universal or universalistic? Or is there some distinctive quality in the nature of the so-called world religions that sets them apart from the particularistic ones? In other words, as Kuenen puts it, is the universality of a religion a question of "*a fact* or a *quality?*" Is the difference between the particular and the universal a matter of statistics or principle? Are we to infer, moreover, that a religion becomes numerically dom-

---

5. The article Tiele refers to is L. W. E. Rauwenhoff's "Wereldgodsdiensten" (1885).
6. Abraham Kuenen, *National Religions and Universal Religions* (1882), 4–5, 8.

inant *because* of its inherently universal (or at least universalistic) nature? Or could it possibly be the other way around?

In the paragraph that follows the passage from his *Encyclopaedia Britannica* article quoted above, Tiele is in some sense responding to this formidable complex of questions. In a sense, he tries to have it more than one way. At the outset it appears that he would settle for the empirical fact-of-transnationality argument and for the pragmatic and nominalist understanding of the category "world religions," but his rationale begins to falter and the distinction is blurred even before the sentence is over:

> Without serving longer to determine the character of certain religions, the term "world religions" might still be retained for practical use, to distinguish the three religions which have found their way to different races and peoples and all of which profess the intention to conquer the world, from such communities as are generally limited to a single race or nation, and, where they have extended farther, have done so only in the train of, and in connexion with, a superior civilization.

Let us first note that the defining characteristics of this seemingly descriptive category include not only the *fact* of "hav[ing] found their way to different races and peoples" but also the express *intention* of "conquer[ing] the world." The second aspect to be noted in this passage is that, as the last part of the sentence clearly indicates, Tiele would admit that there are cases where a particularistic or national religion *happens to have spread* beyond its national boundary owing to historical accident and not on account of its own intrinsic universalistic character. A religion may spread, that is, riding on the back of a "superior civilization," on account of the greater military, economic, or cultural prowess of its carriers. But if such an accidental expansion could happen, how do we distinguish an essentially and inherently universalistic "world religion" from the ones that are only incidentally transnational? And, in the last analysis, could there possibly be more than one religion that can be said to be intrinsically universal, universalist, or even universalistic?

At this juncture, Tiele most probably senses a pitfall. Indeed, here is a yawning abyss that threatens to plunge the fledgling science of religion right back into interminable theological disputations. He immediately puts a stop to this metaphysical slide by making one significant concession. He continues without pause: "Strictly speaking, there can be no more than one universal or world religion, and if one of the existing religions is so potentially it has not yet reached its goal. This is a matter of belief which lies beyond the limits of scientific classification."

Strictly speaking, then, Tiele would admit to the legitimacy of the question in principle and allow that the question as to whether or not there is one single universal world religion, or if so, which one it is likely to be, is not altogether nonsense, as long as it is clearly understood that such a question lies outside the purview of science. This resolution, one might suggest, is a preemptive strike against any partisan, confessional, or apologetic arguments liable to invade the sanctity of scientific impartiality, and given the context of his remarks (an encyclopedia entry, after all), his move here should be appraised as judicious. For Tiele was not so much called upon to preside over or participate in a polemic as he was expected to represent the general state of the scholarship, and this called for a degree of equanimity, if not to say rhetorical legerdemain. Rather than remaining entrenched in his own previously proclaimed position, he chose to resolve the matter in a way that would allow differences of opinion as regards the classification of Islam and at the same time forefront what scholars then could agree upon. At the cost of suppressing his own opinion, then, he manages to reinstate the authenticity and the legitimacy of the categories:

> [T]here is a real difference between two at least of the three [religions] above named, which are still contending with one another for supremacy over the nations of the globe, and the other religious communities which no longer try to make proselytes—between Buddhism and Christianity on the one hand, and Confucianism, Brahmanism, Jainism, Mazdaism, and Judaism on the other. *And this difference, which ought to be maintained, is indeed one of principle, not of fact only.* If the latter, after having been adopted by a nation, have remained stationary for centuries and even are continuously fading away, while the former now embrace many millions of adherents belonging to various nations and races, and ever go on increasing more or less rapidly, *this cannot be due to some fortuitous or external circumstances only, but must have its principal cause in the very nature of each sort of religions.* (Emphasis added)

By opting to mention only two of the three universalistic religions and thus bracketing the case of Islam, Tiele manages to reinstate the all-important distinction between world religions and national religions.

From our point of view, once we see the list of specific religions supposedly belonging to each of these categories, Tiele's distinction may seem puzzling, arbitrary, and finally unsound. In contrast to his elaborate system, our current use of the term "world religions" includes not only the two (or three), but all of the above-named religions and a few others besides; it is not our convention to recognize a separate category of national religions. As we have been accustomed to the more inclusive list, ascribing to some religions while withholding from others either the intention to proselytize or the ability to contend for global supremacy seems strangely misguided, if not to say altogether irrelevant, as a system of classification. It does not seem legitimately scientific, we would likely aver. Less often do we reflect upon the probability that, rather than disappearing from our way of thinking, this peculiar line of distinction authorized by Tiele may have simply shifted location.

Today, the so-called world religions are often classified—perhaps with deliberate imprecision—alongside, and distinct from, those other religions that are perhaps not-quite-world-religions. Included among the latter are those local, generic religions reportedly found everywhere in the remaining underdeveloped recesses of the nationalizing and globalizing world; in short, they are the no-name religions that scholars nowadays prefer to call "indigenous," in part as a way of eschewing the once common, stigmatizing assignation "primitive." Tiele's categorial distinction, it could be argued, thus survived and simply relocated. Be that as it may, for the present context, let us note that the view Tiele articulates here was broadly shared by many earlier *Religionswissenschaftler*.

Only a few years after Tiele's authoritative summary, Pierre Daniël Chantepie de la Saussaye revisited the issue and reaffirmed that the distinction was natural, widely recognized, and very important:

> The distinction between the religion of a country, and the religion of the world, seems to have been adopted for the first time as a principle of division by von Drey [in 1827]. It has become very popular in more recent times. The fact that most religions belong exclusively to one nation, whilst Buddhism, Christianity, and Islam have spread among different races of mankind, is so important that the latter class of world-religions divides itself quite naturally from the rest.[7]

Here, Chantepie renders the singular service of identifying what appears to be the very first instance in which the distinction between national and world

---

7. P. D. Chantepie de la Saussaye, *Manual of the Science of Religion* (1891), 54.

religions was made and, indeed, the first time the phrase "world religion"—albeit in the singular, and in German—definitively appeared in print.[8] Remarkably, Chantepie makes little of the reference, except to say, as we read above, that Drey was the first to adopt the category, and that it has become "very popular" lately.

Johann Sebastian von Drey (1777–1853) was arguably the most prominent German Catholic theologian of his time and one of the founding editors of the *Theologische Quartalschrift*, which was inaugurated in Tübingen in 1819 and remains extant to this day. The article by Drey that Chantepie refers to, "Von der Landesreligion und der Weltreligion," appeared in the journal in 1827. It was of significant length, published in two parts totaling seventy-six pages, and the paired terms "world religion" and "national religion" named its subject. The reference, therefore, is far from tangential.

On the other hand, it is not difficult to imagine why this article might have seemed of little relevance to the concerns of Chantepie de la Saussaye and his colleagues. Drey's own singular focal point was the relation between the institution of the Christian church and the nation-state, or, put more precisely, the church's freedom and independence from any particularistic constraints endemic to the nation-state. It is here that the contrast between the universal (catholic) and the particular (ethnic) shows up in the now familiar fashion. As Drey puts it succinctly in a telling passage elsewhere:

The church is concerned with and seeks to realize the highest end which is given to *human beings*, and this for all people without distinction and in the same way. The church is everywhere the same. The state is concerned with and seeks to realize the highest end which is given to *citizens* and everywhere in different ways; states and people are always different from one another. The Christian church and the state are thus related as a universal human reality and a national one, as a heavenly reality and an earthly one.[9]

8. As far as I know, no one else has made any claim either concurring or contradicting Chantepie on this point.

Coincidentally, 1827 was also the year that Goethe is reported to have coined the term "world literature" (*Weltliteratur*) while in conversation with a young acolyte, Eckermann—who published the record of those conversations some years after the death of the poet—and the concept came to play a seminal role in another comparative enterprise originating in the same era: comparative literature. See David Damrosch, *What Is World Literature?* (2003), 1.

9. Johann Sebastian [von] Drey, *Brief Introduction to the Study of Theology* (1994), 139.

Based on this understanding of the Christian church—and for Drey this means Catholicism—he assigns all other religions to the category of *Landes-religion*, or national religions, much the same way, as we saw, James Freeman Clarke set all "ethnic religions" to one side, apart from the universal religion, Christianity. In Clarke's case, this universal Christianity was implicitly equated with New England Unitarianism, liberally understood, but which he called "catholic" to underscore its universality (see above, chapter 2, section 1). Here is Drey's version of the same argument:

> In Christianity alone is religion simply open to humanity without any connection to nationality or citizenship; thus, the church is free and independent. The religions of the ancient world were thoroughly national, and so the state was itself the church. Mosaic religion was no less national, the union of its members forming a church-state in accord with the theocratic principle of its origin and not a church at all; as a result of the weaknesses of sacerdotal government the church-state became a state-church.[10]

Of course, for all his appeals to universality, Drey's claim is plainly partisan, since he categorically refuses to ascribe this unique quality—transcendence of national boundaries—to any religious community other than the Catholic Church. The exclusivist dogmatism of Drey's use of the term, and the potential danger it presented to the cause of the emerging *science* of religion, could not have escaped Chantepie de la Saussaye's awareness. Therefore, rather than dwelling on the otherwise privileged moment of the first articulation of the term "world religion," Chantepie quickly takes leave of the theologian and instead credits Abraham Kuenen for having "most thoroughly treated the relation of the world-religions to the national religions from which they have sprung." He then goes on to concur with the general (if provisional) conclusion at which Tiele has already arrived: "It is clear . . . that universalism may be accepted as an essential quality. In that sense there can be only one real world-religion, whether such a religion exist already, though not yet fully developed, or whether it is to be expected from the future by a combination of different existing religions."

But no sooner are the categories established and the distinction sharply drawn than Chantepie proceeds to note the difference between religions belonging to the same "universal" class, and this fact, it seems, throws into doubt once again the very distinction just made.

10. Drey, *Brief Introduction*, 105.

[T]hese three so-called universal religions [Christianity, Buddhism, and Islam] are very unequal with regard to their freedom from national limitation, and their power of adaptation to different requirements and circumstances. This inequality has been clearly established by Kuenen, who on this account declines to place Islam among the world-religions. In fact the objections to this classification are so strong, that Tiele, who formerly always followed it, has now entirely surrendered the name of world-religion, and accepts the difference between national and universal religions as no more than a subordinate principle of division. Now, his principal division is that, into natural and moral religions.[11]

These last statements concerning Tiele are true only with qualifications. At least at the time of the 1884 *Britannica* article, Tiele did not so much "surrender" the category of world religions as he subsumed and incorporated it into a larger classificatory system, simply renaming the category without really relinquishing the logic. By calling the category "universalistic religious communities," he in effect explicated what was meant by "world religions" in the first place. It is nonetheless true that, at that historical moment, issues surrounding the notion of world religions were so contentious that it looked as though the category itself was about to be abandoned by the scholarly community, and to be disowned by the fathers of the science who had initially adopted and groomed it for what looked like a promising scientific career. Needless to say, the fact that the phrase did not disappear from common use but, on the contrary, gained much greater circulation in the twentieth century calls for some explanation, and part of this explanation must lie in the currency it came to enjoy in quarters outside the theoretical disputations of academics.

It should be noted first, however, that, in the technically academic and self-consciously untheological sense of the phrase, the problem of the category "world religion" did not remain a concern only among a few professors in Dutch and German universities. The news of the debate had apparently reached the other side of the Atlantic by the turn of the century, as we see it duly registered and ably represented by Morris Jastrow (1861–1921), a distinguished American Orientalist and professor at the University of Pennsylvania. In his useful survey of *Religionswissenschaft* of the time, *The Study of Religion* (1901), Jastrow advised: "As for the supposed universalism of certain religions, the difference of opinion which exists with reference to the religions which merit

11. Chantepie de la Saussaye, *Manual*, 55.

this distinction, makes it advisable to leave this factor out of consideration entirely."[12]

The reasoning behind his opinion is the same as the one already rehearsed by Tiele and Chantepie de la Saussaye. On balance, Jastrow seems even more skeptical about the scientific value of the category than Tiele, and concurring with the latter, he suggests that the universality of any given religion should be considered a matter of confessional claim rather than a quality that can be descriptively and objectively ascertained. As for the empirical reality, he observes:

> Strictly speaking, there is no such thing as a universal religion, since there is no religion universally professed. There are a number which aim to be universal—as Buddhism, Islamism, and Christianity,—and there are others—as Judaism and Zoroastrianism—which contain elements that might under given conditions become the universal property of mankind, but it is manifestly unjust to place tendencies and aspirations on a par with reality. The fact that the doctrines of a religion do not set up national or racial distinctions, does not make that religion universal; and while due allowance should be made for the remarkable scope attained by such religions as Christianity and Islam—accepted by a larger variety of races than any others—it is not proper to allow personal pride in achievement to get the better of one's judgment, and to proclaim a certain religion as containing the elements which are destined to make it universal. It is natural and proper for those who profess Christianity, or Islam, or Judaism, or Buddhism, to hold to this belief, and it is the duty of those so professing to do all in their power towards realizing that ideal; but when we come to the study of facts in religion, the circumstance must be reckoned with that a universal religion, up to the present, remains an ideal which has not been realised by any religion.[13]

This was a severely skeptical estimation of the scientific utility of the category "world religions" at the turn of the century.

Meanwhile, elsewhere in the confessional community, it should surprise no one that the concept of world religion in the strict sense—that is, in the sense

12. Morris Jastrow, *The Study of Religion* (1901), 122. In the second chapter of this book, Jastrow extensively discusses various systems of the classification of religions, including those by Hegel, Tiele, Kuenen, Réville, Max Müller, Eduard von Hartmann, and Raoul de la Grasserie.

13. Ibid., 122–23.

of the single universal religion—proved very useful.[14] Hence, "world religion" as a designation proper only to the truly catholic religion, in other words, as just another name for Christianity and for Christianity alone, became available to men and women of faith as a new conceptual framework, which facilitated the adaptation of Christian absolutism to the modern reality. It allowed any liberal Christian to acknowledge the existence of other religions without ceding Christianity's exclusive claim to universal truth, and at the same time, without having to resort to the theory of "Satan's empire" to explain their existence, as some earlier authors had done. In short, beyond the pale of the academic circles discussed above, we find a different and nearly contemporaneous use of the term at the end of the nineteenth century. "World religion" in this exclusivist sense was not synonymous with, but rather distinct from and diametrically opposed to, the "religions of the world," that is, other religions. Thus we can now make sense of the intriguing title of William Fairfield Warren's book *The Religions of the World and the World-Religion* (1911). By the same token, we understand what John Henry Barrows intended when he chose to call one of his books (based on his Barrows Lectures) *Christianity, the World Religion* (1897), and we can also recognize from its title alone that Samuel Kellogg's *The Light of Asia and the Light of the World* (1885) is a comparison of Buddhism and Christianity that pits a regional religion against the universal religion.[15]

In effect, at the turn of the century, we find the term "world religion(s)" and its cognates in German, Dutch, and possibly other European languages in a state of polyvalence. For now, let us take stock of the consensus reached by the disputants, with the exception of the severely skeptical Professor Jastrow. Beginning with Drey, what was uncontested and seemingly beyond any challenge

14. The exact provenance of this confessional-theological use of the term remains unclear to me for the moment. However, it is useful to remember that this "unique and universal" sense of the term "world religion" in the singular was consistent with the sense in which Drey originally employed it.

15. In contrast to this English terminology, however, we should also note the German use of *Weltreligionen* to signify religions of the world other than Christianity. Thus we find, for instance, the title *Die Weltreligionen und das Christentum* (1923) by Martin Schlunk (1874–1958). In this connection, I learned through the online catalog WorldCat (www.oclc.org) of the existence of a pamphlet by Alfred Wilhelm Martin entitled *Universal Religion and the Religions of the World* (1896) published by the First Free Church of Tacoma, Washington, but I have not been able to locate a copy to inspect the content.

was the assumption that Christianity was one religion endowed with the characteristics of a universal or universalistic world religion. Because Christianity's universalism in one sense or another was assumed, it was generally not discussed at all. Among the Dutch and German pioneers of the science of religion in the late nineteenth century, there was another assumption that was also largely uncontested—and this set these scientists apart from Drey, Clarke, Maurice, and other theological comparativists discussed earlier—namely, that Buddhism was a world religion alongside Christianity. On the other hand, for the time being, these *Religionswissenschaftler* apparently agreed to disagree on the question of Islam. They broadly acknowledged that the case of Islam was controversial; Islam was problematic in a way that the status of Buddhism, apparently, was not.

4

Buddhism, a World Religion

On the whole, the opinions among scientists of religion in the late nineteenth century were unanimous concerning the status of Buddhism but divided with respect to Islam. One might infer from this that the European image of the former was more uniform and unequivocal than that of the latter. As we shall see, however, nearly the opposite was the case. To be sure, scholars disagreed as to whether or not Islam was a "world religion" in the technical sense of the term discussed in chapter 3; yet neither they nor most of their contemporaries outside the field of *Religionswissenschaft* seem to have been in much doubt about what Islam as a religion—or, for that matter, Islam as an ideological and political force—was really like. In fact, for a religion that claimed dominion or at least dominant influence over an enormous, and enormously diverse, area of the world, the European idea of Islam was curiously monolithic and, for the most part, consistently negative.

Meanwhile, the European outlook on Buddhism was anything but consistent. For one thing, compared to Islam, there were major and minor disagreements as to what Buddhism was about. But perhaps more significantly, Buddhism's countenance reflected in the European imagination was marked by what might be called a series of bipolar characteristics, or a jumbled combination of striking extremes. According to the scholarly treatises and the popular accounts then rapidly on the rise, Buddhism was unquestionably foreign and archaic but also unexpectedly modern and resonant with current conditions. In sum, Buddhism came to be viewed, by those who were interested in the subject for whatever reason, as at once alien and familiar, its character rigorously philosophical and indulgently ritualistic, serenely ethical and diabolically corrupt, its adherents sagacious and stultified, austere and indolent. In view of this luxuriant multitude of images parading before the reading public's eye, it should not be surprising if any given reader, whether scholar or amateur, held some or all of these extremely divergent attributes as more or less true, without feeling an urgent need either to rein in the empirical chaos or to check their own thought processes.

1. Before Buddhism

Let us begin by noting the historical circumstances under which the designation of Buddhism as a world religion came about.

At the time of the Dutch-German debates, Buddhism had only recently been recognized as "the same" tradition existing in diverse regions of South, Southeast, East, and Central Asia. Until that time, neither European observers nor, for the most part, native "practitioners" of those various devotional, contemplative, divinatory, funereal, and other ordinary and extraordinary cults that are now roundly called Buddhist had thought of these divergent rites and widely scattered institutions as constituting a single religion. Opinions were divided as to whether these phenomena were related in a significant enough way, except in a certain technical sense, that is, in specialized contexts concerning the scholastic traditions and monastic orders, where the question of lineage was always paramount. In early modern times, then, there was no "Buddhism" to consolidate disparate observations gathered in and about Asia.

The diffused state of European knowledge concerning other religions can be gleaned from some of the texts mentioned in chapter 1, and also from the fact that the guiding principle of classification had been for centuries the four-part division, which subsumed all the non-Christian, non-Jewish, non-Mohammedan nations under one blanket rubric of paganism/heathenism/ idolatry. In accordance with this conventional view, William Turner observed in 1695:

> Heathens [of the biblical times], in respect of Religion, were as diverse as the Countries which they inhabited: Every Nation having peculiar Deities, and Rites of worship. . . . Modern Heathens, are likewise diversified, according to the number of countries, where they inhabit, Tribes or Castes, and sometimes Families and Persons.

In this reckoning, outside of the three recognizable domains of faith, religions are as numerous and diverse as nations; while each one may be as singular and peculiar as another, none is so significant or noteworthy to be individually compared with any of the three principal religions. In fact, the only remarkable thing about heathenism en masse seems to be its countless variety and the sheer magnitude of its spread. According to Turner's calculation: "Christians possess a sixth part of the earth, Mahometans a fifth part, idolaters 2 thirds, or near it. Or thus, divide the world into 30 parts the Christians have 5, Mahometans 6, Idolaters 19."[1] Everything that was later to be recognized as Buddhism, therefore, was submerged in the vast sea of nondescript heathen idolatries, which, no matter how numerous and diversified, were considered in their essential nature everywhere the same; they were differentiated only by contingent local particularities.

To be sure, even if the supposed totality of Buddhism was not yet known, there were observations made by Europeans before the nineteenth century that could be easily recognized, in retrospect, as referring to this religion, or to what we today know as such. For example, we find a curious perspective in Daniel Defoe's *Dictionarium Sacrum Seu Religiosum, or Dictionary of All Religions* (1704).

On the one hand, if we look up any of the nations where Buddhism as we know it is preeminent—China, Tartary, Japan, and so forth—each nation is noted only for rampant idolatry, and little else is mentioned about any of them.[2] But on the other hand, there are also individual entries in Defoe's accounting that provide vague and often confused references to certain aspects of Buddhism avant la lettre. The most notable of all, no doubt, is this brief entry for the name "Fe":

> FE or FO, the name of the Chief Deity of the Chineses, whom they adore as Sovereign of Heaven, They representing him Shining all in light, with his hands hid under his Robes, to shew that his Power does all things invisibly; he has at his Right-hand, *Confucius*, placed by the *Pagans* among the Gods; and on his Left-hand, *Lanza* or *Lanca*, chief of the second Sect of their Religion.

In this entry, then, not only do we recognize the Chinese name for the Buddha (Fo), but we can also detect a degree of discernment regarding what were later to be called the three religions of China: Buddhism, Confucianism, and Taoism. What is different about Defoe's rendition from our contemporary understanding is that they are referred to as so many "sects" of the (national) religion

---

1. William Turner, *The History of All Religions in the World* (1695), 606.

2. In addition to the dominance of idolatry, Defoe also notes the presence or absence of other religions in the region. Thus, in the "Religions" entry, under the subcategory, "Religions of Asia," we read: "The *Chineses* are Idolaters, but the Exercise of the Christian Religion, at least as the *Jesuits* have been pleased to modify it, is permitted there, and that order have Divers Churches in that Country; there are also a great Number of *Jews*, who have their Synagogues by the permission of the Emperor of *China*.

"*Tartary* is subject to Divers Princes, the most Potent of which is the great *Cham*; some of the

of the Chinese, rather than as three distinct religions. It is also of considerable interest that, in separate entries under "Confucius" and "Lancu" (Lao-Tzu), Defoe proffers altogether naturalistic accounts of the original founding masters of these secondary and tertiary "sects." The two sages are both described as "philosophers" who lived in the sixth century BCE, that is, they are regarded as historical figures, only subsequently supernaturalized, deified—"placed among the Gods"—and, inevitably, idolized. Interestingly, the Confucius entry also contains another sketchy reference to Fe (or Fo), an account that hints at a foreign, vaguely Western origin of this "deity":

> [Confucius] openly declar'd he was not the Inventor of this [Confucian] Doctrine, that he only collected it out of his Predecessors Writings, and used to say, there was a very Holy Man in the Western Lands, that he was called, by some *Zeuximgim,* but said no more of him. In the Year 66, after the Incarnation of our Blessed Saviour, the Emperor *Thinti* sent Ambassadors towards the *West,* to seek this Holy Man, but they stopped in an Island near the Red Sea, to consider a famous Idol named *Fe,* representing a Philosopher that lived 500 years before *Confucius;* this Idol they carried back along with them, with Instructions concerning the Worship paid to it and so introduced a Superstition, that in several things abolish'd the Maxims of *Confucius,* who always condemned Atheism and idolatry.

Within the context of this lore, at least, the religion of "Fe/Fo" appears as a fortuitous substitute that effectively impeded the Orientals' quest for the True Religion, about which the sage Confucius may or may not have known. One might say that this account also unwittingly adumbrates some of the later speculations concerning the historical person of Gautama, the Buddha. "Fe/Fo" is here identified as another ancient "philosopher"—like Confucius and Lao-Tzu—whose status, according to many of the nineteenth-century European authors, was subsequently elevated to that of a supernatural being, in other words, falsely deified, thence in reality demoted to an idol. It is no surprise, then, that in the eyes of European commentators the resultant religion revealed itself as at once atheistic and idolatrous.

Sovereigns follow the *Mahometan* Religion, others are *Pagans* and *Idolaters;* there are also *Nestorians* and *Jews,* but such as observe but little of the Law of *Moses.*

"Idolatry Reigns in *Japan,* and since the Persecution of *Taicosama,* who Reigned there in 1630, the Christians have now no Church in that Country, but have had formerly."

2. Europe Discovers Buddhism

The object-formation of Buddhism in the nineteenth century and the primary role played by the European academy in this formation has been most extensively described to date by Philip Almond, although specific moments and components of this historical process continue to be delineated by a number of other scholars.[3] Almond demonstrates how in the nineteenth century Buddhism as a distinct religion came to be recognized among the educated classes of Europe. In the first half of the century, this was largely a matter of coming to recognize the resemblances, links, and genealogical relations among some extremely varied and seemingly discrete instances of cult practice observed in a broad range of territories from Ceylon, Burma, and Siam to Japan, China, and Tartary. The emerging scholarly consensus posited that the historical origin of this vast network of phenomena was in northern India in the sixth century BCE, and attention came to be focused ever more intensely on two factors: first, the legendary but nevertheless reputedly historical figure Prince Gautama, and second, the voluminous lore and writings, extant in several ancient Asian languages, that were produced in the wake of his earthly life of eighty years.

According to the customary origin story of Buddhist studies as told by the pioneering scholars themselves, one of the decisive moments for the serious study of Buddhism came in the form of an event that was at once an act of foresight and a turn of good fortune. Brian Hodgson of the British East India Company, then residing in Kathmandu, came across some Sanskrit manuscripts. He recognized the potential significance of the documents and forwarded them to three learned societies, which he believed possessed proper expertise. The scholarly entities in question were the Asiatic Society of Calcutta, the Royal Asiatic Society in London, and the Société Asiatique in Paris. Nothing much came of the gifts to the first two associations, but the Paris shipment fell into the hands of the now legendary philologist Eugène Burnouf (1801–52). As the most famous of his pupils, F. Max Müller, told the story in 1862:

Unappalled by their size and tediousness, [Burnouf] set to work, and [it] was not long before he discovered their extreme importance. After seven years of careful study, Burnouf published, in 1844, his "Introduction à l'Histoire du Buddhisme." It is this work which laid the foundation for a systematic study of the religion of Buddha. Though acknowledging the great value of the researches made in the Buddhist literatures of Thibet,

3. Philip C. Almond, *The British Discovery of Buddhism* (1988), especially 1–32.

Mongolia, China, and Ceylon, Burnouf showed that Buddhism, being of Indian origin, ought to be studied first of all in the original Sanskrit documents, preserved in Nepal.[4]

The discovery of Buddhism was therefore from the beginning, in a somewhat literal and nontrivial sense, a textual construction; it was a project that put a premium on the supposed thoughts and deeds of the reputed founder and on a certain body of writing that was perceived to authorize, and in turn was authorized by, the founder figure. As Almond observes, in the course of the nineteenth century, those highly valorized sets of texts, qua canon or sacred books of the Buddhists, increasingly came into the actual possession of European scholars and European institutions. At the same time, there were no native adherents to be found in contemporary India, the land of Buddhism's origin. In effect, the very essence of this newly recognized religion was in the hands of European learned society. With the proper critical skills, those highly trained, monumentally devoted scholars would be in the best position, if not to say an exclusive position, to grasp Buddhism's essential character. For all they knew, the true teaching of this singular religion had been scattered abroad, having lost its mooring, and was languishing in sundry Asian nations. There is an obvious analogy here between the fate of this faith and that of the Sanskrit texts, which were badly in need of critical editing in order to remove "corruptions" that had occurred over the centuries, and which European scholarship was now busy restoring. One might say that Buddhism as such came to life, perhaps for the very first time, in a European philological workshop.

Once the singular essence of Buddhism was thus identified, the rich and various manifestations of actual Buddhism observed throughout modern Asian nations came to be understood as so many derivative forms and latter-day innovations and corruptions. In any event, the prestige of the fledgling science of religion and of Buddhism itself was entirely on the side of the ancient texts; it was singularly devoted to the rigorous critical study of these writings and what they presumably revealed, whereas this science generally presumed that what the native adherents of this religion practiced today was of secondary importance. Thus, in the judgment of the scholars, the actual, on-the-ground manifestations of Buddhism were subjects more suitable for the attention of missionaries, casual observers, and travelers chronicling foreign curiosities than for serious-minded philologists, who should dedicate their labor first to the re-

4. F. Max Müller, "Buddhism" (1862), in *Chips from a German Workshop* (1869), 1:197.

construction of "original Buddhism" and subsequently to the study of its historical developments. It was imperative, in other words, that the scholar should understand the order of derivation and the hierarchy of significance in representing Buddhism, from the essential core contained in the canonical texts to the peripheral ramifications exhibited in native beliefs and observances.

This hierarchy of values was established early in the history of European Buddhological scholarship, so much so that, already in the 1850s—that is, even before most of the monumental nineteenth-century monographs on Buddhism were published—Charles Hardwick could pen the following statement, with his characteristic precision and economy of expression:

What I intend by Buddhism, is the system of metaphysical and social philosophy, organised by Sákya-muni, or Gautama Buddha. Neither am I speaking here of Buddhism in its modern development, as modified by intermixtures either with the popular forms of Bráhmanism, or with the older superstitions of the countries where it afterwards gained a footing: for that view of it will come more properly before us, when we pass from Hindústan to China, and the other regions where it still possesses a complete ascendancy. In different words, we shall be dealing now with a philosophy rather than with a religion.[5]

As we recall from chapter 2, Hardwick was an Anglican divine and, although very well read, not himself a scholar of Buddhism. But for that very reason his example strongly testifies to how early this notion of Buddhism—and the privileging of its original metaphysic over and against modern practices and institutions—set in and became a commonplace among educated Europeans.

Among the works by the professional Orientalists of the nineteenth century, none embodied this order of derivation and the hierarchy of values more graphically than Buddhism (1889) by Monier Monier-Williams (1819–99), the Boden Professor of Sanskrit at Oxford University since 1861. The volume is a sizable treatise based on the 1888 Duff Lectures Monier-Williams gave in Edinburgh. The lectures had been established in honor of the Scottish missionary to Bengal, Alexander Duff (1806–78).[6] As Monier-Williams explains in the preface to the published volume:

5. Charles Hardwick, Christ and Other Masters (2nd ed., 1863), 1:217–18.
6. With regard to the relation between Duff's missionary work in India and the philological scholarship of his time, see Martin Maw, Visions of India (1990), 41–50.

[Initially,] I had no intention of undertaking more than a concise account of a subject which I had been studying for many years. I conceived it possible to compress into six Lectures a scholarly sketch of what may be called true Buddhism,—that is, the Buddhism of the Pitakas or Pâli texts which are now being edited by the Pâli Text Society, and some of which have been translated in the "Sacred Books of the East." It soon, however, became apparent to me that to write an account of Buddhism which would be worthy of the great Indian missionary, I ought to exhibit it in its connexion with Brâhmanism and Hindûism and even with Jainism, and in its contrast with Christianity. Then, as I proceeded, I began to feel that to do justice to my subject I should be compelled to enlarge the range of my researches, so as to embrace some of the later phases and modern developments of Buddhism.[7]

It is to his credit, in a sense, that Monier-Williams did not confine his attention to Buddhism in its (reputedly) original form but extended his reach to take into account the later actualities. As a result, not without justice, could he claim that his lectures—they finally grew to the total of eighteen chapters—were the first attempt to "present in one volume a comprehensive survey of the entire range of Buddhism." In so doing, his utmost concern was to help "clear a thorny road, and introduce some little order and coherence into the chaotic confusion of Buddhistic ideas."

This intent is reflected in the way the lectures were delineated in book form. After an introduction (lecture 1), the first topic concerns the Buddha as a personal teacher (lecture 2), followed by lecture 3 on the Dharma, or the law and scriptures of Buddhism, and lecture 4 on the Sangha, or the Buddhist order of monks. The series continues with a chapter each on philosophy (lecture 5) and morality (lecture 6). With these six essays, the account of what Monier-Williams calls "true Buddhism" is complete.

The next eleven chapters (i.e., all the remaining lectures save the last) methodically and serially spell out the subsequent history of Buddhism, presented as a history not of development but of deterioration. In short, it is a story of how

7. Monier Monier-Williams, *Buddhism* (1889), vi-vii; hereafter cited in the text by page number. Spelling out some of the "later phases and modern developments," he continues: "This led me to undertake a more careful study of Koeppen's *Lamaismus* than I had before thought necessary. Furthermore, I felt it my duty to study attentively numerous treatises of Northern Buddhism, which I had before read in a cursory manner. I even thought it incumbent on me to look a little into the Tibetan language, of which I was before wholly ignorant."

the original, august, severely ethical and philosophical (if also abjectly pessimistic) teaching of the founder was transmogrified in myriad ways, turning into so many popular, debased, and hybrid local traditions. Specifically, this second series begins with a chapter on Buddhism's disappearance from India (lecture 7); lectures 8 and 9 deal with theistic and polytheistic Buddhism; and in lectures 10 and 11, we learn how the ever inward-looking, self-absorbed Oriental asceticism bred mystical Buddhism and how the stubbornly undemocratic, hierarchical spirit of Asian peoples produced the hierarchical Buddhism of Tibet and Mongolia, better known as "Lamaism."[8] After two chapters on ceremonial and ritualistic Buddhism (lectures 12 and 13), Buddhism is shown to take the course of all popular religions adapted to the soil. "Sacred Places" (lecture 14), thus traces the development of its peculiar mythological topography, and "Monasteries and Temples" (lecture 15), of its institutional topography. In the ensuing chapter on images and idols (lecture 16), Buddhism finally shows itself as so many forms of idolatry, and by the time we get to the topic of sacred objects (lecture 17), as virtually indistinguishable from fetishism. All in all, if the first six lectures explicate "true Buddhism," the subsequent and more voluminous series address its corruptions and contaminations, or, we might even say, mongrel Buddhisms.[9]

It is worth noting, at the same time, that unlike some other prominent writers who also drew a sharp distinction between the original, true Buddhism and the later, corrupt Buddhisms, Monier-Williams was of the opinion that the

8. Monier-Williams, however, considered that certain mystical contemplative tendencies were original with the founder, whose stamp was left on the religion. In this connection, an earlier lecture contains this interesting paragraph exhibiting a stereotypical image of Mohammed as a deluded fanatic: "We know, indeed, that eleven centuries later [than the time of the Buddha] another great thinker arose among the Semitic races in Western Asia, who went through the same kind of mental struggle, and that Muhammad, like Gautama, having by his long fasts and austerities brought himself into a highly wrought condition of the nervous system, became a fanatical believer in the reality of his own delusions and in his own divine commission as a teacher" (Monier-Williams, *Buddhism*, 37).

9. Monier-Williams himself explicitly mentions this two-part division of the lectures. Lecture 7 begins with this paragraph: "In the preceding Lectures I have confined myself chiefly to the consideration of what may be called *true Buddhism* as taught by its Founder and developed by his immediate followers and disciples during the first two or three centuries of its existence in the land of its birth, India." He describes the intent of the remaining lectures in this way: "[T]o give a very general idea of the nature of the changes Buddhism underwent before it died out in India, and of its corruptions in some of the countries bordering on India and in North-eastern Asia" (ibid., 147).

declivity was inherent in the original form, that the corruption was therefore a natural, in fact necessary outcome of the essential nature of this religion. Contrary to certain other scholars of Buddhism, he saw a radical opposition— rather than affinity—between Buddhism (even in its original, "purer" form) and Christianity. Thus we find the following tendentious claim at the beginning of the first of the chapters on Buddhist schisms and corruptions:

> But here it is important to caution the student of religions against forcing a comparison between two systems of doctrine like Christianity and Buddhism, which are radically and essentially opposed to each other.
>
> The unchristianlike incrustations and divisions which have marred the original teaching of the Head of our religion exist *in spite of* Christianity. They are not the result of any development of its first principles; whereas, on the contrary, the corruptions and schisms of Buddhism are the natural and inevitable outcome of its own root-ideas and fundamental doctrines. (149)

The point is further elaborated and amplified in the last chapter of *Buddhism*, entitled "Buddhism Contrasted with Christianity" (lecture 18). In this final chapter, Monier-Williams cautions that "a superficial study of either is apt to lead to very confused ideas in regard to their comparative excellence and their resemblance to each other." Despite the surface affinity, he sees "the grand fundamental distinction":

> Christianity is a religion, whereas Buddhism, at least in its earliest and truest form, is no religion at all, but a mere system of morality and philosophy founded on a pessimistic theory of life. (537)[10]

For Monier-Williams, who evidently believed that one ought to have a religion and not just a philosophy or a mere system of morality, the difference was

---

10. This was Monier-Williams's articulation of a commonly held view of the difference between the two religions. To wit, whereas Christianity was a genuinely salvific religion, Buddhism was a particular personal ethic elevated (and mystified) to the status of a religion; hence Buddhism is essentially self-centered. For example, Frank Ellinwood wrote: "Buddhism was an afterthought, only reached after six years of bootless asceticism. There is no evidence that when Siddartha left his palace he had any thought of benefitting anybody but himself" (*Oriental Religions and Christianity*, 144).

none too subtle, and the choice, therefore, was "absurdly" clear.[11] But there were others in his time who were less certain as to whether they really needed a religion, or needed that particular religion traditional to Europe rather than any other, or whether a philosophy with no eternal life attached (and no eternal damnation, for that matter) might not be a good thing after all. And there were still others who either suspected, or positively believed, that the affinity between "true Buddhism" and the comparable "true Christianity" was perhaps not so superficial but very deep, hidden, and secret. We will have an opportunity to consider some of these latter writers in chapter 7. For the moment, let us note that it was in this volatile climate of spiritual unrest, or, to put it another way, in this effervescent atmosphere rife with dangerous new possibilities, that the study of Buddhism first made its mark, the scholarship itself being a rather dowdy enterprise, engaged as it was in an "appallingly tedious" task of collecting, editing, and translating what seemed like an interminable volume of ancient texts radiating in strange scripts.

∽

The newly recognized tradition won designation as a world religion, of course, solely on the strength of the original, "true Buddhism," sometimes called "primitive Buddhism" or even "pure Buddhism"—available only to European scholars who read the ancient texts—and not on account of any of its later corrupt forms, that is, the localized, nationalized, and indigenized Buddhisms actually found in modern Asia. In order to assess this crucial turn of events, it may be useful to review the advent of the study of Buddhism more broadly.

To begin, the emerging scholarship on Buddhism privileged above all the historical person of the Buddha and the incipient period of its history. This tendency is well attested by the titles of several preeminent nineteenth-century texts on Buddhism, such as *Life of the Budd'a* (*Leben des Budd'a*, 1823) by Julius von Klaproth (1783–1835) and *The Life or Legend of Gaudama* (1858) by Paul Bigandet

11. The way Monier-Williams renders the choice in the last paragraphs of the last lecture is, I think, particularly revealing. "What shall I do to inherit eternal life?—says the Christian. What shall I do to inherit eternal extinction of life?—says the Buddhist. It seems a mere absurdity to have to ask in concluding these Lectures:—Whom shall we choose as our Guide, our Hope, our Salvation, 'the Light of Asia,' or 'the Light of the World?' the Buddha or the Christ? It seems a mere mockery to put this final question to rational and thoughtful men in the nineteenth century: Which Book shall we clasp to our hearts in our last hour—the Book that tells us of the dead, the extinct, the death-giving Buddha, or the Book that reveals to us the living, the eternal, the life-giving Christ?" (Monier-Williams, *Buddhism*, 563).

(1813–94).[12] Even better known are Buddha and His Religion (Buddha et sa religion, 1862) by Jules Barthélemy Saint-Hilaire (1805–95) and The Religion of Buddha and Its Origin (Die Religion des Buddha und ihre Entstehung, 1857) by Karl Friedrich Koeppen (1808–63), this last being, though not as widely known as Barthélemy Saint-Hilaire's, a work highly recommended by Max Müller on account of its superior scholarly merit.[13] The next generation of European scholars of Buddhism continued the same trend, perhaps best represented by Hermann Oldenberg (1852–1920), whose key work was translated, within a year of its German publication, as Buddha, His Life, His Doctrine, His Order (1882), and T. W. Rhys Davids (1843–1922), who counted among his treatises on the subject Buddhism: Being a Sketch of the Life and Teachings of Gautama, the Buddha (1899) and Early Buddhism (1908).

In this connection, it may be useful to remember more generally that roughly during this same period there seem to have developed two typical, nearly requisite, means of identifying an individual religious tradition as distinct, unique, and irreducible to any other: the naming of an extraordinary yet historically genuine person as the founder and initiator of the tradition, on the one hand, and the recognition of certain ancient texts that could be claimed to hold a canonical status, on the other.[14] All of the so-called great religious systems known to the nineteenth century—or what were soon to be called world re-

12. Von Klaproth's work is mentioned in Raymond Schwab's The Oriental Renaissance (1984), 110. The title of Bigandet's work in its second edition is even more telling: The Life, or Legend, of Gaudama, the Buddha of the Burmese (1866).

13. "To those who may wish for more detailed information of Buddhism, than could be given by M. Barthélemy Saint-Hilaire, consistently with the plan of his work, we can strongly recommend the work of a German writer, 'Die Religion des Buddha,' von Köppen, Berlin, 1857. It is founded on the same materials as the French Work, but being written by a scholar and for scholars, it enters on a more minute examination of all that has been said or written on Buddha and Buddhism" (Müller, "Buddhism," 201). This, however, is not to suggest that Barthélemy Saint-Hilaire was no scholar. To be fair to everyone concerned, it may be noted that, although Barthélemy Saint-Hilaire, like Müller, studied Sanskrit with Eugène Burnouf and wrote several books on Buddhism and other Indian subjects, he was more of a classicist than an Indologist, by far the most monumental work of his being a thirty-five-volume translation of Aristotle.

In addition to those already named, as one of the European pioneers of Indology and Buddhist studies, Müller and others often mention Christian Lassen (1800–1876), whose principal work is published in a five-volume collection, Indische Alterthumskunde (1858–1874).

14. To what extent this presumption of importance of the founder and the text had to do with a parallel development in nineteenth-century biblical studies—especially scientific biblical criticism and the so-called quest for the historical Jesus—is a question that is as obvious as it is understudied.

ligions in the twentieth—met these criteria, with the notable exceptions of Hinduism and Shinto, both of which lacked a discernible founder. It appears, however, that the founder function could be served by a figure with an uncertain historical status and with mostly legendary endowments, such as Zoroaster, the founding prophet of modern Parsiism, or Lao-Tzu, the mythic "old master" of Taoism. As for the cases where no individual progenitor of the tradition could be named, scholars nonetheless managed to "discover" an ample cache of "sacred texts" to authenticate the identity and lineage of the tradition. In the absence of a historical founder figure, in fact, something like "a distinct genius of a nation" could be substituted and designated as the generative force of a tradition.[15]

Not surprisingly, in the context of the nineteenth-century world religions debate, a collectively and anonymously originated religion epitomized the *national religion* (*Landesreligion*). Brahmanism (i.e., Hinduism) was a quintessential case, being the religion of India, supposedly, despite the empirical fact that multiple, often contending, and always polymorphous cultic communities had existed in the Indian subcontinent for millennia. In spite of all that might be implied by the overwhelming multiplicity and heterogeneity of the locale, ever since Europeans learned to read Sanskrit, the spiritual genius of the Indian nation has been claimed to reside above all in the Vedas, styled "the sacred books of the Hindus."[16]

In contrast, from the start, the Indian origin of Buddhism was understood very differently. It is as though its inception in the particular locale was a mere

15. Oldenberg describes how the sultry, torrid climate of India turns its people ever inward and meditative, which in turn determines the essential character of its religion. As he puts it, "Will and action are overgrown with thought." To the Brahman, "the true world, hidden by the images of his own dreams, remains an unknown, which he is unable to trust and over which he has no control: life and happiness in this world break down under the burden of excessively crushing contemplation of the hereafter. The visible manifestation of the world to come in the midst of the present world is the caste of the Brahmans. . . . No one can understand the course which Indian thought has taken, without keeping in view the picture . . . of this order of philosophers, as the Greeks named the Brahmanical caste. And above all it must be remembered that, at that time at least, which has shaped the determinative fundamental thoughts for the intellectual efforts of a subsequent age and for Buddhism also, this priestly class was something more than a vain and greedy priestcraft, that it was the necessary form in which the innermost essence, the evil genius, if we may so call it, of the Indian people has embodied itself" (Oldenberg, *Buddha* [1882], 11–13).

16. Thus we read, as early as 1850s, statements of the following sort: "It is now almost universally admitted that to ascertain the basis of Hindú civilisation, or rather, to become

historical accident; this fact was contingent and circumstantial rather than essential and intrinsic to the nature of the religion. In any event, Buddhism's essential beginning was said to lie in the extraordinary mind of one individual, even if that individual's modes of giving shape to his insight and representing and ministering it to others were deeply embedded in the language and the mores of the times and of the locality. From the early days of European scholarly investigation into the matter, the origin of Buddhism was thus uniquely and exclusively tied to one individual and to his reputedly revolutionary spiritual vision. Similarly, from the early days of the scholarship, the Buddha's rejection of the Vedas, the sacred books of the "Brahmanists," was counted among the most important of his founding deeds. Furthermore, this scholarship would claim that his departure from the textual authority of the preexisting tradition had in turn caused the new religion to generate a whole new set of texts, which became sacred scriptures unique and foundational to it alone.

This all-important notion that the historical Buddha challenged and ultimately rejected Vedic authority presided over by the Brahman priesthood—just as Luther had rejected papal authority[17]—appears to be based upon rather modest textual evidence. It amounts to a few passages in certain Buddhist sutras, where the Buddha chides or ridicules the Brahmans. Hermann Oldenberg specifies three such passages—Ambattasutta (Dìgha-Nikâya), Cankîsuttanta (Majjhima Nikâya), and Kûtadantasutta (Dìgha-Nikâya) to be precise—and he interprets them this way: "Buddha discredited the sacrificial system; he censured with bitter irony the knowledge of Vedic scribes as sheer folly, if not as shameless swindle; Brahmanical pride of caste was not more gently handled."[18]

---

acquainted with the earliest utterances of the Hindú religion, we must have recourse directly to the class of sacred books entitled Védas. . . . I shall exclude from this inquiry all reference to the aboriginal (i.e., non-Áryan) tribes of India. The Védas have been ever the possession of one dominant race,—a race which, having crossed the Indian Alps at some remote period, was gradually diffused into the Panjáb, and ultimately over a large portion of the whole Peninsula. Who and what was the 'barbarian' (mléchchha) they drove out before them; who and what the abject serf, or Súdra, they had forcibly converted to their own religion, are extraneous questions, interesting in themselves, but not admissible within the limits of the present survey" (Hardwick, *Christ and Other Masters*, 1:171–72). As this passage indicates, however, strictly speaking, the spirit of the Indian nation is construed as residing not ultimately in the soil but rather in the blood, insofar as it is the invading Aryans from elsewhere that are considered the agent of the spiritual legacy of India proper.

17. The analogy was a common one. Hence James Freeman Clarke's famous designation of Buddhism as "Protestantism of the East." See his *Ten Great Religions* (1881).

18. Oldenberg, *Buddha*, 172–73.

As for the actual sutra passages expressly quoted by Oldenberg, however, it would take a sensitive palate indeed to taste the bitterness of the "irony" he speaks of. Moreover, these instances of mild rebuke against the Brahmans occur among very many other pronouncements where the Buddha scorns, perhaps with a little more venom, a series of rival schools of metaphysics and neighboring groups of ascetic yogins of one kind or another. It may be fairly said, therefore, that Oldenberg and other European scholars of Buddhism considerably inflated the value of the Buddha's ridicule and elevated it to a matter of vitriolic attack and resolute rejection, with the result that passages such as these were made to signify the Buddha's definitive break from the prevailing tradition of his land and of his time.[19]

19. The relevant sutra passages—as explained and partially quoted by Oldenberg—are as follows. As regards the authority and transmission of the Vedic knowledge: "The pupil believes what the teacher has believed, the teacher what he has received from the teachers before him. 'Like a chain of blind men, I take it, is the discourse of the Brahmans: he who is in front sees nothing, he who is in the middle sees nothing, he who is behind sees nothing, what then? Is not, if this be so, the faith of the Brahmans vain?'

"The classical expression of the views of the old Buddhist Church, and, we may say, of Buddha, regarding the value of the Vedic sacrificial cult, is contained in a conversation of Buddha with a Brahman of position, who asked Buddha about the essentials of a proper sacrifice.

"Buddha then narrates the story of a powerful and successful king of bygone days, who, after splendid victories and the conquest of the whole earth, formed the resolution of making a great offering to the gods. He summoned his family priest and asked his instructions, as to how he should set about his project. The priest admonishes him before offering a sacrifice, to establish first of all peace, prosperity, and security in his kingdom. Not until all injustices in the land are repaired, does he proceed to sacrifice. And at his sacrifice no life of sentient creature is taken; no cattle and sheep are killed; no trees are hewn down; no grass is cut. The servants of the king perform their work in connection with the sacrifice, not under pressure and in tears, in fear of the overseer's verge; each works willingly, as his own inclination prompts him. Libations of milk, oil, and honey are offered, and thus the king's sacrifice is performed. But there is, Buddha goes on to say, yet another offering, easier to perform than that, and yet higher and more blessed: where men make gifts to pious monks, where men build dwelling-places for Buddha and his order. And there is yet a higher offering: where a man with believing heart takes his refuge with Buddha, with the Doctrine, with the Order, when a man robs no being of its life, when a man puts far from him lying and deceit. And there is yet a higher offering: where a man separates as a monk from joy and sorrow and sinks himself in holy repose. But the highest offering, which a man can bring, and the highest blessing of which he can be made participator, is, when he obtains deliverance and gains this knowledge: I shall not again return to this world. This is the highest perfection of all offering.

"Thus speaks Buddha; the Brahman hears his discourse believingly, and says: 'I take my refuge with Buddha, with the Doctrine and with the Order.' He had himself intended to perform

The idea, one might say, is a natural extension of the theory that was widely shared by the early generations of scholars of Buddhism, the theory that Buddhism was a historical reform movement initiated by an extraordinary but historically real individual.[20] In other words, according to the prevailing scholarly opinion, the origin of Buddhism was an exemplary case of a great man heroically standing up against the faceless collective power of society and tradition, thus evoking an image that the modern West has come to champion and idolize. Though this idea of Buddhism as a revolutionary reform movement was certainly prevalent in the educated circles of Europe generally, in few other places do we find it more sharply expressed than in the words of Germany's leading Indologist, Albrecht Weber (1825–1901), professor of Sanskrit at the University of Berlin. Weber purportedly issued the following pronouncement in 1857:

> Buddhism in its origin is one of the greatest and most radical reactions in favour of the universal rights of man, as belonging to the individual, as opposed to the crushing tyranny of the so-called divine privileges of birth and rank. It is the work of an individual man, who at the beginning of the sixth century BC rose up in Eastern India against the Brahmanical hierarchy, and by the simplicity and the ethic power of his teaching, brought about a complete split between the people of India and their past.[21]

The import of the "radical reaction" in the eyes of this scholar is obvious. To defy the Brahmans is to discredit Vedic authority and the social hierarchy allegedly sanctioned by that authority. The Vedas on the one hand and the insti-

---

a great sacrifice, and had hundreds of animals ready for it. 'I let them loose and set them free,' he says, 'let them enjoy green grass, let them drink cool water, let the cool wind fan them'" (ibid., 172–74).

20. One conspicuous exception was the hapless Émile Senart (1847–1928). In a controversial and influential essay originally serialized in *Journal Asiatique* (1873–75), he suggested that the Buddha was a legendary and mythological figure, a solar deity. This challenged majority opinion, which assumed the historical reality of the Buddha. The essay was later published in a single volume (Émile Charles Marie Senart, *Essai sur la légende du Buddha* [1875]). Hermann Oldenberg, among others, strenuously argued against this (*Buddha*, 72–94). On the other hand, Abraham Kuenen, without going so far as endorsing the idea of a purely mythical Buddha, gives a serious consideration to Senart's thesis (*National Religions and Universal Religions* [1882], 275–81).

21. Quoted in P. D. Chantepie de la Saussaye, *Manual of the Science of Religion* (1891), 564. Chantepie dates this statement as written in 1857, without specifying the title of the publication

tution of the caste system on the other, of course, have been the twin pillars by which Europeans came to understand what it meant to be Indian, for together they have defined the very essence of the Indian nation. To reject the Brahmanic tradition in its spiritual as well as its social manifestations—what more direct and succinct way is there for shedding the specifically Indian (i.e., nationalistic, as opposed to universalistic) character of a religion than knocking down these pillars? What other act or attitude proved better than this, that Buddhism was a religion "born of a nation, but *rising above it*"? [22]

In effect, the scholarship on Buddhism was from the beginning constructing—or "discovering," as one might prefer to put it—a decidedly non-national religion, a qualitatively universal(istic) religion, that is to say, a *Weltreligion*, or world religion. This conceptual formation of Buddhism was taking place before the distinction of world religions from national religions had been established, and probably without any of the scholars of Buddhism having any notion of what was being debated elsewhere by some Dutch and German *Religionswissenschaftler*. In any event, once the designation "world religion" became

---

by Weber, presumably included in *Indische Skizzen* (1857). The same passage is quoted by Abraham Kuenen, and he cites his source as Weber's *Indische Streifen*, 1:104, which appeared in 1868. Kuenen also refers to Max Duncker, *Geschichte des Alterthums* (1855–63), and Monier-Williams, *Indian Wisdom*, (1875), who made similar arguments. See Kuenen, *National Religions and Universal Religions*, 254–56; also Almond, *British Discovery of Buddhism*, 69–74.

22. It should be noted, in the interest of precision and accuracy, that Chantepie de la Saussaye, who quoted the Weber passage, himself duly recorded the necessity to revise this view. As he put it in no uncertain terms: "The opinion . . . that a fight against Brâhmanism was the starting-point and principal object in Buddhism, and that what was intended was a breaking with all that existed before in India, is quite wrong. . . . The difference of caste is not done away with by Buddhism. . . . We cannot . . . recognise in this religion any radical overthrow of Hindu customs; in India, also, it was not considered as such, as is proved by the tolerance with which Buddhism and Brâhmanism flourished for centuries side by side" (*Manual*, 564–65).

At the same time, we might also remember that, with certain qualification, the idea of original Buddhism as a reform movement continued to be repeated, and this impression does not seem to have abated today. What the nineteenth century passed on to the next is succinctly articulated by Otto Pfleiderer in his 1906 lecture: "[Buddha] did not deny the Brahman gods nor give up the doctrine of transmigration of souls, nor do away with the differences of caste, but he did render valueless the priestly ceremonial service, the school learning, the authority of the Veda and the separating differences of the castes, by establishing as fundamental, moral purity and goodness. This building up of something new, whereby that which is old falls of itself, is the method of all successful prophets. Although Buddha did not wish to be a social reformer, as has often been thought, yet indirectly he did become one by making caste religiously unimportant" (*Religion and Historic Faiths* [1907], 116).

available, there is little surprise that Buddhism came to occupy the category. The matching of the religion and the category seems to have come about quietly and almost automatically, that is, without either an express endorsement or an audible objection on the part of the scholars specializing in Buddhism. Apparently, this novelty of classification was not one of the problems knocking loudly on the door of their Buddhological workshop. But there were other pressing issues. As it turned out, those other problems had indeed much to do with the question of world religions.

3. Buddhism and the Future of Europe

With the discovery of Buddhism there suddenly appeared on the European cognitive horizon a religion, alongside Christianity, that was transnational and supraethnic, and according to the way the nineteenth century did the counting, whose adherents easily outnumbered Christians.[23] Although Rhys Davids, for example, reminded his readers that "numbers are no test of truth, but rather the contrary,"[24] many Europeans of the late nineteenth century seem to have found the number at once amazing and alarming. Their bewilderment is understandable, it would seem, given that the statistics had to do with a religion that, only a few decades earlier, hardly anyone knew existed. Lest it bring about a crisis of confidence among the Christians, prominent experts on Buddhism such as Monier-Williams and Rhys Davids, who was professor of Pali and Buddhist literature at University College, London, and secretary of the Royal Asiatic Society, as well as Professor James Legge of Oxford, the foremost British Sinologist of the time, chose to address this demographic question when they wrote their treatises, and they did so either by correcting the numbers or by offering an alternative interpretation of the existing numbers.[25]

Monier-Williams, in a postscript appended to the preface to *Buddhism* ex-

---

23. Chantepie de la Saussaye refers to the numbers taken from Hübner, *Geographisch-statistische Tabellen aller Länder der Erde* (1884), which shows figures in millions as follows: "Christians 432 (30.2%); Mohammedans 120 (8.3%); Israelites 8 (0.5%); Buddhists 503 (35%); Brahmans 138 (9.6%); and Worshippers of fetishes 234 (16.4%)." Chantepie also mentions Wichman, *Geographisch-statische Notizen* (1885), Atlas Migeon (1884), as well as Wagner, *Lehrbuch der Geographie* (1882) (Manual, 58–59).

24. T. W. Rhys Davids, *Buddhism* (1899), 3.

25. F. Max Müller, on the other hand, seems to have regarded much of this number anxiety with a measure of detached amusement and irony. See, for instance, his 1895 essay "The Kutho-Daw," in *Last Essays* (1901), 210–30.

pressly for this purpose, states that he is much concerned about "a prevalent error . . . [that] is persistently propagated." He then complains:

> Almost every European writer on Buddhism, of late years, has assisted in giving currency to this utterly erroneous calculation, and it is high time that an attempt should be made to dissipate a serious misconception. It is forgotten that mere sympathizers with Buddhism, who occasionally conform to Buddhistic practices, are not true Buddhists. In China the great majority are first of all Confucianists and then either Taoists or Buddhists or both. In Japan Confucianism and Shintoism co-exist with Buddhism. In some other Buddhist countries a kind of Shamanism is practically dominant. The best authorities . . . are of opinion that there are not more than 100 millions of real Buddhists in the world, and that Christianity with its 430 to 450 millions of adherents has now the numerical preponderance over all other religions. I am entirely of the same opinion. I hold that the Buddhism, described in the following pages, contained within itself, from the earliest times, the germs of disease, decay, and death . . . , and that its present condition is one of rapidly increasing disintegration and decline. (xv)

In effect, the "real Buddhists" do not add up to even a quarter of the Christian population. Here, not only does Monier-Williams dispute the numbers but, more fundamentally, he claims Buddhists are destined for extinction anyway, theirs being a death-embracing pseudoreligion whose ultimate goal is annihilation and nothingness. No doubt intended as an assurance to fellow Christians, his emphatic, double-barreled negation of the preponderance of Buddhism attests to the measure of anxiety felt by European scholars and their audiences.[26]

Somewhat more charitably than Monier-Williams, Rhys Davids suggests that the numbers are in themselves an inadequate indicator of the actual condition, and that they should therefore be left alone. At the same time, in concert with Monier-Williams, he also mentions that Buddhists customarily affiliate themselves simultaneously with other "systems" and cults, and, he avers, none of them is strictly or purely Buddhist; or, as he puts it: "Not one of the five hun-

---

26. To compound this impression, at the very end of the book, Monier-William wrote yet another "postscript" referring the reader to that (first) postscript appended to the end of the preface (see *Buddhism*, 563).

dred millions who offer flowers now and then on Buddhist shrines, who are more or less moulded by Buddhist teaching, is only or altogether a Buddhist." All the same, Rhys Davids puts the numbers into perspective, observing that "these tables cannot fail to show how great is the claim on our attention of that system whose influence over living men they roughly express."[27]

But the question of numbers was only one aspect of the general worry about this suddenly prominent foreign religion. As the reality of the historical Buddha—called Gautama, Siddhartha, or Shakyamuni—as well as dates relevant to the early history of Buddhism, began to be confirmed, scholars came to realize that this religion, rather than Christianity, might prove to be the oldest universal(istic) religion. Moreover, with this awareness came the disturbing suspicion that Buddhism could have influenced Christianity.[28] More disconcerting still was the suggestion that what had hitherto been considered the unique and essential characteristic of Christianity—its universality—could have been *derived* from Buddhism. Could Christianity be, after all, a belated, derivative religion, just as the Christians had hitherto accused Islam of being?

It is only when we understand Buddhism's status specifically as a universalistic world religion that we come to appreciate the enormous stakes for nineteenth-century Europeans—that is, why the discovery of Buddhism mattered and, in fact, perturbed many scholars, clergy, and laypeople alike, in a way that the knowledge of the great antiquity of Egyptian, Israelite, or any other "national" or "ethnic" religion had not. So it came about that, in the latter decades of the nineteenth century, writer after writer would make sure not to over-

---

27. Rhys Davids, *Buddhism*, 4, 7. Similarly, James Legge, in a brief introduction to his translation of a Chinese Buddhist text, expended much of the occasion addressing this issue, beginning with this definitive statement: "In concluding this introduction I wish to call attention to some estimates of the number of Buddhists in the world which have become current, believing, as I do, that the smallest of them is much above what is correct" (introduction to *A Record of Buddhistic Kingdoms* [1886], 5).

28. As will be discussed in another context in chapter 7, there arose a number of prominent and widely popular writers in the last decades of the nineteenth century who suggested the likelihood of Indian or Buddhist influence upon Christianity. In the English-speaking world, Arthur Lillie was arguably the most conspicuous, as he wrote several treatises propounding this theory: *Buddha and Early Buddhism* (1881), *The Popular Life of Buddha* (1883), *Buddhism in Christendom, or Jesus, the Essene* (1887), *The Influence of Buddhism on Primitive Christianity* (1893). In addition, among the books written in English, Ernst von Bunsen's *The Angel-Messiah of Buddhists, Essenes, and Christians* (1880) may be cited as a tract making similar claims. On the other hand, Thomas Sterling Berry, *Christianity and Buddhism* (1891), and Sir Robert Anderson, *The Buddha of Christendom* (1899) exemplify treatises contending against these opinions.

look the thorny issue of the possible influence of Buddhism upon Christianity, or even more threateningly, the Buddhist origin or foundation of Christianity—if only to conclude in the end that such an influence was highly unlikely, or that such an order of generation and derivation was patently impossible.[29]

The state of disquiet is made abundantly clear by a number of publications from the last decades of the nineteenth century generated on both sides of the Atlantic. We get a snapshot of the situation, for example, from the Ely Foundation Lectures delivered by Frank Field Ellinwood at the Union Theological Seminary of New York in 1891.[30] His lecture on Buddhism, tellingly entitled "Buddhism and Christianity," opens with a genial and approving reference to Max Müller, who had recently raised a critical voice against certain widespread speculations concerning Buddhism. Ellinwood's complaints in these lectures vividly convey the conditions of the intellectual and spiritual ferment circa 1890:

New interest has recently been awakened in old controversies concerning the relations of Christianity and Buddhism. The so-called Theosophists and Esoteric Buddhists are reviving exploded arguments against Christianity as means of supporting their crude theories. The charge of German sceptics, that Christianity borrowed largely from Buddhism, is made once more the special stock in trade of these new and fanatical organizations. To this end books, tracts, and leaflets are scattered broadcast, and especially in the United States and Great Britain.

Professor Max Müller says, in a recent article published in *Longman's New Review*: "Who has not suffered lately from Theosophy and Esoteric Buddhism? Journals are full of it, novels overflow with it, and one is flooded with private and confidential letters to ask what it all really means. Many people, no doubt, are much distressed in their minds when they are told that Christianity is but a second edition of Buddhism. 'Is it really

29. T. W. Rhys Davids made this point conspicuously in his Hibbert Lectures of 1881: *Lectures on the Origin and Growth of Religion as Illustrated by Some Points in the History of Indian Buddhism* (2nd ed., 1891). The prominent American Unitarian and well-read amateur comparativist, James Freeman Clarke mentioned in chapter 2, similarly and succinctly stated the argument in the article "Affinities of Buddhism and Christianity" (1883), 467–78.

As for further texts comparing Christianity and Buddhism, the following may be cited in addition: Raffaele Mariano, *Cristo e Budda, e altri iddii dell'Oriente.* (1900), and Friedrich von Rittelmeyer, *Buddha oder Christus?* (1909).

30. As noted in chapter 2, section 4, Ellinwood was the inaugural occupant (beginning in 1887) of the chair in "comparative religion" at the University of the City of New York.

true?' they ask. 'Why did you not tell us all this before? Surely, you must have known it, and were only afraid to tell it.' Then follow other questions: 'Does Buddhism really count more believers than any other religion?' 'Is Buddhism really older than Christianity, and does it really contain many things which are found in the Bible?'" And the learned professor proceeds to show that there is no evidence that Christianity has borrowed from Buddhism. In this country these same ideas are perhaps more widely circulated than in England. They are subsidizing the powerful agency of the secular press, particularly the Sunday newspapers, and thousands of the people are confronting these puzzling questions. There is occasion, therefore, for a careful and candid view of Buddhism by all leaders of thought and defenders of truth.[31]

According to Ellinwood, then, these rampant, dangerously enticing, and highly questionable opinions were fuelled largely by individuals with dubious qualifications, self-aggrandizing obscurantists and suspected charlatans who maliciously averred, or else mendaciously and stupidly believed, that Buddhism had the primary and originary status over Christianity.

If most of the popularizers of these benighted opinions did not possess academic credentials themselves, they were not without recourse to the prestige of the academy altogether, for included among the authorities often cited for their support were highly esteemed scholars like Albrecht Weber.[32] As mentioned earlier, in the 1850s, the German scholar advanced the view that Buddhism was a humanistic and universalistic reform movement that arose in protest against the hierarchical, priestly particularism of Brahmanism, the "race religion" of India, much as Christianity was a universal(istic) religion arising in opposition to the race religion of the Jews. Weber was by no means alone in the academy for upholding this view, and indeed, it was undoubtedly an appreciative outlook from seats of learning that made it possible for others to proclaim sententiously that Gautama, the Enlightened One, spoke in the name of universal

31. Frank F. Ellinwood, Oriental Religions and Christianity (3rd ed., 1906), 140–41).

32. Weber occupied a prominent position in Indology, and his influence was considerable. From 1850 to 1863, he was the principal and founding editor of Indische Studien: Zeitschrift für die Kunde des indischen Alterthums, journal of the German Oriental Society (Deutschen Morgenländischen Gesellschaft). Many of his voluminous publications are highly technical and scholarly; however, his University of Berlin lectures on Indian literature, Akademische Vorlesungen über Indische Literaturgeschichte (1852) was translated into French in 1859 (Histoire de la littérature indienne). The English translation became available in 1878 (History of Indian Literature) and has seen very many editions and reprints, the most recent of which is dated 2000.

humanity centuries before Jesus the Redeemer, that he was the true original, and Jesus was not. To make matters more irritating for Euro-Christian traditionalists, both Gautama's own ministry during his lifetime and the subsequent religious movement in his name seem to have been, on balance, considerably more successful than that of Jesus. It was against the backdrop of such an annoyingly exalted image of the Buddha and Buddhism that Ellinwood positioned himself as a staunch defender of Christian priority, superiority, and supremacy. He attacked what he deemed irresponsible sensationalism perpetrated by "the secular press" in unholy alliance with xenophilic liberal extremists and washed-up skeptics. He labeled his adversaries as "fanatical" and vaguely described them as dubious, although he mentioned no specific names. The point, for him, was that the ideas freely derived from scholars like Weber were all the more dangerous because of their powerful popular appeal. He saw such beliefs and arguments as not only foreign and wrong but also expressly anti-Christian.

Ellinwood's diatribe is but one of countless examples from the period that testify to the enormous trepidations stirred up by the discovery of Buddhism. As we see in the case of Max Müller's unnamed correspondents (referred to by Ellinwood above), even those relatively uninvolved in the occupation of Orientalist scholarship anxiously inquired into the nature and the history of the newfound religion, because the matter actually concerned Europeans' own standing in the spiritual topography and chronology of the world, which seemed to have become increasingly uncertain. For better or for worse, the controversy over Buddhism was thus as widespread and fashionable among moderately educated people as it was annoying to the professional philologists. However exasperated the scholars might have been in the face of the misguided worries of the public, it cannot be denied that the problem was of the academy's own making in more than one sense. Not only had the philological scholarship yielded—discovered, constructed, invented?—Buddhism to begin with, but in so doing, it had created a whole new configuration of nations and peoples, as it opened an entirely new ground for comparison. The full import of this transformation was to become evident only decades later. Or perhaps it should be said that much of the import remains still unexamined and poorly understood to this day.

To review what the present investigation has thus far made manifest, Buddhism as a universal(istic) religion immediately brought itself into competition and contention with what had been until then the only such religion, in fact, the only real religion in the proper sense of the term. Following this earlier train of thought, many nineteenth-century advocates of Christianity habitually called their own religion *uniquely universal*. Once Buddhism came into the field of vision, of course, none of them was to be the only religion—except, possibly, in the eyes of those who believed, as Monier-Williams apparently did, that Buddhism was not a religion but a philosophy. Both Buddhism and Christianity were to be recognized as unique in a certain sense, that is, each in a manner proper to itself. Buddhism was thus accepted as a world religion, that is, as something comparable—at least in a taxonomic sense—to Christianity.

Given the complexity and multiplicity of factors involved in the technical debates of the time, it may not be immediately obvious why European scholarship accorded this status with unprecedented honor to Buddhism rather than to any other religion. As we saw earlier in this chapter, some of the proponents of the fledgling *Religionswissenschaft* would advance a "quantitative" argument, pointing to the empirical fact that Buddhism had in the course of its long history gained a great number of adherents in many nations and thereby had transcended its original boundaries of race, language, and culture. Alternatively, others could opt for a "qualitative" argument in support of Buddhism's status as a world religion, suggesting that Buddhism's essential nature derives from the singular intention of its founder toward something like a spirit of individual freedom and universal humanity soaring above the particularism of national tradition.

The elevation in status of Buddhism to the rank of world religion naturally and perhaps inevitably leads to the question: Why withhold the same privilege from Islam—a powerful, formidable religion long known to Europe, proven transnational from the earliest days of its founding, and emphatically universalistic in its creed? To pose this question more specifically from our own historical standpoint: What accounts for the reluctance or even active resistance on the part of some nineteenth-century scholars to acknowledge Islam as a world religion? What credible argument could have been advanced to differentiate the case of Gautama and his transnational, reputedly universalist protest movement so decisively and categorically from the case of Mohammed and his reformist religion, which Islam undoubtedly and self-consciously was? In fact, why should there have been any controversy about Islam at all?

As will be shown in more detail in chapter 6, some of the protagonists in the nineteenth-century debates maintained surprisingly vociferous opinions on the particularistic nature of Islam, adamantly insisting that it is rigidly national and narrowly racial in its essence despite its apparent transnational and inter-racial spread. In hindsight, these opinions cannot but appear tendentious, too vehement to be taken at face value. In light of such a monolithic, unilateral, and artlessly condescending view of the religion of Mohammed, one is tempted to offer a comparably unsubtle delineation of the difference between the two religions as entertained in the minds of those nineteenth-century European authors. The difference, in effect, may amount to something as simple as this: Buddhism, or true Buddhism, is Aryan; Islam is Semitic.

Not surprisingly, the ascendancy of Buddhism in European estimation was concurrent with the proportionate decline in status of the non-Christian monotheisms, that is, Judaism and Islam. As we recall, before the advent of comparative science of religion, these two were the only "other religions" nominally recognized by Christian Europeans; indeed, as such, they had been grudgingly acknowledged and respected, even as they were feared and hated. This shift in relative positioning was taking place, moreover, at the time of growing recognition of what philologists had begun to call "language groups," which were to give rise to a new classificatory system. As we shall discuss in chapter 5, under this classificatory system, the "original" languages of Islam and Judaism (Arabic and Hebrew) were categorized in one group, while the language of the Christian New Testament (Greek) and, very significantly, the languages of ancient Indian and Persian religions—that is, the "original" languages of Brahmanism, Buddhism, Zoroastrianism (Sanskrit, Pali, Avestan)—were placed in another.

Nor should it be surprising that this shift in the relative value of biblical religions vis-à-vis other "other religions"—formerly known generically as heathenism or idolatry—affected the standing of Christianity itself. True, Christianity now had other religions to contend with. But, even more significant was a new train of thought that suggested something like a composite (rather than unitary) constitution of historical Christianity. Was not Christianity born of the Israelite religion? Did not Jesus himself speak Aramaic, a Semitic language, rather than Greek? By virtue of its birth, then, did Christianity belong to the same "family" as Judaism and Islam, that is to say, to the Semitic family of religions? Was Europe, then, merely in an adoptive relation to the religion that it claimed as its own? Although historically Christendom and Europe had long been conflated,[33] in the minds of some nineteenth-century thinkers, the possibility of a new configuration and realignment of religions began to drive a wedge into this time-honored equation, with as yet uncertain implications. In fact, it might be fairly suspected that the controversies over Islam and the general taxonomic disturbance occurring in the latter half of the nineteenth century were, in the last analysis, all about the positioning of Christianity with respect to the destiny of humankind, or—what in the minds of European intellectuals amounted to roughly the same thing—the hegemonic status of Europe at the helm of the global historical process and, within this framework, Europe's future relation with, or perhaps without, Christianity.

This is as much as to suggest that an adequate answer to the question, Why Buddhism and not Islam? may not be forthcoming until we view the issue from a broader vantage point, until, that is, we recognize the import of this question in its intricate relation to whatever else was percolating in the European imagination concerning their own identity at that historical juncture. For this reason, a detour into adjacent areas of nineteenth-century science and discovery is in order.

33. This is of course a point of view of western Christianity, insofar as it underplays the significance of various long-standing Christian communities in North Africa, Eastern Europe, and Western Asia.

5

Philology and the Discovery of a Fissure in the European Past

By the closing decades of the eighteenth century, there were already soundings of novel ideas about European origins. In the nineteenth century, two distinct sources of "Europeanness" came to be recognized as fundamentally separate and, in certain respects, dichotomous. Matthew Arnold, for example, gave an iconic representation of this duality in a well-known series of essays eventually published as *Culture and Anarchy* (1869).[1] Arnold terms the two sides of Europe's bifurcated taproot "Hellenism" and "Hebraism." Following his cue, one may delineate the dual origin of Europe and its supposed bipolarity in this manner: the mellifluous cultural inheritance of ancient Greece (or, in Arnold's own phrase that has since turned saccharine, "sweetness and light") and the austere spiritual inheritance of ancient Israel, a somber religion of commandments, sin, expiation, and redemption. The Hellenic legacy purportedly includes such vital and felicitous endowments as the capability for comprehensive theoretical knowledge (science), aesthetic sensibility and creativity (art), the spirit of freedom and ennobling will for self-determination (democracy), whereas the Hebraic influence defines a stalwart morality, an unflinching ethics of duty and obedience, and frugality in all other aspects.

It is useful to remember that Arnold was particularly concerned about what he saw as the excess of Hebraism in his own historical moment. In the face of this imbalance, his principal aim in *Culture and Anarchy* is to warn of the peril brought on by this excess, and to restore the ameliorating influence of Hellenism. He repeatedly emphasizes, it is true, that Hebraism and Hellenism are equally "august" and "invaluable," both vitally necessary "*contributions to human development*." (He has little to say, however, as to how peoples elsewhere, remote from these traditions, might participate in "human development.") Yet the particular historical conditions of his time move him to speak as an advocate for Hellenism. According to Arnold, the periodic infusion and

---

1. The following discussion cites Arnold, *Culture and Anarchy*, 93/157. I refer here to the version edited by Samuel Lipman in 1994, which also indicates the pagination of the 1869 edition. The first number refers to the 1994 edition, the second to that of 1869.

the consequent preponderance of Hebraism is nothing new: Hebraism first surged into the arena of European history when Europe first turned Christian, expressly in reaction to the overripe and decadent extravagance of Hellenism in the last days of the Roman Empire. A millennium later, the pendulum swung once again to extreme Hellenism in the wake of the Renaissance—which, in its quintessential form, was largely a Mediterranean phenomenon. Europe saw the resurgence of Hebraism in the form of the Northern Protestant Reformation, whose rippling effects could be seen for centuries thereafter, in Puritanism and, most closely at home for Arnold, in the vociferously sectarian temperament of various Nonconformist churches, a disposition perfectly in concert with the strident industrial modernity of his time.

An implication of arguments such as Arnold's—to name but the most obvious and pressing—is that, somehow, the *religious* heritage of European peoples was genealogically distinct and separate from all other aspects of their heritage. To put it simply, it suddenly appeared that Christianity could be at odds with the rest of what it meant to be European, rather than being its defining characteristic. This may be as much as to say that the very idea of Europe—or, as we say today, the West—was struggling to emerge as an entity apart from the hitherto defining notion of Christendom.

Once the stage had been set in this new way, other questions stood waiting in the wings, the most unsettling of which might be this: Was the synthetic composition of European civilization ultimately providential? Was specifically *Christian* Europe preordained and therefore bound to last until the end of time, or was it essentially contingent and temporary, and the collaboration of Hellenism and Hebraism that had endured for nearly two millennia, however useful and beneficial, fated to expire?

Another way of casting this conundrum—in fact, the one that proved dominant—was to saddle Christianity itself with a composite, split heritage, or at least an apparent split. After all, was not Christianity a messianic Jewish reform movement at its beginning? At the same time, could it not also be said with justice that Christianity became what it is by crossing over from the Jewish to the Gentile world? Was this crossover a merely historical, contingent fact, or was it in the very nature of the new religion to grow beyond the bounds of Judaism, a Semitic religion? If the latter should be the case, perhaps there would be no pressing need for Europe to rethink its relation to what had been its traditional religion. Instead, it would seem, it was high time to reenvision Christianity in relation to its traditional kin, the monotheistic brethren, and to reposition itself among all other historical religions, since there were suddenly so many, and so much about them was rapidly becoming known. As we saw in chapter 2, these were the cardinal concerns that comparative theologians of the nineteenth century were attempting to address and to resolve, in one form or another.

Wherever the fault line, the task at hand for us, then, is to examine whence comes the whole idea of the bifurcated legacy of Christian Europe that seems to have preoccupied the leading men of faith, and how this new idea determined the ways in which nineteenth-century scholars were to classify "other religions."

Neither Hebraism nor Hellenism was an established concept prior to the nineteenth century. They were not in any way elements traditionally considered to be constitutive of Europe—assuming for now, at least, that there was a notion roughly corresponding to Europe in the way we think of it today.[2] They were indeed conceptual novelties, arguably the most important ones to emerge from the provenance of the newly prominent science of philology. Summarily put, it was philological scholarship that generated a new type of distinction among peoples and nations in terms of language groups; the most immediately critical in this context was the distinction between Indo-European (or Aryan) and Semitic language groups. The impact of this scholarship was manifold. The idea of the dual legacy of Europe was only one of its many ramifications that became visible in the course of the nineteenth century.

1. The Discovery of the Indo-European Past

It is now customary to count as one of the founding moments of Oriental philology an epoch-making pronouncement by William Jones in 1786.[3] By then already an acclaimed author of some poetic works, Jones was a serious Orien-

---

2. This binary should not be confused or conflated with the Christian versus pagan dichotomy that personally troubled St. Augustine so much before his conversion. One could conceivably map this dichotomy also onto the Semitic versus the Indo-European only retroactively, that is, anachronistically. Certainly in Augustine's time, there was no equivalent conception of the duality in such a way that one or the other, or both, were constitutive of any specific cultural or racial identity. We would do well to remember that the saint, though he did go to Rome to be baptized, was from Hippo, a North African city.

3. J. P. Mallory, however, returns part of the credit to James Parsons's 1767 study, *The Remains of Japhet, Being Historical Enquiries into the Affinity and Origins of the European Languages*: "Had this work been much shorter, its author might be better remembered. Unfortunately for Parsons, this rather tedious book ensured his obscurity and subsequent neglect in histories of Indo-European studies, a neglect not entirely deserved" (Mallory, *In Search of the Indo-Europeans* ([1989], 10).

talist and prominent colonial official of the East India Company residing in Calcutta. He was one of the first Europeans to learn to read Sanskrit from native Brahman pundits.[4] But even more to Jones's credit was his discovery of the close affinity between the languages of ancient India and Persia on the one hand and the classical languages of Europe on the other. In the celebrated third presidential address to the Asiatic Society of Bengal, Jones declared:

> The Sanscrit language, whatever be its antiquity, is of a wonderful structure; more perfect than the Greek, more copious than the Latin, and more exquisitely refined than either, yet bearing to both of them a stronger affinity, both in the roots of verbs and in the forms of grammar, than could possibly have been produced by accident; so strong indeed, that no philologer could examine them all three, without believing them to have sprung from some common source, which, perhaps, no longer exists.[5]

This oft-quoted proclamation heralded the vogue for not only Sanskrit studies but a broad range of philological scholarship. Possibly because he was a well-known figure and the founder of the first Asiatic Society, or conceivably on account of his prominent position as an established literary figure, or perhaps just because the time was right, Jones's address inspired and captured the

4. This is not to forget, however, the interesting career of Roberto de Nobili (1577–1656), an Italian Jesuit missionary to India in the early seventeenth century, who taught himself not only Sanskrit but also Tamil and Telugu and wrote numerous erudite treatises on religious and philosophical topics of India, where he lived nearly half a century (see Wilhelm Halbfass, India and Europe[1988], 38–43). While he dutifully forwarded these works to Rome, they had little impact, and the learned men of the church seemed more worried about Nobili's accommodating himself too much to the Indian natives than they were interested in the wealth of scholarly material that he collected and the analyses that he produced. As Max Müller put it in 1861: "'Accommodation Question,' as it was called, occupied cardinals and popes for many years; but not one of them seems to have perceived the extraordinary interest attaching to the existence of an ancient civilization so perfect and so firmly rooted as to require accommodation even from the missionaries of Rome. At a time when the discovery of one Greek MS. would have been hailed by all scholars of Europe, the discovery of a complete literature was allowed to pass unnoticed. The day of Sanskrit had not yet come" (F. Max Müller, Lectures on the Science of Language, first Series [1862; 6th ed., 1880], 156–57).

Also mentioned in this context, both by Müller and by Halbfass, is the scholarly labor of another Jesuit, Father (J. F.) Pons, who, Halbfass speculates, was the author of a Sanskrit grammar written in Latin (circa 1733). See also Raymond Schwab, The Oriental Renaissance (1984), 147–48.

5. The Works of Sir William Jones (1807), quoted by Thomas R. Trautmann, Aryans and British India (1997), 38. The same passage, though somewhat shorter, is also quoted in Schwab, The Oriental Renaissance, 41.

imagination of the educated classes of Europe, and he thus proved critical in disseminating the classical literature of India—religious and legal, as well as literary.[6] Thereafter, in a matter of few decades, one could witness regular and prolific discourses on such sonorous "classics" as Shakuntala, Hitopadesha, the Bhagavad Gita, and the Oupnek'hat (the Upanishads). Assuming, as many people then did, that an affinity between languages entailed an affinity, proximity, and probable kinship between the peoples who spoke them, it is not surprising that this discovery of the common origin of languages generated an altogether new quota of energy, stimulating the investigation into what had been until then a rather remote and foreign subject matter. At the same time, the historical, empirical, and scientific study of languages—as philology was and has since been understood to be—opened a new venue to explore and to scrutinize Europeans' own past and future destiny.

It is useful to recall here that it was in the context of this new awareness of Europe's ancestral relation to India and Persia that the word "Aryan" first came to be adopted by the Europeans. As present-day authorities would concur, ārya—meaning, roughly, "noble"—was originally a self-referential term used by ancient Persian and Sanskrit speakers, who presumably did not know or could not have cared much about their possible kinship with the uncouth inhabitants of the distant European peninsula (to borrow a provocative phrase from none other than Max Müller). Millennia later, in the first half of the nineteenth century, "Arya," or more commonly "Aryan," became the accepted nomenclature among European scholars to designate the group of languages

---

6. Jones was by no means the first modern European to undertake a serious study of Indian and Persian literature. However, earlier translators of Indian literature, such as Nathaniel Brassey Halhed, Alexander Dow, and John Zephaniah Holwell, did their work from Persian translations. This is true also of Abraham Hyacinthe Anquetil-Duperron (1731–1805) who translated four Upanishads (Oupnek'hat), whereas this indomitable scholar's lasting fame may rightly depend on his first European translation of the Zend-Avesta, the sacred literature of Zoroastrianism.

For an interesting and informative account of Anquetil-Duperron's work on the Avesta, William Jones's response to Anquetil, and other competitive and contentious exchanges among the eighteenth-century Orientalists often colored by their nationalistic interests, see James Darmesteter's introductory essay to The Zend-Avesta (1880), which constitutes volume 4 of The Sacred Books of the East (general editor, F. Max Müller), xi-cii, especially xiv-xxv.

For a useful and succinct discussion of early Indology, see Halbfass, India and Europe, 54–68. For a detailed and comprehensive documentation, see parts 1 and 2 of Schwab's Oriental Renaissance, 11–128. As an extensive study of the cultural history of Sanskrit scholarship, Trautmann's Aryans and British India is incomparable.

recognized as a family of sorts, also called the "Indo-European," "Indo-German," or "Indo-Celtic" language group. Thus, although initially a term referring to a certain cluster of languages, "Aryan" increasingly was taken to mean an ethnic or, purportedly, racial grouping of peoples.

It is singularly ironic that by the time the name "Aryan" had taken on the virulently racist connotation familiar to us today, the noble Persians and Indians of yore were all but expunged from its meaning, as the term came to signify a certain idea of European identity, that is, the "whiteness" that excluded, above all, the Jews, who in turn were deemed—though not for the first time—"Oriental." This ironic turn, however, was not without a certain tortuous logic, for one of the most significant corollaries of the discovery of the Indo-European language group was the parallel recognition of another set of languages constituting an analogous but separate family. Hebrew, Arabic, Aramaic, Phoenician, Akkadian, among others—these languages are now called "Hamito-Semitic" or, more simply, "Semitic." As we know, this category, too, did not remain a merely linguistic grouping but soon came to be understood in ethnic and racial terms.

Of course, it is a matter of opinion whether Jones's own achievements should be credited or blamed for being the true beginning of Indo-European philology. For one thing, it is uncertain whether an apprehension of the family resemblance among languages really amounted to the recognition of a particular language group—that is, a group of historically and genealogically related languages in contradistinction to some other language groups.[7] For some, rather than generating a new system of difference and classification, this discovery presaged a new, scientific confirmation of an old monogenist idea sanctioned by the Bible: the original unity of all humankind. Indeed, there is much to suggest that the excitement generated by Jones and other early Orientalists could have had just as much to do with the possibility that there was a broader unity

---

7. The principal import of Jones's statement was the affinity, and possible family resemblance, between these languages hitherto thought unrelated, rather than a clear distinction of this particular group from another, namely, Semitic languages. At the same time, we should remember that the above quoted speech by Jones continues as follows: "There is a similar reason, though not quite so forcible, for supposing that both the *Gothick* and the *Celtick*, though blended with a very different idiom, had the same origin with the *Sanscrit*; and the old *Persian* might be added to the same family, if this were the place for discussing any question concerning the antiquity of *Persia*." Léon Poliakov notes that, earlier than Jones, first Leibniz, then Ludwig von Schlötzer (1735–1808) made a distinction between the Semitic and Japhetic family of languages, and included in the latter Armenian and Persian (Léon Poliakov, *The Aryan Myth* [1974], 189).

of nations, that is, the possibility that all languages of the world could eventually be shown to form one single, very large and populous, family.[8] Moreover, some would argue that Jones's discovery was at bottom merely fortuitous, an accidental find of certain similarities of words across different languages, rather than an apprehension of the true structural similarity between the languages. For these reasons and perhaps a few others besides, philologists of later generations as well as cautious historians today seem to prefer to grant him a kind of ceremonial laurel as the honorary originator of Sanskrit studies, while reserving the more substantive position of the founding of comparative philology to a later generation of scholars who clearly discerned the basis of comparison on more solid grounds.[9]

There is no doubt, however, that Jones's discovery in fact served as a launching pad for a torrent of activities, scholarly and speculative, that engaged some of the most remarkable European minds and intellects of the nineteenth century. Regardless of whether the basis of his comparison was sound and scientific or merely intuitive and haphazard, his assertion itself—and its most apparent implication, namely, the probable kinship of India, Persia, and Europe—was approvingly accepted by most aspiring Orientalists of his day. Among the subsequent generation of Orientalists who played crucial roles in the development of the nineteenth-century philology, the most conspicuous and consequential was Friedrich Schlegel (1772–1829).

A philologist with a grand spiritual ambition and a profound enthusiasm for India, Schlegel received Sanskrit instructions in Paris from a British naval officer and scholar, Alexander Hamilton, formerly of the East India Company and one of the founding members of the Asiatic Society in Bengal.[10] Thenceforth Schlegel contributed immensely to the future development of Oriental phil-

---

8. Some enthusiasts in this direction of thought—including Jones himself—were liable to extend the family to include Hebrew, Arabic, and even Chinese.

9. Cf. Poliakov, *The Aryan Myth*, 189–90. For a more detailed and critical historical account of how later generations viewed the accomplishments of the early Orientalists such as Jones, Humboldt, and Schlegel, see Sebastiano Timpanaro, "Friedrich Schlegel and the Beginnings of Indo-European Linguistics in Germany," in Friedrich Schlegel's *Über die Sprache und Weisheit der Indier* (1977), xi–lvii.

10. Schlegel had the good fortune to be in Paris when Hamilton was there also, having been detained while on research, owing to an outbreak of hostility between the host country and his own in 1803. In return for a more kindly treatment than could have been expected under the circumstances, Hamilton gave what amounted to an intensive course of Sanskrit lessons to a handful of scholars, including, in addition to Schlegel, the classicist Jean Louis Burnouf, the father of Eugène.

ology, especially in Germany. His influence, however, was not as a language instructor but rather as a highly visible exponent and emblem of Orientalism as a lofty spiritual mission. To be sure, there had already been a great deal of imaginative musing and wistful fantasizing about things Indian among German intellectuals, and this tendency had been particularly strong among Schlegel's illustrious Romantic circle of friends, which included Novalis (1772–1801); his own elder brother, August Wilhelm Schlegel (1767–1845); and Ludwig Tieck (1773–1853), to whom he famously wrote in 1803: "Here is the actual source of all languages, all the thoughts and poems of the human spirit; everything, everything without exception comes from India."[11]

It is safe to say that this cultural climate rosily predisposed toward the ancient Orient and especially toward India as the land of origin was what had caused Friedrich Schlegel to travel to Paris in the first place. Upon his return, he gave a series of university lectures at Cologne in 1803 and 1805, but it was above all his treatise *On the Language and Wisdom of the Indians* (*Über die Sprache und Weisheit der Indier*), published in Heidelberg in 1808, that elevated the prestige of and fanned the enthusiasm for Indology. The work was instrumental in turning a glorified literary fashion into something more substantive: a spiritual mission and, eventually, a rising science.

The enormous influence of this work can be discerned from a wide range of historical facts. At the same time, its driving force appears to have come from something very personal. In his acclaimed historical study first published in 1950, *Oriental Renaissance*, Raymond Schwab draws particular attention to what he calls Schlegel's "double conversion to Calcutta and Rome," namely, the fact—in Schwab's view, far from coincidental—that the publication of the historic analysis was contemporaneous with its author's conversion (together with his wife, Dorothea, née Mendelssohn) to Catholicism. For Schlegel, the study of classical Indian language and literature certainly was not a matter of mere knowledge for knowledge's sake; nor was it motivated by the sort of prac-

---

11. Quoted in Halbfass, *India and Europe*, 75. Regarding this circle, as Friedrich Schlegel himself remarks in the last paragraph of the preface to his famous essay *On the Language and Wisdom of the Indians* (1808), there was yet another Schlegel brother who was also an aspiring Indologist, Karl August Schlegel, "who died at Madras on the 9th of September, 1789, having in the latter years of his life made many journeys into the country, and had much intercourse with the natives, had commenced a study of the country, the literature and genius of the Indian people, which was prematurely terminated by his early death."

tical interests that initially moved the British colonial government to condone or even encourage some of its officials—such as Jones and Hamilton—to expend their company time on scholastic pursuits. In Schwab's words:

> It was Schlegel who made what could have been no more than a pastime into a vital reality, who created a general cultural movement out of one particular field of knowledge. And he was able to do this because he, alone among all the others, saw this first and foremost as a spiritual event. The convergence of three essential factors in his mind predestined the outcome: his background as a responsible German historian, his romantic veneration for a prevenient Orient whose precedents would determine the literary future of Europe, and, above all, his faith, which led him to choose to relate everything to religious interests.[12]

For this very reason, Schwab expressly and singularly names Schlegel as "the inventor of the Oriental Renaissance." In the preface to *On the Language and Wisdom of the Indians*, Schlegel seems to testify to the justice of this assessment:

> The study of Indian literature requires to be embraced by such students and patrons as in the fifteenth and sixteenth centuries suddenly kindled in Italy and Germany an ardent appreciation of the beauty of classical learning, and in so short a time invested it with such prevailing importance, that the form of all wisdom and science, and almost of the world itself, was changed and renovated by the influence of that re-awakened knowledge. I venture to predict that the Indian study, if embraced with equal energy, will prove no less grand and universal in its operation, and have no less influence on the sphere of European intelligence. And wherefore should it be otherwise?[13]

What was at stake, then, in promoting the study of the Orient was nothing less than the rejuvenation of Europe, not by means of a return to what had been, however, but by mining the hitherto untapped resources for the purpose of charting a new course, for the sake of an unprecedented future for Europe.

---

12. Schwab, *Oriental Renaissance*, 72.

13. I cite E. J. Millington's translation from *The Aesthetic and Miscellaneous Works of Frederick von Schlegel* (1849), 427–28; cited in the text by page number hereafter.

2. The Birth of Comparative Grammar

Among those who heeded the clarion call of the Oriental Renaissance was the young Franz Bopp (1791–1867). Following in Schlegel's footsteps, Bopp sought knowledge of the East in Paris. He crowned his four years of education abroad with a year of Sanskrit study under the tutelage of Antoine-Léonard de Chézy (1773–1832), recently appointed to the new chair of Sanskrit at the Collège de France, the first such position in a European university.[14] Bopp's application to his studies resulted, in 1816, when he was only twenty-five, in the publication of the rather prosaic and didactic title *On the Conjugation System of Sanskrit Language in Comparison with Those of Greek, Latin, Persian and German Languages* (*Über das Conjugationssystem der Sanskritsprache in Vergleichung mit jenem der griechischen, lateinischen, persischen und germanischen Sprache*)—a work generally deemed "definitive" in the establishment of the science of comparative grammar. Indeed, Schwab calls it "the first work in which William Jones's lucky intuition became a method."[15]

In this fashion, the general outlook of the most distinguished philologists of Europe—among whom we should also count H. H. Wilson (1786–1860), Christian Lassen (1800–76), and Eugène Burnouf (1801–52)—turned decidedly scholastic and technical. At the same time, the romance of India did not abate. For these scholars India's immediate and vital relevance to the question of the European past and future was not in doubt. Most conspicuous in its regard for the East was the German-speaking world, though the cultural-linguistic domain of "Germany" itself still lacked unified nation-statehood. Notwithstanding this political disability (or possibly because of it), in various principalities and kingdoms of the Germanic world, particularly in the emergent state of Prussia, the leading men of science and of the affairs of state made concerted attempts to become conversant with Orientalist scholarship. Thus such philo-

14. Schwab informs us that Bopp's initial intention was "to learn Persian with [Antoine Isaac Silvestre de] Sacy and to pursue Semitic studies with [Étienne Marc] Quatremère," but he remained one more year to study with Chézy, who had just been appointed to the Sanskrit chair (Schwab, *Oriental Renaissance*, 78).

15. Ibid., 178. A truly monumental work that was to determine Bopp's position in history, *Comparative Grammar of Sanskrit, Zend, Greek, Latin, Gothic, and German* (*Vergleichende Grammatik des Sanskrit . . . und Deutschen*) first appeared in Berlin in 1833; the posthumously published third edition (1868–71) added to the above list of languages Armenian, Lithuanian, and Old Slavic. In "Friedrich Schlegel and the Beginnings of Indo-European Linguistics in Germany," Timpanaro notes, in addition to Bopp, another German scholar often credited with being an important founding figure of scientific philology: Rasmus Kristian Rask (1787–1832).

sophical luminaries as Hegel (1770–1831), Schelling (1775–1854), and Schopenhauer (1788–1860) regularly consumed the latest output of a rising generation of Orientalist scholars often less than half their age.[16] The same held true for those intellectuals in high positions of power; perhaps most consequential of all was the Prussian minister, diplomat, farsighted educational reformer, and classical scholar in his own right, Wilhelm von Humboldt (1767–1835).

Though Humboldt had been a serious student of world languages since his youth, his deep interest in Sanskrit was awakened when, in 1817 in London, he met Franz Bopp, who had left Paris to study further with the British Sanskritists Charles Wilkins (1749–1836), translator of the Bhagavad Gita, and Henry Thomas Colebrooke (1765–1837). It was from Bopp and August Wilhelm Schlegel—who like his younger brother Friedrich had received Sanskrit instructions in Paris, and likewise had come to London—that Humboldt learned Sanskrit. Shortly thereafter Humboldt returned the favor, so to speak, by establishing

16. As Urs App has shown in some detail, Schopenhauer's interest in Orientalist scholarship goes back to his youth. See Urs App, "Notes and Excerpts by Schopenhauer" (1998), 11–33.

An emblematic episode in regard to the general interest of German intellectuals in the new field of Oriental studies may be the curiously mutual pedagogic relation that developed between Schelling, then in his sixties, and the twenty-year-old Max Müller—already in professional command of Sanskrit—who had lately arrived in Berlin to study philosophy with the legendary professor, as well as to study more Sanskrit with Franz Bopp. From the beginning of their acquaintance, Schelling took the opportunity to interrogate the young man on various points of arcane Indological knowledge and had him translate one of the Upanishads expressly for him. See Müller's *Life and Letters*, edited by his wife Georgina Max Müller (1902), 1:20–25. Later, Müller rendered similar Sanskritic services to Alexander von Humboldt, Christian Bunsen, and others among his benefactors.

In a letter to his mother, translated and included in the *Life and Letters* (23), Müller describes his first meeting with Schelling thus: "I went to announce myself. He receives people at four o'clock. I had not expected much, for I had heard how he had dismissed Jellinick, but I was more fortunate. I asked him if he would continue to lecture next term on the Philosophy of Revelation. He said he could not decide yet, therefore probably only a private lecture again. Then I spoke to him of my time in Leipzig, of Weiss and Brockhaus, and then we came round to Indian Philosophy. Here he allowed me to tell him a great deal. I especially dwelt on the likeness between Sankhya and his own system, and remarked how an inclination to the Vedânta showed itself. He asked what we must understand by Vedânta, how the existence of God was proved, how God created the world, whether it had reality. He has been much occupied with Colebrooke's *Essays*, and he seemed to wish to learn more, as he asked me if I could explain a text. Then he asked where I was living, knew my father [Romantic poet Wilhelm Müller] as Greek poet and a worker on Homer, and at last dismissed me with 'Come again soon,' offering to do anything he could for me."

"the first chairs of Sanskrit in Germany in 1818, one created especially for Bopp at Berlin, and the other for Wilhelm Schlegel at Bonn."[17]

While he thus did much to assist the careers of others professionally engaged in Sanskrit studies and to promote the institution of Indology generally, Wilhelm von Humboldt's involvement in Oriental philological scholarship was by no means merely derivative or vicarious.[18] Throughout his life he took opportunities, as they arose, to study languages as far removed and as wide-ranging as those of the Basques, Native Americans, and South Pacific islanders. At the time of his death in 1835, he was preparing a three-volume work on Kawi, a highly specialized language of Java greatly influenced and reshaped by Sanskritic elements brought onto the island with "Hindu and Buddhist" cultures from India.[19]

Humboldt had planned a monograph-length essay as a substantial introduction to the compendium—hence often known as the "Kawi Introduction." The actual title of the essay testifies to its ambitious goals: *On the Diversity of Human Language Construction and Its Influence on the Mental Development of the Human Species* (*Über die Verschiedenheit des menschlichen Sprachbaus und ihren Einfluss auf die geistige Entwicklung des Menschengeschlecht*, 1836).[20] He makes clear in this introduction his intention to carry out a far-reaching study of comparative philology. The import of comparison was for him far from merely technical. Indeed, the value Humboldt conferred upon the aim of comparative philology is expressed in words no less stirring, and even more profoundly universalistic, than those of Friedrich Schlegel:

17. Schwab, *Oriental Renaissance*, 179. Schwab also relates in this context: "Humboldt was . . . the man who later uttered a resounding shout about the *Bhagavad Gita* and with whom Chateaubriand nearly spoke Sanskrit at the dinner table."

18. It should be noted also that his no less illustrious brother, Alexander von Humboldt (1769–1859)—whose five-year voyage of scientific exploration to the Spanish Americas, the West Indies, and the United States at the turn of the century made him arguably the most celebrated scientist of the early nineteenth century—was also keenly interested in Indology. Max Müller's letters from the 1840s and later recollections document several critical occasions in which the elder scientist—then working on his last grand opus, *Kosmos*, and himself quite impecunious, having exhausted his considerable patrimony on scientific expositions and the publication of the results—personally did much to facilitate the young man's pursuit of the Rig Veda project.

19. His younger brother Alexander edited and published Humboldt's work on Kawi posthumously.

20. I use here Peter Heath's English translation, *On Language* (1999); cited in the text by page number hereafter.

The division of mankind into peoples and races, and the diversity of their languages and dialects, are indeed directly linked with each other, but are also connected with, and dependent upon, a third and higher phenomenon, the *growth of man's mental powers* into ever new and often more elevated forms. . . . This revelation of man's mental powers, diverse in its degree and nature, over the course of millennia and throughout the world, is the highest aim of all spiritual endeavour, the ultimate idea which world history must strive to bring forth clearly from itself. (21)

This conception of the spiritual mission of the comparative study of language sets Humboldt and his goals at a considerable distance from the resolutely empirical objectives of those technophilological Orientalists exemplified by Bopp.[21] At the same time, it is impossible to overestimate the degree to which Humboldt's powerful conviction of a direct connection between the study of languages and the world historical destiny of a nation and ultimately of the human race fostered, legitimated, and glorified the young science and its practitioners, no matter how tediously particular and prosaic their actual scholarly activities. As Humboldt himself puts it: "The *comparative study of languages* . . . loses all higher interest if it does not cleave to the point at which language is connected with the shaping of the *nation's mental power*" (21). Needless to say, the exaltation of comparative philology was made incomparably consequential because it was issued by Humboldt, who at a certain critical period was in the position to put the power of the Prussian state behind it. As already mentioned, he single-handedly caused professorial chairs in Sanskrit to materialize in two German universities, whose prestige in Oriental studies was to endure for generations thereafter.

Despite the obtuseness of his prose, the depth of Humboldt's assumptions deserves some attention. First, he maintains that languages are worth studying comparatively because the differences among languages correspond to the

21. This tension, if not to say opposition, between the more spiritual/speculative aim and the technical/empirical objective of philology manifests itself frequently in Humboldt's text, while he always seems to resolve the matter in terms of the necessary sequence and hierarchy of purposes. For example, this passage: "It is precisely the highest and most refined aspect that cannot be discerned from these disparate elements [or 'infinity of *details*' that constitute the material being of any language], and can only be perceived or divined in *connected discourse*; which is all the more proof that language proper lies in the act of its real production. It alone must in general always be thought of as the true and primary, in all investigations which are to penetrate into the living essentiality of language. The break-up into words and rules is only a dead makeshift of scientific analysis" (Humboldt, *On Language*, 49).

differences among "peoples and races"—not so much peoples who might happen to (or learn to) speak them, but the people who originally generated them. For Humboldt, a language is not a natural environmental formation that spontaneously occurred in a given locality by happenstance; nor is it an instrument that was accidentally discovered by a particular people. Rather, he claims that the relation between a people and their language is essential, vital, and mutually formative. He clearly believes that language formation is a "task" that each people or nation must "resolve"; it is an accomplishment of a people, an expression of their intrinsic nature.

> The *bringing-forth of language* is an *inner need* of human beings, not merely an external necessity for maintaining communal intercourse, but a thing lying in their own nature, indispensable for the development of their mental powers and the attainment of a world-view, to which man can attain only by bringing his thinking to clarity and precision through communal thinking with others. (27)

In short, for Humboldt, "Language . . . is the organ of inner being. . . . It therefore strikes with all the most delicate fibres of its roots into the national mentality; and the more aptly the latter reacts upon it, the more rich and regular its development" (21). It is "the outer appearance of the spirit of a people" (46).

Second, Humboldt definitively asserts that those different peoples, distinguishable by different languages, manifest their unique essences in different times and places, and the totality of these innumerable manifestations, taken together and considered as a single universal historical process, will amount to the collective destiny of the human race (*Menschengeschlechts*).[22]

Obviously, it is in the context of this second assumption that the groupings of peoples and languages become extremely important. But Humboldt's interest here is not the classification of languages as such; rather, he considers the diversity of languages important "as a necessary foundation for the *progress of the human mind*" (90). He seeks to sort languages of the world into groups, not

---

22. "It may well be assumed that the language-making power in man does not rest until, either in individuals or as a whole, it has brought forth that which answers the most and most completely to the demands to be made. In the light of this assumption, therefore, we may be able to discover, even among languages and linguistic families that betray no historical connection, an advancement in varying degrees of the principle of their formation. But if such be the case, this connection of outwardly unlinked phenomena must lie in a common inner cause, which can only be the evolution of the force at work" (ibid., 27).

just to establish a taxonomy, but in order to construct a historical narrative of the advent and the vicissitudes of human race as a whole. The case of Kawi is a particularly useful focal point for such deliberations because, in his view, the island of Java in the course of its long history experienced an extraordinary commingling of languages, cultures, and religions. In other words, he saw in Java what were beginning to be recognized as the three major language groups playing their respective, and rather unequal, parts: the native Malay language (belonging to the noninflecting group of languages, later to be called the "agglutinative," or, by Max Müller and others, the "Turanian" group), Sanskrit brought from India (a fully inflecting language of the Indo-European family), and Arabic (a Semitic language with limited inflection). This commingling, however, is not merely a historical after-effect, but instead, it somehow represents the state of plenum at the origin of all things. And insofar as Humboldt, like Schlegel, saw the origin of Europe ultimately in India, it is not surprising to find him referring, even if rather vaguely, to Asia as the "very part of the world from whence proceed the greatest and most remarkable linguistic phenomena, from the unisyllabic nature of Chinese to the wealth of forms in India, and on top of that again the uniformly fixed pattern of the Semitic language-structure" (22).

There is no strong evidence that Humboldt's posthumous publication on the Kawi language, voluminous as it was, had a scholarly influence of any great significance or an inspirational impact comparable to that of Schlegel's sensational essay of three decades earlier.[23] This notwithstanding, if I dwell on the "Kawi Introduction" at some length here, it is not only because of the unique position of its author as a patron saint of the future commonwealth of philological scholarship in Germany. Even more important, it is because this ponderous dissertation contains, or rather, officially inaugurates, some of the most fundamental, enduring, and gravely consequential assumptions concerning the typology of languages and their hierarchical order. Humboldt's

23. In addition to the Kawi project, Humboldt's other notable foray into the domain of Orientalism included his lectures on the Bhagavad Gita delivered in 1825 and 1826 at the Royal Prussian Academy of Science in Berlin. The lectures were subsequently published in the *Proceedings of the Historical Philological Section of the Berlin Royal Academy* in 1827, and were later reprinted in his collected works (1850–52), under the title *Über die unter dem Namen Bhagavad-Gîtâ bekannte Episode des Mahâbhârata*. Shortly after Humboldt's original lectures, a much disturbed Hegel interrupted the revision of his *Encyclopaedia* (1817) and wrote a two-part response longer than Humboldt's text, published first in 1827 and recently in translation as *On the Episode of the Mahâbhârata Known by the Name Bhagavad-Gîtâ by Wilhelm von Humboldt* (1995).

summary description of the three language groups makes this apparent. Throughout the essay runs a veritable dithyramb in praise of the "Sanscritic family" (later to be called the "Indo-Germanic," "Indo-European," or "Aryan" family of languages):

It is marvellous to see what a long series of languages, equally happy in their structure and equally stimulating in their effect upon the mind, has been engendered by that language which we must place at the summit of the Sanscrit family. (182)

Predictably, this high estimation of the Sanskrit family and the concomitant denigration of non-Indo-European languages lead to a self-congratulation of modern Europe. As facile as this logic may be, and undeserving of his robust intelligence, Humboldt articulates it plainly enough, without a hint of irony.

In the history of nations, the question may well have been raised as to what would have happened in the world if Carthage [a Semitic nation] had defeated Rome and conquered the European West. One might equally well ask what the present state of our culture would be if the Arabs [a Semitic race] had remained, as they were for a time, the sole possessors of scientific knowledge, and had spread throughout the Western world. A less favourable outcome seems to me, in both cases, beyond doubt. It is to the same causes which produced the world-dominance of Rome, namely the *Roman spirit and character*, rather than to external and more accidental circumstances, that we owe the powerful influence of this world-dominion upon our civil institutions, laws, language and culture. Through the turn toward this culture, and through inner kinship, we became genuinely receptive to the Greek mind and language, where the Arabs only adhered, for the most part, to the scientific results of Greek inquiry. Even on the basis of the same antique heritage, they would not have been capable of erecting the edifice of science and art which we may justly boast today. (182)

How, one might ask, does he know this to be true? As he and many fellow metaphysicians of language of his time and thereafter would readily agree, the truth lies in the very nature of the respective languages; such nature is revealed in the language's grammatical *structure*. According to this theory, prevalent at the time, the "spirit and character" of the Semitic language, in comparison to that of the Sanskritic family, is "fixed," "rigid," and inimical to *Bildung* (growth, development, culture).

Much of the text of *On Language* is in fact devoted to a deeply metaphysical contemplation on the origin and development of human language and its diversification. At issue is the process of development from certain rudimentary "sound forms" to language as a system, that is to say, from the first articulation of protowords, or roots (*Wurzeln*)—a root as a primordial utterance that is at once a sound and a signification—to words proper, that is, linguistic units capable of constituting a syntax. At its best, this development occurs from within, as the root word evolves outward, generating its syntactical capabilities out of its own essential being. The resulting grammatical form is *inflection*. Since the development of inflection is an intrinsic self-evolution of the root, this efflorescence is free and prolific yet remains true to its origin; and the development follows its own logic, therefore it is rational. Alternatively, lacking this inner development characteristic of inflection, root words may be contrived to form a language system synthetically, as it were, by a particular sequencing of root words and by artificially inserting additional exterior components or particles to piece them together into syntax. This latter mode of language formation is *agglutination*. While no language is said to be entirely devoid of one or the other of the two types of syntax formation, what Humboldt calls the "Sanscritic family" defines one end of the spectrum, while Chinese, quintessentially, marks the opposite end; the Semitic language family is situated between the two opposing poles, representing the type of languages with *delimited inflection*. Even though he would allow that each type of language formation has its own potential for perfectibility, this taxonomy is not value neutral. In sum, Humboldt maintains that the most authentic and perfect language formation is inflection.

3. The Supremacy of Inflection

On the cardinal point of the supremacy of inflection, Humboldt's speculations are much too abstruse and protracted to lend themselves to succinct and lucid summary; nor is a comprehensive overview of his version of the theory necessary for our present purpose. In fact, when it comes to the relative valuation of inflection over agglutination, he is not entirely original; the gist of his argument had already been laid out by Schlegel in *On the Language and Wisdom of the Indians*.[24] At the beginning of the chapter entitled "On the Division of

---

24. This may be as good an occasion as any to remember that the scholarly credit-debt relation between Schlegel and Humboldt was mutual. Indeed, the relation should be extended to include the Schlegel brothers (Wilhelm and Friedrich) as well as the even more famous Humboldt brothers (Wilhelm and Alexander). In *On the Language and Wisdom of the Indians*, Friedrich

Languages into Two Principal Branches, Founded on its Internal Structure," Schlegel indicates that his objective is to elucidate the "peculiar principle" predominating in the Sanskritic family of languages, marked by "astonishing simplicity," in contrast to "most other languages," whose governing principle he claims is "completely opposite" in nature. He explicates the difference between the opposing types thus:

> Secondary determinations of meaning [die Nebenbestimmungen der Bedeutung] may be produced either by inflection, [that is,] internal alterations of the root-sound [durch inner Veränderung des Wurzellauts],[25] or by annexing to it a certain peculiar particle [durch ein eignes hinzugefügtes Wort], which in themselves indicate the past, the future, or any other circumstance. On these two simple methods we found our distinction between the two principal branches of language. (447)

Schlegel illustrates this contrast with specific examples:

> The Chinese presents a remarkable instance of a language almost without inflection [Flexion], every necessary modification being expressed by separate monosyllabic words, each having an independent signification. The extraordinary monosyllabic form, and perfect simplicity of its construction, make the consideration of it important as facilitating the comprehension of other languages. The same may be said of the grammar of the Malay language. The singular and difficult dialects of America illustrate the most important peculiarities of this entire branch. (447)

In the context of this binary system, Semitic languages occupy a position in-between, part inflectional and part agglutinative, for the reason that their inflection is delimited and constrained. This is because, Schlegel speculates, the inflectional development of these languages began not originally and directly from the root sounds but instead from primitive words already compounded with particles, thus already turned partially agglutinative:

Schlegel duly acknowledges and thanks "the distinguished author, A. von Humboldt, for his kindness in procuring . . . various vocabularies and dictionaries," and anticipates "from the elder von Humboldt, a copious and more especially, a distinct and intelligent analysis of that remarkable language [Basque]" (447).

25. Here, I have modified the translation slightly. In Millington's translation, it reads: "modifications of meaning, or different degrees of signification" and "internal variations of the primitive word" respectively.

An appearance of inflection is sometimes produced by the incorporation of the annexed particles with the primitive word. In the Arabic language, and those related to it, the first and most important modifications, as, for example, the persons of the verbs, are formed by the introduction of single particles, each bearing its own appropriate signification, and in these the suffix not being easily distinguished from the original root, we may conclude a similar incorporation to have taken place in other instances, although the foreign particles inserted may be no longer traceable. (448)

In effect, Schlegel is claiming that, in the case of Semitic languages, the inflectional capability—hence linguistic freedom and mental/spiritual (*geistige*) creativity—was compromised from the start, owing to the incipient agglutination that had already occurred.

In terms of the principles governing various language groups, then, the hierarchy delineated here seems unambiguous enough, descending from the highest (inflected) to the lowest (agglutinative), with a kind of hybrid (partially inflected/agglutinative) in the middle. But when it comes to evaluating actual, specific languages, and the question as to whether any of them are absolutely superior in comparison to another, there are significant qualifications to be noted. For one thing, Schlegel suggests that the agglutinative languages, though crude and artless at the beginning, tend toward gradual refinement in the course of time, "as the subjoined particles become incorporated by degrees with the primitive words"; in contrast, inflectional languages are susceptible to later corruption, as "the first beauty and symmetry of their construction [is] gradually defaced by an attempt to simplify and elucidate it, as may be seen by comparing various dialects of the German, Romantic, and Indian languages, with the original type from which they were framed" (451–52).

To complicate the matter further—and this is even more consequential for our concern—it is not clear whether the mixed and compromised formation of the Semitic languages should necessarily cause them to rank higher in the scale of linguistic excellence than the agglutinative languages. Repeated reference to the alleged rigidity and the stunted growth of the Semitic languages seems to imply that these languages are in fact doubly constrained, unable to evolve or refine, thus unable to develop in either direction. At the same time, the delimited nature of the Semitic languages is sometimes seen as ennobling, as a source of their faithfulness and immunity from change, and therefore as the very characteristic that elevates Hebrew and Arabic above some of the inflectional languages in certain respects. Giving these considerations their due, implicitly or explicitly, Schlegel cautions against presuming any simple evaluative scheme:

> It must not . . . be supposed that I desire to exalt one chief branch of language exclusively, to the neglect or disparagement of the other. The sphere of language is too comprehensive, rich, and grand, and has been too highly developed and investigated for one sweeping decision to accomplish any such object. Who can deny the lofty power and energy of the Arabic and Hebraic languages? (451)

None of these circumspections, however, appears to have altered the basic presumption of the categorical superiority of inflection. Schlegel puts the matter not so much as absolutely axiomatic but simply as self-evident. His statement on this matter is beguilingly cautious and treacherously vague: "It must undoubtedly be admitted, after adequate investigation and comparison, that languages in which the grammar is one of inflexion are usually preferable, as evincing higher art in their construction" (451).

Wilhelm von Humboldt was by no means the sole inheritor of this hierarchical valuation of linguistic structures that placed the Sanskritic family of languages at the top—Sanskrit itself above all, then classical Greek as a close second. What is also notable is that to claim Indo-European superiority always seems to lead not so much to a disdain for the peoples speaking agglutinative language but instead to a peculiarly pointed and dismissive judgment against the Semites, and against the Arabs in particular. To cite but one such example, Léon Poliakov, in his renowned study first published in 1971, The Aryan Myth, reports that Christian Lassen, "pupil and protégé of the Schlegel brothers," asserted the superiority of the Indo-Europeans over Semites with these condescending words: "All [the Semites] have done is to borrow from the Indo-Germans, and it was only the Arabs who did this. Their views and notions so absorb their intelligence that they are unable to rise with serenity to the contemplation of pure ideas. . . . In his religion the Semite is egotistical and exclusive."[26]

The view articulated by Lassen was to prove rather typical of the century and perhaps beyond: the notorious "rigidity" of the Semitic language structure directly corresponded to the limitation of the Semites' mental capacity and to their intellectual inflexibility. Lacking the inherent power of creativity characteristic of Sanskritic peoples, they could not generate original ideas on their

26. Lassen, Indische Altertumskunde (1847), quoted in Poliakov, The Aryan Myth, 197.

own. And whatever they "borrowed," they might contain but could not assimilate; nor could they foster its further growth and efflorescence. The meanness of their mental/spiritual endowment was such that whatever fell into the hands of the Semites from without, their custody would prove an iron cage for the inherited treasure, if not a veritable deathbed and a grave. A philosophical idea might be preserved by them intact, but at the cost of sterilization and ossification; the life goes out of it.

To return now to where we left Humboldt's Kawi treatise, the supremacy of inflectional languages was expected to be obvious enough to any reader who had followed the exposition in *On Language* without dissent. Counting on such a sympathetic reading, Humboldt continues:

> Assuming this [theory of inflection] to be correct, we may ask whether such a preeminence of the peoples of *Sanscrit origin* is to be sought in their intellectual endowments, or in their language, or in more favourable historical circumstances. It is obvious that none of these causes can be regarded as working alone. *Language and intellectual endowment*, in their constant interaction, admit of no separation, and even *historical destinies* may not be so independent of the inner nature of peoples and individuals, for all that the connection is far from being evident to us on every point. Yet this superiority must be discernible from example of the Sanscrit family, [so] we must look into the question of why one language should possess a stronger and more variously creative *life-principle* than the rest. As is plainly visible here, the cause lies in two points, namely that we are speaking of a *family of languages*, not a single one, and beyond that in the individual make-up of the *language-structure* itself. (182–83)

Here, while no unilateral causality is assumed, it is evident that much has been inferred from the perceived excellence of a particular group of languages. It is significant that such a definitive statement of so tenuous an idea—which was to prove extremely powerful and consequential in the centuries to come— was issued by as authoritative a figure as Humboldt, even if he was not the first one to propose it. The articulation in this instance indeed allows us to observe with some clarity the fundamental forces underwriting the European investment in "India" and "Orient" for their own interests. The stress on the divisions between different families of languages (and the concomitant deemphasis of the internal differences within the related languages) leads the way to some of the cardinal assumptions that were to render the Indo-European idea enormously useful.

Most immediately, a "family" of languages implies a distinct genealogy, apart and separate from other families and their respective lines of descent. The notion of linguistic families thus had the effect of suspending and transferring to another plane the controversy that was soon to erupt over the single versus multiple origin(s) of the human species. Philological theories of language groups, such as Humboldt's, effectively preempted this debate from taking place in its own arena, it seems, while implicitly favoring polygenesis over monogenesis.[27] To be sure, comparative philology itself might never reveal the biological beginning of the species, but insofar as this science suggested that several distinct types of languages emerged more or less independent of one another, and that the "spirit" of a people was coterminous with the type of language they generated, it seemed reasonable to infer that the division of the races—here, understood not in terms of differences discernible in bodily features but in terms of spiritual, mental, and intellectual qualities—was fundamental and, in effect, original, since the differences went back all the way to the earliest traceable moment of (pre)history.

This deep division of the "races" implied, conversely, commensurability and commutability of peoples, languages, "geniuses," and "spirits" belonging to the same "family," even if they were separated by a great distance in space or in time. Thus the nineteenth-century Englishman could presume that there was an essential tie between him and an Athenian of the fourth century BCE, whereas a medieval Mohammedan from North Africa, for all his knowledge of Aristotle, presumably could not claim the same kinship. Similarly, an ancient Persian could be claimed by a contemporary Prussian as kin, on account of their presumed common spiritual ancestry, even if there was no subsequent historical relation—let alone relation of descent—directly connecting them.

27. It is necessary to remember, however, that not all philologists of the nineteenth century were unaware of certain political uses and abuses to which their theories were being put, and some even publicly denounced such applications. Most notably, Max Müller made the following public statement in 1861: "In modern times the science of language has been called in to settle some of the most perplexing political and social questions. . . . in America comparative philologists have been encouraged to prove the impossibility of a common origin of languages and races, in order to justify, by scientific arguments, the unhallowed theory of slavery. Never do I remember to have seen science more degraded than on the title-page of an American publication in which, among the profiles of the different races of man, the profile of the ape was made to look more human than that of the negro" (*Lectures on the Science of Language*, 22).

Another implication of the concept of language family seems to be the capacity to isolate any instances of historical—meaning, "accidental"—transmission of language and keep such cases separate from the question of genealogy or descent. Mere transfer of languages from one group of people to another, which might occur because of proximity, conquest or commercial intercourse, for example, would leave intact the original distinctions separating different "families" of people. By this reckoning, learning another's language, or being born into a language of another, would not alter one's inherent identity. An American of African descent growing up speaking English, or even more ironically, generations of Jews speaking Yiddish, the language of their own and of no one else for centuries, would not be considered Indo-European even though their birth languages undoubtedly were. These languages, in fact, would be forever a borrowed tongue for them. In contrast, Germans speaking English or Russians speaking French were merely circulating among their own family, so to speak, and by the same token, the modern European might rightfully claim classical Greek or Sanskrit as his own, as his birthright.

From Schlegel to Humboldt, it is conspicuous that the theory of language groups placed an overwhelming emphasis on grammatical structure. The virtue of any given language is to be assessed ultimately by the nature of its syntax. According to this theory, all other linguistic properties and endowments that might be regarded as meritorious and deserving of attention—such as opulence of vocabulary, sonority and lyricism of diction, intelligence and intricacies of rhetorical figures—are decidedly secondary. For nineteenth-century philologists, nothing seems to have mattered more than grammar and its perceived rationality.[28]

We, on the other hand, are left incredulous that this sweeping hegemonic idea of Indo-European language, culture, and, eventually, "race" could be based

28. It may be variously speculated as to why nineteenth-century philologists put nearly exclusive emphasis on the grammar. That the Greeks, and even more, the ancient Indians valorized grammar undoubtedly influenced or legitimated their views. On Sanskrit grammarians, Max Müller writes: "The Hindús are the only nation that cultivated the science of grammar without having received any impulse, directly or indirectly, from the Greeks. . . . There is no form, regular or irregular, in the whole Sanskrit language, which is not provided for in the grammar of Pânini and his commentators. It is the perfection of a merely empirical analysis of language, unsurpassed, nay even unapproached, by anything in the grammatical literature of other nations. Yet of the real nature, and natural growth of language, it teaches us nothing" (ibid., 116).

on such arcane and seemingly tenuous grounds as the superiority of inflection over agglutination. Nor does it seem to us warranted to draw, as brusquely as the pioneering philologists did, an immediate equation between the nature of syntax and the cultural character of a people or their religious dispositions. But regardless of what we might think about such theories today, it apparently became feasible, even inevitable, to represent the religions of the Semites— particularly Islam—in the shadow of an overwhelming prejudgment that proclaimed their essential inflexibility, which stemmed from, and was unmistakably reflected in, their language. Thence it came to be widely held that, no matter how richly various its worldwide spread, Islam was in its very essence rigid, invariably intolerant and exclusive, incandescently purist, with an inherent tendency toward fanaticism.

Concurrent with this turn of events is a marked change in the image of Muslims. Once represented in earlier centuries by the figure of a languid, indulgent, and dissolute "Mussulman"—epitomized by the fabulously rich, corpulent Ottoman pasha wrapped in silk, lounging in his harem surrounded by all manners of pleasure-giving accoutrements—the quintessential "Mohammedan" now turned into a fierce zealot, a sword-wielding, camel-riding desert nomad; he is an Arab. Here, one might be suitably reminded that, in the nineteenth century, just as now, the total population of the Afghani-, Persian-, and Hindustani-speaking Muslims (who therefore were Indo-Europeans) combined with the Ottoman Turks and other agglutinative language-speaking Muslims of China, Indo-China, and the East Indies, were together far more numerous than Arab Muslims. From this point on, however, in the European mind, this overwhelming majority population of the non-Arab Muslims no longer represented the essential character of their religion.

It is also noteworthy that, in the course of the nineteenth century, the efficacy and the value of this philologically based taxonomy was significantly transformed, or as the case might have been, the hidden logic that had been there from the beginning became overt and pronounced. It became more apparent that the most widely consequential outcome of the classification of language groups was not really the relative value of inflection over agglutination (which separated the Indo-European from most others), but the distinction between languages with full inflection and those with limited inflection, that is, between the Indo-European and the Semitic. By the same token, not surprisingly, the very import of the "Indo-European," and its virtual synonym, "Aryan," increasingly became a matter of defining Europeanness. It might be fairly said that the notion of "Aryan" was part of the new conceptual apparatus contrived to represent the European heritage as a direct descendent of Greco-Roman antiquity, with a definitive emphasis on the Greek portion of the hyphenation. In due course, it became customary among Europeans, in speaking of "the Aryans," to set aside the Persians and the Indians altogether, and to use the term to refer to and distinguish themselves from "the Semites"—above all, from the Arabs (now equated with Muslims) and the Jews.

It may be useful to note in this connection that Wilhelm von Humboldt is remembered today not only for his contribution to Oriental scholarship; he is more famously recognized as a founding father of the science of classical antiquities, or *Altertumswissenschaft*. The emerging science of antiquity was above all predicated on the unique and incomparable status attributed to the Greeks. Ancient Greece was now recognized as the absolute origin of nearly everything that constituted Europe; at the same time, Greek civilization attained a status that was at once suprahistorical and nearly supernatural. This novel idea—a metaphysical doctrine, to be sure, brazenly flying in the face of sound historical science—is epitomized by the following unapologetic statement by Humboldt, which dates back to his youthful, pre-Sanskritic period:

> For us the Greeks step out of the circle of history. . . . We fail entirely to recognize our relationship to them if we dare to apply the standards to them we apply to the rest of world history. Knowledge of the Greeks is not merely pleasant, useful or necessary to us—no, in the Greeks alone we find the idea of that which we ourselves should like to be and produce. If every part of history enriches us with its human wisdom and human experience then from the Greeks we take something more than earthly— something almost godlike.[29]

In his mature years, Humboldt enhanced, rather than tempered, this idea of the primordially generative power of antiquity by extending it further, as it were, beyond Greco-Roman, to encompass Indo-European.

4. The Essential Nature of the Semitic: Ernest Renan

The ramifications of mid-nineteenth-century philological theories of language groups, races, and religions are exemplified in the works of Ernest Renan (1823–92). Born the same year as Max Müller, and in a sense a counterpart to the famous Indo-European philologist, Renan was one of the foremost scholars of the Semitic languages. Despite their initial disagreements over, among

29. Quoted in Martin Bernal, "Black Athena Denied" (1986), 27–28.

other things, the issue of the religious tendencies ascribed to the Semites, Müller and Renan became close correspondents and lifelong friends.[30] Unlike Müller, who came from a liberal German Protestant milieu, the French Catholic Renan had renounced his allegiance to the church that had supported and enabled his education and promised security for his future as a scholar and cleric.[31] Thenceforward independent of clerical support and protection, he went on to have a distinguished scholarly career, marked by several major publications including *Histoire générale et système comparée des langues sémitiques* (1855) and, perhaps most controversially and sensationally, *La Vie de Jesus* (1863). Thus counted among the best academic authorities of the time, Renan, toward the end of his life, and roughly half a century after Humboldt, undertook what was to be the last of his great works, a five-volume history of the Israelites (1887–93).

Early in the first volume of his *History of the People of Israel*, we find the following statement, the gist of which by now seems eminently familiar:

The languages of the Aryans and the Semites differed essentially, though there were points of connexity between them. The Aryan language was immensely superior, especially in regard to the conjugation of verbs. This marvellous instrument, created by the instinct of primitive man, con-

---

30. It appears that the onset of their relationship was rather more contentious than friendly, amounting to mutual attacks, beginning with Renan's sharp criticism of Müller's article on Turanian languages (1854), to which Müller responded by writing a scathing review of Renan's *Histoire générale et système comparée des langues sémitiques* (1855). According to his widow, Georgina Grenfell Max Müller, partly urged by Bunsen, partly because Renan himself wrote him conveying a puzzled reaction to the severity of his counterattack, Müller decided not to publish the pamphlet, "though already printed, and they gradually became great friends" (Müller, *Life and Letters*, 1:172–73). A copy of this suppressed pamphlet, entitled "Reply to Monsieur Renan's Remarks" (printed in London, 1855), is extant in Bodleian Library, Oxford University (Max Müller Papers, shelfmark d.2358, folio 1–25). More pertinent to our immediate interest, however, is that, after the publication of the second edition of Renan's *Histoire générale* (1858), Müller wrote a lengthy critical review arguing against Renan's notion that the Semites are by instinct monotheistic, in contrast to the Indo-Europeans who tend toward polytheism. See F. Max Müller, "Semitic Monotheism" (1860), in *Chips from a German Workshop*, (1869), 1:337–74.

31. The story of his church-subsidized education and his subsequent loss of faith—and his indomitable sister Henriette's role in this latter process—is sympathetically and amusingly narrated by an early biographer, Madame James Darmesteter (A. Mary F. Robinson), *The Life of Ernest Renan* (2nd ed., 1898). Prior to this biography, Renan's pupil and Zend scholar James Darmesteter wrote a lengthy essay narrating and reflecting on Renan's departure from the Catholic Church. "Ernest Renan," in *Selected Essays of James Darmesteter* (1895), 178–240.

tained in the germ all the metaphysics which were afterwards to be developed through the Hindoo genius, the Greek genius, the German genius. The Semitic language, upon the contrary, started by making a capital fault in regard to the verb. The greatest blunder which this race has made (for it was the most irreparable), was to adopt, in treating the verb, a mechanism so petty that the expression of the tenses and moods has always been imperfect and cumbersome. Even at the present time the Arab has to struggle in vain against the linguistic blunder which his ancestors made ten or fifteen thousand years ago.[32]

As fatalistic as it might sound, it is not certain that the linguistic heritage envisioned here amounted to the kind of racial determinism ascribed, since the end of the Second World War, to almost any mention of the term "Aryan" in contradistinction to "Semitic." Although it is useful to remember that what Renan expresses in this passage is by no means atypical of his time, his articulation is exceptionally valuable not only because of his scholarly authority but for the disarming frankness of expression, not to mention the beguiling charm of his prose generally. It is he, moreover, who drew, with far greater clarity than any other scholar hitherto examined, the contrast between the Indo-European and the Semitic "geniuses" and between the respective contributions they supposedly had made to the course of world history; by doing so, he developed most fully the idea of the bifurcated origin of Europe, an idea shared by contemporary European intellectuals, including, as we remember, Matthew Arnold. Renan's pronouncements also proved entirely consistent with the basic orientation of Humboldt, who pursued the study of "Sanscritic" antiquity in order to shed light on the distant ancestry of Europe and, ultimately, for the greater glory of Greece. The very first paragraph of Renan's preface to *History of the People of Israel* demonstrates this affinity well:

For a philosophic mind, that is to say for one engrossed in the origin of things, there are not more than three histories of real interest in the past of humanity: Greek history, the history of Israel, and Roman history. These three histories combined constitute what may be called the history of civilisation, civilisation being the result of the alternate collaboration of Greece, Judea, and Rome. Greece in my opinion has an exceptional past,

32. Throughout this discussion, I cite the translation by C. B. Pitman and D. Bingam, which started to appear within a year of the original French edition: Renan, *History of the People of Israel* (1888–93), 1:7–8; cited in the text by page number hereafter.

for she founded, in the fullest sense of the word, rational and progressive humanity. Our science, our arts, our literature, our philosophy, our moral code, our political code, our strategy, our diplomacy, our maritime and international law, are of Greek origin. The framework of human culture created by Greece is susceptible of indefinite enlargement, but it is complete in its several parts. Progress will consist in constantly developing what Greece has conceived, in executing the designs which she has, so to speak, traced out for us. (1:vii)

A rather odd opening for a five-volume work intended to narrate the history of the Israelites, one might think, yet for Renan, this Hellenophilic pronouncement indeed furnished a proper orientation for any contemporary European who would write such a history. As he saw the matter, everything, or nearly everything had its origin in Greece—everything, that is, but one critical failing, and it was in the task of filling in that gap that the history of Israel finds its sole justification "for us":

> Greece had only one thing wanting in the circle of her moral and intellectual activity, but this was an important void; she despised the humble and did not feel the need of a just God. Her philosophers, while dreaming of the immortality of the soul, were tolerant towards the iniquities of this world. Her religions were merely elegant municipal playthings; the idea of a universal religion never occurred to her. The ardent genius of a small tribe established in an outlandish corner of Syria seemed created to supply this void in the Hellenic intellect. (1:vii)[33]

In effect, Renan suggests, the world historical mission of the Israelites, if not to say of the Semites as a whole, was to serve the one and the only truly original agent of civilization, the Greco-Aryans, who were endowed with the inherent force of progress. (And what is history without progress?) In order to serve this particular purpose, moreover, the character of the Semites had to be decidedly *other* than the grand, beneficent, and genteel disposition of the masters of

---

33. As Renan put it in a later passage: "What Greece was as regards intellectual culture and Rome as regards politics, the nomad Semites were as regards religion. It was by means of religion that these worthy pastoral tribes of Syria reached an exceptional position in the world. The promises made to Abraham are mythical only in form. Abraham, the imaginary ancestor of these tribes, was in reality the father in religion of all peoples" (ibid., 1:22).

history. According to this narrative construction, in fact, it was precisely the mission of the Israelites to be somewhat ill-mannered and cantankerous in their insistence on justice, and on justice alone:

> Israel never stood quietly by to see the world so badly governed, under the authority of a God reputed to be just. Her sages burned with anger over the abuses of the world. A bad man, dying old, rich, and at ease, kindled their fury, and the prophets in the ninth century BC elevated this idea to the height of a dogma. (1:viii)

Thus was born a veritable religion of moral extremism, which featured a doctrine of stringent laws, unforgiving judgment, and hair-raising retribution. This was the unprecedented advent of unadorned ethical monotheism, stripped bare of all ceremonial fineries and meditative unction—a religion that was deadly literal, monolithic, fanatic:

> The Israelitish prophets were impetuous writers such as we of the present day should denounce as socialists and anarchists. They were fanatics in the cause of social justice, and loudly proclaimed that if the world was not just, or capable of becoming so, it had better be destroyed—a view which, if utterly wrong, was very fertile in results, for, like all the doctrines of despair, such as the Russian nihilism of the present day, it led to deeds of heroism and brought about a grand awakening of the forces of humanity. (1:viii)

In Renan's time, this figure of a zealous soldier of divine justice immediately evoked associations with certain revolutionary radicals who were causing political and social unrest, whose dangerous fervor was particularly visible during the revolutionary events of 1848, of which Renan himself was a witness in the streets of Paris.[34] In our own time, this image of the quintessential Semite resonates disturbingly with the figure of Muslim extremists turned Arab terrorists. It is as though the incorrigibly self-righteous, wholly self-absorbed, at

---

34. Renan wrote *L'Avenir de la science* in the wake of 1848 to express his own socialist ideals, which, however, waned shortly thereafter. The manuscript was not published until 1890, two years before his death. The document itself, as well as the fact that he returned to the topic in advanced age, it might be surmised, testify to the deep impression those events of his youth left on him.

once self-sacrificing and other-destroying crusader for the cause of justice has burst straight out of the shell of the prophets of yore.

If such fire-and-brimstone holy outrage was the defining characteristic of Semitic religion, it would seem highly unlikely that this hypercritical force—with an altogether negative, unpromising prospect for a career in constructive history—should have come to play an essential role, perhaps the greatest part ever, on the world historical stage. But this was indeed what happened, according to Renan. This was the miracle of Christianity—that is, insofar as this adamant rationalist would allow any mention of miracles. In Renan's view, the founders of Christianity included not only Jesus and the apostles but also "the second generation of Christians." It was those "direct successors of the prophets," he suggests, who "spent their strength in an incessant call for the end of the world, and, strange to say, did in reality transform the world." In this fashion, the essentially Semitic religion of the prophets, or what Arnold called Hebraism, becomes on a par with the master narrative of history, or Hellenism, at least for a time:

> Christianity, in a word, becomes in history as important an element as the liberal rationalism of the Greeks, though in some respects less assured of duration. The tendency which leads the nineteenth century to secularise everything, to make a host of things lay instead of ecclesiastical, is a reaction against Christianity; but even supposing that it attains its end, Christianity will leave an imperishable trace of its existence. (1:ix)

This pronouncement is ominous, of course, for those Semites who come after Christianity—what might be their raison d'être, now that Christianity has arrived? And what of those who would insist on Christianity beyond this historical moment? The case is clear in Renan's mind: of all the strands of history that have come to constitute the world as "we" know it, eternity lies with the legacy of Greece alone; the rest may have their own day, but their glory is in their respective place, and time, in serving that master history.[35]

---

35. Thus it follows, for Renan, that the most felicitous of all historians are those who write about Greece. And he positions his own mission in life as a Semitic scholar in this way: "Happy will be the man who shall, at the age of sixty, write this history [of Greece] con amore, after having spent his whole life in the study of the works which so many learned schools have devoted to it. He will have for his recompense the greatest joy which man can taste, that of following up the evolutions of life in the very centre of the divine egg within which life first began to palpitate."

All in all, then, there is no surprise that the five volumes of Renan's *History of the People of Israel* should end with the advent of Christianity. Thus we read in the conclusion at the end of the final volume:

> Christianity is the offshoot, or . . . the end or final cause of Judaism. Having given birth to Christianity, Judaism still continues to exist, but as a withered trunk beside one fertile branch. Henceforth the life is gone from it. Its history, though still deeply interesting, has only a secondary importance in a large historical view. There is in this assertion nothing that need sadden the heart of an Israelite, however strong in his own conviction. It is through Christianity that Judaism has really conquered the world. Christianity is the masterpiece of Judaism, its glory and the fulness of its evolution. (5:355–56)

This opinion, as problematic and objectionable as it might sound to our ear, was generally consistent with the traditional Christian view of the Jews; for the post-Christian Israelites had always been deemed, or even venerated in some sense, as living fossils of a superseded stage of providential history. Accordingly, there were few indeed among Renan's contemporaries, who would contradict this notion.[36] What was far more controversial at the time was Renan's suggestion that the time of Christianity, too, shall pass, and that signs of its passing were already in evidence in the world around him:

> Judaism and Christianity will both disappear. The work of the Jew will have its end; the work of the Greek—in other words, science and civilization, rational, experimental, without charlatanism, without revelation, a civilization founded upon reason and liberty—will last forever; and if this globe should ever fail in its duty, there will be others found to push to the end the programme of all life,—light, reason, and truth. (5:361)

And yet does it follow that, because I envy the future historian of the genius of Greece, I regret the Nazarite's vow which attached me early in life to the Jewish and Christian problem? Assuredly not. The Jewish and Christian histories have been the delight of eighteen centuries, and although they are now half vanquished by Greek rationalism, they are extraordinarily effective in the amelioration of morals" (*History of the People of Israel*, 1:x-xi).

36. This is not to forget, however, some important critical voices that began to be raised in the nineteenth century, particularly by the proponents of the so-called Jewish Enlightenment. See Susannah Heschel, *Abraham Geiger and the Jewish Jesus* (1998), and Jonathan M. Hess, *Germans, Jews and the Claims of Modernity* (2002).

Rarely was the rationalist republican creed of the nineteenth century more plainly and more serenely spoken than by this former seminarian, much honored and with little to lose or to fear at the end of his days. This rationalism, lest we gloss over it too quickly, was firmly grounded in a claim for the absolute supremacy of the Aryan genius in the universal march of history. At the same time, Renan insisted with utmost sincerity, that in the legacy of humanity there was and would always remain the unforgettable gift of the Semites, or what he called, rather chillingly, "the trace of Israel."

6

Islam, a Semitic Religion

In light of the generative history of comparative philology sketched in chapter 5, there may be little surprise that Buddhism—recognized from the beginning as a tradition of Aryan origin—was more readily considered on a par with Christianity than was Islam and, frankly, more favorably viewed by the newly ethnoconscious Europeans of the nineteenth century.[1] In fact, in certain cases, Buddhism was regarded by some Europeans as their long-forgotten spiritual heritage and actively appropriated in place of Christianity, whose Semitic origin now struck a discordant note with their supposed Hellenic ancestry. Meanwhile, Islam, an old menace and invincible foe to European Christendom for centuries, had been recast as a prototypically Arab—hence Semitic—religion. In the course of the nineteenth century, Islam thus came to acquire a new alienness. Instead of being begrudged as the luxuriantly overbearing dominion of Eastern infidelity, the rule of Islam was now condescendingly viewed as narrow, rigid, and stunted, and its essential attributes were said to be defined by the national, racial, and ethnic character of the Arabs, the most bellicose and adversarial of the Semites.

This chapter documents in some detail the transformation of the image of Islam under the scrutiny of nineteenth-century European scholarship. After a review of Europe's changing relation to the Muslim world in section 1 and some general observations in section 2 on the infiltration of the new idea of the Semitic in European thought, I turn in sections 3 and 4 to Abraham Kuenen and Otto Pfleiderer, two vocal proponents of the view that the Islam is an ethnic religion of the Arabs, a Semitic race, and therefore does not belong to the class of world religions.

---

1. This outlook seems to be sustained to this day, even if the contrast is less explicitly racialized. On the whole, "typical" Muslims are considered to be prone to militancy, while Buddhists are generally presumed pacific and meditative. Although the sampling is small and highly localized, an interesting empirical study in present day Tübingen, Germany, demonstrates that the stereotypical views of these religions, mainly driven by popular media, agree with these century-old images. Kirsten George, et al., "Das Bild des Islam und des Buddhismus" (1996), 55–82.

The image of Semitic Islam established by the end of the nineteenth century is now eminently familiar to us, so much so that we seem largely oblivious to the fact of its establishment, that there once was a time when Islam presented a rather different countenance to the eyes of Europe. How such a transformation was possible in the first place, and why it occurred when it did, cannot be ascertained merely by peering into the arcane society of nineteenth-century European Scholars. While the focal point of the present study is precisely that scholarly society, I begin this chapter with a consideration of the broader historical context, a rough sketch taken from an existing historical narrative, drawn from a wide array of studies documenting the sea change in the power and fortunes of Europe over the past five centuries.

1. The Problem of Islam for Premodern and Early Modern Europe

It is uncontroversial enough to say that European modernity commenced, for whatever reasons, with a dramatic transformation of Europe's relation to the rest of the world. For centuries, the most proximate of the rest of the world for Europe was solidly Islamic. As we know, the so-called voyages of discovery did not send out the denizens of Europe to hitherto uninhabited, uncharted, or ungoverned places elsewhere. Far from it, much of that "elsewhere" had been the dominion of those whom the Europeans called Mohammedans, who were not of one but of greatly diverse sorts. Europe began to make inroads into this vast and various Islamic dominion and, in the latter half of the nineteenth century, reached a certain watershed. Call it colonial expansion or the progress of modernity, this amounted to a monumental geopolitical shift, a large-scale change in the power relation between the Islamic domain and European Christendom. It is therefore impossible to claim to take seriously either the European discovery of other religions or its refiguration of Islam, or for that matter, the concomitant reconstitution of European identity itself, *apart from* this shift in the position of Europe vis-à-vis the once-invincible Islamic rule.

In the past half century or so, this story of dynamic geopolitical change has been concertedly narrated, analyzed, and critiqued by numerous scholars. This critical literature includes, to cite a few prominent trends, works presenting new global perspectives on modern economy, as exemplified by Immanuel Wallerstein's "modern world-system" theory and many a critical rejoinder thereof, by comprehensive historical studies such as Donald Lach's life-work documenting the "making of Europe" in its dealings with Asia; and by the prolific scholarly output in the wake of Edward Said's epoch-making treatise,

Orientalism.[2] In effect, we are certainly not lacking in the variety of historiographical accounts, which could be employed as a means to orient the topic of this chapter in a larger historical context. Thus, if I choose to utilize for this purpose an older, relatively unknown text instead, it is for a reason.

Asia and Western Dominance: A Survey of the Vasco Da Gama Epoch of Asian History, 1498–1945, by Kavalam Madhava Panikkar (1896–1963), was first published in London in 1953, and as the author himself credibly states, it was "perhaps the first attempt by an Asian student to see and understand European activities in Asia for 450 years."[3] "The Vasco da Gama Epoch" of the subtitle refers, of course, to the period in which Europeans began to explore the world beyond their boundaries and successfully established a new world order in their own terms and to their unparalleled advantage, thereby usurping the Islamic rule that had reigned supreme over the semiglobal trade system until the beginning of that period. From the closing years of the fifteenth century through at least the end of the Second World War, various European powers—multiply contending among themselves and sometimes in complicity with one another—developed technological and strategic means to transport themselves directly to Asian nations. They eventually attained direct control, or at least uncontestable sway and influence over much of the inhabited part of the earth.

What was new in Panikkar's study was that it brought back the broad, semiglobal perspective that had apparently been lost since the nineteenth century.[4] As Panikkar explains in the introduction:

2. To name but a few of the most representative studies, see Immanuel Wallerstein, *The Modern World-System* (1974–89), Eric R. Wolf, *Europe and the People without History* (1982), Andre Gunder Frank, *ReOrient* (1998), in addition to Donald F. Lach, *Asia in the Making of Europe* (1965–93). Cf. also K. N. Chaudhuri, *Asia before Europe* (1990). P. J. Marshall and Glyndwr Williams's useful study of the European conception of the world may also be mentioned: *The Great Map of Mankind* (1982).

3. I refer throughout this discussion to a more recent edition: K. M. Panikkar, *Asia and Western Dominance* (1959), 17; cited in the text by page number hereafter. If Panikkar's claim is true, it seems significant that a pioneering work on the critical study of Orientalism, in the broadest sense, was brought forward by a historian who identified himself as a non-European. Moreover, the relative obscurity of this text and of its author seems all the more remarkable, especially given that Panikkar was far from obscure, being a distinguished historian, diplomat, and prolific writer.

4. I believe it is fair to describe its perspective as semi-global, even if this particular work by Panikkar is principally focused on the relation between Europe and non-Islamic Asia.

Though this epoch, because of its importance, has been the subject of many valuable studies, so far they have been concerned mainly with special areas. No study of the relations of Europe with non-Islamic Asia as a whole has yet been attempted. On the purely historical side there are many works of great value dealing with each country separately and ignoring the basic unity of the problem, which was to a large extent obscured by the position of the British Empire in India which a distinguished Foreign Secretary of that Government once described as neither the Far East, nor the Middle East, but INDIA. The British position in India was thus isolated from the rest of the problem, rendering a correct perspective of Asia difficult if not impossible.

The present attempt, therefore, is to restore that perspective, which was well understood and fully realized in the seventeenth and eighteenth centuries. (17)

It would be worthwhile, indeed, to consider at some length both the circumstances and the probable causes for this loss of perspective, since the amnesia itself may have been an essential condition for the success of the new world order accomplished at the end of the nineteenth century, that is to say, an indispensable condition for European hegemony to seem natural, objective, and necessary.

Let us begin by remembering the indisputable superiority of the Islamic powers on the world stage up to the late fifteenth century, and what that must have meant for the denizens of Europe. With the ancient glories of the Roman Empire and of Alexander's exploits long past and faded, European Christendom was a rather confined area, whose power was only of regional importance. Clearly, it was no match for the enormous reach of the Islamic realm, which by that time spanned North Africa and the islands of today's Indonesia. To be sure, the sheepherder of Fez and the spice gatherer of Batavia may not have had much in common or much to say to each other; at the same time it could be meaningfully said that they did inhabit two geographic extremities of the "same," though far from homogeneous, domain. And this domain at its height was a vast landmass and archipelago covering a multitude of nations, interconnected by an intricate network of regional administrative relations and transregional trade routes, both on land and sea. What we now call in retrospect the Islamic world was thus a broad ribbon of kingdoms and empires extending halfway across the planet, an immense area studded with countless busy ports and prosperous cities teeming with traveling goods, people, and animals, their markets redolent with tropical perfumes and spices, their palaces resplendent with gold, ivory, silks, and brocades from the Far East, . . . or at least that must have been how the Europeans imagined it from afar, judging from the intensity of their age-old longing "to reach India." The memory of this yearning survived well into the nineteenth century, as it moved Hegel to call India, suitably enough, "a Land of Desire."[5] And he was by no means the last to recollect this old yearning.

Notable already in this survey is the deep ambivalence in the European attitude toward the East, manifest in the semantic bifurcation of the Orient into, on the one hand, a land of desire, and on the other, a formidable obstacle to attaining those very objects of desire. This ambivalence is probably less psychostructural than a direct reflection of a particular historical circumstance. As Panikkar points out, "the spice trade with the East, one of the great motivating factors of history and one which yielded the largest profits to merchants as commodities in universal demand, could only come from the Indian ports across the territories controlled by Muslim rulers. . . . Spices which became more and more an essential for European cookery could not be obtained except from India and Indonesia and must come through Persia or Egypt" (22).[6] In short, the more Europeans desired spices, the better business it was for Muslims everywhere. This general situation had obtained since the end of the twelfth century:

> From the time of Saladin, who recaptured Jerusalem from the Crusaders in 1187, Islam based [i]n Egypt had been organized as an immensely powerful barrier between Asia and Europe. The extraordinary burst of energy, enthusiasm and zeal which had moved Christendom in the first three Crusades had come to naught, and the victory of Saladin, from the point of view of later history one of the most decisive in the world, had established

---

5. "From the most ancient times downwards, all nations have directed their wishes and longings to gaining access to the treasures of this land of marvels, the most costly which the earth presents, treasures of nature—pearls, diamonds, perfumes, rose essences, lions, elephants, etc.—as also treasures of wisdom. The way by which these treasures have passed to the West has at all times been a matter of world historical importance bound up with the fate of nations" (Hegel, *Philosophy of History*, quoted in Panikkar, *Asia and Western Dominance*, 21).

6. For a consideration of the impact of the spice trade upon modern European cultural history more generally, see Wolfgang Schivelbusch, *Tastes of Paradise* (1992).

Muslim predominance in the vital area of Syrian and Egyptian coasts for centuries to come. That European statesmen were not unaware of this is proved by the fact that the fifth Crusade (1218–21) was directed against Egypt itself. (22)

Interestingly, the only Europeans who were not particularly encumbered by this situation, but on the contrary handsomely profited from it, seem to have been the patrician families of the mercantile republic of Venice. "By a combination of skilful diplomacy, adventurous spirit and far-sighted policy the Venetians had for long established powerful influence at Cairo and had made themselves the monopolist agents of Eastern trade in Europe. While their fortunes, so far as the land routes were concerned, varied with political changes in Byzantium, the Venetians were able to resist every challenge and to maintain their supremacy in the Red Sea trade" (23). The prodigious wealth and power of this trade monopoly was such that, even today, any visitor to this improbable city, poised on the water as if it were adrift at sea, would not fail to see that five-hundred years of relentless decline has not yet been enough to rub off the gilded opulence and sheer splendor of its premodern economic miracle.

The rest of Europe had been hemmed in, insofar as their external commerce was concerned, not only by the immense unmovable reality of the Ottoman Empire but also by the uncontestable dominance of the tiny Italian city-state that virtually controlled the vital trade routes of the eastern Mediterranean Sea. Consequently, the singular objective of many of the lesser European nations—especially those with limited access to the Mediterranean, such as Portugal, Spain, the Netherlands, and England—was to circumvent the impenetrable Orient, the landmass blockade, and to sail "freely" to the other Orient, the land of desire, to the ethereal font of fragrant treasures. As we know, the most ambitious pioneers among them devised what could only be described as rather outlandish alternative methods of getting to "India." Some took an extraordinary detour circumnavigating the massive continent of Africa, in order to reach the Indian Ocean by way of what they poignantly named the Cape of Good Hope. Others sailed far west into the Atlantic Ocean, in the hopes of eventually getting to the east. Thus commenced the "Vasco da Gama Epoch," or, more commonly, what school children today learn as the "Age of Discovery." As the story told by the triumphalist moderns goes, the irrepressible spirit of freedom—supposedly a natural endowment of the West—stepped up to take the center stage in world history. This innate spirit of the West was at last enabled and empowered by a series of scientific discoveries, technological innovations, and just plain resourcefulness. Thenceforward, the West, mobility (particularly navigational mobility), modernity, and freedom have been presumed to be essentially and constitutionally interrelated in the deepest possible sense. Looking back at this turn of world historical events from a point of view less ideologically blinded and more historically informed, Panikkar's account allows us to see how indispensable—hence how extraordinarily revealing—this conflation of attributes self-ascribed to the West has been to the cause of European hegemony.

Also noteworthy is Panikkar's observation that the nation that initiated this momentous turn of European fortune was Portugal, one of the most zealous and abiding supporters of the cause of the Roman Catholic Church to fight the Mohammedan infidels. Earlier in the fifteenth century, Portugal's single-minded prince Henry, deservedly called the Navigator, reportedly made an extraordinary investment in developing a new navigational technology (in short, devising vessels navigable in the open sea, and fleets and vessels large enough to carry cannons) and in the charting of a new route around Africa. As Panikkar reminds us, in the mind of this prince and of his compatriots, these developments meant more than technical feats and commercial gain:

> The spirit of the Crusades not only survived but flourished with added vigour in the Iberian Peninsula in the fifteenth and the sixteenth centuries. While to the other countries of Western Europe, Islam was but a distant menace, to the people of the Iberian Peninsula, to Castile, Aragon and Portugal, Islam represented something menacing, formidable and vigilant on the doorstep. Other countries became enthusiastic against the infidel by fits and starts; but the Iberian was a Crusader by necessity, every day of his life, for in the Peninsula itself Muslim kingdoms still existed and were flourishing. To a devout and patriotic Iberian, Spaniard or Portuguese, the fight against Islam was a stern imperative, a combination alike of religious duty and patriotic necessity. Islam was the enemy and had to be fought everywhere. Much of Portuguese action in Asia will remain inexplicable unless this fact is constantly borne in mind. (24)

From this standpoint, then, the efforts of early European explorers to reach India were aimed at more than lowering the cost of pepper or outwitting the hated Venetian monopolists; for, in the eyes of those navigational pioneers, their expeditions were veritable missions in the continuing crusade. Their charge, put succinctly, was "to cut at the root of Islam by attacking it from behind" (27).

As we know, the pathbreaking success of the Portuguese was soon overridden by the wily mercantilism of the Dutch, who in turn were to be overshadowed by the concerted colonial enterprises of the more powerful neighboring nations of the eighteenth century. Yet, despite these intraregional transfers of the ruling power over colonial trade, from that critical moment in the late fifteenth century until today, the centrality and the hegemonic position of Europe—and, in time, including all the colonial locations established fully on this Eurohegemonic principle, that is, the West—has not been seriously challenged. Thence comes the inseparability of Eurocentrality and modernity.

The conquest of Islam in this complicated sense, then, was the utmost exigency for European modernity at the moment of its inception. The remarkable success of this project achieved by the end of the nineteenth century was such that, apparently, the very memory of the former condition was nearly effaced.[7] Thenceforward, the problem of Islam seems to have been vaguely felt more as a puzzling nuisance than an active menace, as a strange, alien ethos that remained incorrigible, backward, and recalcitrant. For reasons no longer recognized, then, Islam now appeared as the most peculiar of the "old" religions—all the more irrational and anomalous because, as discussed in chapter 2, it was a latecomer. But in the last analysis, it was liable to be set aside as a moribund tradition just like all other "archaic" religions, as one of the last vestiges of the stubborn premodernity with which the world was still replete.

2. The Problem of Semitism and Aryanism for Nineteenth-Century Europe

With this historical context in mind, we now return to the condition of European self-understanding in light of the new theory of language families, and the novel perspectives on "other religions" that this theory brought about.

The construction of Aryan Buddhism and the reconstitution of Semitic Islam occurred by virtue of the new science of language. As we saw in chapter 5, by the second half of the nineteenth century, these newly minted categories had found their places in a nascent domain of knowledge, the science of religion. Of the practitioners in this emerging field, the Continental scholars, among whom the term "world religion" had begun to have a specific meaning, naturally accepted Buddhism's status as a world religion, thereby attributing to it a cer-

---

7. This is consistent with Panikkar's suggestion above that the global perspective (within which the changing relation between European Christendom and Asia can be adequately comprehended) was "well understood and fully realized in the seventeenth and eighteenth centuries," but not, presumably, since the nineteenth century.

tain universalistic character, if not to say universality outright. This effectively brought Buddhism on a par with Christianity, at least in a certain taxonomic sense. In describing the similarity between Christianity and Buddhism, these scholars would often draw an analogy between the historical origins of the two religions: on the one hand, the emergence of (universal) Christianity out of (national/ethnic) Judaism, and on the other, (universal) Buddhism out of (national/ethnic) Brahmanism.

For some, the analogy went even further. Just as Christianity did not thrive in the place of its origin but rather disappeared from it, so it was suggested, Buddhism likewise vanished in its native India, and both religions came to prosper among strangers in foreign lands. But in the course of their subsequent transnational developments, the ethnic character of the new host nations inevitably colored the outcome such that, just as original Christianity at one point was diverted to gnostic heresies, popish superstitions, and other forms of particularism and divisiveness, the universalistic primitive Buddhism, too, was corrupted and transformed into a variety of peculiar, popular, (non-Aryan) ethnic forms endemic to various South, East, and Southeast Asian nations. By this reckoning, it would appear, it was entirely natural that the essential characteristic of "original Buddhism"—or, as Monier-Williams called it, "true Buddhism"—as a universalistic religion should be more readily recognized and far better understood by European scholars than by native Asian practitioners. For, after all, those Asian Buddhists had little connection or access to the early textual sources of their religion, either through scholarly and intellectual cultivation or through their "racial," ethnic, or national heritage.

Furthermore, if Buddhism was a universal or universalistic religion that was genuinely Aryan in its origin, arising quite independently of Semitic monotheism, it would be feasible to suggest that universality is an intrinsic character of (Indo-)European civilization, while at the same time it would be possible to relinquish the traditional assumption that (Semitic) monotheism is the sole source of universality. As we recall, in earlier centuries, the privileged position of Christianity as universal religion was based on its being a true monotheism, that is, on the unity, singularity, and universality of the Deity.[8] On account of the shared belief in monotheism, moreover, earlier Euro-Christians saw relatively little difficulty in recognizing that their closest kin were Jews and Mohammedans. This was in fact taken for granted, because of their commonality of

8. The idea is typically expressed, for instance, by David Hume's *The Natural History of Religion* (1956), a text originally prepared for publication in 1756 but suppressed until 1777.

origin in the biblical tradition, as well as their subsequent historical relations, even though much of that history consisted of conflict. Despite the recurrent outbursts of animosity, the Euro-Christians of the early modern period acknowledged or assumed the three communities to be fraternal, or even consanguineous. Measured against the trio of monotheisms, all forms of Gentile polytheism were deemed no match, however grand and Olympian they might be, not to mention more humble instances of heathen idolatry, fetishism, or any other veneration of limited and particularistic deities and spirits. Given this evaluative scheme, then, any serious challenge to Christian supremacy could come only from other monotheisms. In fact, in order to demonstrate the superiority of Christianity over all others, it seemed sufficient to show how it and it alone realized and embodied the true universalism of the Sovereign Deity. An argument in favor of Christianity on this score could be made—at least to the Euro-Christians' own satisfaction—by suggesting that Judaism represented an older, undeveloped, fossilized, hence limited universalism, whereas Islam was a latter-day breakaway movement, amounting to a renegade universalism, and both of these definitions, of course, were contradictions in terms.

The nineteenth-century discovery of the Indo-European lineage undermined this basic assumption. In the new, philologically informed perspective, the triune ensemble became a questionable alliance at best, and in the meantime, a hitherto unknown rival had appeared on the horizon. Buddhism, though not exactly a polytheism, is not a monotheism either. Its principle of unity and universality, if there is one, is not tied to the figure of an all-commanding Creator-Judge-God; rather, the unitary principle involved here seems more abstract and philosophical, or so it seemed in the eyes of nineteenth-century Indologists, many of whom were well-schooled in German Idealism. Perhaps it was almost as though they could imagine that something like a Kantian idea of God—what Kant called the ideal of pure reason, qua postulate of reason, that is, as necessary guarantor of the unity of knowledge and therefore of the possibility of science[9]—had long ago been posited by Buddhism in its gloriously plain, primitive Aryan nakedness. The case of Buddhism therefore presented an alternative to the (mono)theistic foundation of universalism, as it pointed to the possibility of universal religion predicated instead on more philosophical, or even "scientific," grounds. Having recognized its origin as essentially Aryan, not surprisingly, some Europeans

---

9. Cf. Immanuel Kant, "Appendix to the Transcendental Dialectic," in *Critique of Pure Reason*, B670–733.

found in Buddhism a new venue in which to reenvision their ancestral roots, to reassemble and to rectify their heritage racially and spiritually.[10]

For the European intellectual and cultural elites who were also cognizant of developments in the emergent human sciences at the end of the nineteenth century, there were several options for envisioning their future destiny. Some, as we have seen already in the case of Ernest Renan, for instance, were not entirely averse to relinquishing Europe's historical ties with Christianity altogether. It seems that some were even prepared to embrace alternative spiritual traditions supposedly original to the Indo-Greco-Germanic or Celtic peoples, including various forms of "polytheism." The lure of pre-Christian paganism seems to have stemmed in part from rising nationalist sentiments and their habitual recourse to mythologies—whether Norse, Celtic, or Teutonic. But the most powerful attraction came from the romance of ancient Greece, whose glorious pantheon was taken to be a monument to what Hegel famously termed "the religion of beauty." What underlies this extolling of Olympian polytheism was a relatively novel and intriguing idea that the polytheistic temperament of the Greeks, combined with their superb sense of order, balance, and proportion, constituted their unique genius, which allowed them—and them alone— to come to terms with the infinite multiplicity of nature. Hence their incomparable ability to represent the world beautifully (their artistic genius) as well as rationally (their scientific genius). As we recall from Renan's musings, it was this felicitous culmination of the aesthetic and the rational that was believed to be the origin of virtually everything that was true, good, beautiful, and therefore universal.

10. I should note here that the function of these racial, ethnic, and religious terms of identity is extremely various and complex. The value of such loosely strung associations is in the volatile nature of each of the terms rather than in any kind of exactitude one might attempt to ascribe. I should therefore note that, in this context, I am not heeding Tiele's fastidiously discriminating use of "Aryan," which he states as follows: "I keep the ugly but established designation 'Indo-Germans,' to distinguish the race from the Aryans proper, who were the ancestors of the Indians and Persians. The name Indo-Europeans is to be rejected on every account. The name Aryans may also be applied to the whole race, and the Indo-Persians may then be called East-Aryans. The name Indo-Germans indicates the two peoples between whom all the others belonging to the race are scattered" (C. P. Tiele, *Outlines the History of Religion* [1877], 107). Similarly but somewhat differently, Chantepie de la Saussaye explicates: "The whole family is named after its two extreme branches, the Indo-Germanic, or more correctly the Indo-Celtic, sometimes called the Indo-European, and also the Aryan, which is hardly as suitable, as it is a name better kept for the more eastern branch: the Indo-Persian" (P. D. Chantepie de la Saussaye, *Manual of the Science of Religion* [1891], 321).

It is in this regard also that the Greeks were said to be radically different from the eastern branches of the Aryan brotherhood. For, in the East—particularly in India, though perhaps less so in Persia—the Aryan sensibility embracing multiplicity went wildly out of control and produced surreal monstrosities. Not only were there countless multitudes of gods and demons, but unchecked by the sense of balance, beauty, and rationality, India generated appalling images of gods with multiple heads, numerous limbs and other body parts, not to mention the grotesque concatenation of animal and human features in a single figure. As Otto Pfleiderer guilelessly rendered this familiar idea:

> One thing which the Indians lacked utterly, the Greeks possessed, namely, a sense of order and proportion, of clearness and beauty. This artistic tendency was the *charisma* of the Greeks, ever present in their religion as in their philosophy, preserving them from the excesses of Indian fanaticism and dreaming. It is this which made it possible for them to exercise a deep influence upon Oriental belief and thought such as had never been possible to Indian wisdom.[11]

In contrast to the chaotic Eastern polytheism, the superbly classical representation of Apollo and Athena in the Greek pantheon was considered the epitome of serenity and order. It was evidently easy for nineteenth-century Europeans to overlook the rampant monstrosities among ancient Greek mythological themes, well documented in art and literature throughout the ages, which included numerous instances of sexual excess, violation of social mores, and breach of cosmic order.[12]

11. Otto Pfleiderer, *Religion and Historic Faiths* (1907), 190–91. This aversion to things Indian on aesthetic and "rational" grounds was shared by some luminaries of an earlier era, Goethe and Hegel most notably. Schopenhauer's leaning toward Buddhism instead of Brahmanism/ Hinduism, too, may be analyzed in view of this general sentiment. Nietzsche's enigmatic co-option of "Zarathustra" may also resonate with Goethe's acknowledged preference for the reputedly more serene Persian tradition over and against the Indian. Cf. also Partha Mitter, *Much Maligned Monsters* (1977).

12. Interestingly, Max Müller seemed particularly sensitive to the monstrosity present in Greek mythology, which he described in another context as "hideous and revolting"; but he expected this atrocious characteristic in any mythology, not only Greek or Indian (F. Max Müller, "Comparative Mythology" [1856], in *Chips from a German Workshop* [1871], 2:1–141). See also the opening paragraphs of "On the Philosophy of Mythology," a lecture given at the Royal Institution in 1871, included as an appendix to his *Introduction to the Science of Religion* (1873). For Müller's views on the essentially grotesque character of mythology, see Tomoko Masuzawa, *In Search of Dreamtime* (1993), 58–75.

Meanwhile, other Europeans, perhaps less sanguine about the prospect of pagan gods returning in droves, and at the same time hesitant to embrace anything so unfamiliar as Buddhism, availed themselves of another option, another way of realigning the place of Christianity in the history of religions, by disengaging their Christianity from its Judeo-Semitic origin. There was apparently more than one way of accomplishing this disengagement. One was to claim that, despite a long-held tradition, Christianity in its essential being (as opposed to its historical beginning) is not to be traced back to Palestine as one of the many Jewish messianic sects; rather, Christianity emerged from the far richer soil of the late Hellenic world, which stretched from the Mediterranean to Persia and Northern India—roughly, the reach of the short-lived Macedonian empire of Alexander the Great. Following this train of thought, Christianity was reenvisioned as something more universal than national or ethnic, or—to say roughly the same thing—more Greek, meaning, more broadly Hellenic and Aryan than Hebraic and Semitic.

Another option for salvaging Christianity from the fetters of Semitic provenance—and this alternative was more immediately compliant with orthodox Christian views than the one just mentioned—was to claim to identify, in the heart of the ancient Israelite tradition itself, something that completely transcended the narrow and particular confines of the Semitic race religion; it was from this transcendent element alone that Christianity presumably originated, that is, without carrying over any ethnic peculiarity of the parent religion. And this transethnic, universalistic element was identified as the prophetic tradition, the most central and essential spirit of the Hebrew Bible. A ready implication here was an idea as bold as it was astonishing, namely, the notion that there was at the very core of Judaism something not really Jewish.[13]

It is difficult to say with certainty when exactly and who specifically originated this powerful, much taken-for-granted idea that the "Hebrew prophets" were incomparably, overwhelmingly important in constituting the essential nature of the biblical tradition and at the same time not strictly Jewish or Semitic. James Darmesteter, distinguished French savant of the Avestan language and of Persian antiquity, credits none other than Renan and his massive *History of the People of Israel* for the revolutionary new perspective. In reviewing Renan's work, Darmesteter opines that "its novelty consists in having made prophecy the centre of interest of the history of Israel" and, in fact, in "making the

---

13. Maurice Olender discusses this "rescue operation" of Christianity from the taint of Semitism specifically in relation to Ernest Renan's work. See *The Languages of Paradise* (1992), 63–79.

central figure of this history not Moses on Mount Sinai, but the company of prophets, the men who spoke to Israel during the last two centuries of the Jewish kingdom, and during the Babylonian captivity, from about 800 to 536 before Christ."[14] Renan's scientific interpretation of the biblical narrative thus relocated the generative moment of Hebrew history, lifting it away from the Garden of Eden (mythical origin) and away from Mount Sinai (sacrohistorical origin), and placing it squarely on the labor of several generations of prophets long after the fall of the Davidic kingdom.

This suggestive reading made Renan a controversial figure in the eyes of church-abiding contemporaries. For, as he more than implied, those prophets—hypercritical denouncers of the world and advocates for the Lord who purported to call the people of Israel back to their earlier covenant—in reality had created, invented, or forged this "forgotten" past and, by the same token, fashioned the Deity himself. As Darmesteter puts it: "The prophets, who according to the traditional conceptions appear in times of defection to recall to Israel forgotten truths, are in reality the creators of these truths, and prophecy, in place of being the flower of Judaism, is its very root." In effect, Renan went so far as to regard "the successive revelations of Jehovah to the legendary ancestors of the race . . . the revelation from Sinai and the colossal figure of Moses transformed from the leader of the exodus to the legislator . . . and all this drama of national history"—in short, all of the narrative history of ancient Israel—"merely a sublime fiction."[15] What was nonfictional and nonmythical, and therefore permanent and true in the ancient Israelite tradition, was the resounding voice of the prophetic exhortation tirelessly admonishing the people to repair themselves to the blessed way of justice and to righteousness.

3. Islam, the Arab Religion: Abraham Kuenen

Abraham Kuenen, the Dutch Arabist and biblical scholar whom we encountered in chapter 3 in the company of Tiele, Chantepie de la Saussaye, and others, was in fact in agreement with Renan, to the extent that he, too, would trace the roots of Christianity back to the Hebrew prophets. Kuenen considered this prophetic tradition not as an ethnic and idiosyncratic disposition of desert nomads but as a kernel of true universalism whose full realization,

---

14. James Darmesteter, "The Prophets of Israel," in *Selected Essays of James Darmesteter* (1895), 23.

15. Darmesteter, "The Prophets of Israel," 23, 27.

however, came about only with the advent of Christianity. The general idea was not new: that the essence of the Israelite religion, which supposedly made this particular Semitic tradition unique and different from all other Semitic religions in the ancient Near East, came to fruition only with Christianity. But what the nineteenth-century formulation added to the familiar idea was that, just as this feature of the biblical tradition was being elevated, it was also lifted away and made separate from the "national life" of the Jews. With this conceptual maneuver, Kuenen made it possible to address the conundrum of how the universal religion of Christ, a world religion, could have originated in anything so particular and localized as the tribal life of the Jews firmly in the grip of a national religion, if ever there was one. As Kuenen puts it in his *National Religions and Universal Religions*:

> If we judge Judaism by its first establishment, we must attribute a rigidly national and exclusive character to it. Though not denying this, I have nevertheless asserted that it was not without the internal leaven of universalism. And if it really had appropriated this treasure bequeathed by the prophets, you may reasonably ask where it had concealed it!
> To begin with, let us note that the Jewish religion was only in appearance a sub-section of the Jewish national life. In reality, it had an independent existence.[16]

Kuenen thus credited the Jews with laying hold of universal religion for the first time in history, and at the same time he granted to them only the custodial status of foster parents who hid the universal genius of their offspring until the appropriate moment, just as the Hebrew parents of the infant Moses are said to have done; and in the end they, too, had to relinquish their right of sole custody.

Thus Kuenen explicates succinctly the fundamental fissure within Jewish history—the splitting of the "leaven of universalism" that lies at the core of Judaism from Jewish national life. Predictably, Kuenen goes on to suggest that this deep inner split finds its "strongest proof" in the subsequent history of the Diaspora. In this view, the Jews themselves came to testify, albeit in a peculiar fashion, to the nonnational, nonethnic universalism inherent in their religion by becoming a nationless nation, by stubbornly insisting on remaining the chosen people of the God who would finally deny them that very status. The

16. Abraham Kuenen, *National Religions and Universal Religions* (1882), 180; cited in the text by page number hereafter.

Jews, in other words, are those who submit to the fundamental contradiction of Judaism. By this reckoning, Christianity became what it is (a distinct and separate religion) by literally growing out of this fix. This could happen because, presumably, the Christians were not "ethnically Jewish," as we say today, and because, somehow, their own nature made them refuse to be bound by such an impossible nationhood.

Seen in this way, the difference in the historical developments of the two world religions becomes clear. On the one hand, the Aryan universalism of Buddhism, once adopted by non-Aryans, turned ethnic and particular and subsequently stagnated hopelessly, languishing until the nineteenth century, when the original font of its universalism was recovered by European philology. The universalism of the Israelite religion, on the other hand, was once and for all liberated by the very people who had usurped and wrested it from its national origin; Jewish universalism was rescued from its own contradiction and was fulfilled precisely by crossing over to the Gentile Christians.

In contradistinction to both these cases, the history of Islam, in Kuenen's relentlessly damning account, represents an instance of reversion and regression from the beginning. It is a case where a particularistic—and, for that reason, arbitrary and capricious—religion is forged out of preexisting universalistic traditions, and the resulting forgery is masqueraded as something universal. As a matter of fact, Kuenen claims repeatedly in *National Religions and Universal Religions*, it was precisely Islam's disregard for the universal that caused it to be successfully imposed upon other nations. His claim, in other words, is that Islam's spiritual narrowness accounts for the high degree of its success in spreading beyond its native (Arab) borders. Here, then, the fact of its transnational existence is judged to be clear proof of its deficiency in universalism. Kuenen puts the onus of this defect squarely on the prophet-founder, Mohammed:

[T]his we may lay to his account—less as a fault than as a striking evidence of spiritual immaturity—that the difference between the national and the universal had never entered into his mind, so that he could see no difficulty in laying upon Persians and Greeks what was exclusively adopted for Arabs. And this, again, is connected with what I might call the artificial origin of Islam. Mohammed made Islam out of elements which were supplied to him very largely from outside, and which had a whole history beyond them already, so that he could take them up as they were without further elaboration. The sifting of the national from the universal, which was accomplished in other instances in and by the life of the people, had not taken place in the preparation of Islam. Inasmuch as Mohammed places himself in the line of God's previous revelations to Israel and to the Christians, and appears as completing them and setting the seal upon them, nothing is wanting to the universalism of his own prophetic consciousness; and yet in his religion itself—just because of its origin—we miss the true character of universalism. (33–34)

The undeniably vast reach of Islam and its de facto transnationality—which could be and in fact were "mistaken" (by Tiele and others) as evidence of its universalism—are said by Kuenen to betray its opposite character. As Kuenen infers from his compatriot Veth's report on Java,[17] far from being the fulfillment of an intrinsic universalism, the hemispheric spread of Islam signifies its disingenuousness, its violence, and the danger it continues to pose to the rest of the world. For one thing, Kuenen points out, Islam in Java is merely "the official cloak that is stretched over native society" and, underneath it all, there is a horrific profusion of particulars that makes a mockery of unity and universality:

If a flap of this cloak be lifted here and there, the Buddhism brought to Java long ago by missionaries from Hindustan is revealed; and side by side, often in grotesque confusion with it, the Siwaïsm [Shivaism] brought by the Hindu colonists from their fatherland; and beneath it all lies the old popular animistic belief that has really lost none of its force for the masses. Nature-worship and spirit-worship are still the religion of the Javanese. Hindu and Mohammedan elements have linked themselves to them, and so that strange compound has been formed which is not inappropriately called "Javanism." (42–43)

Meanwhile, in cases where Islam is not a cloak but in earnest, those "Mohammedans in heart and soul" turn out to be at once victims and perpetrators of "fanaticism, constantly fired by colonists from Arabia and by pilgrims returning from Mekka, infectious too, like all fanaticism, [which] by its very nature, might lay hold of the masses of the population, and certainly makes them very dangerous subjects. But this infectiousness of the political idea of

17. Presumably, Kuenen refers to Pieter Johannes Veth (1814–95), author of several books on the Dutch East Indies, including the three-volume *Java* (1875–82).

Islam is no proof of its spiritual supremacy" (43). In short, the spread of Islam, where it is not a sham, is virulent.[18]

The infelicitous reality of Islam, infecting and endangering the farthest reaches of the globe, is once again attributed to the narrowness of its founder and of the Arab race, for, in Kuenen's judgment, "the Arabic nationality was not the cradle but the boundary-wall of Islam." After improbably remarking that he trusts he has not been unjust despite the stridency of his review, Kuenen goes on to concur with Dante, who in the first book of the *Divine Comedy* (canto 28) consigned Mohammed to one of the lowest circles of hell. As we recall, the poet describes the condition of the prophet's infernal existence roughly in this fashion: his body is split in half lengthwise, his gut spilling out, and in that manner he is marked and punished as "the sower of schism." Here is Kuenen's more technical rendition of Dante's poetic vision:

> For it was thus that [Dante] expressed . . . the fact that Islam is a side branch of Christianity, or better still, as we should now say, of Judaism: a selection as it were from Law and Gospel, made by an Arab and for Arabs, levelled to their capacity, and further supplemented—or must we say adulterated?—by national elements calculated to facilitate their reception of it. Thus derived from the long acknowledged documents of God's revelation, and presently entering the lists against them, Islam was destined, after a very brief period of growth and development, to stereotype itself once for all and assume its unalterable shape. (57–58)

This anti-Islamic (and more broadly anti-Semitic) pronouncement doubtless found considerable resonance among his contemporaries. In fact, this opinion can be safely described as pervasive, and the following passage from John Arnott MacCulloch's *Religion, Its Origin and Forms* (1904), should serve as a

---

18. In this respect, many instances of the early-nineteenth-century European discussion of Java and the Dutch East Indies are particularly revealing. We are already familiar with Wilhelm von Humboldt's work on Kawi, a Javanese language with significant Sanskritic influence, as well as—as it happens—extensive "borrowing" from Arabic. While both are "foreign" imports, the former influence was considered positively transformative and ultimately ennobling, whereas the latter was deemed an alien imposition, destined to remain forever unassimilated, repellent. Even before Humboldt, Sir Thomas Stamford Raffles (1781–1826), a colonial official during the brief British reign on the island, set forth this idea in his two-volume *History of Java* (1817), the first such history to be written by a European. I thank Ronit Ricci for bringing this work to my attention.

good example, as would many others. The opening paragraph of the chapter entitled "Mohammedanism" reads:

Islam, the religion of submission, as it sprung up among a people who had preserved most faithfully their Semitic characteristics, has also remained faithful to Semitic religious conceptions. In nearly every case the gods of the Semites were lofty and terrible deities, before whom man crouched in fear, unlike those of the Aryan race. And Islam in its conception of Allah has made this the foundation-stone of their faith. It is a religion of fear, not of love; it is ultra-Calvinistic in its idea of destiny and its denial of free-will; while every one of its dogmas is marked out with the utmost precision and the frankest literalism. Probably for these very reasons it succeeded from the first among barbaric races, on whom fear, fact, and precision always make a deep impression. Thus the religious experience of an enthusiast, preached with authority, commended itself to millions, mostly of an inferior civilization, and became one of the so-called universal religions.

As to Islam's alleged rigidity and inability for growth, MacCulloch further comments:

More than any other religion Islam has shown itself unable to develop from within and to adapt itself to the varying needs of successive ages. The absolute authority of the Quran is the cause why, as [William Gifford] Palgrave says, "Islam is lifeless, and, because lifeless, cannot grow, cannot advance, cannot change, and was never intended to do so."[19]

In effect, the concept of Islam as the epitome of stifling rigidity, intolerance, and fanaticism was by this time in the public domain; it had become a familiar theme, mechanically repeated by one treatise after another, in flagrant disregard of the diversity and obvious malleability evidenced in the vast domain of the actual Islamic world. It may be added that, despite better, far more extensive scholarship on Islam available today, little has changed about this image.

4. Sufism, an Aryan Islam: Otto Pfleiderer

Although without much Orientalist learning, the German theologian Otto Pfleiderer (1839–1908) had opinions on Judaism and Islam generally consis-

---

19. John Arnott MacCulloch, *Religion, Its Origin and Forms* (1904), 167, 172.

tent with those of Renan and Kuenen. In a series of lectures given in Berlin late in his life, Pfleiderer, too, affirmed the seminal importance of the Hebrew prophets to the biblical tradition, calling the religion of Israel "the prophetic religion in a high sense."[20] Like Kuenen, he also held the attendant view that the ancient Israelites and their direct ethnic descendents, the Jews, were not true to the spirit of the prophets but instead had created around this spiritual core an ossified religion of legalism and ritualism.[21] It was as though, as far as the Jews were concerned, the voice of the prophets had indeed come from afar and from an alien world, bearing a universal salvific message. As this message was showered upon them, they did not grasp its import, but at least they recorded it faithfully. The resultant scriptural legacy, the Hebrew Bible—or as Christians would have it, the Old Testament—was from the beginning a gift to the whole world, yet it was to remain for a time in the hands of a particularly provincial people, or as Renan put it, "a small tribe established in an outlandish corner of Syria." While the treasure had been thus entrusted to the Jews, according to Pfleiderer, Judaism proper—Judaism as the religion of the Jewish people—always tended toward formality and calcification, toward exteriority of laws and ceremonials.[22]

20. Pfleiderer, *Religion and Historic Faiths*, 211; cited in the text by page number hereafter. At the same time, he checks the theologically deviant direction of Renan's thought with these artless words: "Some have thought that the flight of the Israelites from Egypt and the person of Moses are mere fictions. This is going too far; the matter is not as bad as that. As far as the person of Moses is concerned, careful research students of to-day are of one opinion, that, much as legend may have woven fables about him, yet he was a historical figure of great importance" (214).

21. Pfleiderer also opines, however, that the prophetic spirit was not entirely lost to the Jews, and the legacy of the prophets produced further results in the form of certain other "writings" included in the Bible. Yet he argues that these came into existence despite the priestly religion that is the predominant character of Judaism: "Within the hard shell of external legality, the better spirit of the ideal religion of the prophets did live on and produced new and valuable fruit. At the same time that the sensuous sacrificial services which were so little to the taste of the prophets were being carried on with ever-increasing pomp at the temple, there arose the spiritual service of God without sacrifice, through scriptural edification in the synagogue. Where formerly the prophetic belief in God had been the possession of a few individuals, now it could be acquired by all the members of the Jewish congregation as their personal conviction and spiritual attitude. The most beautiful fruits of this internalization and application of religion to the experiences of man's daily life were the Psalms, and the wisdom books (Proverbs, Ecclesiastes, Job). Their ideal of piety is not the ritualistic saintliness of the priestly code, but a clean heart and noble deed in the fear of and the trust in God" (*Religion and Historic Faiths*, 239).

22. Predictably, Christianity is depicted by Pfleiderer with an image that perfectly reverses Judaism's legalistic ceremonialism. He deems the "mythical ideas" of miracles that have been part

Pfleiderer's view of Islam is an extension of this prescribed outlook on the Semitic national character. Whatever narrow and parochial characteristics could be attributed to the nation of ancient Israelites were only amplified in the case of Islam. Indeed, they were exaggerated to the point of appearing at once alarming and ridiculous. Thus Islam is characterized by its vociferous claim and its meritless presumption of universality, by the general backwardness of its subscribers, its belatedness, its derivativeness. There is hardly a more succinct and more revealing example of this quick-stroke caricature than the opening paragraph of Pfleiderer's final lecture in *Religion and Historic Faiths*:

> Islam, the religion of Mohammed, is the latest among the historical religions, a late after-impulse of the religion-forming power of the Semitic race. Founded by the prophet Mohammed under Jewish and Christian influences among the half-barbaric Arabic people in the seventh century, Islamism shares the monotheistic, rigidly theocratic and legalistic character of Judaism, without its national limitation; with Christianity, it shares the claim and propagating impulse of world-religion, but without the wealth of religious thought and motives and without the mobility and the capacity for development which belongs to a world religion. It might be maintained, probably, that Islamism is the Jewish idea of theocracy carried out on a larger scale by the youthful national vigor of the Arabians, well calculated to discipline raw barbaric peoples, but a brake on the progress of free human civilization. (274)

Here, what was implicit in Kuenen's claim becomes overt. The logic seems to be that, despite Islam's de facto transnational spread, it is not to be taken as a world religion because, in reality, it is but an inflated national religion, a national religion transgressing beyond its own proper boundaries; its universal pretensions merely reflect the expansionist ambition of the Arab nation. The much-rumored virulence of Islam, that is, its dangerous character, seems to boil down to this penchant for border aggression. This, one might surmise, is

---

of Christianity and of the New Testament "merely the shell, in which lay hidden the actual experience of the present redeeming power of faith and love." In the last analysis, the relation between Judaism and Christianity becomes more tenuous and contingent than the conjointly canonical status of the Old and the New Testaments might suggest. In his words, "the Christian belief in salvation," which he claims is the essential nature of the religion, "gathered up in itself all the truths contained in the religions and the philosophies of its time," and Judaism turned out to be just one of many such preexisting entities with which Christianity "shares" certain characteristics (ibid., 271).

what makes Islam more menacing than Judaism, for, if the latter represents stubborn resistance to the New Truth, the former threatens violence against it. In either case, the two principal representatives of the Semitic peoples were denied any possibility of transcendence beyond their own narrow ethnicity, whereas, as we recall, the residents of certain city-states in Greece were credited with just such capacity. Why this was so, and why it should be so self-evident, was no longer a question worth expending much European thought on at the end of the nineteenth century. There was only some vague recollection from the previous half century or more, a distant echo of the clamor about the full inflection of the Indo-Europeans versus the inchoate, imperfect, delimited inflection of the Semites.

Pfleiderer's frank expression in the passage quoted above is useful in that it brings into plain view the major components of the stereotypical image of Islam that had by then gained predominance in Europe. The passage also explains why, for Pfleiderer as well as for Kuenen, Islam was not to be considered a world religion, and that this matter, moreover, was a question of quality (i.e., the intrinsic nature of the religion) rather than quantity (the actual number of people or variety of peoples who happened to pledge allegiance to it). More specifically, it was Pfleiderer's opinion that Islam was disqualified from designation as a world religion because of its abject poverty of spiritual substance and, again, its essential nature inimical to "mobility," "development," and "freedom." Indeed, he suggests, the legalism and ritualism characteristic of the Semitic religions were ineluctable consequences of this deficiency: "The greater the poverty of spiritual content in the teaching, the more minute are the details of the ceremonial prescribed, down to the most minute" (283).

Furthermore, although the august singularity of the omnipotent God insisted upon by the Muslims might seem a lofty enough idea, this is no indication of their doctrinal height or spiritual depth, Pfleiderer implies, since this image of the Deity was merely modeled on the all too powerful ruler of the temporal domain, a tyrant typical of Oriental nations:

The fundamental dogma [of Islam] is that of the unity of God; but concerning the nature of God, Mohammed made no deeper reflections. He conceived God as the supermundane, almighty ruler, similar to an Oriental despot; terrible in his anger and then again benevolent, delaying judgment in his benevolence, arbitrary in reward and punishment, with a will irresistible as inconceivable, demanding blind submission of men and even then his grace uncertain. This all-deciding freedom of God's despotic will was expressed, though without logical completeness, in the form of an absolute predestination. Mohammed had no difficulty in contributing even immoral features, such as revenge and deception, which naturally belong to the typical Oriental despot, to his idea of God. (283)

This mirroring of the mundane upon the supermundane, that is, the projection of the attributes of the earthly tyrant upon the figure of the supposedly almighty heavenly ruler, goes hand in hand with Islam's negative vision of this world:

This gloomy view of God corresponds to a pessimistic view of the world; the world is compared to a dung-heap full of decaying bones, and its misery is so great that only the tortures of hell exceed it. Just as horrible as the hell, so joyous is the description of the heavenly paradise, whose drinking-bouts shall compensate the pious for the prescribed abstinence from the enjoyment of wine during life on earth. (283–84)

The gruesome depiction of the world seems to rival, or possibly surpass, that of Buddhism (whose pessimism and turning away from the world, as we recall, was viewed by European observers like Monier-Williams as its worst feature). Not only is such pessimism retrogressive and unmodern, an obvious implication here seems to be that all Islamic theology—its doctrines of God, of salvation, of retribution—is rather silly, well nigh infantile. At the same time, this immaturity of reflective imagination is presumed to be commensurate with the barbarism of the nations who embrace Islam.

It is not clear exactly where Pfleiderer derived these condescending views of Islamic philosophy, as there is no specific citation provided in the published lectures. Nor is it certain, for that matter, to what degree he was acquainted with the actual historical and contemporary conditions of the so-called Oriental nations. It might be fairly surmised that, whatever his immediate sources, those ideas were in the air, since one can easily find them voiced in countless other contemporary texts.

Pfleiderer's lecture on Islam was to be the final of the series he delivered, and it may seem an awkward ending indeed to conclude with such unflattering remarks on the last religion to be discussed, a religion that was purportedly at once late in coming and early in the developmental scale. It was perhaps unfortunate from the standpoint of his narrative design that the latest major religion to appear on the world historical stage was merely a local religion born of a particular Semitic people, for, it would seem, any such provincial tradition would prove ultimately irrelevant to the universal future of humankind.

Not surprisingly, this judgment on Islam stands in sharp contrast to Pfleiderer's concluding statement on Christianity—the subject of the preceding chapter. Christianity is a religion of universal salvation, Pfleiderer proclaims, "gather[ing] up in itself all the truths contained in the religions and philosophies of its time." In this gathering of past wisdoms, ancient Judaism was only one of many tributary streams (272). The all-encompassing capacity of Christianity assures its genuine universality: "Thus it is that Christianity became the religion of the religions, conquered the old world and led up to the new" (273).

As it turns out, however, the exposition on the unreflective parochialism of the Arabs was not Pfleiderer's last word on Islam. As if to salvage, with one small gesture, the entire narrative procession of all the "historic faiths" of the world, he provides at the end of his last lecture several pages in which he discusses certain "unorthodox" strands within the greater fabric of Islam, strands that are said to be distinctly and uncharacteristically rich in philosophic exploration and spiritual contemplation. In particular, he grants the honor of the last and the most prominent place to Sufism. This tradition of Islamic mysticism has often been evocatively represented in the European imagination by the ethereal image of a ring of whirling dervishes in white skirts, entranced in dancing meditation. The first statement Pfleiderer offers regarding this philosophical tribe of elegantly dressed, otherworldly contemplatives is the following:

> A peculiarity of Persian Islamism, not less interesting is Sufism, a mystical-speculative tendency, some of which was deeply pious and given to flights of high thinking. Certain it is that this was not a genuine product of Arabian Islamism, even though it must remain undecided whether it owes its origin to ancient Persian, Indian or Neo-platonic gnosticism. (287)

Here, again, what seems to be the most precious, most profound, and most enduring aspect of this religion—an aspect consisting of deep piety and mysticism, lofty contemplation, and speculative ability—is found to be essentially alien to Islam proper, insofar as the latter is defined as the religion of the Arabs. Should it come as a surprise, then, that this jewel-like kernel, which "Arabian Islamism" has surrounded and entombed for centuries within the iron cage of its ethnicity, turns out to be not Arab in origin at all but perhaps Persian, maybe Indian, or possibly Greek (Neoplatonic)—in whichever case, Aryan? Pfleiderer, at any rate, appears much more at home in expounding the theological details of this purportedly non-Arabic facet of Islam:

> According to the Sufi theory, the world is a flowing out of and flowing back into God. The soul of man is part of the divine being, and its destiny is union with God, which is perfected in three planes. Upon the first plane, the plane of law, God is held to be the Lord beyond who desires to be worshipped with all the traditional ceremonies. Upon the second plane, comes the knowledge that external works are without value for those who know, and in their stead there must be placed an ascetic freeing of the spirit from sensuality. Through continuous concentration of thought, one may arrive finally at the condition of enthusiasm and ecstasy which, by frequent recurrence, leads to the third and highest plane, upon which, God is no longer sought outside of one's self either by ritualistic or ascetic works, but upon which, the immanence in one's own spirit come into consciousness. For the wise man and the mystic who has attained this knowledge, the varying doctrines and ordinances of the different religions have lost their meaning. (287–88)

Thus, in the heart of Sufism, or Aryan Islam, Pfleiderer seems to find himself in strangely familiar territory. Seen through the mystic kernel of Sufism, all the parochial and miserly laws, childish dogmas, and ceremonial encrustations that have constituted orthodox Islam seem to fall away. In effect, through deep contemplation, this kernel would come to seem something other than Islam proper, or Islam in the usual sense.[23] And it seems to promise that those who set their mind to it could hope to enter a realm where "the varying doctrines and ordinances of the different religions have lost their meaning," or, perhaps, somewhere close to where "all the truths contained in the religions and philosophies" of the world were gathered up.

23. A contemporary text by John Arnott MacCulloch mentioned earlier similarly closes the chapter on Islam (also the last chapter of the book) with a laudatory account of Sufism, which simultaneously has the effect of further denigrating what is construed as Islam proper. Sufism, MacCulloch claims, is an attempt to "engraft on Islam principles wholly foreign to it," and it exhibits some pantheistic influence, possibly from Buddhism. He then goes on to conclude: "Obviously this is no native growth in Islam, but it has supplied Islam with some of its most rapturous and beautiful religious aspirations and poetry" (Religion, Its Origin and Forms, 173).

This kernel, in effect, would become a sphere more or less coeval with Christianity or, if not quite that, with something yet nameless but very much like Christianity of the future.

It is evident from a casual survey of the tracts published toward the end of the long nineteenth century that the views articulated by Kuenen and Pfleiderer—their decidedly negative, racially anxious, self-serving opinions about the one-time international superpower that was Islam—found much sympathy among their contemporaries. In the long run, however, Kuenen and Pfleiderer seem to have been on the wrong side of the debate when it came to the question of whether or not Islam should be counted among the world religions. For, by the turn of the century, the other side seems to have quietly won out, as the list of "world religions" by then minimally and unfailingly included Buddhism, Christianity, *and* Islam, and this list of three was already routinely presented with no particular argument or justification. Otto Pfleiderer, reputedly one of the original proponents of the *Religionsgeschichteschule*, may have been voicing his opposition to including Islam as late as 1906. But when a younger and more famous representative of the school, Ernst Troeltsch, wrote the little essay "Christianity and the History of Religion" in 1897, he was already taking the list of three "great world religions" for granted.[24] Two decades later, when Troeltsch's one-time colleague and friend Max Weber was writing a series of massive essays under the general title *Economic Ethic of the World Religions* (*Die Wirtschaftsethik der Weltreligionen*, 1916–1919),[25] the list was expanded still more to include Hinduism and Confucianism, and, with some important qualifications, what Weber called "ancient Judaism" (*das antike Judentum*); along the way, Weber went on to discuss certain attendant traditions, including "Taoism," "Sikhism," and "Shinto," with the result that the list of religions began to resemble ever more closely what is familiar today.

How and why this expansion of the list came about, how the number came to settle around ten, eleven, or thereabouts, why this sedimentation of what

24. Ernst Troeltsch, "Christianity and the History of Religion," in *Religion in History* (1991), 77–86. Concerning both the diversity of opinions and the commonality of intentions within the so-called history of religions school, see Ernst Troeltsch, "The Dogmatics of the History-of-Religions School," originally published in 1913, and included in the same volume.

25. The collection as a whole never came to print, but see Weber's essay of the same name, translated by H. H. Gerth and C. Wright Mills as "The Social Psychology of the World Religions" (1958).

amounts to the standard list occurred in 1920s and 1930s, and why little has changed since then—these are questions requiring an extensive and multifaceted investigation, or rather, a long series of investigations. The third and last part of this book will include a chapter that names—albeit in a preliminary fashion, and without any claim for being exhaustive—some of the possible areas for further inquiry. As for now, in light of the foregoing examination, we may assess the taxonomic transformation and the movement toward the eventual institutionalization of the standard world religions list from the vantage point of the nineteenth century.

First, the specific controversy that made it meaningful to distinguish "world religions" from "national religions" in the first place had lost much of its significance by the beginning of the twentieth century, primarily, it seems, because the latter term fell out of use. At the same time, the decline of interest in this particular principle of classification seems to have left intact the specific representations of several major religions that had been vital components of the nineteenth-century system. These representations of major religions include the following key ideas: (1) Buddhism was originally a humanistic and humanitarian reform movement—much like Protestant Christianity was supposed to have been—that had arisen in opposition to an ethnic religion of India, that is, Hinduism. (2) Islam is an intrinsically Arab religion, Semitic in its essential nature, and its universalist intensions derive partly from the fact that its founder had drawn considerably from Jewish and Christian sources, partly from the Arabs' own transnational political ambition and their resistance to the advancing universalism of Christianity, modernity, and rationality. (3) The spiritual core of the biblical tradition is prophetic and transethnic, whereas rabbinic Judaism, or Judaism proper, is an ethnic tradition-formation endemic to a particular Semitic people. (4) Christianity emerged not from this Semitic religion but directly out of the ancient prophetic tradition, and therefore it was from the beginning transnational and transethnic in nature. Furthermore, what is largely implicit but consistent in all of these representations is the idea that the national spirit of the Semites, apparently by its very nature, was bound to remain just that, national and ethnic, whereas those nations of the Aryans—whether Greece, Persia, or India—had shown in various epochs of their history the capacity to transcend their national particularities, hence, their propensity for universality. Consequently, as this train of thought went still further, it is the Aryan nations who either originated or brought to fruition all of the universals that the modern world would recognize and value, namely, science, art, systems of government based on law and individual freedom, as well as those universal(istic) religions, or "world religions" in the original, strict sense.

It now appears, then, that what should be called "uniquely universal" is not Christianity—a religion saddled with a complicated, compromised, and contested legacy—but instead, the Aryans. At the close of the nineteenth century, it seems, European people everywhere no longer felt the need to wonder why this should have been the case—no need to explain the intrinsic universalism of the Aryans or the inescapable national/ethnic/racial limitation of the Semites and, for that matter, of everyone else. It was as though, at that point in history, the recently established new world order, or European hegemony in the military, political, and economic spheres could be trusted to speak for itself. Only a very faint echo seems to have remained of the idea, once heard distinctly and clamorously, that, somehow, all this had to do with inflection.

7

Philologist Out of Season

F. Max Müller on the Classification of Language and Religion

Even in his own lifetime, it was not infrequently said that Friedrich Max Müller (1823–1900) had outlived his fame and usefulness. His reputation of being already somewhat out of date and out of step with his own time seems rather odd, especially given that he is still acknowledged as one of the most accomplished Sanskritists of the nineteenth century, and his preeminent position among the progenitors of the scientific study of religion remains largely unchallenged.[1] Indeed, whether out of genuine appreciation or merely out of habit, the science of religion today dutifully traces one of its beginnings to Müller's application of a century of philological scholarship—in particular, the genealogical taxonomy of languages—to the classification of religions. This classification system provided the foundation for the fifty-volume compilation he edited, The Sacred Books of the East, the second of his monumental contributions to the emergent field, a project he undertook immediately upon the completion of his much touted critical edition of the Rig Veda. Was he, then, the figure most instrumental in bringing a new classificatory regime to the science of religion, and thus most responsible for establishing and authorizing something very close to today's list of world religions?

An answer in the affirmative is naturally expected—why else would he occupy the founding position?—but the condition for an answer seems to be more complicated than it may first appear. It is true that he introduced a broadly tripartite division of religions based on a philological classification system; he also named eight individual religions—that is, a majority among the most commonly enumerated world religions—as religions of principal importance. His list of major religions thus differed fundamentally from the exclusivist list of universal(istic) world religions debated by scholars such as C. P. Tiele,

1. By far the most substantial consideration of Müller's position in the history of the study of religion is provided by Lourens P. van den Bosch's recent monograph, Friedrich Max Müller (2002). Norman J. Girardot's The Victorian Translation of China (2002) is an even larger monograph, principally focused on the Sinologist, James Legge, but it also offers a valuable detailed view of Müller's activities. For a review of recent publications on Müller, see Tomoko Masuzawa, "Our Master's Voice" (2003).

Abraham Kuenen, and Otto Pfleiderer. In comparison to these scholars, then, Müller appears to have assumed a greater pluralism and more generously inclusive recognition of multiple religions, and thereby prepared the way toward the twentieth-century paradigm. Or so it seems.

Müller's difference from his contemporaries, however, was more than a matter of numbers. Rather, he was preoccupied with altogether different problems and ideas concerning the origin and development of languages and of religions. Some of his ideas were so strange as to put him at odds not only with the fellow scientists of religion but, more fundamentally, with a great majority of the philologists of the century.

Müller's name is closely associated with the term "Aryan," so much so that one easily gets an impression that he either invented or instituted the very notion, and that he generally valorized things Aryan, whether language, religion, culture, or "race." As some of the foregoing expositions have begun to make evident, this impression is largely incorrect.[2] To begin, since Müller was a student of Eugène Burnouf and of Franz Bopp, he belonged to the third or the fourth generation of European Sanskritists. Furthermore, the highly charged speculative thinking about "Aryans" and "Semites" dates back to decades before his birth, when there was not yet settled terminology for these categories. What is less obvious and perhaps more surprising than this plain historical fact is how greatly Müller's own position diverged from those of his predecessors and his contemporaries, and how little this divergence has been noted to this day. He articulated some of these differences in published lectures and articles as well as personal letters, while some other differences are marked only by his silence. An example of the latter is what may be described as his profound indifference to the debate concerning the theoretical distinction between partic-

2. Often the ascription of "Aryanism" to Müller seems to be based on mere association. For instance, we find the following sequence of statements by J. P. Mallory: "Following the West's discovery of the wealth of Indic and Iranian literature, European scholars looked beyond Eden to seek their own more illustrious forebears in Central Asia, Iran and India. Although Indo-European and Indo-Germanic had both been coined early in the nineteenth century, Max Müller, and other linguists, encouraged the use of Aryan to describe the ancient Indo-Europeans. Naturally, if these early Aryans were the ancestors of the Europeans, then they too must have been part of the superior white race" (In Search of the Indo-Europeans [1989; reprint ed., 1999], 267). The rampancy of this association, leading to racist allegations, causes me to suspect that, in some instances, Friedrich Max Müller may have been confused with a Viennese philologist, Friedrich Müller (1834–98), author of the four-volume Grundriss der Sprachwissenschaft (Foundation of the science of language, 1876–88), a scholar with opinions on race and language significantly different from those of our Müller.

ularistic national religions (*Landesreligionen*) and universalistic world religions (*Weltreligionen*).

Silence, of course, does not necessarily imply active dissent. But whether or not he paid any attention to this Continental scholarly concern in the 1880s, he had already proposed altogether different grounds for classifying religions more than a decade earlier. At first sight, his system of classification seems to reproduce more faithfully than any other the taxonomy established by philology. As we have seen in the preceding few chapters, this taxonomy generated and endorsed the strongly hierarchical ordering of nations by attributing authenticity, creativity, freedom, and therefore the capacity for indefinite growth and expansion to some nations (variously called Sanskritic, Indo-European, or Aryan), while relegating other languages and nations to various branches of developmental dead-ends. This difference among peoples, according to the prevailing philological view, stemmed from the presence or absence of a particular grammatical form in their respective languages: inflection. As we shall see, Müller's peculiarity was due above all to his rejection of these inferences that animated the rest of the philological field.

In 1870 Müller gave a series of four lectures at the Royal Institution of Great Britain under the title "Introduction to the Science of Religion." After a few years of unofficial circulation in private and pirated editions, those lectures were finally published as a single volume in 1873. Some ten years earlier, he had taken the same podium for the first time, to deliver an also highly successful series of lectures on the topic of the science of language, and these lectures of 1861 were committed to print the same year.[3] It may be useful to consider, therefore, the origin of the science of religion out of the science of language—or, comparative religion out of comparative philology—as an arc spanning this

3. Müller began lecturing on the subject of comparative philology in 1851 at Oxford University, when he was appointed Deputy Taylorian Professor of Modern European Languages, apparently substituting for the incumbent, who had fallen ill and whom Müller succeeded in 1854 (F. Max Müller, *Life and Letters* [1902], 1:116–23). The first series of lectures was officially entitled "History and Origin of Modern Languages," but handwritten lecture notes (dated 1851) at the Bodleian Library shows an inscription on the back in Müller's hand: "My first course Comp. Phil." (Max Müller Papers, shelf mark 2353).

Müller actually gave two separate series of lectures on the subject at the Royal Institution, both published under the title *Lectures on the Science of Language*. The first series consisted of nine lectures delivered in April, May, and June of 1861, and the second series was delivered in twelve installments from February through May of 1863.

decade. The inextricable relation between the history of language and that of religion was such that, often during his lectures on the science of religion, he is found discoursing on the deeper stratum of language, dwelling tirelessly on what Humboldt once called "infinite details"—roots, syntax, and word endings—and seldom rising to the sphere of generality adequate for the presentation of any "characteristic features" or "defining beliefs" of this or that religion.

1. The Aristocracy of Book Religions

Both the venue in which Müller's lectures were delivered and the life circumstances of the lecturer at the time may be of some importance in situating the inaugural moment of the science of religion. The Royal Institution of Great Britain, founded in London in 1799, was one of several such organizations to arise in Europe following the first wave of the so-called scientific revolution and amid the industrial revolution, but also in the shadow of the momentous political revolution in France. It was established as a philanthropic society with the express purpose of promoting scientific research, disseminating knowledge, and facilitating the judicious application of new knowledge and technology for the betterment of the life of the commonwealth.[4] In material terms, the institution's considerable assets and operating costs were provided by proprietary donations and subscriptions from some of the wealthiest families and individuals of London society, some of whom were themselves scientists or science enthusiasts. For both the landed gentry and the lately affluent industrialists and financiers, science was of keen interest, as many of them were persuaded that the advancement of scientific knowledge and its application were vitally necessary for greater productivity of the land, factories, and mines they owned. At the same time, science and technology also promised to improve the lot of the poor (on whose labor their prosperity depended), hence reducing, as they hoped, the likelihood of underclass discontent, social unrest, and revolt against the existing regime. In addition to these long-range benefits, the proprietors and subscribers could also enjoy the privilege of attending lectures and demonstrations performed by some of the leading scientists of the day for their own edification and amusement. Thus it was that the Royal Institution became

4. For general information on the Royal Institution, the following publications narrate its history: Gwendy M. Caroe, The Royal Institution (1985), Morris Berman, Social Change and Scientific Organization (1978), Thomas Martin, The Royal Institution (1949), Frank A. J. L. James, ed., The Common Purpose of Life (2002). The Royal Institution still operates today at the same address in the same building as at the time of its founding. Its website (http://www.rigb.org) provides some useful information about its history.

the host to the illustrious careers of such aristocratic socialite-scientists as Sir Humphrey Davy—whose many useful inventions included the Davy lamp, an illumination device with lower risk of causing explosions in the mines—as well as enabling the extraordinary achievements of Davy's successor, a great scientist of extremely humble origin, Michael Faraday.

It was in this atmosphere of cutting-edge science (in particular, of natural philosophy, or what we today tend to call simply "science"), with politically conservative yet socially liberal philanthropic goals, that Max Müller brought his lectures on language.[5] Already a prominent scholar at the relatively young age of thirty-seven, Müller found before him what must have been an imposing audience, which included such Victorian luminaries as Frederick Denison Maurice and John Stuart Mill, not to mention Faraday himself, then in his last year as the director of the Royal Institution. Four months earlier, Müller had suffered a significant professional setback, failing to attain the chair of Sanskrit at Oxford University. According to the majority opinion then and now, this was a position he fully deserved, and it was denied him, reportedly, because of his foreign nationality as well as his questionable Christian orthodoxy in the eyes of the Anglican establishment.[6] (The position went to Monier Monier-

---

5. See note 3 above for background on the lectures of 1861 and 1863. Müller's were among the earliest lectures given at the Royal Institution on topics of human sciences. Coincidentally, an archival record at the Royal Institution shows that, concurrent with Müller's first few lectures on the science of language in April of 1861, Hermann Helmholtz (1821–94) was giving a total of nine lectures on topics ranging from "the natural law of conservation of energy" to "musical acoustics."

Early on in the very first lecture of 1861, Müller expressly claimed that the science of language, or comparative philology, was one of the natural sciences (or, in his own terminology, "physical sciences") rather than human sciences (or, as he calls them, "historical sciences"). See F. Max Müller, Lectures on the Science of Language, first series (1862), 31–32. This claim was repeatedly ridiculed by William Dwight Whitney, American Sanskritist and professor at Yale (see his Max Müller and the Science of Language [1892]). Whitney also scoffed at the very idea of the science of religion in his article "On the So-Called Science of Religion" (1881).

6. His candidacy had come about as a result of the sudden death of H. H. Wilson, his mentor and the supervisor of his Veda project since 1848. In addition to this loss, Müller's long-time benefactor and personal friend Baron Bunsen died the same year (1860). As for the record of his candidacy and the ensuing controversy, see "Testimonials and Letters Relating to the Election for the Boden Professorship of Sanskrit at Oxford, 1860–1861," Bodleian Library, Oxford, "Max Müller Papers," shelf mark c.2807. There is a wealth of contemporary evidence that this incident was much talked about internationally in academic circles, especially among Sanskrit scholars. Albrecht Weber, for example, wrote to Brian H. Hodgson in March 1861, referring to "Müller's defeat" at Oxford owing to "fanaticism in England." Weber comments that he was appalled

Williams instead.) In retrospect, however, this misfortune had the effect of launching Müller on a new career, as it ushered him into uncharted territory, to which his name came to be forever attached.[7] As it was reported later, it was in recompense for this disappointment that Oxford moved to create a new professorship in comparative philology specifically for him.[8] The new appointment came in 1868, making that year another significant landmark in the history of comparative studies.

Müller proposed a tripartite division, consisting of Aryan, Semitic, and a category he preferred to call "Turanian," as the governing taxonomy both in comparative philology and, a decade later, in comparative religion. When applied to the classification of religions, however, this system was predicated on another distinction, the one roughly corresponding to the present-day distinction (often silently but effectively maintained) between world religions and the rest (otherwise called primitive religions, or synonyms thereof). This latter divide was essentially a matter of literacy, that is, whether or not the technology of writing constituted an authoritative component of the tradition: there were those religions with sacred books, and those without. It might be suspected that this stress on the significance of scriptural culture and of writing technology reflected the proclivity of the philologists, professionally obsessed as they were with dead letters. In *Introduction to the Science of Religion*

"to see that such things are possible in England, the fatherland of freedom and progress" (B. H. Hodgson's autograph book, folio 98, Hodgson Papers, Royal Asiatic Society, London).

7. As his widow related in 1902: "There can be no doubt that it was a keen disappointment to Max Müller, but he lived long enough to trace his almost unique position later in the world of letters, and the influence he was able to exert on religious thought in England, to this very disappointment. Had he been successful, he . . . would no doubt have remained to the last . . . 'the first Sanskrit scholar in Europe.' It was the Chair of [Comparative] Philology, founded some six years later specially for him . . . that led him on from the Science of Language to the Sciences of Thought and Religion" (*Life and Letters*, 1:242).

8. "During the winter months a movement had been going on in Oxford for the foundation of a Chair of Comparative Philology, which was carried out in the May Term, with the proviso in the statute of foundation that Max Müller was to be the first Professor, if he would accept the post. He was deeply gratified by this mark of esteem from the resident members of the University, and it relieved him of the duties of the Chair of Modern Languages, added to his salary, and enabled him to devote all his time and energies to his own line of studies. . . . 'Professor Max Müller,' says a contemporary notice, 'enjoys the high honour—an honour the more signal as he is a foreigner—of occupying the first Professorship ever founded at Oxford by the University Corporation itself; all previous Professorships having been established either by royal benefactions or private announcements'" (ibid., 350).

(1873), however, Müller ascribes the valorization of "book religions" to the Orientals themselves:

> Among Eastern nations it is not unusual to distinguish between religions that are founded on a book, and others that have no such vouchers to produce. The former are considered more respectable, and, though they may contain false doctrine, they are looked upon as a kind of aristocracy among the vulgar and nondescript crowd of bookless or illiterate religions.[9]

Following his assertion about the source of this distinction, Müller duly cautions that those prized canonical texts are not really records of the original doctrines, as the texts themselves often claim, but rather later reflections or reconstructions. Even so, he then goes on to muse, "how few are the religions which possess a sacred canon, how small is the aristocracy of real book-religions in the history of the world!"

Among the world's aristocracy of literate nations, Müller naturally grants priority to two groups in particular, or as he puts it in language reminiscent of other philologists of his time, "the two races that have been the principal actors in that great drama which we call the history of the world, the Aryan and the Semitic." This opinion, however, does not lead him along the usual route to the presumption of predestined hegemony for Euro-Christianity. Instead, in an ensuing passage, he observes matter-of-factly that in the Aryan family as well as in the Semitic,

> two members only of each race can claim the possession of sacred code. Among the Aryans, the Hindu and the Persians; among the S[e]mites, the Hebrews and the Arabs. In the Aryan family the Hindus, in the Semitic family the Hebrews, have each produced two book-religions; the Hindus have given rise to Brahmanism and Buddhism; the Hebrews to Mosaism and Christianity. Nay, it is important to observe that in each family the third book-religion can hardly lay claim to an independent origin, but is only a weaker repetition of the first. Zoroastrianism has its sources in the same stratum which fed the deeper and broader stream of Vedic religion;[10]

---

9. F. Max Müller, Introduction to the Science of Religion (1873), 102; cited in the text by page number hereafter.

10. Müller was to revise this opinion of Zoroastrianism somewhat later, especially after he became cognizant of James Darmesteter's work on the Zend-Avesta.

Mohammedanism springs, as far as its most vital doctrines are concerned, from the ancient fountain-head of the religion of Abraham, the worshipper and the friend of the one true God. (103–4)

Here, six of the time-honored "book religions" of the world are identified in their genealogical relation to one another.[11] In addition to rendering the configuration of the two groups in a diagram (reproduced opposite), Müller also delineates the parallelism in the later development of the "two religious stems":

Buddhism, which is the offspring of, but at the same time marks a reaction against the ancient Brahmanism of India, withered away after a time on the soil from which it had sprung, and assumed its real importance only after it had been transplanted from India, and struck root among Turanian nations in the very centre of the Asiatic continent. Buddhism, being at its birth an Aryan religion, ended by becoming the principal religion of the Turanian world.

The same transference took place in the second stem. Christianity, being the offspring of Mosaism, was rejected by the Jews as Buddhism was by the Brahmans. It failed to fulfil its purpose as a mere reform of the ancient Jewish religion, and not till it had been transferred from Semitic to Aryan ground, from the Jews to the Gentiles, did it develop its real nature and assume its world-wide importance. Having been at its birth a Semitic religion, it became the principal religion of the Aryan world. (105–6)

The two lines of descent of the Aryan and the Semitic religion groups—if we can refer to them as such, in analogy with language groups—are indeed remarkably symmetrical in Müller's configuration.[12] Extending this diagram further, Müller adds to the list of six Aryan and Semitic religions two more, rep-

11. The terminology, of course, diverges slightly from present-day conventions; thus "Mosaism" for "Judaism," "Brahmanism" for "Hinduism."

12. Since this delineates the relation of descent, it would be awkward to make the case that Christianity was the culmination and fulfillment of all other religions, as many contemporary theologians did, or that Christianity was the embodiment of what was inherently universal. Nor would it be particularly compelling to claim that what was universal in ancient Judaism was not really Jewish, as some other, more philologically inclined scholars did. One context in which Müller does definitively champion Christianity as "universalistic" is in his suggestion that "[i]t was Christianity which first broke down the barriers between Jew and Gentile, between Greek and barbarian, between the white and the black. Humanity is a word which you look for in vain in Plato or Aristotle; the idea of mankind as one family, as the children of one God, is an idea of

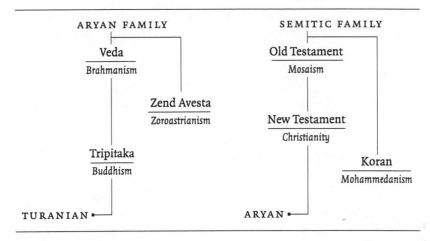

resenting the "aristocracy" of the Turanian group, but both originating in a single nation: "China became the mother, at almost the same time, of two religions, each founded on a sacred code—the religion of Confucius . . . and the religion of Lao-tse, the former resting on the Five King and the Four Shu, the latter on the Tao-te-king."[13] Without so much as a pause, he goes on to sum up: "With these eight religions the library of the Sacred Books of the whole human race is complete . . . written in Sanskrit, Pâli, and Zend, in Hebrew, Greek, and Arabic, lastly in Chinese" (106). In a way, then, Müller's list of eight defines the

---

Christian growth; and the science of mankind, and of the languages of mankind, is a science which, without Christianity, would never have sprung into life" (*Lectures on the Science of Language*, 128). It is noteworthy here, however, that the contrasting examples for national or ethnic culture, for him, is not the Hebrews or the Semites but the Greeks.

13. The prestige of the ancient Chinese religion and civilization in the eyes of Europe is of course older than the European discovery of Sanskrit; this prestige was especially tied to their much venerated classical texts. As late as 1812, this respectful view of the Chinese "sacred books" was expressed, in the context of a theory—by then rather archaic—which suggested that no one, including the Chinese, was originally ignorant of the five books of Moses: "The theology of the ancient Chinese, who lived before the time of Moses, was, as to its juridical and moral institutions, much the same as is contained in the ancient part of the Bible; but the ancient Chinese, who lived after the time of Moses, followed the order of the Hebrews, by dividing their Shu-King, or SACRED BOOK, into five parts. They seem to have approved of the Pentateuch, like the sacred code of the Samaritans, and of their Persian neighbours, the laws and precepts of their SHU-KING are much the same. This book is held in the highest estimation among them, for knowledge concerning the origin of the world, the fall of man, and the worship of one God" (John Bellamy, *The History of All Religions* [1812], 131–32).

purview of the science of religion in the strictest sense; the science of a religion is fully realizable only through a close and concerted study of some long venerated texts and, of course, their language.

This is not to say, however, that Müller recognizes no other religion beyond this literate aristocracy. Far from it, as he explains:

> But after we have collected this library of the sacred books of the world, with their indispensable commentaries, are we then in possession of the requisite materials for studying the growth and decay of the religious convictions of mankind at large? Far from it. The largest portion of mankind,—ay, and some of the most valiant champions in the religious and intellectual struggles of the world, would be unrepresented in our theological library. (116)

Indeed, according to Müller, there are countless other religions, both lofty and humble, some known to the present only through archaic monuments, fragmentary myths, and undecipherable inscriptions, some others discernible to the European eye only by the columns of smoke that rise from their rustic altars deep in the forest, far across the sea. The "sacred books" of such religions are either irretrievably lost or materially nonexistent to begin with. Book or no book, Müller asserts, religion is and has been everywhere in the world where humans have lived.[14] In a swift sweep across the globe in a matter of several paragraphs, Müller unfurls what he calls a "world-wide panorama" of religions (122). Having thus impressed upon the reader the formidable breadth of such a survey, he proceeds to address the fundamental question, namely, how to begin, how to go about understanding the vast and various panorama of religions. Müller responds to this question with one of his most celebrated sayings, "Divide et impera," which he calls an "old saying" and translates "somewhat freely" as "Classify and conquer." How, then, do we classify?

The distinction between national religions and world religions apparently

---

14. It is significant, though hardly surprising, that Müller presumed the absolute universality and ubiquity of religion across the world and throughout history. But what comes on the heels of this assumption is a distinction, somewhat less typical of his time, between religion as a universal, permanent endowment of humankind and religion as particular, varying, and changeable phenomenon. This distinction shows itself, for instance, in the following phrasing: "I do not mean religion as a silent power, working in the heart of man; I mean religion in its outward appearance, religion as something outspoken, tangible, and definite, that can be described and communicated to others. We shall find that in that sense religion lies within a very small compass" (Müller, *Introduction to the Science of Religion*, 153).

has no role in Müller's classificatory system. The pairing of the two terms does not occur anywhere in his lectures.[15] Instead, he considers at some length a few of the more traditional categories, and in particular he dwells on the time-honored distinction between revealed religions and natural religions, if only to dismiss in the end all of the traditionalist distinctions as scientifically useless.[16] Having thus done away with the prevailing systems of categorizing religions, he avers at the conclusion of the second lecture that

> [t]he only scientific and truly genetic classification of religions is the same as the classification of languages, and . . . particularly in the early history of the human intellect, there exists the most intimate relationship between language, religion, and nationality—a relationship quite independent of those physical elements, the blood, the skull, or the hair, on which ethnologists have attempted to found their classification of the human race. (143)

Here, while establishing the identity of language, religion, and nationality in the prehistoric or early historic times, Müller pointedly dissociates the question of language from those factors pertaining to physiological and biological determination. As we have seen in the previous chapters, these factors, components of the racialist notion, were coming into prominence just at that time, and they subsequently came to be associated with the idea of Aryan supremacy.[17] At this particular juncture, however, Müller does not belabor the

15. Nor does it occur anywhere else in his corpus that I am aware of. I must concede that this is only to the best of my knowledge. Müller's textual production is very large even for a Victorian writer, and I have not read all of his writings with this particular question in mind. However, I believe I have covered a significant portion thereof—and the most likely places—and found no mention of national versus universal religions. The term "world religion" itself is generally absent from his writings.

16. Müller contends that the question as to whether a given religion is founded on revelation—meaning, roughly, religious authority descended from suprahuman source—cannot but be a matter of religious advocacy, not an impartial description. To call a certain religion "revealed" amounts to claiming it is a true religion coming from above, in contradistinction to others that are "natural," that is, grown from the ground up, or mundanely and humanly manufactured, hence made-up, "false" religions. Likewise, with respect to classification in terms of national versus individual religions, and in terms of monotheistic, dualistic, and polytheistic religions, Müller discounts the scientific viability of these categories (Introduction to the Science of Religion, 122–43).

17. As will be discussed presently, for the rest of his life, Müller was to insist on the distinction between the classification of language on the one hand and the divisions of people in terms

point but instead moves on to consider briefly—in a speculative fashion, leaning on such philosophical authorities as Schelling and Hegel—the initial unity of language, religion, and nationality before the historical processes of dispersion, contact, and conquest came to complicate the relation.

With the genealogical isomorphism—but not identity—between the language groups and the religion groups thus established, Müller raises an unexpected question next: Why such groupings in the first place? This is an odd question. If one's theory of the origin of language is really genealogical, or "genetic" as Müller frequently calls it, the question as to whence comes the "family resemblance" among the closely related languages is seemingly nonsensical, since it would be answered tautologically. The answer, in effect, would be that the resemblance is among kin, and the matter calls for no further explanation. That such a question could arise at this point for Müller therefore must be a warning: it suggests that in his frame of mind there was a significant difference, in fact a disjuncture, between the descent of language and the "natural" descent of a family, supposedly determined by biology and genetic transmission.[18] Here is Müller, describing the "descent" of the three distinct groupings of religions and of languages:

> These three classes of religion are not to be mistaken, as little as the three classes of language, the Turanian, the Semitic, and the Aryan. They mark three events in the most ancient history of the world, events which have determined the whole fate of the human race. (Müller, Introduction to the Science of Religion, 159)

But is a sequence of generations, or descent, an event? What sort of "event" does Müller have in mind?

This may be the first moment in Introduction to the Science of Religion that allows us to detect Müller's unannounced, hitherto undetected departure from the prevailing theory of the origin, development, and diversity of human language. As it becomes evident presently, Müller dismissed unequivocally the idea that language grew and took shape as an outward expression of the innate spirit of

---

of physiological features, even though, he had used the word "race" to describe the former, much in line with the older (roughly, pre-1850s) usage of the term. See for example, "Philology versus Ethnology; Letter to H. H. Risley, Esq.," in Biography of Words (1888), 243–51.

18. That is to say, "family" understood in a somewhat erroneous, naturalistic sense. For, as we know, family descent is no more a natural process than it is a complex system of social practice and contractual relation.

a people, nation, or race, thus directly contradicting the philological credo upheld since the reign of Schlegel and Humboldt. The formation of a "language family," in Müller's view, was not to be construed as a self-propelling development intrinsic to some unique inner essence but rather as a process far more incidental, contingent, and synthetic. How the groupings came about, he suggested, was a process of consolidation, a fortuitous solidification of certain structures, in three distinct moments or localities, which took place sometime in the course of the history of the human species, but not at the very beginning of it. Let us trace this train of thought, which is of crucial significance in Müller's theory of language and race, in his own words.

Müller presupposes a prehistoric condition—that is to say, time before history proper—before these distinct groupings emerged, when there was nothing but a vast, utterly polymorphous sea of nondescript growths. In this scene of the prehistoric imaginary, language is little more than a natural process. A peculiar endowment of the species though it may be, the vicissitudes of such "natural language" in constant flux could hardly be considered a historical development. He describes this natural, precultural state of human speech thus:

> There was language and there was religion everywhere in the world, but it was natural, wild-growing language and religion; it had no history, it left no history, and it is therefore incapable of that peculiar scientific treatment which has been found applicable to the study of the languages and the religions of the Chinese, the Semitic, and the Aryan nations. (160)

At the origin of each of these distinct groups of languages/religions/nations, it is supposed that there was a certain "arrest" of the cycle of natural growth and decay, a cessation caused by "social, religious, political, or at all events by extraneous influences" (162). Evidently, Müller finds nothing predestined about the commencement of this history, or histories. There was nothing inevitable about the distinctive formations, and in fact, he implies that the actual fact that a given grouping took place at all is unexpected and indeed surprising.

> Families of languages are very peculiar formations; they are, and they must be, the exception, not the rule, in the growth of language. There was always the possibility, but there never was, as far as I can judge, any necessity for human speech leaving its primitive stage of wild growth and wild decay. If it had not been for what I consider a purely spontaneous act on the part of the ancestors of the Semitic, Aryan, and Turanian races, all

languages might for ever have remained ephemeral, answering the purposes of every generation that comes and goes, struggling on, now gaining, now losing, sometimes acquiring a certain permanence, but after a season breaking up again, and carried away like blocks of ice by the waters that rise underneath the surface. Our very idea of language would then have been something totally different from what it is now. (161–62)

This process of linguistic group formation implies a fundamental difficulty for the science of language, according to Müller. Because the history of civilization has unfolded along the streams of three language groups only, all the cultural resources and conceptual apparatuses that outfit our faculty of thinking and theorizing are exclusive attributes of "exceptional formations." All the highly specialized intellectual endowments that facilitate civilized knowledge—including philosophy, historiography, and the science of language itself—are the products of these "exceptional" developments. Therefore, it must be assumed, these tools and strategies of knowledge are fundamentally dissonant, ultimately incompatible with the character of prehistoric language in the near-natural state. Any theory of language devised by a "civilized" nation is thus ill suited to understand the process of the formation of "exceptional" languages because it does not understand language in its wild, natural state. In order for the "civilized" intellect to conceptualize the transition from natural to historical, it seems, one would have to turn one's thoughts inside out, as it were, or to think beyond one's means. This is a mental maneuver, Müller observes, directly contrary to our inclinations:

> We first form our idea of what language ought to be from those exceptional languages which were *arrested in their natural growth by social, religious, political, or at all events by extraneous influences,* and we then turn round and wonder why all languages are not like these two or three exceptional channels of speech. We might as well wonder why all animals are not domesticated, or why, besides the garden anemone, there should be endless varieties of the same flower growing wild on the meadow and in the woods. (162; emphasis added)

The analogy of garden flowers and domestic animals leaves no room for doubt: Müller conceived of the formation of "exceptional channels" of language as a contingent process extraneously wrought. There was nothing inherent in any language to instigate its own growth in a particular direction, that is, from its germinal monosyllabic state into intricately arranged forms, any more than any animal species had an internal urge to become domesticated, or any anemones had an inherent proclivity to turn themselves into the garden variety of their own accord.

But if each of the three "exceptional" language families (or groups) is ultimately a fortuitous formation caused by historical accidents, what is the ground for supposing that one formation is more authentic, closer to the original spirit of the nation or people (Volk), freer, and inherently more capable of developing than another? In other words, whatever happened to the theory of the essential and inalienable power of inflection, upon which so much of the characterization and valuation of the Aryan language seems to have been based?

The question, in fact, might have already occurred to those who were present at Müller's lectures on the science of language a decade earlier, and if so, they had already been given an answer on that occasion.

2. On the Possibility of the Common Origin of Languages

Similar to Müller's series on the science of religion, the series published as *Lectures on the Science of Language* takes the form of a comprehensive historical overview.[19] Along the way, readers would learn the foundational premises as well as some basic material data that informed the science in Müller's day. A critical moment in this detailed survey of the science of language comes at the beginning of the sixth lecture, where the subject turns to "comparative grammar," which is equivalent to saying the science of language proper. As we discussed in chapter 5, this science began in earnest when the comparison of languages was no longer a matter of collecting and sorting *words* according to their superficial resemblances but became a comparison of grammatical *forms*. This means that the labor of the scientist of language is not to pore over the primitive word component, or what are known as roots or radicals, but rather to engage in a systematic analysis of the variations and mutations of those secondary elements that allow the formation of syntax, or what Müller calls "formal elements." In the simplest terms, he says, the comparative philologist's ques-

19. Throughout the following discussion, unless noted otherwise, I refer to the first series of 1861 rather than the second series of 1863 and quote from the second edition published in 1862; cited in the text by page number hereafter. See also note 3 above.

tion comes down to this: "What is language that a mere formal change, such as that of I *love* into I *loved*, should produce so very material a difference?" (215). How did these formal elements (which are in themselves devoid of meaning yet essential in constructing a syntax) and the rules governing the syntax (which seem so arbitrary) develop?

Before he discloses the scientific answer to the problem of the origin of grammatical forms, Müller briefly surveys two preexisting theories, both of which he deems inadequate. The first is a kind of contract theory, which postulates that these forms and rules are purely conventional, that is, the result of some mutual agreement made among the original speakers of the language. The proponents of this theory, Müller observes, "if they were asked why the mere addition of a d changes I *love* into I *loved*, or why the addition of the syllable *rai* gave to *j'aime*, I love, the power of a future, *j'aimerai*, they would answer, that it was so because, at a very early time in the history of the world, certain persons, or families, or clans, agreed that it should be so" (216). Müller regards this imaginary congress of prehistoric protohumans negotiating about grammatical forms—but by what means?—as a fairytale. He therefore judges this first theory to be entirely unscientific. As to the second theory:

> [The first] view was opposed by another which represents language as an organic and almost a living being, and explains its formal elements as produced by a principle of growth inherent in its very nature. "Languages," it is maintained, "are formed by a process, not of crystalline accretion, but of germinal development. Every essential part of language existed as completely (although only implicitly) in the primitive germ, as the petals of a flower exist in the bud before the mingled influences of the sun and the air caused it to unfold." This view was first propounded by Frederick Schlegel, and it is still held by many with whom poetical phraseology takes the place of sound and severe reasoning. (216–17)

Müller's judgment on the two theories of the origin of grammatical forms is definitive: "The science of language adopts neither of these views." While his own prose was seldom free of poetical phraseology, Müller's dismissal of the second, imaginative, idealist theory—which at least could boast a far more illustrious list of supporters than the first—is sobering:

> As to imagining language, that is to say, nouns and verbs, endowed with an inward principle of growth, all we can say is, that such a conception is

really inconceivable. Language may be conceived as a production, but it cannot be conceived as a substance that could itself produce. (217)

Here, Müller does not take time to demonstrate further the conceptual fault of this second theory or to confront directly its metaphysical underpinning, to which the name of Schlegel is conspicuously attached.[20] Instead, he immediately sounds a markedly positivist note: "But the science of language has nothing to do with mere theories, whether conceivable or not. It collects facts, and its only object is to account for these facts, as far as possible."

Whatever the value of this remark, it is clear that his apparent dodging of the metaphysical in the name of "facts" and "science" amounts to a direct offensive against the idealist theory of language, that is, against the theory of pure, original inflection. This theory had been the keystone of the claim for the supremacy of the so-called Indo-European languages, or as one might say from Müller's more critical secularist standpoint, this theory had served as the basis for the idol-worship of the Aryan language that had entertained the poetic imagination of many a European philologist, from the Schlegel brothers

---

20. Müller nonetheless appends a lengthy footnote, quoting an unidentified author and article, presumably his own, which renders the gist of Schlegel's theory and its obscurantism (Müller cites *Transactions of the Philological Society* 2:39, but I have not been able to verify the source): "It has been common among grammarians to regard those terminational changes as evolved by some unknown process from the body of the noun, as the branches of a tree spring from the stem—or as elements, unmeaning in themselves, but employed arbitrarily or conventionally to modify the meanings of words. This latter view is countenanced by Schlegel, 'Languages with inflexions,' says Schlegel, 'are organic languages, because they include a living principle of development and increase, and alone possess, if I may so express myself, a fruitful and abundant vegetation. The wonderful mechanism of these languages consists in forming an immense variety of words, and in marking the connection of ideas expressed by these words by the help of an inconsiderable number of syllables, *which, viewed separately, have no signification*, but which determine with precision the sense of the words to which they are attached. By modifying radical letters and by adding derivative syllables to the roots, derivative words of various sorts are formed, and derivatives from these derivatives. Words are compounded from several roots to express complex ideas. Finally, substantives, adjectives, and pronouns are declined, with gender, number, and case; verbs are conjugated throughout voices, moods, tenses, numbers and persons, by employing, in like manner, terminations and sometimes augments, which by themselves signify nothing. This method is attended with the advantage of enunciating in a single word the principal idea, frequently greatly modified, and extremely complex already, with its whole array of accessory ideas and mutable relations'" (in Müller, *Lectures on the Science of Language*, 216–17).

and Wilhelm von Humboldt to Müller's own contemporary and friend, Ernest Renan.

Müller continues without pause:

> Instead of looking on inflections in general either as conventional signs or natural excrescences, [science] takes each termination by itself, establishes its most primitive form by means of comparison, and then treats that primitive syllable as it would treat any other part of language,— namely, as something which was originally intended to convey a meaning. (217–18)

At this crucial point in Müller's argument—even though he frames his move here as if it were nothing more than a delineation of scientific method and its analytic procedure—he takes definitive steps to undermine the second, idealist theory of the origin of inflection. Müller proposes, first, that "each termination," that is, every "formal element" is to be taken "by itself"; he implies that science demands this. Second, this formal element, no matter how devoid of meaning it may seem, should be traced, by means of comparative analysis, back to its most primitive form possible; and this primitive form, moreover, should be assumed to have been "originally intended to convey a meaning." In effect, the inflectional ending—that is, the purely formal element seemingly devoid of semantic content—must have been, at the beginning, just another word, or more precisely, word root. This idea is announced explicitly toward the end of the same paragraph:

> What is grammar after all but declension and conjugation? Originally declension could not have been anything but the composition of a noun with *some other word expressive of number and case*. (218; emphasis added)

Thus argues Müller, but at this juncture he cannot yet claim to have proven these assertions conclusively. In the rest of lecture 6, however, he purports to make good on his argument by demonstrating, through several examples taken from the history of the Indo-European language family, how such tracing to earlier forms is possible, and how this method always leads to a linguistic unit that is meaningful, which is to say, to an independent word. For example, the mysterious termination -*rai*, which makes a future out of j'*aime* (I love), resulting in j'*aimerai* (I will love), is traced to the auxiliary verb *avoir*, and this path is made visible by an intricate comparison with Latin, Spanish, and Provençal, among others. Likewise, Müller tracks the termination -d, which changes many English verbs from present to past ("I love" to "I loved"), through an enlightening detour into Gothic and Saxon to the auxiliary verb "to do" in Anglo-Saxon (219–34).

Moreover, this comparative method makes evident that the loss of meaning—that is, the process in which the original meaning of the added component becomes unintelligible—is a result of something quite material, mechanical, and inadvertent, namely, phonetic decay. An ever so slight slippage of sound, a little contraction, a small extraneous sound thrown in to help ease the pronunciation, and so on—these mindless, meaningless, or semantically inattentive alterations lead to the deterioration of meaning of the help word that has now become melded into the dominant word, becoming, in other words, a mere word *ending* without a recognizable meaning of its own.

At the conclusion of these deliberations, Müller is prepared to make this astonishing claim:

> Now, in this manner, the whole, or nearly the whole, grammatical framework of the Aryan or Indo-European languages has been traced back to original independent words, and even the slightest changes which at first sight seem so mysterious, such as *foot* into *feet*, or I *find* into I *found*, have been fully accounted for. This is what is called comparative grammar, or a scientific analysis of all the formal elements of a language preceded by a comparison of all the varieties which one and the same form has assumed in the numerous dialects of the Aryan family. (234)

The implication of the new findings of comparative grammar is thus obvious. The origin of inflection is agglutination. Every grammar without exception begins with the compounding and coalescing of root words. No word ending would ever grow *out* of a word root on its own. Some languages (such as Chinese), says Müller, remained in the predominantly compounding mode and never developed the formal elements or "termination" proper.[21] Other languages became more agglutinative, and still others finally became inflectional. All this leads ineluctably to this conclusion: there is no such thing as an origi-

---

21. "There is one language, the Chinese, in which no analysis of any kind is required for the discovery of its component parts. It is a language in which no coalescence of roots has taken place: every word is a root, and every root is a word. It is, in fact, the most primitive stage in which we can imagine human language to have existed. It is language *comme il faut*; it is what we should naturally have expected all languages to be" (ibid., 272–73).

nally inflectional language. By the same token, there is no tenable categorical distinction between pure inflection and limited inflection (i.e., between languages that were purportedly inflectional from the beginning and those that developed inflection after agglutination had already taken place).[22]

Müller was even more explicit and unequivocal on this point on another occasion some years later. In 1868, Müller gave a Rede Lecture at Cambridge University under the title "On the Stratification of Language," wherein he proclaimed:

> No language can by any possibility be inflectional without having passed through the agglutinative and isolating stratum; no language can be agglutinative without clinging with its roots to the underlying stratum of isolation.[23]

So much, then, for the purity of the Aryan language and its original, pure inflection. As Müller saw the matter, it was none other than the science of comparative grammar itself—the product of the initial enthusiasm surging around the discovery of Sanskrit, the "perfect" inflectional language[24]—that destroyed the myth of inflectional purity.

In sum, according to Müller, there are not different scenarios in the histories of the grammatical formation of the Aryan, Semitic, and "other" language groups, since every one of them started out the same.[25] The difference is in the

22. As we recall, this was the primary structural difference between the Aryan and the Semitic languages, according to Schlegel and others. See chapter 5, section 3 above.

23. F. Max Müller, *On the Stratification of Language* (1868), 20.

24. As we know, "Sanskrit" means, in its own vocabulary, "perfect."

25. Müller is also explicit in pointing out that this erroneous conception of inflection is present in Humboldt. In a passage a little earlier in the Rede Lecture, he states: "Those who are acquainted with the works of Humboldt will easily recognise in these three stages or strata, a classification of language first suggested by that eminent philosopher. According to him languages can be classified as isolating, agglutinative, and inflectional, and his definition of these three classes agrees in the main with the description just given of the three strata or stages of language.

"But what is curious is that this threefold classification, and the consequences to which it leads, should not at once have been fully reasoned out; nay, that a system most palpably erroneous should have been founded upon it. We find it repeated again and again in most works on Comparative Philology, that Chinese belongs to the isolating class, the Turanian language to the agglutinative, the Aryan and Semitic to the inflectional; nay, Professor Pott and his school seem convinced that no evolution takes place from isolating to agglutinative and from agglutinative to inflectional speech. We should thus be forced to believe that by some inexplicable gram-

degree of development along the same path—that is, over the course of gradual coalescence, phonetic decay, and loss of meaning. Or, to put it more precisely, it is simply a matter of different strata in which the "arresting" and solidification of the language occurred.[26]

> The first stage, in which each root preserves its independence, and in
> which there is no formal distinction between a root and a word, I call the
> *Radical Stage*. This stage is best represented by ancient Chinese. Languages
> belonging to this first or Radical Stage, have sometimes been called *Mono-
> syllabic* or *Isolating*. The second stage, in which two or more roots coalesce
> to form a word, the one retaining its radical independence, the other sink-
> ing down to a mere termination, I call the *Terminational Stage*. This stage is
> best represented by the Turanian family of speech, and the languages be-
> longing to it have generally been called *agglutinative*, from *gluten*, glue. The
> third stage, in which roots coalesce so that neither the one nor the other
> retains its substantive independence, I call the *Inflectional Stage*. This stage
> is best represented by the Aryan and Semitic families, and the languages
> belonging to it have sometimes been distinguished by the name of *organic*
> or *amalgamating*. (286–87)

This is a good moment to note that there is a significant divergence between,
on the one hand, Müller's morphological classification of languages (taxonomy in accordance with the stages of development or stratification) and, on the

---

matical instinct, or by some kind of inherent necessity, languages were from the beginning created as isolating, or agglutinative, or inflectional, and must remain so to the end. It is strange
that those scholars of language who hold that no transition is possible from one form of language to another, should not have seen that there is really no language that can be strictly called
either isolating, or agglutinative, or inflectional, and that the transition from one stage to another is constantly taking place under our very eyes" (ibid., 17–18).

The deeper background of this pointed pronouncement by Müller was as follows. In response to Müller's Turanian essays (discussed in sections 3 and 4 below), in 1855 August Friedrich Pott (1802–87) published a sixty-page polemical paper, "M. Müller und die Kennzeichen
der Sprachenverwandtschaft," in the *Journal of the German Orientalist Society* (*Zeitschrift der deutschen
morgendländischen Gesellschaft*), in addition to two other shorter reviews of Müller's publications
(see Joan Leopold, *The Letter Liveth* [1983], 24–25). In the following year, Pott also published an
essay on the inequality of the races, argued primarily on philological grounds: *Die Ungleichheit
menschen Rassen* (1856).

26. It is important to note that the "arresting" he refers to in relation to the formation of a language family/group is markedly different from the "stunting" of growth that both Renan and

other, the familiar, tripartite genealogical classification in terms of the Aryan, Semitic, and Turanian families or groups. Particularly striking in Müller's account is the (dis)location of Chinese. As we recall, in Müller's addendum to the genealogical chart of the aristocracy of great religions, ancient China is called the birthplace of the two "Turanian" book religions, namely, Confucianism and Taoism; but in the morphological mapping of languages, Chinese seems to represent not the Turanian (terminational stage) but the pre-Turanian (monosyllabic or isolating stage).

There are several things to be said about this apparent discrepancy, and some of these things may shed further light upon the peculiarity of Müller's system of classification and, by the same token, on the rather unique position in which Müller stood in relation to many of his predecessors and contemporaries, with respect to both the theory of language and the classification of religions.

3. The Trouble with the Turanian

It has never been a secret that Müller's notion of the Turanian was controversial, and that what he said in relation to this subject caused him a good deal of trouble across the full length of his career. Just what kind of trouble this was for him, however, may not be immediately obvious, and it is certainly not well known. To begin, the term "Turanian" itself never managed to settle into a definitive meaning but remained malleable, now seeming to denote one thing, now another. At times, it appears that Müller wanted it to refer to all of these shifting domains of meaning combined, in all their indefiniteness and incon-

---

Kuenen mentioned with regard to Semitic language/religion. As we recall from a passage quoted earlier, for Müller, every formation of a language group is an arresting of the "natural" process of "wild growth and wild decay," that is, arresting the constant flux and ending the non-formation of such particularized form.

As for Müller's rejection of the idea that the inflectional and agglutinative languages differ constitutionally and originally, there are numerous citations that could be given in support, throughout his writing career. In the most immediate context, see for instance: "The chief distinction between an inflectional and an agglutinative language consists in the fact that agglutinative languages preserve the consciousness of their roots, and therefore do not allow them to be affected by phonetic corruption; and, though they have lost the consciousness of the original meaning of their terminations, they feel distinctly the difference between the significative root, and the modifying elements. Not so in the inflectional languages. There the various elements which entered into the composition of words, may become so welded together, and suffer so much from phonetic corruption, that none but the educated would be aware of an original distinction between root and termination, and none but the comparative grammarian able to discover the seams that separate the component parts" (*Lectures on the Science of Language*, 324–25).

gruity, and this indeterminacy seems to have been a problem. Rather surprisingly, however, Müller apparently had a peculiar investment in this imprecise concept. Upon close inspection, one may begin to discern a certain logic in his tenacious attachment despite the shiftiness of the idea.

Like "Aryan," "Turanian" is a term derived from a word in the Indo-Persian language family, namely, "Turan," meaning "Turkestan" in Persian. Müller's name is closely associated with both these terms; he has been recognized as the figure most visibly responsible for having introduced or popularized each in European discourse. With respect to the term "Aryan," he had proffered a detailed and didactic account of its etymology in one of his 1861 lectures on language, and from that point on, he continued to return to the concept and to secure its meaning with ever greater precision, though, in reality, his efforts were increasingly running against the tide of rampant misuse. It must be admitted that his repeated attempts at protecting its proper sense were ultimately in vain, for, as we know, soon thereafter the term slipped entirely out of philological control and went on to have a monstrous life of its own, leaving behind any memory of the ancient Persians, the Vedas, Sanskrit grammar, and all the rest that had given rise to the idea in the first place. The career of "Turanian," on the other hand, never even got off the ground, and the term seems to have become an archaism almost immediately; it was variously replaced by other terms and concepts, which were purportedly endowed with greater semantic precision and, supposedly, with greater empirical reality. Like the concept of ether, "Turanian" is remembered primarily for what was wrong with it, rather than what it was meant to denote.[27]

When Müller initially used the term Turanian to speak of the non-Aryan (also understood as pre-Aryan) inhabitants of the Indian subcontinent, he presumed their barely visible yet deep linguistic affinity and kinship with a very broad range of peoples scattered about the world. One of the earliest articulations of the Turanian concept occurred in a lengthy essay that was to remain controversial for years, entitled On the Languages of the Seat of War in the East (1854), where Müller explained Turanian in the following terms:

It comprises all languages spoken in Asia or Europe not included under the Arian and Semitic families, with the exception perhaps of the Chinese

27. Today, a typical dictionary entry for "Turanian" would refer to the people of "Ural-Altaic stock," together with secondary and tertiary references to "Turkic or Tartaric" peoples, or even to "a nomadic people held to have preceded the Aryans in Europe and Asia." Cf. for example, Webster's Third New International Dictionary (1993).

and its dialects. This is, indeed, a very wide range; and the characteristic marks of union, ascertained for its immense variety of languages, are as yet very vague and general, if compared with the definite ties of relationship which severally unite the Semitic and the Arian.[28]

The capaciousness of the category alone was likely to invite skepticism. To claim any kind of genealogical relation among peoples of so diverse an area—possibly, the whole world—in the absence of credible historical evidence of migration and dispersion, seems a recklessly speculative move. If the spread of this family is so vast, is it not equivalent to saying simply that this is a family of "the rest"? Can any group or any language that is neither Semitic nor Aryan, no matter how unusual and singular, be excluded from this third category? True, the genealogical relation of at least some of the languages within this broad category had been established, and large divisions or groupings within the category had been recognized, with the result that the empirical reality of this family might become more palpable as time passed and as science progressed.[29] But even so, the very diversity within the category would remain problematic; in fact, he does concede: "[I]t will be difficult to exclude from the same system the other provinces of speech which lie scattered throughout on the map of Asia and Europe" (86).

Given this concession, it is rather surprising that, instead of retracting the category as untenable or at least mitigating the assertion, Müller goes on to suggest, in effect, that this very diffuseness is a distinct characteristic of this family of languages. As he puts it: "The absence of that close family likeness which holds the Arian and Semitic languages together, becomes itself one of the distinguishing features of the Turanian dialects. They are *Nomadic languages* as contrasted with the Arian and Semitic dialects, which may be called *State* or *political languages*" (86). Fundamentally inimical to settlement and to consolidation, it is as though this "family," this band of languages on horseback, never prone to take root or to conform to any place, any form, any rule, or any collective memory, had roamed the earth from time immemorial, and that is why

---

28. F. Max Müller, *The Languages of the Seat of War in the East* (1854; 2nd ed., 1855), 86; cited in the text by page number hereafter. See 86–95 especially.

29. Müller explicates the particular nature of the affinity among some of the Turanian languages—distinct and different from the nature of the affinity among the Semitic or Aryan language group—in the first lecture of the second series he gave at the Royal Institution in 1863. See *Lectures on the Science of Language*, second series (1864; new ed., 1880), 33–50.

today their descendents are found everywhere around the globe, but without any recollection of their distant common past.

Müller's argument here is evocative and no less poetical than Schlegel's idea of a primordial spirit-language; it is a difficult case to make in the name of science. It is therefore all the more noteworthy that from that point onward, Müller persisted in this undeniably speculative theory of the origin of the Turanian peoples and that he never relinquished it completely. Rehearsing the same argument in the 1861 lecture series before the Royal Institution, Müller avers, "[T]his Turanian family comprises in reality all languages spoken in Asia and Europe, and not included under the Aryan and Semitic families, with the exception of Chinese and its cognate dialects." And for this reason, he admits, "[s]ome scholars would deny it the name of a family; and if family is only applicable to dialects so closely connected among themselves as the Aryan or Semitic, it would no doubt be preferable to speak of the Turanian as a class or group, and not as a family of languages." But then he goes on to claim, "[T]his concession must not be understood as an admission that the members of this class start from different sources, and that they are held together, not by genealogical affinity, but by morphological similarity only" (288–89).

His reasoning as to why the category should not be construed merely morphologically is the same as before, but he is now more explicit and deliberate in making the case:

No doubt if we expected to find in this immense number of languages the same family likeness which holds the Semitic or Aryan languages together, we should be disappointed. But the very absence of that family likeness constitutes one of the distinguishing features of the Turanian dialects. They are Nomad languages, as contrasted with the Aryan, and Semitic languages. (290)

In these three sentences, we find, first, an admission of the diffuseness of this "family"; then a refusal to concede, combined with something of a turnabout, that is, the conversion of a seeming difficulty into a defining characteristic; this is followed by an astonishingly simple explanatory claim: Turanian languages are nomadic.[30]

30. Or as Müller says plainly enough a little earlier, "The name Turanian is used in opposition to Aryan, and is applied to the Nomadic races of Asia as opposed to the agricultural or Aryan races" (Lectures on the Science of Language, 289). This claim interestingly contradicts the more prevalent notion that the epitome of nomadic culture was represented by the Indo-Europeans,

Yet this is not all. The argument is further elaborated by contrasting the Aryan-Semitic (inflectional) type and the Turanian type. In the Aryan and Semitic languages

> most words and grammatical forms were thrown out but once by the creative power of one generation, and they were not lightly parted with, even though their original distinctness had been blurred by phonetic corruption. To hand down a language in this manner is possible only among people whose history runs on in one main stream; and where religion, law, and poetry supply well-defined borders which hem in on every side the current of language.

In contrast:

> Among the Turanian nomads no such nucleus of a political, social, or literary character has ever been formed. Empires were no sooner founded than they were scattered again like the sand-clouds of the desert; no laws, no songs, no stories outlived the age of their authors. (290)

But this scattering of the desert sand, this evanescence of "empires"—does this not threaten the very possibility of constituting a nation, a people? Does it not, by the same token, undermine the assertion that any of their languages form a family? Müller's position here is a difficult one to maintain. The argument is obviously strained. It is as though, just like a Turanian nomad needing to found an empire in every generation, he needed to reiterate this theory and to reinstall the reality of the Turanian family at every turn, against the ineluctable erosion that comes at the end of each enunciation.[31] Once we recog-

---

who probably originated somewhere in the steppes of Western Asia and who first domesticated horses, and possibly invented the war chariot. From this plausible theory derives the less credible but ever popular image of the Proto-Indo-European as mobile warriors and invaders. Cf. Mallory, *In Search of the Indo-Europeans*, for various references to that horse culture. The 1999 paperback edition of this volume sports a photograph of a "[b]ronze figure of an Iranian steppe nomad taking a classic 'Parthian shot' over his shoulder." The warrior depicted, naturally, is astride a galloping horse.

31. For instance, this passage occurs a little later in the same lecture series: "The traces by which these languages attest their original relationship are much fainter than in the Semitic and Aryan families, but they are so of necessity. In the Aryan and Semitic families, the agglutinative process, by which alone grammatical forms can be obtained, has been arrested at some time, and this could only have been through religious or political influences. By the same power through which an advancing civilization absorbs the manifold dialects in which every spoken

nize that this indeed is the tenor and the intent of Müller's argument, what should draw our attention is not only its tenuousness, but even more his adamant insistence on this singular theory of the Turanian.

At this juncture, it also becomes apparent why Chinese in particular was a rather fascinating, ultimately unresolvable problem for Müller. Naturally, his first inclination was to distinguish and separate the redoubtable ancient Middle Kingdom from the ranks of free-ranging nomads with short memory. But if the Chinese were an exception, their language certainly did not suggest any closer affinity to other instances of the exceptional, that is, the linguistic solidification and settlement of the agrarian Aryan or pastoral Semitic peoples. On the contrary, the Chinese language marked exactly the opposite end of the stratification schema. European philologists called Chinese an "isolating" language, considering it the epitome of the elemental and radically noninflectional; by all counts, then, its characteristics were supposed to be even more unfettered and unsettled than those of the horde of nomadic Turanians. In fact, virtually without any coalescing of root words and with a syntax governed by mere ordering of monosyllabic components—or so the philologists claimed—the Chinese language might be envisioned as an enormous swarm of free-floating, free-associating radicals. Hence this paradoxical outcome for Müller: if the Chinese language, nation, and religion were to be installed as the aristocracy among the Turanian nations—which is precisely what happens in Müller's 1870 lectures on the science of religion—this must be so by virtue of the Chinese language's peculiar nature as an extreme exaggeration of Turanian nomadism. All in all, then, the actual historic grandeur and legendary stability of the Middle Kingdom, not to mention its vast sedentary population, would have to be construed as a miracle of sorts, or, what might amount to the same thing, an ultimate contradiction.

---

idiom naturally represents itself, the first political or religious centralization must necessarily have put a check on the exuberance of an agglutinative speech. Out of many possible forms one became popular, fixed, and technical for each word, for each grammatical category; and by means of poetry, law, and religion, a literary or political language was produced to which thenceforth nothing had to be added; which in a short time, after becoming unintelligible in its formal elements was liable to phonetic corruption only, but incapable of internal resuscitation. It is necessary to admit a primitive concentration of this kind for the Aryan and Semitic families, for it is thus only that we can account for coincidences between Sanskrit and Greek terminations, which were formed neither from Greek nor from Sanskrit materials, but which are still identically the same in both. It is in this sense that I call these languages political or state languages" (Müller, Lectures on the Science of Language, 334–35).

4. The Real Trouble with the Turanian

The case of China, however, was not what caused trouble for Müller and out-raged some of his detractors. The focal point of the controversy occasioned by his early pronouncements on the Turanian language lay elsewhere. As Müller himself relates on several later occasions, much of the dispute started immediately following the publication of an essay called "Last Results of the Turanian Researches," but more simply known as "On the Turanian Languages." Although it is also often referred to as a "letter" and is in fact written in an epistolary mode, this rather lengthy essay—well over 250 pages, including various charts and appendices—was hastily composed in 1853, at the request of his older friend and benefactor, Christian Bunsen, and it was published a year later as a section of the latter's multivolume work *Christianity and Mankind*.[32] Eight years later, toward the end of his first series of Royal Institution lectures, he had occasion to reiterate the intent of that essay and to defend himself against some of the charges brought against him in the meantime.

As he explains in *Lectures on the Science of Language*, this youthful tract had become the target of "fierce attacks," and he clearly identifies his opponents as the polygenists, or in his words, "those who believe in different beginnings of language and mankind" (338). At the same time, he adamantly insists that he himself was not propounding a monogenist theory or purporting to prove conclusively the unitary origin of the humankind:[33]

32. Georgina Max Müller explains that the essay was included in the third volume of Bunsen's *Christianity and Mankind* (1854), under the title, "Last Results of the Turanian Researches Respecting the Non-Iranian and Non-Semitic Languages of Asia or Europe, or the Turanian Family of Language." Bunsen's multivolume work was also known by several titles. Volumes 3 and 4 were issued separately as *Outline of the Philosophy of Universal History applied to Language and Religion* (1854), 263–521.

33. Müller was also criticized, somewhat unjustly, for allegedly advocating a similarly speculative theory of the origin of language. In the preface to the sixth edition of the 1861 lecture series—included in the edition published in 1880—he expends much effort to correct this misperception, the insistent tone of which is an indication of the tenacity of the charge against him: "Though I have protested before, I must protest once more against the supposition that the theory on the origin of the roots which I explained at the end of my first course, and which I distinctly described as that of Professor Heyse of Berlin, was ever held by myself. It is a theory which, if properly understood, contains some truth, but it offers an illustration only, and in no way a real solution to the problem. I have abstained in my Lectures from propounding a theory on the origin of language, first, because I believe that the Science of Language may safely begin with roots as its ultimate facts, leaving what lies beyond to the psychologist and metaphysician; secondly, because I hold that a theory on the origin of language can only be thoroughly treated

The real object of my Essay was therefore a defensive one. It was to show how rash it was to speak of different independent beginnings in the history of human speech, before a single argument had been brought forward to establish the necessity of such an admission. The impossibility of a common origin of language has never been proved, but, in order to remove what were considered difficulties affecting the theory of a common origin, I felt it my duty to show practically, and by the very history of the Turanian languages, how such a theory was possible, or as I say in one instance only, probable. (339)

In tracing the history of comparative philology (see chapter 5), we have already learned something about the impediments and "difficulties" standing in the way of a viable theory of a unitary origin of all human language—difficulties that Müller had indeed removed. As we recall, Schlegel and his followers had claimed that some languages, namely, what Schlegel called "Sanscritic" but were later to be called the Aryan, had been *from the beginning* inflectional, whereas certain others, the Turanian, began with agglutination, and yet another group, the Semitic, adopted a composite or compromised method of development, and on this basis they drew the conclusion that, since the differences among these three groups are historically irreconcilable, it is impossible to establish a common origin among them.[34] But this conclusion is precisely what Müller has rejected in claiming that *all* languages must be presumed to

---

in close connection with the theory on the origin of thought, i.e. with the fundamental principles of mental philosophy. Although in treating of the history of the Science of Language I found it necessary in my Lectures to examine some of the former theories on the origin of language, and to show their insufficiency in the present state of our science, I carefully abstained from going beyond the limits which I had traced for myself" (*Lectures on the Science of Language*, new ed. [1880], viii).

34. Müller in fact credits Wilhelm von Humboldt with identifying clearly these distinct phases of the development of grammatical forms but also charges that he drew a wrong conclusion from this insight. After an extensive quotation from Humboldt's own summation—as it appears in his 1822 essay *Über das Entstehen der grammatischen Formen und ihren Einfluss auf die Ideenentwicklung*—Müller comments: "After this lucid statement of the gradual growth of grammatical forms, it is extraordinary that Humboldt should still have doubted a possible historical transition between the different forms" ("Last Results of the Turanian Researches," 283). Müller goes on to show that Otto von Boehtlingk (1815–1904), who also noted the same non sequitur in Humboldt, unaccountably ends up drawing the same conclusion himself. Müller quotes from Boehtlingk: "It is inconceivable how, with such a view on the origin of inflection [as Humboldt's], any one can doubt for a moment about the possibility of two such languages as Chinese and Sanskrit having the same origin. I say the possibility, not the historical reality, because all

have begun the same way, that is, from the "monosyllabic" or "isolating" system. True, some time later, many languages entered the stage of agglutination, and some among them went further to turn inflectional. At the same time, Müller maintains in no uncertain terms that there is *no* originally inflectional language. Reiterating this cardinal point, he quotes again, twice, from his 1854 essay: "Nothing necessitates the admission of different independent beginnings for the *material* elements of the Turanian, Semitic, and Aryan branches of speech," which is to say, there is a theoretical possibility that the roots in these three language groups may be traced to a single source. Furthermore, "[n]othing necessitates the admission of different beginnings for the formal elements of the Turanian, Semitic, and Aryan branches of speech" (339)[35]

In short, as Müller saw the matter, the real point of contention was not merely a particular factual question of whether the non-Aryan languages of India were Turanian rather than Semitic—even though he had written "Last Results of the Turanian Researches" expressly to support Bunsen, who held this view. Nor was it merely the technical question as to how closely or how distantly they were related to Turkic, Malay, or Chinese.[36] Rather, he recognized the attack against him in this way:

> I have been accused of having been biased in my researches by an implicit belief in the common origin of mankind. I do not deny that I hold this belief, and, if it wanted confirmation, that confirmation has been supplied by Darwin's book "On the Origin of Species." But I defy my adversaries to

---

attempts at *proving* such a common origin ought from the very beginning to be stigmatised as vain, futile, and therefore unprofessional." Of course Boehtlingk does not explain what exactly "stigmatizes" such an attempt so definitively.

35. These two points, which "Comparative Philology has gained," are stated in full, with emphasis as shown, in the original essay ("Last Results of the Turanian Researches," 479–80).

36. On this point, Müller finally remained ambivalent, as we see in the concluding paragraph of the "introductory remarks" of "Last Results": "Even now, in answer to your [Bunsen's] kind inquiries, I should rather have adopted the negative method of arguing; I mean, I should rather have exhausted possibilities, and proved that these same languages cannot be referred to any other race from which, as far as history and geography go, they might possibly have sprung. I might have endeavoured to show they are neither Semitic, nor Chinese, nor Indo-Chinese, nor Malay, nor idioms transplanted from the east coast of Africa. . . . However, as you wish it, I shall lay my case before you in a more positive form, leaving it to you to judge whether, even in its imperfect state, it deserves the consideration which you were kind enough to accord it" (ibid., 268–69).

point out one single passage where I have mixed up scientific with theological arguments. (340–41)

Clearly, then, he took the charges of his critics as an affront to his scientific
credibility. In a rather modern move, he asserted his rights to hold religious
convictions and keep them separate from the practice of his science, and to
have his science judged on its own merit.[37]

Among his more vociferous opponents seeking to foreclose the possibility
of a common origin of all languages were those who conflated—in Müller's
view, wholly illegitimately—the classification of language with the supposedly
physiological and biological classification of "race." Müller's defense of the
science of language therefore most often took the form of an indictment of the
racialist understanding of the language families or groups, an idea that was
then becoming increasingly influential.

In retrospect, however, it must be judged that Müller was on the losing side
of the contention, and he was keenly aware of his failure, as well as the failure
of comparative philology more generally to put a stop to this development that
was of its own making.[38] His personal stance on this issue remained constant
throughout his career, though as he grew older, the tone of his protest became
noticeably acerbic.

Late in his life, when he delivered three lectures at the Oxford University
Extension Meeting under the familiar title of "The Science of Language" (1889),
he devoted much of the last lecture to this particular problem. With the telling
title "Thought Thicker than Blood," this third lecture served as yet another occasion for him to refer back to his early controversial essay:

> I have always, beginning with my very first contribution to the Science of
> Language—my letter to Bunsen "On the Turanian Languages," published
> in 1854—I have always, I say, warned against mixing up these two relation-

37. This assertion of the legitimacy of the separation between scientific and religious views,
commonplace as it may seem to our ear, is extremely important in enabling the science of religion in particular as a justifiable endeavor. Müller was by no means the first one to advocate it,
but his clear political stance on this was consequential. Concerning the significance of this maneuver, first recognizable in David Hume's writing on religion, see Tomoko Masuzawa, "Origin," in Willi Braun and Russell McCutcheon's *Guide to the Study of Religion* (2000), 209–24.

38. See *Three Lectures on the Science of Language*, based on the series delivered at the Oxford University Extension Meeting (2nd ed., 1895), 54–55. Throughout the following discussion, I refer
to this second edition; cited in the text by page number hereafter.

ships,—the relationship of language and the relationship of blood. As these warnings however, have been of very little avail, I venture to repeat them once more. (43)

And in fact, he goes on to quote from the 1854 essay for the next two pages, re-producing verbatim much of the section originally called "Ethnology v. Phonology," including statements such as the following:

> The philologist should collect his evidence, arrange his classes, divide and combine, as if no Blumenbach had ever looked at skulls, as if no Camper had ever measured facial angles, as if no Owen had examined the basis of a cranium. His evidence is the evidence of language, and nothing else; this he must follow, even though it were in the teeth of history, physical or political. (44)[39]

Here we see the evidence that, as a young scholar with only a modest claim to authority, Müller stated his position bluntly enough, and that he understood the stakes to be necessarily political.[40] Nor was he poorly informed as to what kind of racialist ethnological theories were being propounded at that time, and who among the better authorities had a definitive critique of such theories, that is, a critique backed by science and empirical facts. Thus he went on to observe, as he quotes himself in his Oxford lecture:

> Ever since Blumenbach tried to establish his five races of men (Caucasian, Mongolian, American, Ethiopian, and Malay), which Cuvier reduced to three (Caucasian, Ethiopian, and Mongolian), while Prichard raised them to seven (Iranian, Turanian, American, Hottentots, Negroes, Papuas, and Alfourous), it was felt that these physiological classifications could not be brought to harmonise with the evidence of language. . . . This point was never urged with sufficient strength till at last [Alexander von] Hum-

---

39. The section appears on pages 349–53 in the original essay. The only notable difference is that "phonology"—Müller's name for the science of language at the time of the early essay—is properly replaced by "philology" when he quotes the passage in the 1889 lecture.

40. Elsewhere in the same section, "Ethnology v. Phonology," he asserts: "There ought to be no compromise of any sort between ethnological and phonological science. It is only by stating the glaring contradictions between the two sciences that truth can be elicited. I feel no doubt that the only natural solution of the problem would have been found and accepted long ago, had it not been for this baneful spirit of accommodation and mutual concessions" (Müller, "Last Results of the Turanian Researches," 351).

boldt in his *Kosmos* . . . stated it as a plain fact, that, even from a physiological point of view, it is impossible to recognise in the groups of Blumenbach any true typical distinction, any general and consistent natural principle. (44)[41]

Meanwhile, Müller was also alert to the changing definition of "race," so much so that in the end he appears to have come to the conclusion that the term would have to be given up for lost. At the time of the first Turanian essay, when explaining the term "race," Müller, the consummate philologist, commented as follows: "If 'race' is derived, not from 'radix' ['root'] as was hitherto supposed, but from the Old High-German reiza, line, lineage, it might be retained as a technical term." But such an etymologically pure, technical sense of the term was not to be preserved. He soon came to realize that he could no longer cleave to the old meaning of "race" against the overwhelming trend of his time. Similarly archaic was Müller's early use of the term "blood." There was at least one instance in which he spoke of "blood" not in the biological sense but the metaphorical sense pertaining to succession and lineage. In the introductory remarks to the Turanian essay, while describing the affinity between such languages as Bengali, Hindi, Marathi, and Gujurati, he states that they are "all of Arian descent . . . the blood that circulates in their grammar is Arian blood." Needless to say, no kind of "blood" other than the metaphorical would be capable of running through a "grammar."[42]

By sacrificing the words "race," "blood," and even "descent" to the enemy camp, then, it looks as though Müller had hoped to fend off the incursions

41. It is important to remember that the author of *Kosmos*, to whom Müller is referring here, is not Wilhelm von Humboldt, but his younger brother Alexander, eminent explorer and natural scientist, the convener of the first international scientific congress in Berlin. Alexander Humboldt—as he preferred to be called, without the aristocratic "von"—also supplied much linguistic information to his brother, which he gathered, together with countless geological, botanical, and zoological data, in the course of his expedition in South and North America and the Caribbean. He lived to great old age and in his later years helped many aspiring young scientists of all branches, among whom was Max Müller (see chapter 5, note 16 above). For an attractively illustrated biography of Alexander von Humboldt, see Douglas Botting, *Humboldt and the Cosmos* (1973).

42. Müller, "Last Results of the Turanian Researches," 473n and 268. This is not to forget that, even for a race theory presupposing biological determinism, the relation between race/descent and "blood" is merely metaphorical. It would be absurd to suggest that parents transmit their blood to a child literally, as it would be comical to think that blood transfusion would change one's "race."

from the race scientists and their appropriation of philological categories and taxonomies. He had said as much in the early essay, and quotes himself again in the Oxford lectures:

> From a physiological point of view, we may speak of varieties of man,—no longer of races, if that term is to mean more than variety. Physiologically the unity of the human species is a fact established as firmly as the unity of any other animal species. So much then, but no more, the philologist should learn from the physiologist. (45; emphasis added)

In sum, according to Müller, the ethnologists are in error on more than one account. First, they are wrong to confuse physiological data with matters pertaining to language, and to poach on philological territories for possible support for their prescribed conclusions, where there is no such support to be had. Second, they are wrong to defy the very findings of ethnological or biological science, insofar as this science definitively demonstrated, to his mind, the unity of human species.[43] As he put it in the concluding paragraph of the section "Ethnology v. Phonology" in the original essay (though not quoted in the Oxford lectures):

> The interval between the first beginnings of the natural history of man, and the times to which we can ascen[d] through the evidence of language, may be so great as to make it impossible to gather up the threads of the one, and connect them with those of the other period. It may be . . . impossible to strengthen the arguments of physical science in favour of a common origin of mankind, by evidence derived from phonological [philological] researches; but it should not be attempted again to disprove the unity of the human race by arguments derived from the apparent diversity of human speech.[44]

This was the young Müller, at scarcely thirty years of age. And if the scientific authority of figures like Alexander von Humboldt, to whom he appealed for support, began to seem a little out of date, in 1889, the much older Müller could appeal in his Oxford lectures to another figure of eminence:

43. Regardless of the intentions of the ethnologists, Müller insisted that this was the only conclusion to be drawn from their research: "Physiological Ethnology has accounted for the varieties of the human race, and removed the barriers which formerly prevented us from viewing all mankind as the members of one family, the offspring of one parent" (ibid., 474).

44. Ibid., 352.

I have made this long extract from a book written by me in 1854, because it will show how strongly I have always deprecated the mixing up of Ethnology and Philology, and likewise that I was a Darwinian long before Darwin. At that time, however, I still entertained a hope that the physiologist might succeed in framing a real classification of races, on the evidence of skulls, or the skin, or the hair, as the philologist has succeeded in framing a real classification of languages, on the evidence of grammar. But in this hope we have been disappointed. Mankind has proved obstreperous; it has not allowed itself to be classified. According to Darwin, all men form but one species. (45)

This amounts to a wholesale rejection of race theory—that is, a negation of divisions among human species on physiological grounds, unless it is a simple recognition of their vast and unclassifiable *varieties*. The old man Müller had much to regret about philology's participation in those attempts to establish divisions and hierarchy within humankind, which he saw as essentially political, rather than scientific.[45] Yet he concludes this train of thought, at least on the occasion of the 1889 Oxford lectures, with a somewhat more hopeful, ameliorating evaluation of the science:

If the Science of Language has encouraged these various national aspirations in places even where separation and national independence would mean political annihilation; if it has called forth a spirit of separatism, it has also another lesson to teach, that of an older, a higher, a truer brotherhood—a lesson too often forgotten, when the opposite lesson seems better to answer political ends. As dialects may well exist by the side of a national speech, nay, as they form a constant supply of life, and vigor, and homely grace to the classical language, so imperial rule does not exclude provincial independence, but may derive from the various members of a great empire, if only held under proper control, its best strength, its permanent health, and that delightful harmony which is the reward of all true and unselfish statesmanship. (55)

---

45. "My memory reaches back far enough to make me see the real and lasting mischief for which, I fear, the Science of Language has been responsible for the last fifty years. The ideas of race and nationality, founded on language, have taken such complete possession of the fancy both of the young and the old, that all other arguments seem of no avail. . . . [E]loquent agitators know how to fan a new, sometimes a dangerous fire" (Müller, *Three Lectures on the Science of Language* [1895], 43).

The language of empire and universal brotherhood may sound to our ears distinctly old-fashioned, and even disturbingly imperialist. But many critics of his own day objected to this for another reason. They thought of their own polygenist theory of human origins as a mark of scientific independence from the biblical authority vested in the story of Adam and Eve in the Garden of Eden, and saw Müller's penchant for monogenesis as evidence of his sentimental attachment to traditional religion.[46] This perception may have contributed to the easy dismissal and continued neglect of his trenchant opposition to the dominant tendencies generated or encouraged by the science of language. Nor is there much evidence that Müller had many sympathizers within his own profession; no other prominent philologist spoke in strong support of his protest against the racialized use of philology.

Thus, the figure most representative of the scholarly propagation of "Aryan"— it was under Müller's watch that the current orthography, instead of "Arian," was established—was, in fact, a vocal opponent of Aryanism, or what might be more precisely called Aryan separatism. Yet the failure of his efforts to convince others was so complete that the fact of his opposition seems to have been largely erased. Indeed, he has been often relegated to the camps of his enemies.[47]

Léon Poliakov, for example, in The Aryan Myth, conflates Müller's position with that of his friend, Ernest Renan. The latter is described by Poliakov as "the

46. An earlier passage, it is true, sounds an even more traditionalist note: "Blood, flesh, and bone are not of our true essence. They are in a constant flux, and change with every year, till at last they return to the dust. Our body is our uniform, very tight sometimes, very painful to don, very painful to doff, but still our uniform only. It matters very little whether it is black or white. Language, on the contrary, is the very embodiment of our true self. Take away language, and we shall indeed be mere animals, and no more. And, besides that, it is language that binds individuals together into families, clans, and nations, and survives them all in its constant growth, thus enabling us to base our classification on general and permanent characteristics, and not on peculiarities which, for all we know, may be the result of climate, diet, and heredity" (ibid., 49).

47. It was a posthumous misfortune that subsequent racist tracts often co-opted Müller's name for their cause. One of the most glaring examples of this may be Duren Ward's 1909 publication innocuously entitled, The Classification of Religions, in which he favors "classifications from racial relationships and from actually traceable mutual historical influences (including linguistic and other genealogical schemes)" (3) and goes on to discuss Müller's Science of Religion extensively (53–64) under the rubric of "classifications based on racial relationship," immediately before going on to disclose his own openly racist system.

chief scientific sponsor of the Aryan myth in France," and "as a propagandist for the Aryan Myth . . . deserves to be placed side by side with his friend Max Müller." Acknowledging the subsequent "retraction" of their supposed earlier views, Poliakov nevertheless goes on to say, of both Müller and Renan:

> The warnings which both of them issued *after* 1870–71 against seeking political advantage from the confusion between languages and races must be placed to their credit. This *implied self-criticism* had little effect, however, while their writings before the Franco-Prussian war continued to make headway in one encyclopaedia after another and to spread their influence through a series of textbooks.[48]

As we have seen, however, Müller's indictment of the racialist ethnology was not implied but quite explicit; nor could it be called self-criticism if we take into account, as he never tired of reminding his readers, that he had always disapproved of it and pronounced his opposition to it in public from the beginning of his career. Poliakov's rather inexplicable account here, therefore, should be viewed as evidence of Müller's almost total failure to get his point across to this day.[49]

48. Léon Poliakov, *The Aryan Myth* (1974), 206; emphasis added.

49. There is a troubling aspect to Poliakov's misperception in that he equated the matter of racialist/racist Aryanism with that of German nationalism. (Hence the significance of 1870–71, the years of Franco-Prussian War, as a watershed.) In a later passage, he further says of Müller: "[T]his man of good will publicly proclaimed his revision of the anthropological ideas he had held until then"—here, he does not specify any particular earlier works—and then goes on to cite Müller's address at Strassbourg criticizing German nationalism, adding, however, that "his timid retraction passed almost unheeded" (ibid., 213–14).

The actual historical circumstance was roughly as follows. Müller certainly had a share in German nationalist sentiments, at least for a time. In the years leading up to and during the war, he was living in Oxford with his English wife and their four children, while his mother and many of his friends and colleagues lived in Germany. At the same time, he was personally acquainted with members of both the German and the English royal families, as well as with the British prime minister Gladstone. Müller thus found himself in a difficult position. In those years, he often publicly and privately spoke and wrote in defense of his fatherland and expressed views that were more sympathetic to the German cause, represented then by the militant figure of Otto Bismarck, than many of his English and French friends and colleagues would have liked, whereas, after the war, amid the triumphalist jubilation of his compatriots, he made critical statements concerning German nationalism.

In view of these records, it may be concluded that Poliakov's claim that Müller at one time expounded "anthropological ideas" regarding language and race which he later "implicitly" and "timidly retracted" is altogether unfounded. On the other hand, Poliakov's claim would be true

It appears that Max Müller, the nineteenth-century's most celebrated scholar representing that branch of science promoting and advancing the knowledge of the Aryan language, maintained throughout his life a position opposed to racialist philology and Aryan separatism, and the textual evidence he left behind seems unequivocal on this point. To be sure, this is an issue separate—or at least separable in principle—from the question as to whether he personally harbored views and opinions about Europeans and non-Europeans that we may find objectionable or censorable, and the textual traces we have pursued thus far do not adequately address this latter question. What they do bring to light—and this, I think, is of a more immediate consequence to the theoretical constitution of the science he is supposed to have helped found—is twofold: on the one hand, he was atypical and even eccentric in view of the prevailing opinions of the philologists and comparative religionists of his time, and on the other, he utterly failed in having his opinions recognized, let alone in persuading others to agree with him.

Just what caused him to remain so stubbornly out of step with the times is difficult to ascertain. An answer to this may not be forthcoming merely through continued close reading of his voluminous corpus. Nevertheless, if for no other reason than the historical interest—and, after all, we are interested in the history of the academic field that was largely responsible for authorizing today's world religions discourse, the field that habitually declares itself beholden to Müller—it may be worthwhile to examine in some detail at least one manifestation of Aryanism, which he did not so much openly fight against but did his best to undermine, so it seems, by all but denying its very existence. This particular form of Aryanism not only greatly annoyed Müller, but in his view, it posed a direct affront to the fledgling science of religion.

5. A Tale of Two Burnoufs

One of the conceptual options available to nineteenth-century intellectuals sufficiently intrigued or troubled by emerging theories of race, religion, and nation was to rethink and reconstitute the origin of Christianity, their tradi-

---

if he said, instead of "Müller's anthropological ideas," "Müller's German nationalist views." This seemingly unconscious conflation of racist Aryanism on the one hand and German nationalism on the other is a serious misstep in Poliakov's otherwise important work. This easy equation would cause us to misconstrue the nature of the Aryanist ideology deeply entrenched in nineteenth-century Europe, which, as we have seen, was by no means limited to the German-speaking world.

tional religion. As we discussed in chapters 5 and 6, it was typically claimed by such thinkers that the historical origin of Christianity—despite its apparent and exoteric ties to the ancient nation of the Israelites and to the Old Testament—was not to be sought in the religion of a Semitic race but more broadly in the soil of the late Hellenic world. This world was said to be a legacy of Alexander's brief but brilliant career, which momentarily brought under one Grecian wing a vast territory ranging from Egypt to Northern India. Though in political terms the youthful conqueror's empire was short-lived, its cosmopolitanism, it has been said, had a lasting effect on the course of world history, resulting as it had in the efflorescence of great seats of learning exemplified by Alexandria. It was this urbane pan-Hellenism of Mediterranean late antiquity that was the most significant setting for the birth of the religion of Christ. This was an opinion greatly favored by savants of more "Hellenic" inclinations, but its popularity was by no means limited to scholarly circles.

An extreme variant of this idea was the theory that this Hellenic world was under direct and extensive Indian and Persian influence, and that Christianity originated from this largely Indianized—that is, overwhelmingly Aryanized—milieu. The Judaism of Jesus' time, especially the "higher form" of Judaism, so some argued, in fact was rather less Semitic and rather more Aryan. Arthur Lillie, one of the British exponents of this theory, put it succinctly in a publication with a telling title, *Buddhism in Christendom, or Jesus, the Essene* (1887):

> About two hundred years before the Christian era a remarkable mystical movement arose amongst the Jews. It came from Alexandria, but its head-quarters in Palestine nestled amongst the protecting malaria of the shores of the Lake Marea, for it was bitterly persecuted. In Egypt these mystics were called Therapeuts; in Palestine, Essenes and Nazarites. In the view of Dean Mansel,[50] this movement was due to Buddhist mission-

50. Presumably, this is Henry Longueville Mansel (1820–71), dean of St. Paul's, Regis Professor of Ecclesiastical History at Oxford, and author of *The Gnostic Heresies of the First and Second Centuries* (1875). As a more conservative Christian, Mansel's purpose in postulating this connection between gnosticism and Buddhism was entirely different from Lillie's; nonetheless, we find in this work some familiar notions expressed, beginning with these statements: "Of the two great divisions of the Indian religion, Brahmanism and Buddhism, the latter is that with which we are chiefly concerned as the channel through which Indian belief and speculation obtained an influence in other countries. The Brahmanical religion was founded upon the total isolation of the Indian people and its castes, and admitted of no communion with other nations; the Buddhist faith was designed for all mankind, and its disciples were zealous and successful

aries, who visited Egypt within two generations of the time of Alexander the Great. . . . [Moreover,] the rites of this, the higher section of Judaism, were purely Buddhist, and . . . two remarkable works, which embody their teaching, minutely reproduce the theogony of Buddhism. These works are the "Sohar" of the "Kabbalah," and the "Codex Nasaraeus."[51]

Lillie explicitly alleges here that the Indo-Persian influence reportedly widespread in the ancient Mediterranean world was due to Buddhist missionary activities, and that the new movement pervading the area as a result was mystical in nature. Rather than excluding Judaism altogether from this pan-Aryan sphere of influence, Lillie's theory instead sought to include and co-opt that aspect of the Jewish tradition deemed by many modern scholars as most esoteric and spiritual, namely, Cabbala. In near perfect symmetry with the case of Sufism and Islam, then, this strand of Jewish mysticism could be disengaged from the staunchly Semitic Jewish orthodoxy and made more "universal"; at the same time, the historical origin of this deeply spiritual Jewish mysticism could now be claimed to be actually Indo-Persian, hence Aryan, just as has been said of Sufism (see chapter 6, section 4).

As this theory of the Indo-Persian origin of the universal makes evident, to situate the source of Christianity somewhere to the east of Palestine was not an accommodating gesture toward Asia, especially toward contemporary inhabitants of Asia. On the contrary, it was a high-handed strategy for the solidification of an idea of purely Aryan Christian Europe. This conceptual mechanism had been set in motion decades before Lillie.

The first writer to achieve international fame and notoriety for proposing a theory of the Indian origin of Christianity was Louis Jacolliot, author of the once much adored, if also much maligned, and now mercifully forgotten bestseller La Bible dans l'Inde, vie de Iezeus Christna (1869). A poetic and evocative dissertation with no particular pretensions to be scholarly, and with no footnotes—other than the author's note of assurance that he had duly conversed with brahmins, pundits, and fakirs—it makes its case through a series of bizarre, assuredly nonphilological comparisons of names, terms, and mythic themes. (Let the "Iezeus" and "Christna" of the subtitle be telling examples.)

---

propagandists. The principal points of contact however between Indian philosophy and Gnosticism may be regarded as common to both branches of the former" (Mansel, Gnostic Heresies, 29).

51. Lillie, Buddhism in Christendom (1887), 2.

But the foundation, or platform, of his argument was the conviction that it was impossible for the culture of the Hebrews, a minor people of servile origin, to have been the source of the religion that compelled and conquered all of Europe, and now, possibly the entire world.[52]

No doubt, the popular appeal of Jacolliot's treatise emanated not only from the sheer novelty of his demonstration but at least as much from its theory of a de-Semitized and re-Aryanized origin of Christianity. The sensational success of this book was such that, scarcely a year after its publication on the Continent, Max Müller was moved to offer some words of caution in his 1870 lecture on the science of religion at the Royal Institution. In brief, he asserts, Jacolliot's speculations are based on bad sources; the author has evidently been deceived by unscrupulous native informants:

> No Sanskrit scholar would hesitate for one moment to say that they are forgeries, and that M. Jacolliot, the President of the Court of Justice at Chandernagore, has been deceived by his native teacher. We find many childish and foolish things in the Veda, but when we read the following line, as an extract from the Veda: 'La femme c'est l'âme de l'humanité,—' it is not difficult to see that this is the folly of the nineteenth century, and not of the childhood of the human race. M. Jacolliot's conclusions and theories are such as might be expected from his materials. (32–33)

Müller's pronouncement in the public forum of the Royal Institution is thus suitably circumspect, pretending to give the Frenchman the benefit of the doubt, exonerating him from the charge of fabrication while passing the blame to his unnamed native informants. Privately, however, Müller expressed his disapproval of Jacolliot's treatise—and his exasperation at its popularity—in a more pointed tone, as we see in a letter he posted on June 29, 1869, addressed to his friend Arthur Penrhyn Stanley, the dean of Westminster:

> That book of Jacolliot's is as silly, shallow, impudent a composition as ever I saw. It is sad to think that people can still be taken in with such a book. Would you believe that Gladstone was reading it in the midst of the Irish debate! The book quotes from the Veda! The extracts are no more from the

---

52. See especially part 2, "Mosès ou Moïse et la société hébraïque," chapter 8, "Impossibilité de l'influence biblique sur le monde ancien," in Jacolliot, La Bible dans l'Inde (1869), 202–8.

Veda than from the *Koran*. I felt so disgusted that I could read no more; and then people ask me to review such a book—they might as well ask me to fight a shoe-black![53]

Unfortunately for Müller, Jacolliot's was not the only instance of this type of wild speculation.[54] For, in the meantime, evidently unbeknownst to him, a highly fashionable Parisian literary journal, *Revue des deux mondes*, was turning out a series of articles by a certain E. Burnouf, who proclaimed that there once was a primitive Aryan religion—much as many philologists maintained that there once was a proto-Aryan language—and he further claimed to demonstrate that it was from this proto-Aryan religion that not only the religions of the Veda and the Avesta and of Greco-Roman antiquity arose but also Christianity itself. In effect, according to this Burnouf, Christianity was an Aryan religion from the beginning, and it had little to do with the Semitic religion of the Jews. These essays, which originally appeared from 1864 to 1868, were subsequently published as a single volume in 1872, under the title *La Science des religions*, no less, thus preceding by one year, albeit in French, Müller's official publication of his Royal Institution lectures by the same name.[55]

One of the early readers of this controversial French treatise was Matthew Arnold, who thoroughly disapproved of it and lost no time saying so in print.[56] Having seen the upstart "science of religion" for what it was, Arnold thought, he declined to predict any hopeful future for the new enterprise and went on to dismiss it. This summary dismissal in turn moved Max Müller to respond, and he did so in *Introduction to the Science of Religion* only a few pages after his comments on Jacolliot quoted above. His tone on this occasion, responding to Arnold, indicates less a cool condescension than befuddled amazement:

I do not wonder at Mr. Matthew Arnold speaking scornfully of *La Science des Religions*, and I fully agree with him that such statements as he quotes would take away the breath of a mere man of letters. But are these state-

53. Müller, *Life and Letters*, 1:367.

54. Jacolliot himself went on to write *Le Spiritisme dans le monde* (1875), another sensational treatise on "occult science in India," extending this view.

55. Émile Burnouf, *La Science des religions, sa méthode et ses limites* (1872), translated by Julie Liebe as *The Science of Religions* (1888).

56. Matthew Arnold, *Literature and Dogma; An Essay towards a Better Apprehension of the Bible* (1883). Müller refers to an 1871 publication by the same title but with different pagination. I have not been able to locate this (presumably original) edition of Arnold's essay.

ments supported by the authority of any scholars? Has anybody who can read either the Vedas or the Old and New Testaments in the original ever maintained that "the sacred theory of the Arya[n]s passed into Palestine from Persia and India, and got possession of the founder of Christianity and of his greatest apostles, St. Paul and St. John"? (35)

After citing some more examples of scholastic outrage of this sort from the Burnouf articles (all quoted by Arnold), Müller eventually concludes his paragraph thus:

Mr. Arnold quotes indeed the name of Burnouf, but he ought to have known that Eugène Burnouf has left no son and no successor. (36)

Müller's indignation is understandable if we consider that, for him personally, this was not only an attack on the "science of religion" but also a senseless denigration of his late beloved Sanskrit teacher, or at least the Burnouf family name. In hindsight, however, it appears that this was a case of misunderstanding—mostly on Müller's part. What Arnold had actually said in the passage Müller referred to was by and large factually correct; for in that context, Arnold was clearly speaking of the author of *La Science des religions*, Émile Burnouf (1821–1907), whom he described as "the accomplished kinsman of the gifted orientalist Eugène Burnouf."[57] As it turns out, the author of the controversial treatise was in fact a cousin of the great E. Burnouf (Eugène), and he, too, could in fact read the Vedas in the original. Whether he indeed consulted any real Vedas for this work, to be sure, is another question; it must be admitted at least that he had the requisite Sanskrit training.[58]

Incidentally, Müller was by no means the only one who seems to have been muddled about the identity of the lesser E. Burnouf. For, with the notable exception of Raymond Schwab, virtually everyone who ever mentioned the two different Burnoufs, or rather, everyone who commented on the monographs respectively authored by one or the other of the two, seems to have confounded them in one way or another.[59] The mistake in their identity can be detected from the otherwise dependable early historian Louis Henry Jordan (who misattrib-

57. Ibid., 106.

58. Although Émile Burnouf reportedly received his doctorate for his work on Plato, his Sanskrit training was evidently of high caliber, so much so that he is credited with the compilation of a Sanskrit-French dictionary (*Dictionnaire classique sanscrit-français*, 1865).

59. After months of perplexity and frustration concerning the identity of the Burnoufs, I came across a critical footnote in Schwab that resolved my predicament. My immense gratitude

utes their works in the index) all the way to a present-day library catalog on the web.[60] But it seems surprising that Müller should have been unaware of his teacher's cousin, who was a Sanskritist of sorts, and who was appropriating the very nomenclature "science of religion" for his own dubious scholastic enterprise. But if indeed Müller was unaware of this situation, he missed a choice opportunity to demonstrate, through a concrete example, how the biological line of family descent is by no means a sure pathway through which such personal attributes as character, talent, and intellectual capabilities are transmitted. For, in sharp contrast to the irreproachable erudition and scholarly circumspection of Eugène—as exemplified by his tour de force *L'Introduction à l'histoire du buddhisme indien* (1844)—his cousin's book is an odious racist tract, wildly speculative, which solicits no support from any kind of scholarship, philological or otherwise.[61]

Like Jacolliot's *La Bible dans l'Inde*, the principal argument of the lesser Burnouf's *Science des religions* is that the essential origin of Christianity was in the primitive Aryan race, and that its nature was therefore less Mosaic than Vedic. As the writer of the preface to the 1888 English translation, *The Science of Religions*, summarized it cautiously but sympathetically:

---

for this clarification moves me to quote the footnote in its entirety: "There were three philologists with the name Burnouf: Jean-Louis (1775–1844), the Latinist and translator of Tacitus and Pliny the Younger and a student of Sanskrit under Chézy before his son Eugene. His nephew Emile-Louis, born in 1821, was also a serious Indic scholar and a Hellenist by profession; Emile founded the Ecole Indianiste at Nancy and was later director of the Ecole d'Athènes. One is surprised to find René Guénon, in *Introduction générale a l'étude des doctrines hindoues*, confusing Eugene with Emile Burnouf when he attacks *La science des religions*, which was the work of the latter. Jean-Louis, born in 1775 near Valognes (the son of a weaver), was a professor of Latin oratory at the Collège de France in 1817, a friend of Bopp and Chézy, and a character in the tradition of Postel" (Raymond Schwab, *Oriental Renaissance* [1950], 494).

One of Schwab's sources here could have been Ernst Windisch's comprehensive history of Sanskrit philology and ancient Indian studies published in 1917 and 1920, where both Jean-Louis and Eugène Burnouf are discussed in some detail. Interestingly, however, Windisch does not mention Émile Burnouf. Cf. Ernst Windisch, *Geschichte der Sanskrit-Philologie und indischen Altertumskunde* (1992), 1:123–40.

60. The online catalog WorldCat (www.oclc.org) attributes a 1973 Paris edition of the translation of *Le Lotus de la Bonne Loi* (originally published in Paris, 1852) to Émile Burnouf, instead of Eugène.

61. The banality of Émile Burnouf's racism is consistent with that of Jacolliot, who also ascribed to the Hebrews (and to the Semites generally) not only a total lack of "spirituality" but also base sensuality and blatant immorality. Cf. Jacolliot, *La Bible dans l'Inde*, 213–14.

Burnouf contends, that if we trace the religious systems of ancient India and Persia to their source, we come to a primitive Âryan religion, which sprang from a deep insight into the principles of nature, and which was, in fact, a refined system of metaphysics founded on a thorough grasp of physical facts. According to Burnouf—and this is the great distinctive feature of his teaching—this primitive Âryan religion was not only the fountain-head of the religions of the *Vêda* and *Avesta*, but also of Christianity itself.[62]

According to Émile Burnouf, moreover, nothing more is needed to apprehend the truth of this "teaching" than "a perfectly unprejudiced mind." Thus he claims, in a crucial chapter entitled "The Action of Races":

> When, with a perfectly unprejudiced mind, we begin to study the written or figured monuments of Christianity, we soon perceive that the metaphysics they disclose have much more in common with that of Persia and India than with the doctrine of the Semites, and that it is identical with that of the *Vêda*. We do not find the nature of God declared in a dogmatic and definite manner in that work. (196)

In this passage we again come across the familiar image of the rigid dogmatism of the Semites, an effective backdrop against which to throw into relief the gracious ease and sophistication of Aryan-Hellenic spirituality generally, and now, of Christianity specifically.

Thus, as always, it is in the explication of the difference between the Aryan and the Semitic that racialist assertions become intensified. What is distinctive and particularly pronounced in Burnouf's version is that the openly ethnological delineation of the difference comes to take on an aspect less of "anthropology" than physiology, physiognomy, or possibly zoology, as in the following passage:

> Those scholars who have studied anthropology almost all agree in placing the Semites between the Âryans and the yellow peoples: not that their distinctive traits betoken a medium condition between those of our race and those of eastern Asiatics; but notwithstanding their being far superior to the yellow races, they betray with regard to us such disparities as to pre-

---

62. E. J. Rapson, preface to Burnouf, *The Science of Religions* (1888), vii; the translation is cited in the text by page number hereafter.

vent their being confounded with Indo-Europeans. A real Semite has smooth hair with curly ends, a strongly hooked nose, fleshy, projecting lips, massive extremities, thin calves and flat feet. And what is more, he belongs to the occipital races; that is to say, those whose hinder part of the head is more developed than the front. His growth is very rapid, and at fifteen or sixteen it is over. At that age the divisions of his skull which contained the organs of intelligence are already joined, and in some cases even perfectly welded together. From that period the growth of the brain is arrested. (190)

Here, then, we find the recurrent theme of stunted growth and "arrested" development particular to the Semites. In contrast:

In the Âryan races this phenomenon, or anything like it, never occurs, at any time of life, certainly not with people of normal development. The internal organ is permitted to continue its evolution and transformations up till the very last day of life by means of the never-changing flexibility of the skull bones. When in the latter years of life our cerebral functions get out of order, this derangement is not due to the external conformation of the head, but in all probability to the ossification of the arteries. (190–91)

The defining characteristic of the Aryans is the capacity for indefinite growth and never-ending development; this familiar idea is given an explicitly physiological explanation here. And this fact of the anatomy, for Burnouf, immediately entails the chasm between the Aryan and the Semitic temperaments that necessitates a clear distinction between the religion of Christ and Semitism of any kind, despite the fact that both these races have been prominent players— or exclusive ones—in the course of human history. They played their respective crucial roles, so he suggests, precisely because they are diametrically opposed: universality on the one hand, exclusivity on the other:

The two tendencies to which the better members of the human community are submitted gather without doubt beneath the banner of Christian metaphysics, making a truly universal religion of Christ. The real Semitic beliefs, on the other hand, spring from one belief exclusively, to which the name of monotheism has been given—an ill-chosen name, for at heart Âryan pantheism admits the unity of God no less so than the doctrine of the Jews or the Arabs; only that unity is differently understood. All exclusiveness in Semitism has had two consequences, which history unfolds to us thus: in the matter of religion, the Semites have kept themselves aloof from all foreign influence; they propagated their dogmas to outsiders only by violence. The Jews never attempted to convert other nations; they rejoiced as privileged beings, superior to other men in their own estimation. (79)

What this passage accomplishes, clearly, is that the sublime majesty of one true God is wrested away from the religion of the monolithic, narrow, exclusivist Semites, and reassigned to the prolific, all-inclusive, universalist Aryans, and thus, by implication, to European Christianity. This is but one more turn given to the momentum driving the more respectable theory offered, for instance, by Renan.

If sheer repetition can impress an idea upon our mind regardless of its intrinsic sense or nonsense, having observed the arguments of Kuenen, Pfleiderer, and Renan, we can now easily predict what is to come next: Burnouf's discussion at this point shifts from the Jews to the Muslims. The recalcitrant minority enclave of the self-aggrandizing Jews—an insignificant minority in the judgment of Émile Burnouf or Jacolliot—is perfunctorily set aside, and a full explication of the essential character of the Semites is then displayed in the historical theater, or rather on the anatomy, of the Arabs, who in the eyes of these authors stand for Muslims in general. And this character, again, can be summarized in one word: violence. Thus Burnouf continues immediately:

> The growth of Islamism belongs to political and military history rather than to the science of religions. It spread itself among peoples of Âryan origin in central Asia and India, as well as among the yellow populations of several countries of Asia; but only with the sword did it conquer, and by force retain. The people who embraced Islamism were ever after noted for the violent energy which animated them, and it became the most prominent trait of their character; and that which may be said of the white or yellow races semitised by Mohammedanism is particularly applicable to black races. (79)

The true nature of the Semitism having been revealed in full, Aryan Christianity can be understood with all the more clarity:

> Christianity then inherits its natural gentleness from the Âryan race amongst whom it grew and unfolded itself, and not from any lingering element of Semitism. Intolerance, of which it is sometimes accused, does

not exist at the fount of its dogmas or in its spirit, which is a spirit of meekness. (79–80)

Having followed the lesser Burnouf thus far, his racialist language appears far more censurable than those of some other authors encountered earlier, even though the premise and the logic of their arguments are essentially the same. Those generally more respectable—Kuenen, Pfleiderer, Renan, and others who are better remembered than Burnouf—had, as grounds for their racialist assumptions, the opinions of many contemporary philologists, who had expounded, in a highly philosophical and technical manner, on the marvels of certain grammatical forms and on the freedom and the originality of inflection. Émile Burnouf, in turn, did not appeal to philological scholarship for support because he did not need to; his own theory was secured, instead, by the reputedly scientific study of skulls, bones, and arteries.[63] Max Müller was intent on rejecting both these grounds without reserve. Hence his oddity, his isolation.

It has occurred to me more than once that, when Müller complained in apparent puzzlement that Matthew Arnold inexplicably had cast aspersions on "Burnouf" and on the science of religions, this might not have been a case of misunderstanding after all. Admittedly, I have no definitive evidence at hand to support the hypothesis that Müller knew of the lesser Burnouf and his work, his appropriation of the term "science of religions," as well as his "blood" relation to the great Burnouf, Müller's teacher. There is only its strong likelihood. For one thing, the original series of Burnouf's articles appeared over four years in a prominent Parisian journal, to which Müller's friend and close correspondent Ernest Renan was also a frequent contributor. It also seems exceedingly strange that, as well connected as Müller was, he did not know of a philology professor from Paris, the compiler of a major Sanskrit-French dictionary and close correspondent of the great Eugène Burnouf, his cousin.[64] Is it possible,

63. Émile Burnouf was by no means the last one to proclaim this racialist understanding and classification of religions in the name of science. Explicitly racialist and openly racist expositions of the differences among religions continued to be produced, as we see, for instance, in the case of Duren J. H. Ward (1851–1942). As mentioned earlier, he left many tracts, pamphlets, and sermons, which include the following titles: The Biography of God as Men Have Told It (1925), The Classification of Religions (1909), A Receivership for Civilization (1922), The Human Races (1922).

64. Based on the extant correspondence, it is reported that the relationship between the two cousins, though twenty years apart in age, was intimate and warm. See Akira Yuyama, Eugène Burnouf (2000), 48.

then, that Müller, having understood the import of the Burnouf tract only too well, in which he could see the pernicious coagulation of Aryan separatism, simply chose not to acknowledge it, that is, chose to disavow its very existence entirely?[65]

"Mr. Arnold ought to have known," Müller said, "that Eugène Burnouf has left no son and no successor." Certainly no offspring such as this. We may take this as a forewarning, then, that Müller was ready to disown, in advance, any such ramifications of his science of language and of religion.

This total silence over Émile Burnouf, the author of La Science des religions—as well as other key aspects of Müller's career we have traced in this chapter— leaves finally inconclusive Müller's precise position with respect to the development of the twentieth-century classification of religion.[66] In fact, this uncertainty renders all the more questionable the relation between the science of religion and the now prevalent discourse of world religions. Despite appearances, Müller did not endorse the classificatory logic devised by philology or its rationale for characterizing individual religions. Meanwhile, other nineteenth-century pioneers of the field did not resolve the question of the division be-

65. In this connection it might be noted that it is also highly peculiar that Müller, for all his love of music and his intimate familiarity with the German music scene since his childhood, never mentions Richard Wagner, arguably the most prominent composer of his time and avid Aryanist and Buddhism enthusiast. For a discussion regarding Wagner's involvement with Buddhism, see Urs App, Richard Wagner und der Buddhismus (1997).

66. It is indeed difficult to reconcile the facts, on the one hand, that there were serious objections to his classificatory system, and on the other, that Müller has been held in great respect as one of the founding figures of the science of religion, and his lectures of 1870 continue to be cited as one of the seminal moments of this science. This is all the more puzzling when we realize that many of the early scholars of comparative religion (or historians of religion) found fault with Müller's theory, particularly his classificatory scheme. In his survey of the study of religion at the turn of the century, Morris Jastrow describes Müller's system as something "proposed by Professor Max Müller many years ago and to which he clung to the last." He then continues incredulously: "It is rather surprising that so acute a thinker as Max Müller should have been led to such an arbitrary system of classification. One might have expected such a scheme from one who was 'merely' a philologist, who might be pardoned for looking at all phenomena through the spectacles of linguistics, but not from a scholar of Max Müller's remarkably broad range, combining in his person the poet, historian, philosopher, and linguist" (Morris Jastrow, The Study of Religion [1901], 81). Rather than taking Jastrow's disbelief as merely rhetorical, it may be well advisable to ponder seriously why indeed Müller clung to the matter of language so tenaciously, why he refused to let the classification of religion float on its own.

tween universal world religions and particularistic national religions, or between religion as such (necessarily particularistic, according to some) and science and rationality (reputedly of Aryan origin yet supposedly universal, according to many); these scholars therefore cannot be credited with having abandoned the theoretical underpinnings of their contentions and having ushered in the new era of a less discriminatory, or one might say laxly inclusive pluralism.

This largely negative result—a disappointing one if the expectation has been a discovery of a definitive causal nexus behind the emergence of the world religions discourse—is instructive nonetheless. What this investigation into the nineteenth-century scholarly world reveals is a complex bundle of concerns and contestations over the spiritual legacy of Europe, concerns that can be read as a series of attempts at theorizing and historicizing Europe, no longer as a mere geographic location but as an identity—an identity that is distinct, in principle, from Christendom. That these thought experiments were left unresolved at the close of the nineteenth century is as significant as the sudden rise of a new conceptual regime in the early twentieth, when the flatly monotonous pluralism of world religions discourse replaced nearly a century of conceptual unrest and quickly became a uniformly adopted convention. And if the new convention seems to have overcome or overridden the concerns of the previous generation by ignoring them, this may be a notable fact still, as it may be an evidence of a certain method of inheritance and continuity all the same.

Perhaps instigated by external reasons, the contentious hypothetical propositions of the previous century were suddenly co-opted and converted to placid facts. Viewed diachronically, there is indeed little difference between the nineteenth-century characterization of various religions and the general description of the same religions under the new discursive regime of the twentieth; in either context, Buddhism generally appears to be benignly compassionate, contemplative, and metaphysical at the core, if also tending toward effete quietism; Islam, on the other hand, is considered fastidiously elemental and constant, tending toward fanatic militancy. The nineteenth century devised some daring theories about these purported characteristics; the twentieth century forgot them. What has thus become invisible under the new discursive regime, then, is the very speculative logic that rationalized and legitimized these commonplace characterizations in the first place.

PART 3

8

Interregnum
Omnibus Guide for Looking toward the Twentieth Century

It remains to be seen what forces contributed most to the determination of the classificatory scheme of the world religions system, and what factors were most instrumental in its eventual installation in the early twentieth century. We have yet to explain not only the particular time in which this occurred, but also the specific character of the new taxonomy. What individual religions beyond the nineteenth-century triumvirate of Christianity, Buddhism, and Islam were named and distinctly recognized, and subsequently came to be included regularly in the list of world religions? And what of the reasons for the remarkable stability of the system for the past century?

This book's scope does not allow a full consideration of the twentieth-century occurrence. The questions enumerated above, in fact, circumscribe a domain of investigation altogether too large for a single study, and the present study is primarily focused on the preceding century. But in the course of examining the nineteenth-century history, I have come upon a number of subject areas that invite further investigation in this chronologically forward direction. In this chapter I will identify several of these areas in a preliminary manner. Some of these topical areas are not entirely new to historical scholarship. My principal purpose in cataloging them here is to suggest that, in some future research, these factors may be profitably considered in relation to the changing classificatory regime and the eventual stabilization of the world religions system.

1. Bequest of the Nineteenth Century: *The Sacred Books of the East*, 1879–1910

Among the gifts of nineteenth-century scholarship on religion to the general public, few were more concrete, compact, and widely disseminated than *The Sacred Books of the East* (1879–1910). Being the first material presentation of the full range of "Oriental religions," the fifty-volume series was compiled under the general editorship of F. Max Müller, and the roster of the translators and collaborators of the project was as illustrious as it was international. The resulting collection was an irreproachable scholarly achievement that made hitherto arcane Oriental classics readily and efficiently accessible to the

English-speaking public, and it became a source to which the students and scholars of religion throughout the twentieth-century have referred time and again. The event and the circumstances of the historic publication, not to mention the actual processes of the project's coordination and the editorial decisions, therefore comprise an important domain of inquiry, which a comprehensive account of the genealogy of the world religions discourse can ill afford to overlook.

That this collection effectively defined the parameters of the "major religions of the world"—which generally corresponded to those belonging to what Müller termed the "aristocracy of book religions"—can be illustrated in a number of ways. To begin with the most immediate, the very idea of compiling what was intended to be a comprehensive collection of such religions must be cited as a significant new objective. The ambitious scope of the project may not be as readily perceptible today as it once was, for nowadays in most American research libraries, the customary Library of Congress cataloging system forces these fifty volumes to be scattered throughout different sections. In contrast, in libraries where the Dewey decimal or some other similarly archaic system still rules, one can share in the full impact of the presentation, as one can behold so many eloquently lettered "great religious systems," each with wondrous ancient roots, lined up in identical costly spines, emanating an air of indisputable facticity.[1]

That there was no established, self-evident list of "great" religions prior to this collection is evident from the fact that the project was carried out incrementally, rather than with a presumption of a predetermined totality, or at least there was no public announcement of any presumption of the sort. The amorphousness of such a project, and the indeterminacy of what counted as the sacred traditions of the non-Western world in the mind of the public, is humorously illustrated by an anonymous letter to the editor of the *Times* (London?), signed "Bibliophilus," dated February 14, 1876(?). Responding to the initial announcement of the publication plan, Bibliophilus writes:

Dear Sir: Prominently among the Notes and News in last Saturday's *Academy* appeared the startling announcement that "Professor Max Müller has

---

1. I became aware of this at Duke University Divinity School Library, where I initially came across many of the nineteenth-century texts discussed in this book. It may be mentioned in this connection also that a singular classificatory system of the library at the Union Theological Seminary (New York) subscribes to another interesting method of representing the "religions of the world."

undertaken to edit for the University Press all the sacred books of the world, except the Bible and the Chinese Scriptures, which last will be allotted to the eminent Sinologue, Dr. Legge." Taking for granted that the Delegates of the Oxford University Press are not cognizant of such a gigantic scheme, may I venture to ask whether the writer of the paragraph in question has the vaguest idea of the comprehensive nature of the term "sacred scriptures of the world?"

The concerned writer goes on to predict that, even if the labor of the editors and collaborators could be offered gratis, which was unlikely, the cost of printing "the gigantic series" alone would be enough to cause financial ruin not only of the press but of all the colleges of the university combined; therefore, he opines: "Instead of securing for Oxford the magnificent future predicted in the *Academy*, as the result of this measure, it would, unless the programme were considerably reduced in its dimensions, involve the University in speedy bankruptcy."[2]

As we know in hindsight, when the project was finally completed over thirty years later, the series turned out to be a relatively concise set of fifty volumes, and the finished product indeed added considerably to the glory of the Oxford University Press. The copies of the individual titles and often the whole set found their way into countless private and public libraries throughout the world. This certainly did much to spread the name of Max Müller, certainly to a far greater extent than his earlier publication of the extremely costly, highly technical six-volume critical edition of the Rig-Veda, set in beautiful Devanagari script as it was, useful only to Sanskrit scholars.

If we sort the forty-nine volumes—the fiftieth volume being a seven-hundred-page general index—in accordance with the category of what we now consider to be world religions, the following results obtain:

Hinduism/Brahmanism (21 volumes)
The Satapatha-Brahmana (5)
The Vedanta-Sutras (3)
Vedic Hymns (2)
The Upanishads (2)
The Grihya-Sutras (2)
The Sacred Laws of the Aryas (2)
Hymns of the Atharva-Veda
The Bhagavad Gita (and other
    selections from the Mahabharata)
The Institutes of Vishnu
The Laws of Manu

---

2. This newspaper clipping is found among the Max Müller Papers at the Bodleian Library, Oxford, shelf mark 2808, folio 152.

Hinduism/Brahmanism (continued)
The Minor Law-Books
Buddhism (10 volumes)
Vinaya Texts [Pali] (3)
The Questions of King Milinda
[Pali] (2)
The Saddharma-Pundarika
["Lotus Sutra"; Sanskrit]
The Fo-Sho-Hing-Tsan-King
["Life of the Buddha"; Chinese,
original in Sanskrit]
The Sutta-Nipata [Pali]

Buddhist Suttas [Pali]
Buddhist Mahayana Texts
[various languages]
Zoroastrianism (8 volumes)
The Zend-Avesta (3)
Pahlavi Texts (5)
Confucianism [Classical Chinese]
(4 volumes)
Taoism [Classical Chinese]
(2 volumes)
Jainism [Sanskrit] (2 volumes)
Islam Qur'an [Arabic] (2 volumes)

The overwhelming number of the texts written in Indo-Persian languages (all but nine of the volumes) may attest to the general inclinations of the philological scholarship of the time, heavily favoring the traditions of Aryan antiquity. The predominance of the volumes pertaining to Hinduism, moreover, may suggest that at this time, or at least in the context of this collection, it was no longer considered merely an indigenous ethnic religion of Hindustan from which a veritable world religion (Buddhism) developed, but rather it had acquired a status very much of its own as the orthodox faith of India.

Aside from Judaism and Christianity, whose cannons were excluded from the series, against the general editor's wish, the only "world religions" missing from the collection are Sikhism and Shinto.[3] Sikhism had been for a long time, and to some extent still is, considered something new and syncretistic, combining elements of Hinduism and Islam, hence not a distinct religion in its own right. (The justice or injustice of this judgment, of course, is a matter of much debate.) As for Shinto, beginning in the middle of the nineteenth century, the Japanese imperial government was busy consolidating it as a religion, or more precisely, as a unique form of national polity and spirituality set apart from all religions. Otherwise, the spectrum covered by this collection approximates the contemporary list of world religions closely.

The publication of this collection also testifies to the overwhelming im-

3. On July 27, 1879, Müller wrote to Victoria Welby (who had supplied him with the text of the epigraph to the first volume of the Sacred Books series): "I look forward to the time when those who objected to my including the Old and New Testaments among the *Sacred Books of the East* will implore me to do so" (F. Max Müller, *Life and Letters* [1902], 2:67).

portance given to textual traditions.[4] To be sure, the privileging of the written text may be said to be a natural inclination of the professional philologists themselves, who after all were dedicated to the life of dead letters. At the same time, the penchant for the authority of writing may also be a reflection of a religious ideology upholding the primacy of revelation, that is, the preeminence of the sacred books *as* revelation. As noted earlier, Müller claimed that this tendency to privilege "book religions" was an attribute of certain "Orientals" themselves, rather than an occupational prejudice of European philologists.[5] Whether or not this was so, there is little doubt that the idea of the primacy of written text and revelation was effectively utilized by some non-Europeans of the nineteenth century. For example, certain intellectual elite natives of Hindustan subscribed to this idea when they objectified Hinduism as an authentic indigenous religion, as opposed to foreign Islamic tradition; on the special authority of the Vedas, they managed to postulate the unity, singularity, and continuity of what were (or appeared to be) greatly multifarious, disparate cults. One of the most illustrative instances may be Swami Vivekananda's renowned address at the World's Parliament of Religions in 1893, in which he com-

4. The presumption of textual primacy may also explain the long-standing protocol that always recognized Zoroastrianism (or "Parseeism," literally, "Persianism") as a distinct religion and one among the great religions of the world from early on, despite its historically localized existence, and despite the relatively small number of the contemporary adherents. It might be suggested that Zoroastrianism owed its independent status first of all to the ancient recognition of the prophet Zoroaster (or Zarathustra), as well as to the prestige of the Zend-Avesta and of the Persian language.

In this connection we may also recall that Persian was one of the first Oriental languages in which Europeans acquired familiarity and competence. This came to pass above all because it was the official administrative language of the Mughal Empire, and the European traders and early colonists of Hindustan had little choice but to come to terms with it. For a long while, Persian had to pass as the language of "India." Until the end of the eighteenth century when a few Europeans like William Jones and Alexander Hamilton began to learn Sanskrit, most classical Indian texts known to the Europeans, such as they were, came in the form of incomplete, often spurious Persian translations. See Raymond Schwab, *Oriental Renaissance* [1950], 26–33; also Thomas R. Trautmann, *Aryans and British India* (1997).

5. Müller might have been referring to the fact that, at some crucial moment in the history of Islam, the enterprising denizens of the expanding Islamic world, when they first reached Hindustan, ingeniously stretched the notion of "the people of the book" in order to accommodate into the Islamic ulema certain non-Muslims, who could then be deemed faithful to some kind of sacred book, though the book in question might be of a kind quite different from the Bible or Qur'an.

menced his exposition of Hinduism—defined explicitly as "the religion of the Vedas"—in all-encompassing terms:

> Sect after sect have arisen in India and seemed to shake the religion of the Vedas to its very foundation, but like the waters of the seashore in a tremendous earthquake, it receded only for a while, only to return in an all-absorbing flood, a thousand times more vigorous, and when the tumult of the rush was over, they have been all sucked in, absorbed and assimilated in the immense body of another faith.
>
> From the high spiritual flights of Vedantic philosophy, of which the latest discoveries of science seem like the echoes, the agnosticism of the Buddhas, the atheism of the Jains, and the low ideas of idolatry with the multifarious mythology, each and all have a place in the Hindu's religion.
>
> Where then, the question arises, where is the common center to which all these widely diverging radii converge; where is the common basis upon which all these seemingly hopeless contradictions rest?
>
> The Hindus have received their religion through their revelation, the Vedas. They hold that the Vedas are without beginning and without end.[6]

In this manner, the text-centric ideology, whatever might have been its origin, was skillfully employed by a colonial native spokesperson in order to assert most dramatically the reality and the predominance of the legacy of his people, which he claimed constituted a particular religion, Hinduism, with a tremendous reach, in space, in time, and in variety.

None of this, however, implies that the formation of the final docket of world religions resulted from a unilateral creative projection by European scholars. Nor does it mean that the presumed descendants of the authors of these sacred texts (present-day non-European inhabitants of India, for example) played only a reactive role in the process; we have already caught a glimpse in Vivekananda's gesture as evidence to the contrary. Rather, the situation strongly suggests that even an activity as seemingly cerebral and academic as philology or the compilation of critical editions is thoroughly and ineluctably intertwined with larger social and political processes and therefore must be contextualized and analyzed accordingly.[7]

---

6. Vivekananda, "Hinduism," in Richard Hughes Seager, ed., *The Dawn of Religious Pluralism* (1993), 421.

7. For example, essays included in Donald S. Lopez Jr.'s compilation *Curators of the Buddha* (1995) explore various aspects of the development of Buddhology from this angle. Similarly but

The Sacred Books of the East was a broadly international collaborative work, carried out during the decades when European colonial rule reached global proportions, and completed on the eve of the First World War. It may therefore be a particularly fruitful site for detailed analysis. Given the initial celebrity of the publication, the magnitude of its immediate impact, as well as the scope and the longevity of its influence generally, it may be reasonably assumed that it played not an insignificant role in the development of the world religions discourse in the twentieth century, and perhaps even in its persistence.

2. The World's Parliament of Religions, 1893

Early in chapter 1, we observed how the list of world religions familiar to us today came to be more or less standardized in the 1920s and 1930s, which also happened to be the period of curricular development of new college courses in "great religions" and "living faiths" of the world, especially in North American institutions of higher education. This general condition may in fact indicate that the solidification of the world religions framework as a pedagogical prototype was first of all an American phenomenon.

In this connection, it may be worth recalling the results of a survey taken by Louis Henry Jordan in the early years of the twentieth century, which presented the first comprehensive view of existing "comparative religion" curricula in colleges and universities around the world.[8] What this study indicates is that, as much as a hundred years ago, the basic structure of the world religions schema—that is, the laterally arranged, actively comparativist representation of multiple religions—had a stronger institutional showing in the United States than in the leading European universities, which had up to that point produced the great majority of historians, philologists, and ethnologists whose works had become the basis of comparative studies.[9] Even if one takes into account

---

less analytically, Neil Asher Silberman's *Digging for God and Country* (1982) interestingly narrates the development of biblical archaeology in relation to the colonial interests of various European nations. Among the recent titles dealing with the political and ideological context of the scholarship on religion are Timothy Fitzgerald, *The Ideology of Religious Studies* (2000), Richard King, *Orientalism and Religion* (1999), and Bruce Lincoln, *Theorizing Myth* (1999).

8. See one of the many useful appendices to his *Comparative Religion*, especially chart 4, "The Present Position of Comparative Religion in the World's Universities, Colleges, etc," as well as extensive explanatory notes on individual entries on the chart (Louis Henry Jordan, *Comparative Religion* [1905], 580–604).

9. See, in this connection, an appendix entitled "Germany's General Attitude towards Comparative Religion," in ibid., 512–16.

the fact that as a Canadian Jordan's own vantage point was North American and therefore his views might have been biased in the direction of overemphasis, the survey results still seem to bear out his general observation that the United States is "a country in which the study of the Science of Religion has made phenomenally rapid strides, and in which the number of younger men at present engaged in this inquiry is . . . large and . . . rapidly growing."[10]

In addition to these curricular developments statistically documented by Jordan, one event stands out as an emblem of the nascent American century: the first modern interfaith assembly of a global proportion, part of the world's fair held in Chicago to commemorate the quatercentenary of Columbus's arrival in the New World.

It is reported that on September 11, 1893, marking the commencement of the first World's Parliament of Religions, the Liberty Bell at the Columbian Exposition in Chicago was sounded ten times in the honor of "what were [then] considered the world's ten great religions: Hinduism, Buddhism, Jainism, Zoroastrianism, Taoism, Confucianism, Shintoism, Judaism, Christianity, and Islam."[11] Assuming that this lore is true, it seems significant, first of all, that someone was doing the counting. Indeed, the count was just one short of the present-day standard list of eleven. In other words, only Sikhism—"a relatively modern group," in the words of the editor of the 1993 centenary volume of the Parliament proceedings—was missing.[12] Admittedly, it is now generally acknowledged that the representation in this assembly was wildly disproportionate in favor of Protestant Christianity. Nonetheless, those ten religions did in fact send delegates to the Parliament, where each religious group was asked to "make the best and most comprehensive statement of the faith it holds and the service it claims to have rendered to mankind."[13]

That this congress took place at all may warrant the assumption that, by that time, each of the designated groups somehow recognized itself as a distinct re-

10. Ibid., 462. The information on Jordan's North American background is from A. M. Fairbairn's introduction (vii–ix), according to which Jordan was native of Canada, received his B.D. from Edinburgh, and traveled and studied widely in British, European, and American universities.

11. Richard Hughes Seager, introduction to *Dawn of Religious Pluralism*, 15.

12. Ibid., 8.

13. Joseph M. Kitagawa, "The History of Religions in America," in *The History of Religions* (1987), 5.

ligion, or else a distinct enough sect within a religion. Each religion or sect sent one or more representatives who were empowered and authorized, in some un-specified way, to speak for their "faith."[14] Whatever may be said concerning the fairness or unfairness of representation on the occasion, it cannot be denied that this was the first modern parliament of world religions taking place in, and under the auspices of, the West. The question for us now is to what extent this conspicuous event, which was certainly not without religious as well as geo-political significance, was instrumental in legitimatizing the world religions discourse overall, and possibly also in furthering the cause of the fledgling sci-ence of religion based on comparison.

At present, the received wisdom, especially in the United States, is that the 1893 World's Parliament of Religions marked the symbolic beginning of to-day's pluralistic attitude toward the question of religion, an attitude quintes-sentially embodied by American society.[15] It is even suggested that this event signified the veritable "dawn of religious pluralism," as Richard Hughes Sea-ger, the aforementioned editor of the centenary volume, puts it in his intro-duction, and as Diana Eck concurs in her foreword to the same volume. Both Seager and Eck qualify their assertion with an admission that the pluralism realized in that particular occasion was "limited by today's standards,"[16] that there was not much equity in the way various religions were actually repre-sented, and that there were too many groups not represented at all. These qualifications notwithstanding, both Seager's and Eck's historical assessment of the Parliament is unambiguously positive and celebratory. Their language echoes a familiar view, a largely unconscious but surely nostalgic, harkening back to a brief moment of hope, to the days of a peaceable world gathering just before omens of the world war began to darken the horizon. To see continuity between then and now, overlooking the chasm of political disruptions and vio-lence in the meantime, is a form of optimism to say the least, and possibly a wishful assumption of progress hitherto accomplished: what began a century ago ever so imperfectly as a first attempt at interreligious accord has undergone

14. The case of Taoism was rather peculiar and exceptional in that it was "represented" by an anonymously written essay lamenting the present state of its degeneration into priestly super-stitions, while calling attention to its ancient, philosophically, ethnically, and spiritually pure foundations in the texts of Lao-tzu and Chuang-tzu.

15. For existing deliberations on the impact of the Parliament generally, see Richard Hughes Seager, *The World's Parliament of Religions* (1995), and Eric J. Ziolkowski, ed., *A Museum of Faith* (1993).

16. Seager, introduction to *Dawn of Religious Pluralism*, 8.

in the intervening years very many improvements (if also trials and tribula-
tions) to become today's more inclusive and representative pluralism. According to Eck, those improvements include, first, a greater and more sincere recognition of the plurality of religions, instead of a mere presumption of unity
or facile universalism, and second, a more genuine self-representation of each
group, large or small. She seems to surmise, moreover, that the actual ethnic
diversification of the population in most American cities, and the explicitly representational identity politics emerging in those increasingly cosmopolitan
communities, are felicitous features of American society as a whole, and that
these features have directly contributed to improvements in the pluralist project, which she and others visibly promote.[17]

The optimistic sentiment of these contemporary scholars is generally consistent with the attitude of the Parliament organizers and participants themselves. They, too, were of the opinion that American society uniquely possessed
some propitious qualities that fostered an ecumenical spirit, making possible
such a momentous event as the World's Parliament in the first place. To be sure,
this nonsectarian Americanness, in their late-nineteenth-century minds, was
inseparable from Christianness, or a certain type of liberal Protestantism. The
welcoming address of John Henry Barrows, president of the Parliament, com-
municates this sentiment well:

> You agree with the great mass of Christian scholars in America in believ-
> ing that Christendom may proudly hold up this Congress of the Faiths as
> a torch of truth and of love which may prove the morning star of the twen-
> tieth century. . . . Justis Ameer Ali, of Calcutta . . . has expressed the opin-
> ion that only in this Western republic would such a congress as this have
> been undertaken and achieved. . . . Christian America . . . welcomes to-
> day the earnest disciples of other faiths and the men of all faiths who, from
> many lands, have flocked to this jubilee of civilization.[18]

These writings about the Parliament, then and now, thus emphatically claim
that a congress such as this was possible only in America, the vanguard of an

---

17. Diana L. Eck, foreword to Seager, *Dawn of Religious Pluralism*, xvi–xvii.

18. Barrows nonetheless qualifies his remarks in this fashion: "I do not forget—I am glad to
remember—that devout Jews, lovers of humanity, have cooperated with us in this Parliament. . . . But the world calls us, and we call ourselves, a Christian people" (John Henry Barrows, "Words of Welcome," in Seager, *Dawn of Religious Pluralism*, 25).

emerging global civilization, and that it was appropriate, moreover, that it was not held in one of the stodgier, more dignified localities of the Eastern Seaboard such as Boston, New York, or Philadelphia, but instead in the bustling midwestern city of Chicago.[19] The Parliament certainly put Chicago on the map, and the publicity it generated also boded well for Chicago's newly instituted, vigorously growing eponymous university—financed by American industrialists, most notably, the Haskells and the Rockefellers[20]—where John Henry Barrows, was soon to be appointed the Haskell Lecturer on Comparative Religion.[21]

It is still debatable, however, whether something like the passing of the torch from the old world to the new—that is, the transfer of authority and dominance of the kind imagined by some American scholars then and now—was actually taking place at the time of this celebrated occasion. Nor is it immediately obvious, for that matter, what precisely was the special significance of the Americanization of "comparative religion." It remains to be examined whether this transmission and transformation, if it really occurred, had any bearing on the seeming disappearance of the more technically scientific debate about the universality of *Weltreligionen* (in contradistinction to *Landesreligionen*) and the concomitant surge of the more populist world religions discourse. Similarly, it is yet to be determined whether the Americanization of

19. Seager reports that in the mid-1880s New York and St. Louis were also under consideration as a possible site for the Columbian Exposition. "After lengthy public debate and private lobbying, Washington gave the nod to Chicago, then still the 'great metropolis of the West' and a city rebounding from its devastating Great Fire of 1871. New Yorkers were skeptical about the ability of a city best known for its slaughterhouses, grain and lumber exchanges, and sprawling, smoky railroads to mount a suitably august world's fair, so national promoters of the Exposition set as their standard the most important fair since London's Crystal Palace Exposition of 1851— Paris's 1889 *Exposition Universelle*. As a result, the World's Columbian Exposition was a synthesis of Chicago 'can-do' energy and a canon of taste established by the more Francophilic East" (Seager, introduction to *Dawn of Religions Pluralism*, 3).

20. In this connection, it is also useful to remember the contentious rivalry between some New York Baptists and their counterparts in Chicago, who vied energetically for John D. Rockefeller's attention in order to finance the founding of a Baptist university. The initial pledge by Rockefeller was $400,000—he actually gave $600,000 to start, in 1889—a paltry sum in comparison to Johns Hopkins's bestowal of $7,000,000 in 1867 (one half to found a hospital and the other half, a university); but the Rockefeller gift was singularly instrumental in establishing an institution in the midwestern city. See W. Carson Ryan, *Studies in Early Graduate Education* (1971), especially 91–105.

21. Jordan, *Comparative Religion*, 445–46.

"Western" discourse about religion had anything to do with the decline of the academic preoccupation with classifying and analyzing religions and the simultaneous rise in prominence of more religious concerns.

It was undoubtedly the faith communities in America, primarily interested in the future survival of religions, who groped for ecumenical, universalist, and pluralist strategies for "uniting all religions against all irreligion." To what degree, if any, did the overtly religious and confessional agenda of the Parliament affect the more self-consciously scholarly study of religion? How much sympathy and confidence did this enthusiasm for the ecumenical unity inspire in the minds of the *Religionswissenschaftler* when President Barrows called the Parliament the "first school of comparative religions"? What degree of accord did it find among scholars when Charles Carroll Bonney, in another welcoming speech, stated the purpose of the Parliament in the following terms: "Without controversy, or any attempt to pronounce judgment upon any matter of faith or worship or religious opinion, we seek a better knowledge of the religious condition of all mankind, with an earnest desire to be useful to each other and to all others who love truth and righteousness"?[22]

With regard to these questions, a survey of retrospective evaluations by some of today's academicians seems to indicate that opinions vary, possibly along national boundaries. For example, Diana Eck, professor of comparative religion and Indian studies at Harvard University, is of the opinion that the Parliament gave an impetus to "the academic field of the comparative and historical study of religion, especially in the United States." Emphasizing what she takes to be the scholarly tenor of this unquestionably religious congress, she mentions how "six European scholars of comparative religion—F. Max Müller, J. Estlin Carpenter, Albert and Jean Réville, C. P. Tiele, and Charles D'Harlez—sent addresses to the Parliament." The topics of their addresses appear to be suitably academic:

Estlin Carpenter (Oxford), "The Need for Wider Conception of
   Revelation, or Lessons from the Sacred Books of the World"
C. D. d'Harlez (Louvain), "The Comparative Study of the World's
   Religions"
F. Max Müller (Oxford), "Greek Philosophy and the Christian Religion"
Albert Réville (College de France), "Conditions and Outlook for a
   Universal Religion"

22. Charles Carroll Bonney, "Words of Welcome," in Seager, *Dawn of Religious Pluralism*, 21.

Jean Réville (Sorbonne), "Principles of the Scientific Classification of
   Religion"

C. P. Tiele (Leiden), "On the Study of Comparative Theology"

Judging from these titles alone, it seems that this illustrious slate of scholars
addressed issues that were at once proper to their individual scholarly expertise
and at the same time relevant to the ecumenical concerns of the Parliament. It
therefore appears that the old professors indeed rose to the occasion and did
their pedagogic best, even if, without exception, they chose to do this from afar,
sending their papers to be read, rather than appearing in person at the "jubilee
of civilization." To be sure, since the center of Occidental civilization had on
this occasion moved very far to the west from the European point of view, it is
not surprising that the lengthy journey required for attending the event was not
undertaken by the aging savants of the old world. (In 1893, Max Müller was to
turn seventy, Albert Réville sixty-seven, and Tiele sixty-three.) Be that as it may,
the fact of their physical absence at the congress does not seem to have affected
Eck's estimation of the import of their participation. She thus closes her brief
essay on the Parliament by claiming that "the study of world religions as an academic field today can be traced through numerous threads that lead back to
the Parliament."[23] She does not specify, however, any of these strands of connection; nor does she explain in what sense exactly "the study of world religions" constitutes "an academic field."

An altogether different view of the event is presented by Eric Sharpe, a British
scholar and well-known authority on the history of comparative religion. He
prefaces his remark on the Parliament with a brief paragraph reminding the
reader of the following fact: "The first genuinely scientific congress of comparative religion was held in 1900, in Paris." He is referring, of course, to the
Congrès International d'Histoire des Religions held in conjunction with the
Exposition Universelle. This scholarly gathering was the inaugural event of
what was later to become a regular congress organized, as of 1950, by the International Association for the History of Religions (IAHR). He admits, however, that there had been a couple of congresses prior to that date, "which are
deserving of mention" in some way. One of those precedents is what he terms
"the celebrated (some would say notorious) World's Parliament of Religions,
convened in Chicago in 1893."[24]

---

23. Eck, foreword to Seager, *Dawn of Religious Pluralism*, xiv–xv.
24. Sharpe, *Comparative Religion*, 138.

Sharpe helps contextualize the event by noting that the World's Parliament, though by far the most famous, was not the only religious assembly that took place at the Columbian Exposition: "Under the heading of 'religion' there were in fact forty-one separate denominational and inter-denominational congresses.[25] The actual Parliament of Religions was meant as a demonstration of world brotherhood, and in the eyes of its organisers at least, succeeded in its aim." As this guarded phrasing signals sufficiently, Sharpe's own assessment of the Parliament's success is rather negative. As he puts it presently: "[T]he humanitarian unity toward which the parliament strove probably existed only in the minds of its organisers, and in a few of the delegates. It was bitterly attacked by many orthodox Christian agencies" and was quipped "a menagerie of religions," an outrage, and so on.

Sharpe is even more skeptical in his estimation of the Parliament's contribution to the science of religion proper. This is not to say that he found nothing of scholarly merit among the congress proceedings; but on the whole, the precious little that he could recognize of value turned out to be exceptions that proved the general case: "Some scholarly addresses were given, and amid the welter of sentimental euphoria and the incredible prolixity of the proceedings, some wise words were being spoken." Clearly, Sharpe believes that those eminent scholars who sent their papers but did not appear in person had good reason for not getting fully involved, that is, some reason other than their frailty. In Sharpe's opinion, then, the congress was a sensational success in the eyes of some people (all of the organizers, many of the participants, and the multitude of like-minded suppliers and consumers of the American popular press), an outrage and sacrilege in the eyes of some others (mostly religious traditionalists). But above all, Sharpe implies, the whole affair must have been a mortifying embarrassment for bona fide scholars of religion. Far from being a propitious beginning of scholarship of any kind, he contends, the Parliament posed a real danger to the emerging science of religion because it "tended to associate at least some comparative religionists (those who dared to associate themselves with it) with an idealistic programme of world peace and understanding." Naturally, in this historian's view, such an association was most unwelcome from the scholars' standpoint. In sum, he concurs with the American

25. According to Charles Carroll Bonney, the general president of the World's Congress of the World's Columbian Exposition, however, there were in fact forty-six divisions under the Department of Religion. See Bonney, "A Prefatory Sketch of the World's Congress Work and the World's Parliament of Religions," in Edmund Buckley, ed., *Universal Religion* (1897), first course, 8.

opinion up to a point, but only to draw a sharply negative conclusion concerning the impact of the event upon the well-being of scholarship on religion:

> Observers were right when they pointed out that this meeting could only have been held in brash, sentimental, pluralistic America. But the ideals which were so desirable in the Chicago of the 1890s were not necessarily those of, for instance, the European universities, where the science of religion was slowly finding its feet. It was perhaps permissible for Max Müller to associate himself *in absentia* with the parliament; his reputation could bear it. Others held themselves firmly aloof—and have continued to hold themselves aloof from any further such gatherings simply on the grounds that whatever the need for inter-religious understanding, the scientific study of religion, committed to the quest of truth for truth's own sake, ought not to be saddled with such an onerous and subjective incidental. This is not to say that there have been no scholars who in later years have embraced a refined form of the Chicago programme. There have been many, not least in America.[26]

The acerbic tone of this judgment may suggest that perhaps more is at stake than the relative value of a particular historical event. What is striking is the way in which an Atlantic divide is drawn by means of a series of associations. "Brash" and "sentimental" is on the side of American pluralism, whose predominant concern with "inter-religious understanding" is finally deemed a matter of "subjective incidental"; whereas European universities are aligned with the science of religion proper, which serves no other objective than truth itself, truth for its own sake, and the attitude of scholarship is characterized as at once circumspect ("slowly finding its feet") and resolutely and necessarily aloof.[27] An intriguing question arises at this juncture with particular clarity and simplicity: does religious pluralism really have anything to do with scientific comparativism?

Meanwhile, we may observe that it is still a matter of smoldering trans-

26. Sharpe, *Comparative Religion*, 139.

27. It remains to be investigated whether the European scholars of the time recognized an Atlantic divide of the sort Sharpe has formulated here. For one thing, Max Müller—whose scholarly credentials were strong enough, according to Sharpe, to sustain at least some form of association with the questionable enterprise—left a considerably more charitable, if not to say enthusiastic, view of the Parliament. See F. Max Müller, "The Parliament of Religions, Chicago, 1893" and "Letter to the Rev. John Henry Barrows, D.D., Chairman of the General Committee [April 2, 1893]," in *Last Essays*, 2nd series (1901), 324–45.

atlantic debate, a century later, whether the Chicago Parliament was in the long run a good thing to have happened for the academic well-being of comparative religion and for the science of religion. This is not yet a moment to judge or attempt to arbitrate between the sharply contrasting perspectives represented by two contemporary scholars hailing from two different shores. While we await the results of a more thorough and comprehensive investigation into the impact of the Parliament, the following statement by Joseph Kitagawa, dated 1959, may afford us a somewhat balanced view, if for no other reason than that it acknowledges both the disjuncture between religious pluralism and scientific comparativism and the collusion of the two interests particularly prevalent in America:

> Among the participants [of the Parliament] were many notable scholars, including historians of religions, but they attended the parliament as representatives of their faiths or denominations and not of the discipline of the history of religions. Nevertheless, in the minds of many Americans, comparative religion and the cause of the World Parliament of Religions became inseparably related. What interested many ardent supporters of the parliament was the religious and philosophical inquiry into the possibility of the unity of all religions, and not the scholarly, religio-scientific study of religions. Nevertheless, the history of religions and comparative religion, however they might be interpreted, became favorite subjects in various educational institutions in America.[28]

3. Amateur Interests Have Their Say: Private Foundations and Endowed Lectureships

The World's Parliament of Religions was by no means the only instance in which religiously grounded interests made themselves felt in the scholarly domain, be they instances of intrusion and obfuscation or, on the contrary, of positive incentive in the form of material and moral support. Among the "pluralist" and "comparativist" endeavors of the late nineteenth century, as we have already seen to some extent, scholarly and evangelical enterprises coexisted in many inextricable ways. The preponderance of "comparative theology" in the latter half of the nineteenth century—an endeavor ultimately aimed at demonstrating the superiority or supremacy of Christianity—over and above the more scholastic comparative history of religions, has been noted already in chapter

---

28. Kitagawa, "The History of Religions in America," 5–6.

2. There was a great proliferation of books and lectures discoursing on various religions of the world from this theologically interested perspective, and this alone would indicate that the educated classes of Europe and North America were drawn to this topic primarily for religious reasons. It therefore seems reasonable to assume that, in the long run, this broader base of interested public was far more significant for the dissemination and sedimentation of the world religions discourse than any intramural dispute among the scholars.

As we have seen, some of the high-profile lectures on comparative theology were addressed expressly to future missionaries. It was felt that such instructions were most necessary for those willing soldiers and servants of the Lord, as they prepared to venture into the spiritual wilderness. They would soon come face to face with those of other faiths and, therefore, must be outfitted with the best informed and the most effective means of contending with heathen resistance, in order best to propagate the one and the only universal religion. Also among the audience were those who intended to become colonial officials or otherwise engage in commercial enterprises in foreign territories; they might not be called upon to convert any idolaters but would in time come into the position of governing, managing, and pacifying the heathen population. Still others were homebound bourgeois readers simply curious about, or vaguely frightened by, the recent eruptions of the esoteric and the exotic in their midst. Their increasingly cosmopolitan society was replete with fashionable novelties ranging from Spiritualist séances and Theosophical lodges to fleeting glimpses of transplanted Hindu sadhus and fakirs, whirling Dervishes, and dancing Red Indian medicine men on tour. As numerous contemporary accounts testify, those European men and women of leisure who came in contact with these uncanny foreign elements characteristically exhibited what Rudolf Otto famously described as the attitude of the religiously awestruck: fear, dread, and bottomless fascination all at once. It was in part in response to the demands of such an audience, predisposed to the *mysterium tremendum*, that the magisterial proclamations of expert academic authorities were being offered. Those authorities in turn tempered the fear and quenched the thirst for knowledge for a time, all the while propelling the European desire ever more deeply into the regions of the unknown.

As the nineteenth century wore on, a growing number of experts professionally trained in one or more of the non-Christian traditions—those who had acquired the necessary linguistic competence as well as a privileged access to some of the venerable old texts written in those languages—became regularly available to deliver public lectures and addresses. There is hardly a scholar at the turn of the century renowned for specialized scholarly accomplishments who did not engage the lay audience through public forums of one kind or another. Whether or not the scholar drew any appreciable remuneration from such activities, it is reasonable to infer that the overall standing of those engaged in arcane scholarship on religions was enhanced, if not to say supported and justified, by these more visible services they could render to the public.

One of the remarkable features of the history of the science of religion in Great Britain and the United States is the prominent role played by private donors and foundations who initiated and promoted various educational programs in the interest of the new, nonecclesiastical, nondenominational, and often interreligious approaches to the subject of religion.[29] Frequently, these individuals and organizations chose to institute public lecture series to be delivered by eminent scholars, while utilizing some of the most prestigious academic and cultural venues. The scope of lecture topics was often designated as "natural theology," "history of religion(s)," or "comparative religion." In earlier chapters, we became acquainted with some of these lecture series, including two of the oldest: the Boyle Lectures (established in London in 1691) and the Bampton Lectures (inaugurated at Oxford in 1780).[30] The ever dependable Louis Henry Jordan, in his 1905 study, mentions other series, together with the list of individual topics in some cases: Congregational Union Lectures (London, 1833), Baird Lectures (Glasgow, 1873), Cunningham Lectures (Edinburgh, 1864), Croall Lectures (Edinburgh, 1875–76), Ely Lectures (New York), Morse Lectures (New York), Stone Lectures (Princeton). But by far the most celebrated and significant for

29. The role of private foundations makes all the more pronounced the difference between, on the one hand, the British and American situation and, on the other hand, the countries where the business of science and higher education have been more directly and firmly in the hands of the state, such as the Netherlands, France, and Germany. In the latter locations, either princely, electoral, or at times dictatorial authorities made key decisions affecting the fate of the study of religion, for instance, to establish a chair in comparative religion, or to create a religion faculty independent of the church (sometimes, independent of the state church, as in the case of the Netherlands). Needless to say, the origin and growth of the idea that the public or the state should support the study of religion is a matter deserving extensive study.

30. It seems significant that, as mentioned earlier, at the time of the inauguration of the series in 1699, the Boyle Lectures were actually called "sermons" rather than "lectures." The Bampton Lectures, which became effective as of 1779, pursuant to the will dated 1751, were called "Divinity Lecture Sermons." See Jordan, *Comparative Religion*, 562. It is also noteworthy that the Bampton lecturers were by decree limited to members of the Church of England.

the emergent science of religion were the Hibbert Lectures (1878), Gifford Lectures (1888), and the American Lectures on the History of Religions (1895).[31]

While these lecture series were, and continue to be, peculiarly British and American phenomena, the roster of lecturers was decidedly international. The most famous Dutch pundits of their time, C. P. Tiele and Abraham Kuenen, were recipients of the honor of delivering the Gifford and the Hibbert Lectures respectively. Among many German scholars, Otto Pfleiderer served in both series, as did Max Müller, who was the inaugural lecturer in both.[32] Müller's French friend and Semitic philologist, Ernest Renan, as well as Albert Réville, the first occupant of the university chair in comparative religion in France, delivered Hibbert Lectures; so did the Belgian scholar, Count Goblet d'Alviella. Legendary American philosophers Josiah Royce and William James crossed the Atlantic one after the other in 1899–1900 and 1900–1901 to deliver the Gifford Lectures in Aberdeen and in Edinburgh respectively.[33] James's justly renowned treatise *The Varieties of Religious Experience* (1902) was based on these lectures.[34]

Let us also note a few more American foundations, which had a significant impact on the career of some of the principal figures in twentieth-century comparative religion. It was the Haskell Foundation of Chicago that financed, for

31. See Jordan, *Comparative Religion*, 385–88, 562–72. The last named American lecture series was the fruit of a cooperative committee with members from "Columbia, Cornell, Johns Hopkins, Pennsylvania, Yale, and other leading American Universities" (571).

32. Technically speaking, there were four inaugural lecturers for the Gifford series. The term of the bequest was such that a series of lectures were to be given at brief intervals in each of the four Scottish universities every year. Hence Max Müller, who delivered his at Glasgow, shared the distinction with Hutchison Stirling (Edinburgh), E. B. Tylor (Aberdeen), and Andrew Lang (St Andrews).

33. James and Royce also gave the Ingersoll Lectures on "the immortality of man" (in 1897 and 1899 respectively). The series was established by Caroline Haskell Ingersoll around 1893 in accordance with the will of her father, George Goldthwait Ingersoll, to be delivered at Harvard University, his alma mater.

34. The twentieth-century list of the Gifford lecturers yields an interesting array. It includes philosophers ranging from Bernard Bosanquet, Alfred North Whitehead, John Dewey, Gabriel Marcel, Frederick Copleston to A. J. Ayer and Hilary Putnam; midcentury theologians such as Rudolf Bultmann, Emil Brunner, Karl Barth, Reinhold Niebuhr, Etienne Gilson, John Macquarrie, and Jürgen Moltmann, as well as historians and theorists of religion, including J. G. Frazer, R. R. Marett, Arnold Toynbee, Owen Chadwick, R. C. Zaehner, Nathan Söderblom, Seyyed Hossein Nasr, Jaroslav Pelikan, and Annamarie Schimmel. In more recent years, the speakers have included some vocal proponents of particular theological positions (Alasdair MacIntyre, Stanley Hauerwas), prominent cultural observers (George Steiner, Iris Murdoch), as well as a latter-day speculative theorist of the origin of religion (Walter Burkert).

instance, the institute that resulted in Eustace Haydon's *Modern Trends in World-Religions* (1934), discussed in chapter 1. Caroline E. Haskell had initiated the work in support of comparative religion by establishing the Haskell Lectures at the University of Chicago in 1895. No more than a year later, she also provided for the Barrows Lectures—named, as we have seen, after the president of the 1893 World's Parliament of Religions—to be "delivered in various cities of India." In accordance with the benefactor's wish, John Henry Barrows inaugurated the series in 1896–97 with seven lectures published under the revealing title *Christianity, the World-Religion*. In time the foundation came to serve various communities of the midwestern United States and provided the venue, for instance, for Rudolf Otto's celebrated series of lectures on mysticism, initially delivered in the winter of 1923–24 at Oberlin College in Ohio and published in 1932 as *Mysticism East and West*. Mircea Eliade gave the 1956 Haskell Lectures at the University of Chicago, shortly before he was appointed professor in the same university.

The Terry Foundation Lectures at Yale University over the years hosted a number of highly visible and controversial figures ranging from C. G. Jung, whose 1937 lectures resulted in the well-known *Psychology and Religion* (1938), to the Swiss Catholic theologian Hans Küng, whose *Freud and the Problem of God* appeared in 1979, shortly before Pope John Paul II barred him from calling himself a Catholic theologian or from teaching in the Catholic faculty. As it turned out, the Terry Lectures—the deed of the endowment specifies that they be "on Religion in the light of Science and Philosophy"[35]—was an opportune stage for Küng because, already in 1963, American bishops had banned him from speaking in any Catholic institutions in the United States. On many occasions, then, these lectures (almost always held on university campuses) effectively functioned as a platform for theology by other means.

It may be argued that no other private organization influenced and colored the enterprise of comparative religion in America and at the same time assured the viability of the world religions discourse more intently and conspicuously, or with deeper pockets, than the Bollingen Foundation. Named after C. G. Jung's private place of retreat in a Swiss village, the foundation began as something of a personal mission of Mary Mellon (1904–46). In 1937 she met Jung

---

35. The deed of gift declares that "the object of this foundation is not the promotion of scientific investigation and discovery, but rather the assimilation and interpretation of that which has been or shall be hereafter discovered, and its application to human welfare, especially by the building of the truths of science and philosophy into the structure of a broadened and purified religion" (quoted at the beginning of Hans Küng, *Freud and the Problem of God* [1979]).

in New York on his way back from New Haven, where he had just delivered the Terry Lectures, and she became at once his protégée, benefactor, and ardent promoter. After her death at the age of forty-two, the work of the foundation was passed on to her husband Paul (son of the Pittsburgh banker Andrew Mellon) and his associates, who compounded the endowment manyfold over the years. The Mellons in effect handsomely supported and powerfully promoted Jung and increased the visibility of his novel mythicoscientific theories in America, especially after the Second World War. The foundation accomplished this through such acts as arranging, financing, and publishing the English translation of the entire Jung corpus with unusually lucrative royalty arrangements for the author.[36] Although in time the foundation's publication and fellowship programs came to include many illustrious titles and individuals outside the Jungian framework, it was nonetheless an express intention of Mary Mellon to have Jung "as the keystone" and to have the foundation do its best to "disseminate his teaching." The Bollingen colophon, which she personally chose, embodies this intention rather well, as well as the implicit world religions ideology: "the eight-spoked wheel" with four little circles wedged, or as the Bollingen chronicler William McGuire describes it, "a Buddhist or Jain symbol."[37]

Indologist Heinrich Zimmer, Persianist Henry Corbin, American ethnologist Paul Radin, comparative mythologists Mircea Eliade and Joseph Campbell were among those intimately involved in the operations of the foundation in various capacities for many years. D. T. Suzuki, Gershom Scholem, Louis Massignion, Walter T. Stace, Erwin Goodenough, and Georges Dumézil are some of the well-known religionists and historians of religion also associated with it. Gary Snyder and Alan Watts each received a Bollingen fellowship for their study of Zen.

36. In so doing, the Mellons effectively rescued the mission of Eranos, an older organ closely associated with Jung, founded by Olga Froebe-Kapteyn, who had single-handedly financed and operated Eranos but whose funds were depleted by the late 1930s. The Bollingen historian William McGuire informs us that, at the beginning of Froebe-Kapteyn's venture, Rudolf Otto "responded warmly to Olga's plan for a lecture program" to facilitate the "meeting of East and West," which she proposed to hold regularly in her private estate in Ascona, Switzerland. It was Otto who suggested the name "Eranos," meaning, in Greek, "a shared feast" (William McGuire, *Bollingen* [1982], 23–24).

37. Mary Mellon's letter to C. G. Jung, February 1942, quoted by McGuire (ibid., 48–49); on the colophon, see 70–71.

The extent of support and the range of incentives given by these private donors and foundations to the study of religion for over a century has been incalculable, or at least we should say that it remains uncalculated. We have yet to find a way of gauging their significance for the formation of the science of religion, analyzing the direct and indirect influence of their interests on the directions that science has taken, and determining their role in the public discourse about religion and religions. These endowments and programs resulted from extraordinary and conspicuous acts of generosity on the part of very wealthy individuals who had a special interest in the subject of "religion," whatever that meant for them. The circumstances of their bequests differed significantly, as did the nature and the source of their wealth, and most probably their motives and intentions. Sometimes the gifts were mediated by the executors of a will, or by a board representing the prestigious venues in which such lectures were often delivered.

Particularly well documented is the case of the renowned Gifford Lectures, a distinguished and exceptional series in many respects. Not only was the amount of the initial gift extraordinary, the deed of the bequest was spelled out with unusual clarity and care by the benefactor himself. Gifford specifically designated the academic senate of each of the four Scottish universities—Edinburgh, Glasgow, Aberdeen, and St. Andrews—as "patrons" of the lectureships, as he called them, who were thus charged with the power and the duty to carry out the series program, including the selection of the individual lecturers each year. The gift amount for the four universities totaled £80,000 (in contrast, the Hibbert lectureship was based on £4,000). The sum represented a considerable portion of the benefactor's fortune. This is all the more remarkable in light of the fact that, though he eventually rose to the position of judge and thereby became Lord Gifford, Adam Gifford was a leatherworker's son, and for much of his life, he did not live in wealth, privilege, or in a scholarly environment.[38]

Perhaps most extraordinary of all, Lord Gifford defined the qualification of the lecturers, or rather, he expressly dissuaded the trustees from placing any religiously grounded restrictions on the platform. He stipulated that "the lecturers appointed shall be subjected to no test of any kind, and shall not be re-

---

38. An intimate portrait of Lord Gifford was recorded by his brother and his sister under the title "Recollections of a Brother." Though the document was originally meant "only for the use of his relatives," it is now reproduced in Stanley L Jaki, *Lord Gifford and His Lectures* (2nd ed., 1995), 103–28.

quired to take any oath, or to emit or subscribe any declaration of belief, or to make any promise of any kind," and that, moreover, "they may be of any religion or way of thinking, or as is sometimes said, they may be of no religion, or they may be so-called sceptics or agnostics, or free-thinkers." It is evident that this benefactor sought to secure, in perpetuity, a forum that had a religious as well as academic importance, a venue marked by extreme liberality and generosity of the spirit, which, for all we know, was consistent with his character.

His stipulation for the lectureship, in fact, is less a statement of requirement than a benediction:

> I wish the lecturers to treat their subject as a strictly natural science, the greatest of all possible sciences, indeed, in one sense, the only science, that of Infinite Being, without reference to or reliance upon any supposed special exceptional or so-called miraculous revelation. I wish it considered just as astronomy or chemistry is. I have intentionally indicated, in describing the subject of the lectures, the general aspect which personally I would expect the lectures to bear, but the lectures shall be under no restraint whatever in their treatment of their theme; for example, they may freely discuss (and it may be well to do so) all questions about man's conceptions of God or the Infinite, their origin, nature, and truth, whether he can have any such conceptions, whether God is under any or what limitations, and so on, as I am persuaded that nothing but good can result from free discussion.[39]

Much less clear, and perhaps for that very reason all the more intriguing, is the case of the Hibbert Lectures. What exactly transpired between Mr. Hibbert's death and the inauguration of the lecture series financed by his bequest? Louis Henry Jordan tells us this much:

> For a considerable period, the income of the Hibbert Trust was used almost exclusively in aiding the researches of students of superior mental endowment who were looking forward to the ministry; for Mr. Hibbert expressly stated that expenditures might be incurred in any way that would prove "conducive to the spread of Christianity in its most simple and intelligible form, and to the unfettered exercise of private judgment in

39. Adam Gifford's will is printed in its entirety in ibid., 91–102; the quotations are from pages 99 and 100.

matters of religion." Shortly prior to 1878, however, an influentially signed letter was addressed to the Trustees, praying that some portion at least of the funds should be devoted to the establishment of a Lectureship, under whose auspices the various religious Faiths of mankind might receive capable and exhaustive treatment; and it was suggested that Specialists of international rank should be invited to render this service.[40]

Evidently, the influential signatory's prayer proved effective. Today, the Hibbert Lectures are broadcast nationwide in Britain through the good offices of the BBC.

4. Colonial Self-Articulation

The dominant and essential role played by the European academy, by philology in particular, in the objectification of the world's "great religions" has been the principal concern of the present study. At the same time, it is beyond doubt that the European-initiated ideas of Hinduism and Buddhism, for example, could not have acquired such an overwhelming sense of reality had it not been for those who positively and actively identified themselves as Hindus or Buddhists, or at least those who would not—could not, or did not bother to, for whatever reason—contest being identified as such. What remains yet to be studied concertedly is the very process of mutually interactive development, on the one hand, of European representations of non-Christian religions and, on the other hand, the native appropriation, reaction, or resistance to such representations.[41] Without a comprehensive study of this process, we would not be in the position to understand how certain local practices and regional traditions came to be consolidated and how something like "Hinduism" came to be reified as a religion and came to be considered one of the world religions. This, moreover, has never been merely a matter of international trade in concepts, as it were; rather, it took place in the context of colonialism, or under forceful impact of the European epistemic field, or in any event, under the condition of globalization under duress. Typically, it was a symbiotic process in which the natives came to articulate their own identity by utilizing concepts and ideas initially forged by others, and in which the native articulation came to feed into

---

40. Jordan, *Comparative Religion*, 568–69.

41. The word "native" here is a somewhat unhappy shorthand for "non-European residents of the region." The term is not strictly descriptive or literally accurate, since every community of people, if its history is sufficiently known, appears to have migrated from elsewhere, so that no one can be said definitively to be indigenous.

the reality status of these ideas in a complicated way. These occurrences must be investigated, not generally and abstractly, but in each specific colonial or contact situation.

One of the areas hitherto more extensively explored in this regard is "India" and its correlate, "Hinduism."[42] Wilhelm Halbfass, Partha Mitter, Gyan Prakash, and others have drawn attention especially to the nineteenth-century phenomenon variously called Neo-Hinduism or Hindu Modernism.[43] The principal proponents of this movement were leading Indian intellectuals of the time, who played a major role in forging a new identity for India and for "the East," as they saw themselves emerging into a world on the way to becoming concertedly and irreversibly *modern*. But this new sense of Indian identity also entailed a fresh assessment and a selective recuperation and revivification of the past. It is above all in relation to this project for recovery and revaluation that one could cite the works of such figures, also well known to the West at the time, as Rammohun Roy, Keshub Chunder Sen, Debendranath Tagore, and Swami Vivekananda. It could be argued that, in their speeches and writings addressed to an audience inside as well as outside of India, these nineteenth-century modernists were effectively underwriting the notion of Hinduism. According to their projective view, "Hinduism," though the term itself may be a neologism, refers to the ancient faith of India, a religion that was originally and essentially monotheistic, and whose ancient wisdom is encapsulated in certain select but voluminous canonical texts, which were beginning to be known in the West as early as the eighteenth century: the Vedas, the Upanishads, and the great epics of Ramayana and Mahabharata, the Bhagavad Gita constituting an especially prominent portion of the latter.[44]

42. The quotation marks signal the older conceptual territory coextensive, more or less, with Hindustan, as distinct from the present nation-state by that name.

43. Halbfass attributes the more or less interchangeable use of both terms to Paul Hacker, who wrote extensively on the subject. See Wilhelm Halbfass, *India and Europe* (1988), 219; also John Nicol Farquhar, *Modern Religious Movements in India* (1915); Dittakavi Subrahmanya Sarma, *Studies in the Renaissance of Hinduism* (1944); and more recently, Gyan Prakash, *Another Reason* (1999). Although the following discussion on the case of "Hinduism" is primarily based on the works of the Indologists named above, Richard King's 1999 study *Orientalism and Religion* is an important contribution on the historical "construction" of Hinduism. See also an earlier identification of the problem by Timothy Fitzgerald, "Hinduism and the 'World Religion' Fallacy" (1990).

44. The alternative names "Brahmanism" and "Vedism" seem to have waned gradually as "Hinduism" gained ground. On Hinduism's essential monotheism, see Partha Mitter, "Rammohun Roy and the New Language of Monotheism" (1987), 177–208.

Almost always the first to be mentioned in the history of Neo-Hinduism is Rammohun (or Rammohan) Roy (1772?–1833), the founder of the Brahmo Samaj (or Somaj), one of the so-called Hindu reform movements, based in Bengal.[45] Son of a wealthy brahmin family and himself a successful businessman (primarily in banking and real estate), Rammohun is said to have been well versed in Arabic and Persian literature before he learned English through his dealings with the British East India Company. In many ways a willing and active assimilator of European ideas and ideals, he was also one of the few Indians of his time to cross the ocean and travel abroad. He died in Bristol, England, the port city that had prospered and symbolized, until the eighteenth century, British colonial trade spanning several continents, especially in tobacco and slaves.

Although scholars have pointed out the considerable Islamic influence on Rammohun's religious writings, what he absorbed most fundamentally and consequentially—if not entirely self-consciously—appears to have been views of the new generation of British Orientalists and their roundly positive image of Indian antiquity. In describing the eighteenth-century shift in European views about India, Thomas Trautmann has noted:

> What P. J. Marshall (1970)[46] calls "the British discovery of Hinduism" had a sudden onset in the second half of the eighteenth century. British merchants had been trading with India for the better part of two centuries before the Battle of Plassey turned them into territorial rulers, but the new Orientalism perceived itself in terms of a sharp discontinuity with the past. In the accounts of the 1760s[47] . . . is a breathless sense of having just come upon the literature of a vast and ancient religion that had been vaguely known and thoroughly distorted by all the Europeans who came before.

This marked the beginning of the phase of British Indomania, as Trautmann calls it, a period of great enthusiasm for India, which, for the most part, was a

---

45. See David Kopf, *The Brahmo Samaj and the Shaping of the Modern Indian Mind* (1979).

46. P. J. Marshall, ed., *The British Discovery of Hinduism in the Eighteenth Century* (1970).

47. Trautmann lists Luke Scrafton's *Reflections on the Government . . . of Indostan* (1761), John Zephania Holwell's *Interesting Historical Events, Relative to the Provinces of Bengal, and the Empire of Indostan* (1765–71), and Alexander Dow's introduction to Firishtah's *History of Hindostan* (1768), and adds several later works in the same vein, by Quentin Craufurd, Nathaniel Brassey Halhed, and the Reverend William Robertson.

product of philology, and which has had an enduring impact on many cultured Europeans ever since, as we have seen in the previous chapters. Given this new investment in India, it should come as no surprise that, as Trautmann continues,

> [t]he portrait of the Hinduism that is discovered in these [late-eighteenth-century] publications is highly favorable; indeed it consistently shows a disposition to put the most favorable construction upon the information the writers have managed to acquire of Hindu religion and history. The main features, which are more or less the same in all the renderings, are two: that Hinduism is basically monotheistic, and that the benevolence of its religion and laws made India a prosperous and peaceful country before foreign conquest.[48]

What is noteworthy here is the claim that true Hinduism was the beneficent, dignified, monotheistic religion of classical India, and not what was generally observable throughout India in modern times. If, therefore, an earlier generation of Europeans had fostered a malignant image and judged that the religion of non-Islamic India was nothing but depraved idolatry and polytheism, this was an inference drawn from the observations of its present corrupted state, not an assessment of its original, essential nature. This view, which valorized the ancient/classical/original religion of India prior to Islamic "conquest," came to be shared, for different yet entangled reasons, by Indophilic European Orientalists and elite Indian natives eager for reform and rectification.

In the minds of the Orientalists, the idea that there was a covert tie between the crude superstition of the present-day masses on the one hand and the august principle of classical monotheism on the other, as dissimilar as they were—was consonant with a familiar anticlericalism typical of the Deists. Those eighteenth-century paragons of rationalism took it for granted that ruling religious elites everywhere were in fact consummate rationalists who themselves believed none of the mystical obscurantism that they regularly doled out to the gullible populace. Transcribed to the Indian situation, as Partha Mitter explained, the European Orientalists surmised that "a learned Hindu Brahmin," actually believed that "the many deities were symbolic representations of the supreme principle, whilst the monstrous polytheism was deliberately manufactured by the Brahmin priests to keep the ignorant under control."[49]

48. Trautmann, *Aryans and British India*, 64–65.
49. Mitter, "Rammohun Roy and the New Language of Monotheism," 188.

Following this line of thought, then, it was possible to postulate that the idolatrous Hinduism of the masses was but a grossly distorted version of the pristine religion of their distant ancestors. This of course implied some duplicity on the part of the brahmins, but on the other hand it left open the possibility of reforming and restoring Hinduism to its original purity.[50]

It was above all this view of Indian religious history that Rammohun Roy and other European-influenced, reform-minded Indian elites of the nineteenth century presupposed.[51] Far from being mere passive recipients of European-generated views, however, as Halbfass and others have shown, intellectuals among the colonized population actively engaged with those compelling images of their nationhood, sometimes with an intent to resist the European ideology of civilization and its one-sided universalism, but more often with an aspiration to forge their own destiny against the current of European colonialism, against what pretended to be an inevitable march of world history toward universal modernity. The important issue for us here, then, is not where and with whom the idea of the ancient glory of monotheistic Hindu India originated;[52] a more profitable query rather is how such disparate parties inhabiting different worlds, with divergent and sometimes contradictory interests, could have contributed to a singular result, namely, the objectification and reification

50. In addition, this view of ancient India as the Hindu nation was generally consistent with the notion that the long-standing Muslim presence in the land was after all a result of a foreign invasion (hence the contrast between the Hindus as native residents and the Muslims as outsiders), a notion that both Muslims and non-Muslims for different reasons had interests in upholding.

51. As Partha Mitter put it: "The belief in an innate rational faith reigning over society during the golden age was no doubt part and parcel of romantic primitivism that for instance viewed the unadorned Doric columns of early Greek temples as perfection from which art had gone steadily downhill. It informs much of the new enthusiasm for Hinduism in the works of Halhed, Holwell, Dow, Wilkins and Jones. This enthusiasm was to create the modern image of Hinduism in the West, whose most extreme statement was the German romantic paeans to the sublime and primitive wisdom of the Brahmins as revealed in their sacred and secular writings. Soon after, when the Rg Veda was to be properly edited by the German Orientalist Max Müller, this text was to be consecrated as the repository of primitive Aryan wisdom, produced in 'le berceau de l'humanité.' Coming at a period when India had been brought under the military and political control of the British East India Company, this flattering Western image interpenetrated the self-image of the Hindus themselves" (Mitter, "Rammohun Roy and the New Language of Monotheism," 187).

52. Trautmann rightly cautions that it would be rash to conclude that the notion of Hinduism and the concomitant theory of the ancient Indian nationhood is entirely a Western invention (Aryans and British India, 66–68).

of Hinduism and the elevation of its status and its eventual promotion to the ranks of world religions.

In the face of encroaching unilateral universalism of the West, perhaps encouraged by the ideas of the Indophilic and Indomaniac Orientalists of the West, Rammohun counterposed and claimed as his own an essentially rational, ethical, and monotheistic Hinduism. This version of Hinduism is of course not unlike the liberal Protestantism of the West, only less fastidious and more tolerant, or rather, more generously accommodating toward other faiths. In this move, it may even be suggested that Rammohun anticipated and provided for the future career of Hinduism as a world religion. He entitled one of his last publications "The Universal Religion: Religious Instructions Founded on Sacred Authorities" (1829), a treatise based exclusively on Hindu sources.[53]

The notion of universal Hinduism, not to mention the idea of the commodiously proprietary relation between Hinduism and other religions, appears to be strikingly isomorphic with the logic of Christian universalism propounded by many of the comparative theologians we examined earlier. The claim of Hindu universalism was a fundamental concern for the generations of Indian intellectuals and religious leaders who came after Rammohun Roy, including Debendranath Tagore (1817–1905), Keshub Chunder Sen (Keshab Chandra Sen, 1838–84), Ramakrishna (1836–86), and Vivekananda (1863–1902), who were therefore contemporaries of the theological comparativists of Europe. According to Halbfass, "Keshab was much more inclined than Debendranath to search for 'inspired' sources outside of Hinduism as well and to demonstrate the universal harmony among the traditions by compiling exemplary records of religious experience"; his proclamation in 1880 of the "New Dispensation"—the third dispensation following the Old and the New Testaments—was "intended to establish the universal church and the harmony of all religions." Indeed, Keshub freely spoke of

the Church Universal which is the deposit of all ancient wisdom and the receptacle of all modern science, which recognizes in all prophets and saints a harmony, in all scriptures a unity and through all dispensations a continuity, which abjures all that separates and divides, always magnifies unity and peace, which harmonizes reason and faith, yoga and bhakti, asceticism and social duty in their highest forms and which shall make of all nations and sects one kingdom and one family in the fullness of time.

53. Halbfass, *India and Europe*, 215.

But if such soteriology is no longer specifically Indian—hence no longer sub-stantively "Hindu"—Halbfass reminds us nonetheless that "Keshab consid-ered himself to be essentially the fulfiller and executor of Hinduism: Hinduism alone has been called to lead Christianity to its true universality and to simul-taneously perfect itself therein. . . . The Hindu tradition of inclusivism is placed under the name of Christ: the 'Christianization' of India is simulta-neously the Hinduization of Christianity."[54]

Here, as we observe the isomorphism of the claims for Hindu universalism and Christian universalism respectively, we may gain another insight: we begin to discern a conceptual maneuver through which representatives of two reli-gions, both with universal claims, could negotiate the terms of their coexis-tence and nonaggression, cooperation, or possibly even incorporation in the future. We may detect here, in other words, a tacit bargaining for a virtual land-for-peace agreement between two, ultimately mutually contradictory posi-tions. How can two "world religions" in the strong sense—that is, two self-styled universal religions—seek to accommodate each other? An answer might be through a mutual "respect"—even "sympathy"—that takes the form of complete and willful disregard for the other side's exclusivist claim for totality and universality.[55]

This peculiar, if also very familiar, inclusivism is even better represented by the figure of Ramakrishna. As Halbfass puts it, with Ramakrishna, inclu-sivism's "very 'openness' is a form of self-assertion," and as such, it in fact pre-sented a powerful resistance to the efforts of the Christian missionaries," that is, against the engulfing tide of Christian universalism.[56] The rival universalism presented by Ramakrishna was therefore no mere syncretism but "an extrapo-lation of Hinduism itself, an answer to the Europeans coming out of the tradi-tion of Tantric Vedānta." Ramakrishna's Hinduism—or more accurately, the

54. Halbfass, India and Europe, 226.

55. For an early-twentieth-century Christian articulation of this pluralist-universalist logic, consider Ernst Troeltch's argument, discussed in the chapter 9.

56. Among many instances attesting to this point, B. B. Nagarkar, the outspoken represen-tative of the Brahmo Samaj at the World's Parliament of Religions in 1893, commented: "We are ready and most willing to receive the truths of the religion of Christ as truly as the truths of the religions of other prophets, but we shall receive these from the life and teachings of Christ Him-self, and not through the medium of any church, or the so-called missionary of Christ. If Chris-tian missionaries have in them the meekness of purpose that Christ lived in His own life and so pathetically exemplified in His Glorious death on the cross, let our missionary friends show it in their lives" (B. B. Nagarkar, "Spiritual Ideas of the Brahmo-Somaj," in Seager, Dawn of Reli-gious Pluralism, 438).

highly stylized and mythicized Hinduism represented by his followers in his name—"appears as an open, yet in itself complete, framework of encounter and reconciliation with other traditions, as the timeless presence of the religious per se, to which nothing new can accrue."[57]

Outfitted with such an extraordinarily powerful universalist platform, enlivened by an ever more ardent belief in the inexhaustible wisdom and grace of true Hinduism, many Indian intellectuals after Rammohun came to promote the idea that theirs was a uniquely universal, essentially religious and spiritual (as opposed to political and material) civilization.[58] They emphasized the contrast between the boundlessly protean India and the rigidly unyielding Europe, between the spiritual East and the material West. In their view, the primacy of the spiritual over the material was a characteristic not only of the cultures of Hindustan but it held true, mutatis mutandis, for all of Asia. In sum, these Indians proclaimed the general superiority of the East in the realm of spirituality, just as they conceded that, at least at the present time, the superiority of the West in the realm of materiality, science, and technology was undeniable.[59]

Further advancing this line of thought, Vivekananda, who saw Ramakrishna as "the representative and quintessence of spirituality," spoke to the Indian audience in the following manner:

> Let others talk of politics, of the glory to acquisition of immense wealth poured in by trade, of the power and spread of commercialism, of the glorious fountain of physical liberty; but these the Hindu mind does not understand and does not want to understand. Touch him on spirituality, on religion, on God, on the soul, on the infinite, on spiritual freedom, and I assure you, the lowest peasant in India is better informed on these subjects than many a so-called philosopher in other lands. . . . we have yet something to teach to the world.[60]

57. Halbfass, *India and Europe*, 227–28.

58. Nicholas Dirks, in his 1992 article "Caste of Mind," also argues that this representation of India as an essentially religiously constituted nation, governed by a religiously sanctioned social order, namely, caste, and hence lacking a genuine political culture, was consistent with the British colonial policy, and that it therefore implicitly helped justify the British rule.

59. Ursula King has documented these developments among Indian intellectuals of the nineteenth century. See both *Indian Spirituality and Western Materialism* (1985) and "Some Reflections on Sociological Approaches to the Study of Modern Hinduism" (1989). See also Richard King, *Orientalism and Religion*.

60. Vivekananda, *Complete Works*, 3:148; quoted in Halbfass, *India and Europe*, 231.

∽

It is noteworthy, if also somewhat predictable, that the universalist appeal of these Neo-Hindus turned self-appointed spokespersons for the Spiritual East was not always met by genial responses from their counterparts in other Asian nations. In an intriguing study published in 1970, Stephen N. Hay considered the career of Rabindranath Tagore (1861–1941), the more famous son of Debendranath Tagore, as just such a messenger of the Spiritual East. He was effectively anointed in this role by "a crown from the West," when he received the 1913 Nobel Prize for Literature. With a hope of uniting the venerable Asian nations for a more effective, concerted revitalization of the East and for the ultimate betterment of the world as a whole, Tagore brought his message to Japan in 1916, and to China and again to Japan in 1924. (In this connection, it should be of some interest to us that, while his speeches expressed unmistakable Hindu-universalist views, more or less identical with those of the nineteenth-century Hindu Modernists, when he brought his brotherly message to the East Asian nations, he presented himself as a man from "the land of the Buddha." Despite his awareness of the Confucian, Taoist, and other native traditions of these regions, he chose to characterize both China and Japan as, in the last analysis, Buddhist nations.)[61]

As Hay documented, both in Japan and in China, Tagore was received with great respect, honor, and dignity, his lectures and receptions attended by the highest government officials and the most illustrious of various intellectual communities, an occurrence truly exceptional for a visit by a private person. But in each country, the extraordinary advance publicity and enthusiastic anticipation that greeted him at the moment of arrival sharply contrasted with the deafening silence that followed the delivery of his message. Saddened and puzzled by the realization that there was to be no outpouring of sympathy or any sense of accord from his Asian brethren, Tagore was in no condition to probe very deeply into the reasons for the palpable failure of his message.[62]

The impact of Tagore's spiritualized message upon the native intellectuals of

---

61. This may be construed as an expedient gesture on his part, and apparently it was effective. He is reported to have said that he "had only found the 'true' Japan at Shizuoka [an unremarkable provincial town west of Tokyo], where the Buddhist priests 'brought their basket of fruits to me and held their lighted incense before my face . . . wishing to pay homage to a man who had come from the land of the Buddha" (Stephen N. Hay, *Asian Ideas of East and West* [1970], 69).

62. Tagore was neither comforted nor enlightened by the stereotypical explanations offered by some American and European residents of Japan at the time. According to these foreign ob-

Japan and China was apparently minimal. Whatever was most responsible for this failure, it was not helped by the directions these nations took soon thereafter—the extreme nationalism, militarism, and colonial aggression against other Asian nations in the case of one, and large-scale civil wars, trauma of colonial occupation, and a communist revolution in the other. Despite Tagore's best intentions, the imaginary of the East, an identity predicated primarily on the hopeful—but ultimately reactive and defensive—idea of the supremacy of the spiritual over material, did not find its feet anywhere on solid ground.

5. Transitional Systems

Finally, and perhaps most obviously, the post-nineteenth-century development of the taxonomic regime may come to light if we examine the gamut of texts published in the first half of the twentieth century belonging to the genre of the world religions survey, under whatever name it may have appeared. We have noted already the surge of publications of this kind toward the end of the nineteenth century; but both the phenomenon of proliferation and the content of these numerous texts have yet to be subjected to any systematic, statistically keen analysis.

The present study has focused on the taxonomic and discursive transformation traceable mostly in the British and American contexts because, as it now appears, the transposition of the Dutch and German concept on to the Anglophone milieu was the most critical moment in the emergence of the world religions discourse. Furthermore, we have reasons to surmise that the subsequent forgetting and occlusion of the issues originally at stake provided a precondition for the eventual efflorescence of this discourse. Meanwhile, other European nations and linguistic regions also continued to produce texts on the general subject of "religions of the world," with or without any association with the concept of world religions per se. Consideration of these other, chronologically

---

servers, in Japan, the government (or some such corporate body) dictated individuals' thoughts, and somehow the government was against Tagore's message; or else, they speculated, the Japanese were at the moment veritably possessed by a foreign spirit, specifically, the spirit of Western materialism, which rendered them impervious to spiritual messages of any kind, Hindu, Christian, or any other (ibid., 72–73). In this connection, some two decades earlier, Percival Lowell sought to explain the remarkable Japanese "success" in rapid adaptation to Western science, technology, and the modernization of its military by suggesting that the national character of the Japanese amounts to "susceptibility to foreign possession." He proposed this theory in his popular monograph, *Occult Japan, or the Way of the Gods* (1895), which was one of the earliest treatises on Shinto, which Lowell characterizes as a spirit possession cult.

parallel developments will have to be an important agenda for a comprehensive investigation in the future.

One of the more peculiar national differences can be detected in the case of France, a difference that seems to have roots in earlier times. This singular character, or what might be roundly described as an adamant secularism, may have contributed to the fact that the body of scholarship on religion generated in France remained always at some distance from the Euro-American stream. Despite the apparent centrality of the French academy in the development of modern science generally, there is little evidence that either the expertise of French religion scholars or the interests of the laity had much to do with the emergence of world religions as a discursive construct. And when it comes to the science of religion in the narrower sense, Francophone scholarship appears to have been less than fully integrated into the disciplinary history, as this history is principally told from the northern European Protestant perspective.[63] At the same time, it is also a conspicuous historical fact that there have been several exceedingly popular and internationally notorious works surveying the religions of the world written by the French, works that are marked by overtly naturalist or expressly materialist opinions. Two such examples immediately come to mind. The older work is a seven-volume treatise authored by Charles François Dupuis (1742–1809) entitled *Origine de tous les cultes, ou Religion universelle* (1795), the target of a particularly pointed criticism, as we recall, by Archdeacon Hardwick, in his *Christ and Other Masters*.[64] Curiously, the central thesis of this work, namely, that all religions originated in some form of nature worship, or more specifically, in sun worship, is often attributed in the English-speaking world to F. Max Müller.[65] As well-read Europeans of the nineteenth century must have known, however, long before Müller, the solar myth theory of the origin of religion had already been widely circulated thanks to Dupuis

63. This is evidenced, for instance, by the relatively marginal position occupied by figures such as Albert Réville and Maurice Vernes—deputy-director of the École des Hautes-Études (Sorbonne), and author of an important early history of comparative religion, *L'Histoire des religions* (1887)—as well as by the inadequate attention given to important new institutions such as the first journal specifically devoted to the science, *Revue de l'histoire des religions* (cofounded by Vernes and Réville), or the Musée Guimet (founded in Lyon in 1879, relocated in Paris in 1888), the first large-scale museum of the history of religions, with a well-stocked library.

64. An abridged version of Dupuis's work was translated as *The Origin of All Religious Worship* (1872).

65. It is questionable how significant the so-called solar myth theory of the origin of religion was in the work of Müller, even though he was certainly made famous by this particular idea. Cf. Tomoko Masuzawa, *In Search of Dreamtime* (1993), 58–75.

and, with it, a provocative suggestion that the divinity of Christ should be likewise traced to the same natural provenance.[66] In comparison to some other French treatises of the period, it is true, Dupuis's was not as overtly antagonistic to the established church or acutely satirical of Catholicism and Christianity generally; however, the darkly threatening implications of his thesis were evidently not lost on many of his foreign readers, and the publication immediately solicited a barrage of responses, exemplary of which may be John Prior Estlin's pamphlet with the pointed title *The Nature and Causes of Atheism . . . To Which Are Added Remarks on a Work, entitled, Origine de tous les cultes; ou, Religion universelle, par Dupuis* (1797).

But neither the northern Protestants' pious outrage against Gallic irreligion nor their horror at the supposed political consequences of such brazen atheism as lately seen in the French Revolution, of course, put an end to the republican tradition of producing ever more flagrantly naturalist dissertations, some of which were profoundly hostile to church authorities, Catholic or otherwise.[67] More than a century after Dupuis, another French scholar, the classicist and archaeologist Salomon Reinach (1858–1932), published an enormously successful work on the general history of religions entitled *Orpheus* (1909).[68] Perhaps not quite as monolithic a scheme as Dupuis's purported discovery of the singular origin of all religions in natural causes, Reinach's work, too, is thoroughly secularist in its orientation and the author makes no apology for its lack of piety.

Early in the first chapter, Reinach observes pragmatically: "The word religion being what custom has made it, it is necessary that a minimum definition, as Tylor calls it, should be applicable to the term in all its acceptations." Apparently finding Tylor's own minimalist definition (belief in spiritual beings) not broad enough, and also being of the opinion that the likely lowest common denominator of all religions is not so much an idea or a doctrine as it is a certain

---

66. The connection, or equation, between sun worship and Christ worship continued to be an attractive idea to many, especially once this equation became mediated by the idea that the cult of the sun might be an attribute of the Aryan race. C. G. Jung is among the best-known proponents of this latter notion. For a highly critical appraisal of Jung's theory, see Richard Noll, *The Jung Cult* (1994), 58–137, and *The Aryan Christ* (1997), 98–119.

67. Another voluminous and well-known French work that features naturalistic tendencies is *De la religion* (1824–31), by Benjamin Constant (1767–1830), reissued in 1999 as a single volume.

68. Page references are to the English translation of *Orpheus* that appeared the same year. Additionally, Reinach published five volumes on the subject, *Cultes, mythes, et religions* (1906–23).

mental disposition—a sense of sanction, prohibition, or taboo—Reinach concludes: "As there are a great many religions, so there are a great many limitations, and I propose to define religion as: *A sum of scruples which impede the free exercise of our faculties.*"[69]

It is true, he concedes, "scruple" is rather vague, and this definition has the effect of eliminating from the concept of religion "God, spiritual beings, the infinite, in a word, all we are accustomed to consider the true objects of religious sentiments"; but this elimination, he goes on to argue, is a distinct advantage. For, as he explains, it is his intention to demonstrate, through a survey of all known religions, that it is just such an opaque, obtuse, and nonspecific mental disposition best described as "scruples" that is indeed "the irreducible basis of all religions"; meanwhile, he will show, those patently religious objects—God, spiritual beings, the infinite, and so on—are in fact merely secondary, derivative formations.

Therefore, in sharp contrast to the majority of the religion surveys written in English in the nineteenth and early twentieth century—which were generally consistent or at least minimally compliant with churchly doctrine on the point of the decisive superiority and irreducible singularity of Christianity—we seem to find hardly any prominent French works of similar religious persuasions. Instead, the best-known French treatises are deeply agnostic, unequivocally anticlerical, and, in particular, openly hostile to the Jesuits, who had been in control of both the church and the academy for some time; Reinach's was no exception.[70] Whether it was ultimately because of its thoroughgoing secularism or in spite of it, Reinach's book sold exceedingly well internationally, and

---

69. Reinach, *Orpheus*, 2–3; emphasis in the original. Incidentally, the idea of sanction/prohibition was also fundamental to the idea of religion proposed by another renowned French scholar and contemporary of Reinach, Emile Durkheim. See *Les Formes élémentaires de la vie religieuse* (1912), translated by Karen E. Fields as *The Elementary Forms of Religious Life* (1995).

70. Reinach's incisive and largely unsympathetic analysis of the nineteenth-century resurgence of the Jesuits in the Catholic hierarchy is interestingly detailed in his later work, *A Short History of Christianity* (1922), 172–89. It remains to be seen if the anti-Jesuit sentiment was something of a common denominator among the French historians of religion at the time. Certainly this temperament can be discerned in Renan, who after all had a good personal reason for the animosity, but also in others who had no conspicuous history of confrontation with the church and who were not known to be excessively irreligious. For example, Max Müller recorded in his diary (March 1845) his first meeting with Eugène Burnouf with these words: "Went to Burnouf. Spiritual, amiable, thoroughly French. He received me in the most friendly way, talked a great deal. . . . 'I am a Brâhman, a Buddhist, a Zoroastrian; I hate the Jesuits'—that is the sort of man. I am looking forward to his lectures" (*Life and Letters*, 1:34).

by 1922 the author could boast that "in spite of the war, more than 30,000 copies have been sold" and that "it has been translated into English, German, Russian, Italian, Spanish and Swedish."[71] Testifying to its further success beyond that year, Eric Sharpe offers this guarded remark: "The popularity of this work (and perhaps its lack of competition) can be judged from the fact that when a new English edition appeared in 1930, *Orpheus* had seen no less than thirty-eight French editions—eloquent testimony to the appeal of a book whose chief claim to fame is that it contains the most tendentious definition of religion ever seriously put forward."[72]

Whether or not this tortuous estimation by the English historian should be read as a mark of national difference in its own right remains to be debated. In any event, it is readily understood that Reinach for one had no particular use for the notion or the logic of "world religions."

Meanwhile, the discursive development in Germany appears to have been quite otherwise. As we have seen, the concept of *Weltreligion(en)* was native to its soil, and it is therefore only natural that the term should have had a continuous, though transformative, history of its own. In most German texts of the early twentieth century, the category "world religions" (*Weltreligionen*) is not collapsible to "religions of the world" (*Religionen der Erde*).[73] At the same time, some of these texts seem to exhibit traces of the transition from the narrower definition of "world religions" to the later, more inclusive sense. A didactic collection of essays appropriately titled *Religions of the World* (*Die Religionen der Erde*), edited by Carl Clemen (1865–1940), is a specimen of this transitional type.

Originally published in 1927 and translated into English in 1931, the book consists of a series of essays, each written by a leading authority in the field, and expressly addressed to a general audience with palpably pedagogic intentions.[74] The table of contents signals the transitional character of the classifying principles governing this volume:

71. Reinach, preface to *A Short History of Christianity*, v.

72. Sharpe, *Comparative Religion*, 123.

73. In contrast, a large majority of the works in English published in the twentieth century do not seem cognizant of the theoretical principle demarcating world religions from other "religions of the world."

74. The scientific and educational intent of the book is explicitly stated when, for instance, Clemen explains that the illustrations included in the collection are meant to illustrate the text, rather than being aesthetic embellishments. (Carl Clemen, *Religions of the World* [1931], vii).

I. Prehistoric Religion

II. Primitive Religion

III. Ancient National Religions

   1. Babylonian Religion

   2. Egyptian Religion

   3. Chinese Religion

   4. Indian Religion

   5. Persian Religion

   6. Greek and Roman Religion

   7. Celtic Religion

   8. Teutonic Religion

   9. Slavic Religion

   10. Japanese Religion

IV. The World Religions

   1. Religion of the Hebrews

   2. Buddhism

   3. Christianity

   4. Islam

Several things are noteworthy in this listing. One is the deftly inconspicuous interweaving of different organizing principles: chronological order, typological order, and quasi-developmental order. As Clemen explains in the brief preface, the individual items within each of the last two categories—"Ancient National Religions" and "the World Religions"—are listed chronologically, that is to say, one presumes, in the order of the dates of their appearance or their supposed founding. This order does not take into account any genealogical line of descent or of development; it is strictly a matter of which religion supposedly came on the scene earlier than another. In contrast, the overall organization of the four divisions seems to defy any simple chronology but presupposes instead a certain typology, and these typological differences are also suggestive of distinct developmental stages.[75] Clemen makes a point of claim-

75. In this respect, a three-volume work of the post–World War II era, *Christus und die Religionen der Erde* (1951), edited by Franz König, echoes this complicated scheme, while at the same time approximating the more recent schema typically represented, for example, by later editions of Ninian Smart's *The Religious Experience of Mankind*. The basic divisions of König's collection are: (1) the primal and prehistoric region (*ur- und vorgeschichtliche Bereich*); (2) religions of ancient peoples and cultures; (3) the living non-Christian high religions (*lebenden außerchristlichen Hochreligionen*), which includes sections on Islam, religions of India, Indian Buddhism,

ing that it is something of a novelty that his volume offers a section on "prehistoric religion" set apart from either "primitive religion" or "ancient national religions." All the same, there is a palpable presumption that prehistoric religion and primitive religion are somehow in proximity to each other; they both represent the not-yet-civilized, the level of culture that is still more or less tribal, in contrast to large-scale nations and empires.[76] The overall effect is a strong suggestion that the book offers some basic types of religions past and present, and, in so doing, it exhibits a sweeping pseudodevelopmental scheme consistent with the pattern of development of social organization and political technology: beginning with the tribal, then to the national, and finally to the modern-imperial-global-universal.[77]

Second, despite these complicated ideas schematically deployed in the organization of the book as a whole, Clemen says nothing to explain or to legitimate the fundamental divisions and the principle of their ordering. As a matter of fact, even the use of the term "world religions" seems self-effacing, if not to say also implicitly defensive. The phrase "what is commonly understood under the name of the world religions" is all we hear in the way of explanation as to why Judaism, Buddhism, Christianity, and Islam should be treated separately from all other historical (nonprimitive, non-prehistoric) religions. This conspicuous silence seems to achieve two things simultaneously: on the one hand, for those readers who are already familiar with the distinction between the

---

Chinese religions, and Japanese religions; and (4) Christianity (which includes sections on ancient Judaism).

76. The treatment of the prehistoric and the primordial in adjacency—and both always at the beginning—is one of the conventions of contemporary world religions texts. One of the more prominent examples is the work by Ninian Smart mentioned in the previous note, which, starting with the third edition of 1984 began to split the primitive religions of the earlier editions into two: prehistoric and primal.

77. A similar developmental scheme is represented, rather theatrically, by a popular American treatise of the same period: Gaius Glenn Atkins, *Procession of the Gods* (1931). The chapter titles and divisions, indicated below by a double slash (//) are worth listing in full: (1) "Faiths of the Dark and the Dawn," (2) "Sphinx-Guarded Gods of the Nile," (3) "Gods and Faiths of Babylon and Nineveh" // "A Prologue: The Aryan Begins His Procession," (4) "Zoroasterianism: The Religion of Embattled Light and Darkness," (5) "The Old Faith of Old Aryan India," (6) "Gautama Sits under the Bo-Tree," (7) "And Joins the Procession of the Gods Himself," (8) "Immemorial Faiths of India," (9) "Confucianism: The Religion of Heaven and Humanism," (10) "The Gods Come to Mount Olympus," (11) "The Gods Come to Rome: Religion Wins an Empire" // "A Prologue: The Children of the Tent of Hair," (12) "Mohammed: Prophet of Arabia and Islam," (13) "The Hebrew Prophet Challenges the Procession of the Gods" // "An Epilogue: The Twilight of the Gods" // "A Prologue: A New Order," (14) "Christianity," (15) "Conclusion."

national and the universal religions—those who are informed by the earlier controversies among Dutch and German academicians—the categories are to be assumed by virtue of that scholarly history; on the other hand, for those who are less cognizant or less interested in such academic hairsplitting of yester-year, the contested grounds for the distinction are not to be noticed.

Third, and perhaps most interesting, a fourth world religion has been added, something that looks like Judaism, but is called "Religion of the Hebrews." The article was authored by the renowned rabbi Leo Baeck (1873–1956) of Berlin, whose treatise *The Essence of Judaism* (*Das Wesen des Judentums*, 1905) had been rec-ognized as a powerful response to Adolf Harnack's bestseller *The Essence of Chris-tianity* (*Das Wesen des Christentums*, 1900).[78] As befitting the leader of progressive German Jewry of his day, Baeck's essay in the Clemen volume is written, as the English translator notes, "in a style of great dignity."[79] The opening paragraph is indeed exemplary, in that it proclaims, in no uncertain terms, the status of the religion of his people, *Judentum*, as a bona fide world religion:

> With the Hebrew religion an entirely new formative principle appeared among mankind. In the history of religions it stands for a revelation or, what is the same thing, a revolution, and as such it has been one of the most powerful forces of civilization and become a world religion.[80]

Here, the religion of the ancient Hebrews is not merely one of many pre-Christian national-ethnic religions. Instead, it is accorded the position as the singular point of origination for something utterly new, different, and global, and as such it marks a seismic shift in the course of world history.[81] In effect, it is implied, all of the world religions excepting Buddhism were made possible

---

78. Adolf Harnack's *Das Wesen des Christentums* (1900) was translated by Thomas Bailey Saun-ders as *What Is Christianity?* (1957), presumably to distinguish it from a well-known nineteenth-century treatise by Ludwig Feuerbach by the same title.

79. Clemen, *Religions of the World*, v.

80. Leo Baeck, "The Religion of the Hebrews," in Clemen, *Religions of the World*, 268.

81. Baeck goes on to say: "In revolution . . . we hear the voice of something that is funda-mentally new. It is the first expression of an entirely different way of thinking. It claims to be an absolute beginning, and therefore it completely rejects all that has hitherto existed. It de-mands a breach with the entire past, with all that has been and with all, other than itself, that is. It claims to be, not an evolution, but a new creation. Even from a purely historical point of view, therefore, and apart from the supernatural, a religion that thus appears on the scene as a revolution bears the character of a revelation, a new beginning from which everything must proceed" (ibid., 265).

owing to the spiritual breakthrough that occurred in the form of this ancient, prophetic Hebrew religion. As Baeck states in the closing paragraph of his essay:

> The importance of the religion of Israel lies not in its extensive, but in its intensive aspect, not in its geographical expansion, but in its living power. It has never been able to boast large numbers, but it has been the most influential religious principle in the world. This principle has lived and worked for two thousand years in other religions and philosophies, but its truest content and value have been evinced within the Jewish community itself. It is a world religion both in other religions and apart from them.[82]

It would be a matter of speculation whether or to what extent Clemen and other contributors concurred with Baeck's assertion here when the editorial decision was made to include Judaism, the modern heir to the religion of the Hebrews, among the world religions instead of among the national religions. Whatever that may have been, it is useful to recall that the case for Judaism's inclusion in the league of world religions had been prepared, in a way, by a particular mode of reasoning developed within Christianity. A number of Christian thinkers since the time of the Reformation, especially among evangelical German theologians and scholars of the Hebrew Bible, had been stressing the importance of the Old Testament as an indisputable and inalterable foundation of Christianity, thereby espousing a view of the Israelite religion very much resonant with Baeck's. As we have seen in earlier chapters, in the course of the nineteenth century, this general view culminated in the idea that the essential character of the ancient Israelite religion was above all prophetic; that this religion was staunchly ethical and radically spiritual. Whereas Ernest Renan considered this complex of attributes to be a hallmark of the Semitic race as a whole, many of his contemporaries—who, unlike Renan, did not renounce their Christianity—were of the opinion that the sobering religiosity of the Old Testament was by nature diametrically opposed to the religiosity of the surrounding (mostly Semitic) nations of the ancient Near East, which were on the whole more urbane, decidedly more luxuriant and sophisticated culturally, but less august spiritually. It was in this singularly alien prophetic monotheism of the Hebrews that Gentile theologians customarily sought, and found, the essential beginning of their own "unique and universal" religion. This is the view that informed not only Abraham Kuenen's and Otto Pfleiderer's works in the

82. Ibid., 298.

nineteenth century, but also scholarship in the twentieth, as we see, for instance, in William Albright's once widely read *From the Stone Age to Christianity* (1940). We see it, perhaps even more influentially, in the disposition of Neo-Orthodox theologians epitomized by Karl Barth (1886–1968) and Emil Brunner (1889–1966), as well as of some of the leading American theologians of mid-century, such as Reinhold Niebuhr (1892–1971), whose *The Self and the Dramas of History* (1955) exemplifies this tendency.

Henri Frankfort edited an influential volume of essays that also embodies this opinion. *The Intellectual Adventure of Ancient Man* (1947) comparatively explores the civilizations of Egypt, Palestine, and Mesopotamia. Included in the volume is an essay by William A. Irwin (1884–1967) that bears a conspicuous resemblance to Baeck's, emphasizing as it does "the direct indebtedness of the modern world" to the ancient Israelites:

> Their basic convictions on the ultimate character of the world, their view of the nature and place of man, their social ideals, and their political principles have become so large a part of our common heritage today—and that in general by an immediate and demonstrable line of descent—that with full recognition of the profound contributions of Greece and Rome one may well question whether any other nation has so profoundly influenced the course of human life or has contributed comparable impulse to the thought and action of our day.[83]

In the Frankfort volume, the supposed uniqueness of the Hebrews is thrown into relief, vividly contrasted to the older civilizations of Egypt and Mesopotamia.[84] In effect, the religion of the ancient Israelites, and by implication, the contemporary Jews, achieved its distinct status by positing itself as wholly unlike any other religion, so utterly out of the ordinary that it was nearly suprahistorical, or in such a way that its essence directly connected to the pith of civilization itself, and thus to the present.[85]

83. William A. Irwin, "The Hebrews," in Henri Frankfort et al., *The Intellectual Adventure of Ancient Man* [1947], 359.

84. See John A. Wilson, "Egypt," and Thorkild Jacobsen, "Mesopotamia," in Frankfort et al., *The Intellectual Adventure of Ancient Man*, 31–122 and 125–218 respectively.

85. In several other works on the biblical and prophetic themes, including *The Old Testament* (1952), William Irwin expands on this general thesis. In this respect, the exceptional and suprahistorical status ascribed to the Hebrews is analogous to the status given to the ancient Greeks by scholars ranging from Wilhelm von Humboldt to Ernest Renan.

This privilege, of course, was not without cost to Jews and Judaism, for, in this instance, Judaism gained entry into the ranks of world religions by identifying itself exclusively as the ancient prophetic faith of the Hebrews, and by letting itself be called the absolute origin of civilization as "we," Europeans, knew it. In effect, Judaism shed its long-standing ethnic-nationalist label and claimed its universal essence just as it was co-opted into a dominant universalist scheme of Christianity, particularly of Protestant Christianity, which appropriated the austere Hebraism of the prophetic tradition for itself, in part against Catholicism, but also against various forms of secularism then on the rise.

The rehabilitation of Hebraism-Judaism and its incorporation into the mainstream saw an even more dramatic turn in the far western satellite region of Euro-Christendom, namely, in the United States, beginning in the late 1920s and early 1930s. This was the period in which an alliance of Judaism and Christianity became a matter of great political exigency for the mixed population of that country, when the surging tide of fascism threatened Europe, and when the Americans were about to enter the fray. In this moment of crisis—and no doubt also in reaction to the new domestic situation where they began to see a swelling number of immigrants from Asia and other non-Christian territories—certain liberal Protestants, Jews, and some Catholics in tow attempted to form a united spiritual front of "Judeo-Christian" tradition. It may be surmised that, in view of the discursive history delineated in previous chapters, such a hyphenated identity would have been exceedingly odd—if not to say altogether incoherent—to most Europeans of the nineteenth century.[86] But the situation in America was now different, and urgent. In effect, the "Judeo-Christian" tradition, the self-styled alliance of the "religions of democracy,"[87] was forged

86. To be sure, there were exceptions. Yet the only people for whom this "hyphenation"— here, merely figurative, because German, for instance, does not utilize hyphens in this way— had any sense and utility in the nineteenth century seem to have been those intent on rejecting both elements with a single stroke. One would readily think of Nietzsche in this connection. This is not to suggest, however, that there necessarily was a greater social chasm between the Jewish and Gentile populations in nineteenth-century Europe than in early-twentieth-century North America. Rather, I merely refer to the oddity of articulating an identity by means of this particular religio-ethnic hyphenation (or conjoining) in the historical context described in the preceding chapters.

87. The phrase was first made prominent by the publication of Louis Finkelstein et al., *The Religions of Democracy* (1941). See also Robert Gordis, *The Judeo-Christian Tradition* (1965), 9–10.

as a unified front not only against the urbane, cultured secularism of Western Europe and the outright atheism of the Bolsheviks, but above all against the pernicious Aryan separatism cum genocidal anti-Semitism of the Third Reich, which, after all, had claimed for itself a form of radically de-Semitized Christianity.[88]

One of the earliest advocates of this hyphenated coalition in America—since this was most decidedly an American phenomenon—was Morris S. Lazaron, the rabbi of the Baltimore Hebrew Congregation who had served as a military chaplain in World War I. In 1930, he published an omnibus biography of ten world-famous Jews, the mere recitation of whose names strongly suggests the direct line of descent from the biblical-prophetic past to Euro-American modernity. In effect, the list comprised by *Seed of Abraham* (1930) amounts to a series of Jewish culture heroes through the ages, into which the founding of Christianity itself is seamlessly enfolded: Moses, David, Jeremiah, Mary, Jesus, Spinoza, Heinrich Heine, Karl Marx, Benjamin Disraeli, and Theodor Herzl. Lazaron expounded further on the theme of organic unity of the Judeo-Christian tradition and its centrality to the American sociopolitical identity in subsequent publications: the monograph *Common Ground: A Plea for Intelligent Americanism* (1938) and the revealingly titled article "Judaism, a Universal Religion" (1939), which appeared in the prominent nondenominational weekly *The Christian Century*.

The "Judeo-Christian tradition" as a core constituent of American values, at once pluralist and unitary, thus gained momentum through the American experience during the Second World War and has by now become a commonplace, so much so that the term has the appearance of being merely descriptive.[89] Today, the idea of the Judeo-Christian West seems to have displaced and

88. Or what they called "positive Christianity." See Richard Steigmann-Gall, *The Holy Reich* (2003).

89. In "Jewish GIs and the Creation of the Judeo-Christian Tradition" (1998), Deborah Dash Moore has pointed out the significance of the experience of the American Jews serving in the military in the formation of the Judeo-Christian identity. Jesse T. Todd has noted the critical importance of the 1939–40 World's Fair in the emergence of the Judeo-Christian notion, as he argued in his 1997 paper "Producing the Judeo-Christian Tradition at the New York World's Fair, 1939–1940."

Like the term "world religions" itself, the idea of the Judeo-Christian tradition, as ubiquitous as it is, seems to have been paid remarkably little critical attention. When a question is raised about the cogency of the hyphenation, it seems to be always from the "Judeo-" side of the hyphenation. Cf. Robert Gordis, *The Judeo-Christian Tradition*, Arthur A. Cohen, *The Myth of the Judeo-*

occluded the notion of Christian Europe and usurped the subject position of the world historical unfolding. The concept is now readily available for all forms of conceptually imprecise, politically charged usage. To be sure, it remains a matter for debate and future investigation as to how this displacement and occlusion amounted to further obscuring, and at the same time sheltering and preserving, the hegemonic logic of the epistemic regime formerly instituted on the authority of Euro-Christendom.

Although Judaism's ascendancy to the ranks of world religions was thus multiply significant, this is not to suggest that the expansion of the category came about only along this particular path. In fact, it was not generally the case that Judaism was the next in line, after Christianity, Buddhism, and Islam, for admission to the ranks. Rather, there were other paths, alternate logics in accordance with which the early-twentieth-century transformation of the category of world religions seems to have taken place. One such alternative has been already suggested by the self-consciously universalist articulation of Hinduism voiced by a number of Indian modernists since the nineteenth century. Equally significant, and even more broadly consequential, was the development of the notion of world religions that divested itself of an overt claim to universality. A pivotal figure in this line of transformation was, without a doubt, Max Weber (1864–1920).

Weber counted five world religions, adding Hinduism and Confucianism to the previously established three. As with others of his time and thereafter, while availing himself of the term, Weber did not in any way attempt to theorize "world religions" as a category. Nor is there any evidence that he expended much thought upon the question of how he arrived at the opinion that there were five such religions. Given that Weber is considered one of the most lastingly influential figures in the history of the science of religion, it seems surprising that he made no theoretical contribution to the development of the world religions discourse. But then, neither did Max Müller. In fact, in characterizing their respective roles in the formation of the world religions discourse,

---

Christian Tradition (1969), Mark Silk, "Notes on the Judeo-Christian Tradition in America" (1984), and the exchange between Marshall Grossman and Yerach Gover (Grossman, "The Violence of the Hyphen in Judeo-Christian" [1989], Gover, "Why Be a Nebbish?" [1989], Grossman, "Come to the Movies Yerach" [1989]). For a useful overview of the historical emergence of the Judeo-Christian concept in America, see Mark Silk, *Spiritual Politics* (1988).

it might be reasonably concluded that Müller's significance was in that he never had any use for the category and did not even mention the term, let alone take note of the controversy raging around him, whereas Weber's significance was that he for all intents and purposes authorized the circulation of the term without any deliberation, explanation, or regulation, all the while ignoring entirely the logic and the scruples voiced by his predecessors.[90]

Despite the foundational status accorded to it, Weber's work on the sociology of religion—or what he preferred to call more precisely the comparative sociology of religion (vergleichende Religionssoziologie)—is incomplete and fragmentary. Its component parts began to appear incrementally, beginning with The Protestant Ethic and the Spirit of Capitalism, by far the best-known title in the Weberian corpus, which appeared initially in 1904 and 1905, in two installments in the Archiv für Sozialwissenschaft und Sozialpolitik, the journal Weber co-edited with Werner Sombart and Edgar Jaffé. Weber then initiated a series of studies on the world religions, which were expected eventually to form a massive comprehensive treatise. The project in its entirety was to be called the Economic Ethic of the World Religions (Wirtschaftsethik der Weltreligionen). After the endeavor was cut short by Weber's premature death in 1920, what remained of the project—both previously published and unpublished—was issued in a three-volume collection under the title Collected Essays in Sociology of Religion (Gesammelte Aufsätze zur Religionssoziologie, 1921).[91] This collection included a lengthy

90. Among such predecessors was C. P. Tiele, of whose work Weber was intimately knowledgeable. See Hans G. Kippenberg, "Max Weber und die vergleichende Religionswissenschaft" (1995).

91. This collection also includes the following shorter essays: Die Protestant Sekten und der Geist des Kapitalismus, a piece related to the more famous Protestant Ethic essay,; a substantial introductory essay, originally published independently in Archiv für Sozialwissenschaft und Sozialpolitik in 1915 and translated as "The Social Psychology of the World Religions," in From Max Weber: Essays in Sociology (1958); a preface (Vorbemerkung) to the whole collection, which, according to Talcott Parsons, Weber wrote in 1920 (see Parsons "Translator's Preface" in The Protestant Ethic and the Spirit of Capitalism [1992]). Furthermore, between the original publication of the essay on Chinese religion and that on Indian religion, Weber wrote an important comparative and connective essay, didactically entitled "Zwischenbetrachtung: Theorie der Stufen und Richtungen religiöser Weltablehnung" (Interim reflection: Theory of the stages and directions of religious world-negation, 1915). This was translated and loosely retitled by H. H. Gerth and C. Wright Mills as "Religious Rejections of the World and Their Directions" and included in From Max Weber. The translators give no indication as to how this essay is related to the world religions project. Nor do they explain the reasons for the change in titles.

study each on "Confucianism and Taoism," "Hinduism and Buddhism," and "ancient Judaism," which were published in translation as separate monographs: *The Religion of China* (1951), *The Religion of India* (1958), and *Ancient Judaism* (1952). As has been reported by Talcott Parsons and others, in addition to the material published in the collection, Weber was also working on studies on Islam, early Christianity, and Talmudic Judaism respectively.[92]

This ambitious but incomplete extent of Weber's literary remains represents the range of individual religious traditions that claimed his interest. As is already evident from these titles, while he names five world religions, they do not necessarily constitute clear boundaries that define specific domains of analysis. Instead, he found it more effective for his purpose to consider one world religion in conjunction with another world religion (in the case of Hinduism and Buddhism), or one world religion in relation to another, non-world religion (Confucianism and Taoism), while, in some other cases, the "same" religion is considered in different moments (ancient Judaism separate from Talmudic Judaism, and Protestant Christianity separate from early Christianity). In effect, for Weber, neither the category "world religions" itself nor any of the individual religions so categorized constitutes any fixed analytic boundaries, distinct subject fields, or units of referential constraints; rather, they seem to function more or less malleably, fungibly.

This unusual—one might say singular—use of the category is discernible from the very beginning of Weber's project, even though at first blush his language might seem innocuously conventional. In the introductory essay he published in 1915 under the same name as the entire projected work, "Economic Ethic of the World Religions"—which, however, the English translators unaccountably rendered as "The Social Psychology of the World Religions"—he states:

In addition to the material contained in the three-volume collection mentioned above, Weber's work on comparative sociology of religion also includes a substantial assortment of fragmentary texts, which were reportedly written in the early 1910s. These pieces represent part of another massive unfinished work, whose extant chapters and fragments were published as *Wirtschaft und Gesellschaft* (1956) and in the two-volume translation *Economy and Society* (1978). For a useful discussion on the circumstances of Weber's writing and the publication history, see Guenther Roth's introduction to *Economy and Society*, 1:lxii–lxv, especially lxxvi–lxxvii. Chapter 6 of *Wirtschaft und Gesellschaft* had been previously translated into English and published as a separate volume under the title *The Sociology of Religion*, trans. Ephraim Fischoff (1963).

92. According to Parsons, those manuscripts were left "not yet in a condition fit for publication in any form." Talcott Parsons, "Translator's Preface," in *The Protestant Ethic*, 10.

By "world religions," we understand the five religions or religiously deter-mined systems of life-regulation which have known how to gather multi-tudes of confessors around them. The term is used here in a completely value-neutral sense. The Confucian, Hinduist, Buddhist, Christian, and Islamist religious ethics all belong to the category of world religion. A sixth religion, Judaism, will also be dealt with. It is included because it contains historical preconditions decisive for understanding Christianity and Islamism, and because of its historic and autonomous significance for the development of the modern economic ethic of the Occident—a significance, partly real and partly alleged, which has been discussed sev-eral times recently. References to other religions will be made only when they are indispensable for historical connections.[93]

From this programmatic statement, some general observations may be drawn. Weber was clearly not party to the debate as to what essential and qual-itative differences might exist between the world religions and the non-world religions. Rather, he appears to have settled for a seemingly mechanical, somewhat arbitrary criterion of merely statistical significance—sheer num-bers, that is, what Kuenen and Chantepie de la Saussaye earlier referred to as "a matter of fact rather than quality." As if to underscore the point, Weber pro-claims here, in his trademark phrasing, that the term "world religions" is used "in a completely value-neutral manner" (in ganz wertfreier Art). We count five world religions because, according to Weber, these five happen to "have known how to gather particularly large numbers of confessors" (besonders große Mengen von Bekennern um sich zu scharen gewußt haben). This prima facie explains why Hinduism and Confucianism should belong to the category of world religions in his view—that is, on account of the large population of the nations in which these religions are dominant. As we recall from chapter 3, however, such an un-derstanding of the category is contrary to the opinion of virtually everyone in-volved in the earlier debate. For, according to those others, what distinguished world religions from all others was not a matter of mere numbers, and, further-more, it was then beyond dispute that Hinduism and Confucianism, together with Judaism, were exemplary cases of ethnic or land-specific religions, that is to say, national religions (Landesreligionen).

"National religion," however, is not a viable category in Weber's work. The

---

93. Max Weber, "The Social Psychology of the World Religions," in *From Max Weber*, 267. The original passage appeared in "Die Wirtschaftsethik der Weltreligionen. Vergleichende religion-ssoziologische Versuche: Einleitung," in *Gesammelte Aftsätze zur Religionssoziologie*, 1:237–38.

passage just quoted is but one indication, for Weber, that non-world religions are simply "other religions" (*andere Religionen*). Even more important, in his understanding of the matter, all religions—or, in his characteristic rephrasing, all "religiously determined systems of life regulation" (*religiös bedingten Systeme der Lebensreglementierung*)—bear the mark of historical, geographical, and political particularities, regardless of whether a given religion is designated as a world religion or not.[94] In effect, all of what Weber calls world religions are, in the language of the nineteenth-century *Religionswissenschaftler*, national religions.

This is as much as to suggest that, without ever referring directly to the preexisting scholarly tradition, Weber preempted the scruples of the previous generation, as he declined to entertain altogether any possibility of substantive difference between national religions and world religions.

In this omnibus of a chapter, I have identified several domains where further and more substantial investigations may bear useful results in the future. My preliminary deliberations here are drawn—with the exception of sections 1 and 5—almost entirely from information available in secondary sources; but undoubtedly in each of these domains lies a great deal of primary and archival material awaiting scrutiny. The series of tentative forays executed here may also hint at the immensity of the task involved if an exploration in any of the areas is to be carried out in earnest.

In a way, what allowed the present project to sustain its focus on the scholarly world was the fact that, in the nineteenth century, the incipient concept of world religions, or even the concept of the "major religions of the world," was a concern mostly confined or controlled within the purview of academically positioned intellectuals, and to that extent it was possible to bring its vicissitudes to light by a monolithically intellectualist method. It was possible, in other words, to conduct an extended analysis of the logic of classifying religions—or more precisely, the destabilization, the collapse, and the reconstitution of the classificatory logic—by following in the tracks of a handful of philologists,

94. As he puts it, "[A] religiously determined way of life is itself profoundly influenced by economic and political factors operating within given geographical, political, social, and national boundaries" (Weber, "The Social Psychology of the World Religions," 268). This passage occurs in a well-known paragraph in which Weber stresses the fact of mutual and multilateral determination of economic ethic and religion, and shortly thereafter he comments: "We should lose ourselves in these discussions if we tried to demonstrate these dependencies in all their singularities."

Orientalists, and amateur comparativists. But when it comes to the twentieth century, the discourse of world religions is now truly in the public domain. It therefore does not easily yield to interpretive tactics of the kind I employed for the nineteenth-century material. In short, as of the early twentieth century, the world religions discourse is no longer contained in the sphere of intellectual history proper but abundantly spills over onto all other domains, into social and institutional history.

9

The Question of Hegemony
Ernst Troeltsch and the Reconstituted European Universalism

For reasons variously stated in earlier chapters, the present study does not provide a unifying conclusion. While it may be reasonably claimed that the foregoing deliberations on the nineteenth-century discursive transformation are crucial first steps in understanding the eventual outbreak of the familiar pluralist episteme, couched in the language of world religions, I am under no illusion that this study fully accounts for the installation of that discourse in its historical entirety. In lieu of a conclusion, then, this last chapter presents a tableau vivant in words, a staccato mark accentuating and punctuating a historical narrative that does not come to an end.

The scene is the early twentieth century, when the ideological cathexis that had been accumulating around the notion of world religions had swelled to the point of crisis. It features an intellectual of a novel sort—call him a religious sociologist or sociohistorical theologian. Ernst Troeltsch (1865–1923) represented a new breed of modernist Christian not uncommon in Germany at the time: the liberal, socially conscious, scientifically minded man of faith. A friend and colleague of Max Weber,[1] Troeltsch was an internationally renowned figure, and his struggle with the problem of Euro-Christian dominion under the condition of religious pluralism was by no means merely a personal question. The question had to do with whether and how Europe, or the West, might continue to assume the subject position in the unfolding of world history when the totality of the world was no longer a matter of cosmological imaginary but, in variously volatile and disturbing ways, was becoming a material reality.

1. It is widely acknowledged, including by Weber himself, that Troeltsch's *The Social Teaching of the Christian Churches* (*Die Soziallehren der christlichen Kirchen und Gruppen*, 1912) built upon and far extended Weber's work in *The Protestant Ethic and the Spirit of Capitalism*, and partly on that account Weber "abandoned the topic of Protestantism" in order to pursue instead "a broadly comparative treatment of religion and society," i.e., his world religions project (Reinhard Bendix, *Max Weber* [1984], 49n).

The career of Ernst Troeltsch roughly coincided with the period of change in the meaning of the term "world religions," from the highly selective and frankly evaluative sense (universal or universalistic religions as opposed to national or ethnic religions) to the avowedly neutral and inclusive sense (any major living religions of the world). Chronologically posited at the pivot in this historic turn, Troeltsch's position can be described in multiple ways: while he was thoroughly schooled in the idealist and historicist traditions of the nineteenth-century German academy, he increasingly had gained an audience in the English-speaking world; while he was a systematic theologian, he is also included among the new kind of Wissenschaftler, counted as one of the earliest sociologists of religion. He was a leading Christian spokesperson by profession, and at the same time a pioneering historian of religion of a particular sort.

During the nineteenth century—as mentioned in section 2 of the introduction—"history" as a discursive practice was undergoing a significant transformation. It was emerging as a bona fide academic field and vocation, no longer a matter of mere antiquarian interests. As the modernist self-description of the academic field goes, "history" at that point ceased to be fodder for morality plays to be staged in some distal regions of the past; instead, it reconstituted itself as a scientific discipline foundational to all arenas of human science. It is generally understood, moreover, that German universities in particular were the fountainhead of this intellectual current running across Europe and beyond. Concurrently with the emergence of historical science, or history as a science, "comparative religion" and "history of religion" were becoming familiar designations for a new type of discourse about religion, which means, roughly, those endeavors mobilized and sustained by philological, archaeological, and anthropological research, as opposed to those motivated by dogmatic, apologetic, and evangelical interests.

An exponent of Religionsgeschichteschule, or the history of religions school, Troeltsch was arguably the most prominent among the systematic theologians who took the empirical reality of other religions to heart. As his 1897 essay "Christianity and the History of Religion" announces in no uncertain terms, his highly cultivated historical consciousness drove him to concede that "the rise of a comparative history of religion has shaken the Christian more deeply than anything else."[2]

This sentiment—that the recognition of other religions and other cultures

---

2. Ernst Troeltsch, "Christianity and the History of Religion." I refer in this discussion to the translation in Religion in History (1991), 77.

had a profoundly unsettling effect on the self-confidence of Christian orthodoxy and its institutions—has been broadly and persistently pronounced to this day. In fact, it is so familiar to our ear that probably few among us would deem it necessary to transport our imagination back to that time and ask why such a momentous crisis of confidence should have taken place just then. It occurs to us even less to question the veracity or cogency of the sentiment. But this supposed atrophy of confidence could not have been caused by Europeans' sudden change of heart. Indeed, to take a long historical view, it certainly does not appear to be the case that at the beginning of the twentieth century educated Europeans and Euro-Americans suddenly began to entertain more elevated opinions of Oriental societies and their spiritual cultures. In fact, the opposite was sometimes true, as we have seen in the increasingly virulent European view of Islam, particularly of the Arabs.

More generally, prior to the nineteenth century, European literati had been in the habit of harboring highly laudatory, unrealistically exalted, images of venerable Oriental societies. This was particularly evident with respect to their views on the ancient Egyptian and Chinese dynasties. These regimes were typically fantasized and praised, especially by the Freemasons and other exponents of the so-called Radical Enlightenment, as epitomizing the equanimity and stability of the civilization governed by Reason.[3] At the same time, the Orientomania of eighteenth-century Europeans proved no detriment to their self-esteem or to their own universalist ideals. The image of the rational empire of the East was simply a very useful tool for sharply criticizing and denigrating, by means of contrast, what the proponents of the Enlightenment perceived as grievously benighted, hidebound institutions within their own society, in particular, the Catholic Church. Meanwhile, much to the annoyance of such radical Enlightenment intellectuals who would have liked to see it topple, the ancient regime of European Christendom and its functionaries, far from faltering in the face of increasing reports about other religions, remained recalcitrant, defiant, unshaken.

To be sure, it is often pointed out that what proved unsettling in Troeltsch's time was not mere knowledge of the existence of non-European and non-Christian societies, be they glorious or ignominious, but rather the discovery

3. See Margaret C. Jacob, The Radical Enlightenment (1981). For the pre-nineteenth-century European views on the Orient, see, for example, Adolf Reichwein, China and Europe (1925); P. J. Marshall and Glyndwr Williams, The Great Map of Mankind (1982); Martin Bernal, Black Athena (1987), 161–88; as well as Donald Lach's multivolume work, Asia in the Making of Europe (1965–93), mentioned earlier.

of historicity itself—the realization, in other words, that no one, no body of knowledge, and no vantage point, no matter how powerfully compelling, could escape the pall of historicity, that is, escape the particular and contingent determinations of its own moment. The new historical sensibility did more than bring to the forefront the incontrovertible actuality of non-Christian peoples; a more devastating consequence for "us," Troeltsch argued in the 1897 essay, was that it brought home "the mutability of Christianity. . . . [I]t destroyed the Catholic fiction that the church simply represented the continuation of original Christianity, as well as the Protestant fiction that the Reformation represented its restoration."[4] Historical consciousness had, or was felt to have had, a profound leveling effect on all truth claims and values, including the truth claims of religion. It seemed to cut Christianity down to size, relegating it to the status of just one of the many religions around. As Troeltsch puts it: "Christianity lost its exclusive-supernatural foundation. It was now perceived as only one of the great world religions, along with Islam and Buddhism, and like these, as constituting the culmination of complicated historical developments" (78).

This relativizing tendency of thought, as we recall, had been summarily denounced as "the most prevalent form of unbelief" by Frederick Denison Maurice only half a century earlier. But now it appears that even the paragons of systematic theology, the official spokespersons for the confessional community, could not dismiss it. Equipped with ever greater knowledge of the past and a heightened sense of historicity nurtured by Germanic scientific training, Troeltsch could no longer respond to the challenges of history by simply reiterating and amplifying the universalist-supremacist claim of Christianity, as Maurice, Archdeacon Hardwick, Bishop Wordsworth, and James Freeman Clarke had done a generation or two earlier. Inevitably, then, the theologian came to confront perturbing questions:

> What would become now of Christianity's exclusive truth or even of its decisive superiority? Above all, what would become of the belief in an exclusive revelation? (78)

Troeltsch does not issue an answer to these ominous questions. What is remarkable indeed is that he, without missing a beat, changes the subject. He converts what is clearly a problem of threats specifically directed to the authority of Christianity in particular (threats to its exclusive validity over and against

---

4. Troeltsch, "Christianity and the History of Religion," 77; cited in the text by page number hereafter.

all other religions) into a problem of threats to *religion in general*. Thus he continues without pause:

> But the consequences go even further. Not only the truth and validity of Christianity but also those of religion itself, as a unique sphere of life, disappear in this maelstrom of historical diversity. (78)

This immediate and thus nearly invisible conversion of the problem is without explanation or apology, so that the reader is given no time to take stock of its momentous significance. Troeltsch himself, however, is obviously aware of the jarring transitive moment, if only to encourage the reader to believe that this shift is but a matter of certain consequences "going further."

But, surely, it is more than a question of going further. At this crucial textual juncture, not only does Troeltsch shift the attention away from the immediate difficulty facing the confessional Christian community, but by so doing he also conjures up, out of thin air, something like "religion itself, as a unique sphere of life."

Of course, it is difficult for us today not to be taken in by this rhetorical sleight of hand. It is almost natural for us to be fooled by the move that glosses over this evasion, this non sequitur. But if this is so, it must be because our default position on the subject of religions is likewise saturated by the world religions discourse, which thrives and survives precisely on this easy slippage from the particular (Euro-Christianity) to the general (religion as such). For, even without a thorough historical analysis, it seems obvious enough that the discourse of world religions takes for granted the idea of "religion itself" as a "unique sphere of life," and that it presumes that this sphere is prevalent throughout the world and its history. Nor was Troeltsch in his own day lacking in a sympathetic audience among the comparative historians of religion. From Rudolf Otto and Gerardus van der Leeuw to Mircea Eliade, the majority of the comparative historians of religion had, like Troeltsch himself, not only a personal alliance with, or affirmation of, Christianity but, more important, a sentimental attachment to the seemingly charitable notion that all human beings without exception were endowed with some distinct and irreducible capability or sensibility specific to the Infinite, the Holy, the Absolute. On the basis of this conviction, they probably could take some comfort in the thought that this meant that all human beings were *potential* Christians, even if they were not actually and officially so at the moment. In short, by the early twentieth century, liberal Christians like Troeltsch and Otto were generally prepared to accept the fact of religious diversity and to respect the viability, in principle, of other religions. To take this stance has been more or less a matter of good public policy ever since, and a number of religionists—including various representatives of particular faith communities—have willingly assumed this public position, provided that they remained entitled to their own convictions with respect to the absolute universality of their own religion as a *private* matter of faith.

Notwithstanding the compelling power of these opinions, and notwithstanding, moreover, our own well-schooled habit of believing, rather moralistically, that somehow mere segregation of the private from the public, and the nonaggression pact that this arrangement makes possible, is all for the good of humanity, let us take a moment and insist on this disquieting question that Troeltsch himself raised: Whatever happened to the question of the "decisive superiority" of Christianity? What about its "belief in an exclusive revelation"? Why does Troeltsch evade this issue? And if the answer seems rather too obvious, we might as well ask: Whence comes this new problem, this challenge suddenly brought against "religion itself, as a unique sphere of life"?

In the paragraphs immediately following the passage quoted above, "religion itself," which has made its appearance out of the blue, comes to be endowed with a sense of reality of majestic proportion, not through some evidential demonstration, but by the sheer force of elocution. Here, it is "history" that turns around and comes to the aid of the theologian. As Troeltsch goes on to suggest, if historical-scientific knowledge is what has brought about the crisis of faith, it is also a historical science (specifically in the form of the new discipline of the comparative history of religion) that may bring new knowledge to bear on the reality of the "unique sphere" that is religion.[5] But in order for that to happen,

> [w]e simply must learn to view religion more sympathetically; to free ourselves from doctrinaire, rationalistic, and systematizing presuppositions; and to focus more intently on the characteristic, distinctively religious phenomena and personages rather than on average people. *Then the deepest core of the religious history of humanity reveals itself as an experience that cannot be further analyzed, an ultimate and original phenomenon that constitutes, like* moral judgment and aesthetic perception and yet with characteristic dif-

---

5. In this respect, Mircea Eliade echoed Troeltsch almost exactly, though he added further embellishment. See essays included in *The Quest* (1969), especially "A New Humanism," "The History of Religions in Retrospect," "The Quest for the 'Origins' of Religion," "Crisis and Renewal."

ferences, *a simple fact of psychic life. Everywhere the basic reality of religion is the same: an underivable, purely positive, again and again experienced contact with the Deity.* This unity has its ground in a common dynamism of the human spirit which advances in different ways as a result of the mysterious movement of the divine Spirit in the unconscious depth of the human spirit, which is everywhere the same. Unable to attain its goal in the short span of individual life, this movement is effected through the co-operative efforts of countless generations as they are grasped and led by the divine activity, surrendering to it and experiencing its true import in ever greater fullness and profoundness. (79; emphasis added)

The passage seems to signal at least three cardinal points. First, "sympathy" is needed in properly approaching any religion, beyond calcification of dogmas, creeds, and apologia. Second, there is an essential unity and sameness in all religions when thus approached, and this essence is revealed at their irreducible core. Third, realization occurs over many generations of the different paths to fulfillment of the various spiritual destinies, though all are divinely ordained.

A little later, Troeltsch reiterates this grand thesis about the affinity, if not identity, of all religions— expressed in the above paragraph in more or less theological terms—in a manner somewhat more resonant with the ecumenical language of historical scientific comparativism:

If we go beyond the accidents of time and space, personality and tradition, we find everywhere a very similar truth. We note a great sense of awe before the mystery of a supersensible world that speaks its word within the course of everyday life: whether it comforts people or frightens them, it always disrupts the slumber of a purely innerworldly existence. We also note the manifestation of divine forces in nature, and the authorization of moral and legal norms on the part of the Deity. Above all we note the higher goods of eternal blessedness and the rise of the belief in redemption. All these phenomena are properly viewed as belonging together, as requiring a unified, comprehensive treatment. (81)

The frankness of these assertions is useful. Even if this undisguised universalism expressed by sheer force of dogmatic declaration is unnerving to the contemporary scholar of religion, it would be admitted that the idea itself is generally consistent with those of the key twentieth-century exponents of history and phenomenology of religion, including Rudolf Otto, Gerardus van der

Leeuw, Mircea Eliade, and countless others. That this idea of unity and universality mobilizes and justifies much of the discourse of world religions seems at once too self-evident and too overwhelming a reality to lend itself to a tidy demonstration.[6] It is impossible to appraise summarily the full implications of the fact that this idea, together with the broadly ecumenical—hence, one might venture to say, uncritically monolithic and universalist—sentiment behind this idea, is deeply ingrained in the enterprise of the contemporary study of religion.

To be sure, many of today's scholars would likely contest, rather than accept, this presumption that the unity of "religious experience" should be the basis of the study of religion as an academic discipline. Yet, despite the vocal protest of some within the field, it is equally undeniable that the academy of religion scholars as a whole is publicly perceived, justly or unjustly, as firmly allied with this idea.[7]

6. As we saw in chapter 2, the idea of the fundamental unity of religions—or what may be reasonably termed liberal universalism—has been in evidence in much of the comparative enterprise since the nineteenth century, including among those with clearly hierarchical views (such as F. D. Maurice and J. F. Clarke, among others). Even the religious conservatives who were openly critical of this universalism (such as Charles Hardwick and John Wordsworth) identified this impious and dangerous tendency in the religious comparativism surging around them, and that was the reason for their opposition. There were of course many Christian liberals who embraced this idea whole-heartedly and thus paved the royal road to today's predominance of the world religions discourse. A proclamation of this universalism is heard, for example, in the following anonymous statement quoted on the opening page of *Religious Systems of the World* (1891) from the *Universal Review* of December 1888: "A new Catholicity has dawned upon the world. All religions are now recognised as essentially Divine. They represent the different angles at which man looks at God. Questions of origin, polemics as to evidences, erudite dissertations concerning formulae, are disappearing, because religions are no longer judged by their supposed accordance with the letter of the Bible, but by their ability to minister to the wants and fulfil the aspirations of men. The individual, what can it make of him? As it raises or debases, purifies or corrupts, fills with happiness or torments with fear, so is it judged to accord with the Divine will. The credentials of the Divine origin of every religion are to be found in the hearts and lives of those who believe it. The old intolerance has disappeared, and the old indifference, which succeeded it, has well-nigh disappeared also. The new tolerance of faith recognises as Divine all the creeds which have enabled men to overcome their bestial appetites with visions of things spiritual and eternal."

7. To cite an incident illustrating this point, in 1996, a popular American public television host, Bill Moyers, broadcast his interviews with Huston Smith entitled "The Wisdom of the Faith." In his prepublicity postcard sent to the American Academy of Religion membership, Moyers describes the Academy as an organization "dedicated to exploring, affirming, and educating the public about the religious dimension of human existence," and his guest, also a mem-

Now, it might be observed that there is nothing really new in the idea of the complementary contrast between the surface differences and the depth affinity of all religions; this is an old idea put to a new use—an idea at least as old as English Deists, many of whom opined that "religion" as a genus is one, whereas its "sects" and "denominations" as species are many.[8] The difference is that, whereas the Deists often got into trouble with authorities for their views in their day, we on the contrary would be hard pressed to find a religion writer who would set out to contradict the notion of the fundamental commonality or unity of religions. On the whole, the disciplinary establishment of so-called religious studies, for whatever reason and with whatever justification, seems to hold fast to this bottom line: Religion is found everywhere; it is an essential and irreducible aspect of human life; it should be studied. And if we take into consideration the constitution, for instance, of the American Academy of Religion as a whole, it also seems to imply something else in addition: Religions should be studied concertedly, comparatively.

It is to his credit, however, that the lessons of history that Troeltsch drew rendered his own thoughts considerably more nuanced and thoughtful than the above quotations from "Christianity and the History of Religion" might suggest. This becomes more evident in an essay he wrote a quarter of a century later, "The Place of Christianity among the World Religions" (1923). In this late work he stated unequivocally: what history was apt to exhibit was not unity and universality at all, but on the contrary, individuality:

> History cannot be regarded as a process in which a universal and everywhere similar principle is confined and obscured. Nor is it a continual mixing and remixing of elemental psychical powers, which indicate a general trend of things towards a rational end or goal of evolution. *It is rather an immeasurable, incomparable profusion of always-new, unique, and hence individual tendencies, welling up from undiscovered depths,* and coming to light in each case in unsuspected places and under different circumstances. . . . Thus the universal law of history consists precisely in this, that the Divine Reason, or the Divine Life, within history, constantly manifests itself in

---

ber of the Academy, as one who "has immersed himself in the world's great religions, seeking to discover the distilled wisdom of the human race."

8. Cf. Nicholas Lash, *The Beginning and the End of 'Religion'?* (1996), and David A. Pailin, *Attitudes to Other Religions* (1984).

always-new and always-peculiar individualizations—and hence its tendency is not towards unity or universality at all. . . . It is this law which, beyond all else, makes it quite impossible to characterize Christianity as the
reconciliation and goal of all the forces of history, or indeed to regard it as
anything else than a historical individuality.[9]

Here, with a single stroke empowered both by the authority of systematic
theology and by the equally formidable authority of historical science,
Troeltsch definitively severs the question of the absolute validity, or absoluteness, as he puts it, of Christianity from the question of its universality in the
empirical-objective sense. What he says here amounts to a declaration that, for
any foreseeable future, or perhaps for the entire duration of history that remains, the claim for the universality of Christianity—of any religion, for that
matter—is destined to remain strictly a matter of conviction interior to a person or to a race, and that the source of such conviction is ultimately "the evidence of a profound inner experience" (26) and nothing else. It is above all this
interior "experience" that he admonished us, in his 1897 essay, to view "more
sympathetically." Accordingly, we have been advised, we must "free ourselves
from doctrinaire, rationalistic, and systematizing presuppositions," so that we
may discern "the deepest core of the religious history of humanity" (79).

In sum, the question of the absoluteness and the universality of Christianity
is finally brought to a standstill, as the problem comes to rest in a state of profound ambivalence. On the one hand, it is no longer tenable, if one is to remain
consistent with the lessons of history, to count on the future hegemony and
universal reign of Christianity in any overt, material, and historical sense. But
on the other hand, the dream of unity and universality remains very much viable, it seems, in the domain of "undiscovered depths" that are said to be revealed time and again in certain recondite recesses of human experience, the
kind of experience "that cannot be further analyzed, an ultimate and original
phenomenon that constitutes . . . a simple fact of psychic life." This latter domain, for all its inaccessibility—or precisely because of it—constitutes a much
more durable, difficult to refute, morally sacrosanct basis for a belief in unity
and universality, whether such a belief is held as an article of faith or as a heuris-
tic principle of a science of religion.

There is, however, a significant price to be paid for the reconfiguration and

---

9. Troeltsch, "The Place of Christianity among the World Religions," in Baron von Hügel's
compilation Christian Thought (1923), 44–45; cited in the text by page number hereafter.

reauthorization of theological absolutism. By psychologizing the question of absolute validity in this manner, and by turning the meaning of the absoluteness of a theological claim into something strictly interior to a person or to a "race," Troeltsch implicitly accepts as given the individuality and plurality of believers and of races. The elemental assumption here is that different persons and different peoples adhere to different ideas of foundational truth within their own personal or racial psychic life, and that each of these ideas carries with it its own absolute conviction and universalistic appeal, and these separate psychic interiors are mutually inviolable, nonnegotiable, and irreconcilable; they are private. What, by contrast, can be defended and advocated in the exterior realm—that is to say, in nontheological, nonconfessional public discourse, to which the discourse of science should belong—is therefore no longer Christianity or any other religion in particular, but "religion itself, as a unique sphere of life." Troeltsch's formulation of the historical science of religion allows this.

If the situation delineated by Troeltsch here seems rather grim for confessional theologians—indeed, disastrous for their prospects as public intellectuals—it was in turn a great boon for the historians of religion then in ascendancy. This critical juncture, as exemplified by the turn of Troeltsch himself, was an unprecedented opportunity for the discourse of the *science* of religion to surge forth, and after a fashion to reconfigure and refit a theologian for a new career as a historian of religion.[10]

At the same time, this juncture also makes visible a moment of origin of the suddenly powerful idea of "religion itself." This concept of religion as a general, transcultural phenomenon, yet also as a distinct sphere in its own right, is a foundational premise essential to the enterprise of the history of religions as envisioned by Troeltsch, and by many others since. But if we recall the moment of its sudden appearance in "Christianity and the History of Religion," the concept is patently groundless; it came from nowhere, and there is no credible way of demonstrating its factual and empirical substantiality.[11] Only when we are already compelled, as we often seem to be, by the assumption that religion is

10. This, of course, is not to suggest that Troeltsch in any way ceased to be a theologian at some point. On the contrary, it is because he does not abandon his identity as a theologian and confessional Christian by becoming a historian that makes his example particularly instructive, as he makes visible the nature of the relation and the tension between the two.

11. To be sure, Troeltsch was not the only one to produce the notion of "religion itself," and others who did so did not derive it from this particular textual moment in Troeltsch. But I have yet to encounter any instance in which this notion is brought up in any other way, that is, other

thus unique and universal, are we sure to find it confirmed everywhere, like a figure in the carpet. Furthermore, from the very beginning this idea came fully endowed with all the weight and moral cathexis that was once proper to liberal Protestant theology. This load of ideational energy has now been dislodged from that original site and transferred to "religion itself," now that the very theology has run up against the wall of its own undeniable historicity.

∾

But this was not all. Troeltsch's intellectual passage eventually went beyond this well-rehearsed terrain of classic world religions discourse, where historians strive to recover the unique genius of each "tradition," where comparativists attempt to demonstrate diversity, plurality, and affinity among "traditions," and where theologians seek to confess and to confirm the absoluteness of their limited particular "tradition" when they are among their own kind and, when with others, speak the language of ecumenical empathy, and where, in the end, all parties claim to believe in the authenticity of experience and in the deep unity of all religions in their universal yearning for spirituality and for something like world peace. Such is the state of the world maintained—and suspended—by the discourse of world religions, the condition Troeltsch clearly recognized. Yet, in a certain critical respect, he went further.

As we recall, Troeltsch argued that the absoluteness of (each) religion is not only a matter of individual personal conviction but also something intrinsic and interior collectively to a particular "race." This, as it appears, is a necessary implication of his understanding that all cultures and religions are historically determined and therefore particular. In his view, the dominion of a religion gradually comes to be shaped and circumscribed by a specific race in the course of history, irrespective, it seems, of the place of origin of that religion. What this means in the case of Christianity, according to Troeltsch's essay of 1923, is as follows:

It is historical facts that have welded Christianity into the closest connection with the civilizations of Greece, Rome and Northern Europe. All our thoughts and feelings are impregnated with Christian motives and Christian presuppositions; and, conversely, our whole Christianity is indissol-

<hr>

than out of the blue, already fully lined with given religious universalist sentiments, however vague.

ubly bound up with elements of the ancient and modern civilizations of Europe. From being a Jewish sect Christianity has become the religion of all Europe. It stands or falls with European civilization; whilst, on its own part, it has entirely lost its Oriental character and has become hellenized and westernized. Our European conceptions of personality and its eternal, divine right, and of progress towards a kingdom of the spirit and of God, our enormous capacity for expansion and for the interconnection of spiritual and temporal, our whole social order, our science, our art—all these rest, whether we know it or not, whether we like it or not, upon the basis of this deorientalised Christianity. (24–25)

This view, as we have seen, is consistent with those of many nineteenth- and twentieth-century writers intent on appropriating Christianity fully and exclusively for the West while drawing a delicate line of separation between European Christianity and its Semitic-Oriental origin. Once the Christian religion is permanently, "indissolubly" fused with the historical destiny of Europe and its recent triumphs, there resurfaces anew, in Troeltsch's writing, the question of the universality of Christianity and, concomitantly, the question of its *exclusive* validity. This resurgence, as might be expected, is not without some ominous implications.

Troeltsch himself does not seem to harbor any misgivings—or irony, for that matter—when he finally proclaims that Christianity's "primary claim to validity is . . . the fact that only through it have we become what we are." And when he avers, moreover, that without Christianity "we can lapse either into a self destructive titanic attitude, or into effeminate trifling, or into brutality" (25), there is nothing particularly anxious or self-critical about this assertion, as it becomes evident presently. Scarcely a page later he goes on to proclaim, with sobering clarity, this:

Christianity could not be the religion of such a highly developed racial group if it did not possess a mighty spiritual power and truth; in short, if it were not, in some degree, a manifestation of the Divine Life itself. (26)

There is something nearly fatalistic—in fact, tragic, in a certain Romantic sense of the word—about this sense of European destiny, which is now for Troeltsch a palimpsest for the religion of a self-sacrificing god. For, as he goes on to reflect—the year is 1923—in the wake of the Great War and in the shadow of his own approaching death, our life is a consistent compromise as little unsatisfactory as we can manage between [Christianity's] lofty spirituality and our practical everyday needs. . . . This tension is characteristic of our form of human life and rouses us to many a heroic endeavor, though it may also lead us into the most terrible mendacity and crime. Thus we are, and thus we shall remain, as long as we survive. We cannot live without a religion, yet the only religion that we can endure is Christianity, for Christianity has grown up with us and has become a part of our very being. (25)

What is most remarkable here is not the melodramatic, self-congratulatory appraisal of Christian Europe—after all, there is nothing new about that—but rather the forcefulness of the fusion between a religion (Christianity) and a particular historical cultural domain (Europe), and, as its corollary, the notion that Christendom qua Europe constitutes a well-bounded totality. Some of the immediate consequences of these ideas are of course highly disturbing. For one, this would mean that only those Europeans who "have grown up" with Christianity—for generations, presumably, and not those opportunistic or recent converts—would count as real Europeans. This would immediately put into question, most obviously, the status of European Jews. Conversely, those who are Christians but whose birthplace or ancestry lies elsewhere would be only secondarily Christians, as it were. In sum, those who fall outside the bounds of Euro-Christianity are either the fossil remnants of some stunted growth or illicit offshoots that failed to become part of the vital mainstream (a host of heretics, renegades, para- and pseudo-Christians), not to mention recent converts, such as those in the colonies, who are only vicariously or subordinately Christian. In any case, according to this view, the identity of a non-European Christian, just as that of a non-Christian European, has to be presumed essentially split. One is then left to wonder how such a person or such a people, burdened with a constitutionally divided subjectivity, is to be positioned with respect to the absoluteness of Christianity.[12]

This momentous conundrum aside, with regard to the question of the validity of religions other than Christianity, Troeltsch's position is likewise problematic. He does acknowledge the legitimacy of their truth claims in principle—and he assumes that religions do make truth claims, and that they could

12. Furthermore, in this conceptual framework, where a religion and a civilization are made coeval and considered a totality, it is difficult to conceive of any kind of border region without evoking the problematic notion of syncretism, or any kind of dissent or displacement without the even more suspect notions of impurity and inauthenticity.

stand or fall with the validity of such claims—and he suggests that they be measured by the same yardstick as the one applied to Euro-Christianity. Certainly, he would allow, all the successes and advantages that Christian Europe has enjoyed in recent centuries do not necessarily or automatically "preclude the possibility that other racial groups, living under entirely different cultural conditions, may experience their contact with the Divine Life in quite a different way, and may themselves also possess a religion which has grown up with them, and from which they cannot sever themselves so long as they remain what they are. And they may quite sincerely regard this as absolutely valid for them" (26–27).

It is however unnecessary and injudicious, in his view, to ascribe to every existing religion the possibility of its being *absolutely* valid in this manner. Most of the lesser religions, Troeltsch opines, do not even aspire to be absolute or universal; they are not, in effect, "world religions." Presumably, one can set aside those modestly finite religions, content as they are to remain within the bounds of their own particularity, from the grandly universalistic religions. The rule of thumb amounts to this: a universalistic religion is distinct and unique in its character, its identity is consistent and constant, and above all, it flourishes and endures:

We shall, of course assume something of this kind [i.e., universalistic or absolutist character] only among nations which have reached a relatively high stage of civilization, and whose whole mental life has been intimately connected with their religion through a long period of discipline. We shall not assume it among the less developed races, where many religious cults are followed side by side, nor in the simple animism of heathen tribes, which is so monotonous in spite of its many variations. These territories are gradually conquered by the great world religions which possess a real sense of their own absolute validity. But among the great spiritual religions themselves the fundamental spiritual positions which destiny has assigned to them persists in their distinctness. If we wish to determine their relative value, it is not the religions alone that we must compare, but always only the civilizations of which the religion in each case constitutes a part incapable of severance from the rest. (27)

In the end, then, we find Troeltsch in close proximity to Abraham Kuenen, Ernest Renan, and a like company of elders, speculating on, and investing in, the continuing prosperity of the European expansion project, with a promise and hope of possibly large future returns.[13] Perhaps in the end, even the return of the unencumbered absoluteness and true universality of Christianity may not have been out of reach.

Unconcluding Scientific Postscript

Today, many historians of religion would likely opine that Troeltsch went too far, that it was unnecessary and injudicious of him to take this last step beyond the tensely quiescent pluralist truce, where multiple traditions of absolutes could coexist, with each universalist claim strictly controlled and bound within its own historicity, yet each inspired and enlivened by its own national, ethnic, or racial genius and, possibly, by "the mysterious movement of the divine Spirit in the unconscious depth of the human spirit," as Troeltsch himself would have it. We, the epigones, are inclined to distance ourselves from his final position by saying that it was finally his religious imagination (as opposed to his scientific acumen) that forced him beyond the state of disciplined suspension and gratuitously reached out to the universe of all-out war, where each of those individual absolutisms was made to don the full armor of a particular historical civilization with all of its material accoutrements and do battle with one another, first for survival, and then for eventual mastery over all challengers. With certain benefits of hindsight, today's historians of religion would likely judge this final vision of Troeltsch's as a transgression against the limits of science and scholarship.

13. It is noteworthy that not only was Troeltsch thoroughly familiar with the world religions debate of the nineteenth century but, with respect to Kuenen, he explicitly states his agreement with the latter's theory, down to the graphic detail concerning Islam. "If we make [Kuenen's] distinction [between national and world religions] the basis of our investigation and comparison, we at once perceive that Judaism and Zoroastrianism were explicitly national religions, associated with a particular country and concerned with tasks presented by a particular type of civilization—in the case of the Jews primarily with questions of national loyalty and national aspiration. Islam, too, is at bottom the national religion of the Arab peoples, compelling by the sword recognition of the prophetic claims of Mohammed in all the countries to which the Arab races have penetrated. Where, on the other hand, it has spread beyond the boundaries of Arabian territory, it has not as a rule attempted to convert unbelievers, but has simply maintained them as a source of revenue. And where Islam has developed great missionary activity, as, for example, in Africa and in the islands of the Malay Archipelago, it shows itself to be bound to certain conditions of civilisation which render it more readily acceptable to primitive races than Christianity, but which prove it, at the same time, to be indissolubly connected with a particular type of civilisation. Finally where it has adopted Persian or Indian mysticism, or Greek or modern philosophy, it loses its essential character, and becomes no more than a sign and a proof of national autonomy" ("The Place of Christianity among the World Religions," 18–19).

But how do we avoid such a violation—if that is what it was—and how can we ensure that the science of religion henceforth will not to be in collusion with such malign forces of absolutism in the name of pluralism, with its hidden supremacist pretensions and exclusivism? Or, to shift the ground of the query and bring the matter closer to our contemporary professional concerns: Can a science of religion worthy of its name really be founded on the basis of the world religions discourse as the latter has unfolded hitherto, that is, on the basis of its pluralist ethos, on its doctrine of parliamentary comparativism?

It has not been my express purpose in the present study to furnish an answer to this question one way or another. It has been my hopeful expectation, nonetheless, that some of the deliberations herein may interrupt, or momentarily snag, the overwhelming current of thought that has rushed to answer in the affirmative for the last hundred years. A brief pause may allow us to think refreshed, and perhaps even to imagine differently.

Not without reason, however, today's historians of religion may still insist, despite Troeltsch's own excesses, that it is possible to remain in a state of disciplined suspension, that it is possible to prevent the pluralism of culture-specific absolutes—presupposed and guaranteed by the world religions discourse—from leading to the kind of global competition and battle of the continents that Troeltsch envisioned. They may claim that his conclusion was an illicit extension of the pluralist discourse, and that this transgression had the effect of plunging him right back into the domain of dogmatic theology.

Certainly, it would seem, the end result of Troeltsch's train of thought counterbalanced, if not contradicted outright, the presumably humbling effect of the discovery of radical historicity. And it may be comforting to think that Troeltsch's transgression was a simple misstep, resulting from his being too much of a theologian and not enough of a historian. History is said to have taught him and his fellow Christians the mutability and the irreducible particularity of their religion, but perhaps there was not quite enough instruction in his case. The lessons of history were supposed to have compelled him to realize that his, too, was just another religion ardently claiming to be absolutely valid and uniquely universal. Should the lessons of history be made louder still? But the question that looms larger, it seems to me, is not about how well he learned the lesson; it is about the lesson itself: Is this recognition of historicity, this hard-won new knowledge of historicism, all that humbling?

The notion that "historical consciousness" somehow chastised the West continues to be as strong as it remains questionable.[14] One might imagine that one could be prevented from taking Troeltsch's transgressive last step if only one took care to abstain from indulging in one's own religious presumptions and remained, instead, resolutely historical. But such a blanket belief in the morally curative or prophylactic power of historical consciousness—which, incidentally, is often touted as a prize possession proper only to the West—is suspect. This notion seems to have given cover (if not to say false consciousness) even to some historians of religion; it may have led them to imagine that they are somehow inoculated against theological dogmatism and racial and cultural bigotry solely by virtue of their being pluralistic in orientation and historical in method, whatever is meant by this well-worn mantra: "being historical."

The question for us now, in any event, is whether this limit, this line of demarcation between academic science on the one hand and dogmatic theology on the other can be maintained by fiat, whether it is in truth anything that can be drawn distinctly enough to reduce or eliminate violations of the sort supposedly committed by this particular systematic-theologian-turned-almost-historian. The question is not about the difficulty of remaining in a state of suspension. My question, in any case, stems from the distinct impression—in part, resulting from the soundings of the nineteenth century, to which I lend ear in the present study—that this very threshold of the new discourse of religious pluralism may be bewitched.

What is at stake here is far more fundamental than the problem of border violations between historical science and theology; rather, it is a question of whether the world religions discourse can be in any way enlisted, and trusted, on the side of historical scholarship. Or, put another way, whether the idea of the diversity of religion is not, instead, the very thing that facilitates the trans-

14. Many years after Troeltsch, in 1964, Mircea Eliade voiced the following opinion concerning what he termed "the grave crisis brought on by the discovery of the historicity of man": "This new dimension, the historicity, is susceptible of many interpretations. But it must be admitted that from a certain point of view the understanding of man as first and foremost a historical being implies a profound humiliation for the Western consciousness. Western man considered himself successively God's creature and the possessor of a unique Revelation, the master of the world, the author of the only universally valid culture, the creator of the only real and useful science, and so on. Now he discovered himself on the same level with every other man, that is to say, conditioned by the unconscious as well as by history [emphasis added]—no longer the unique creator of a high culture, no longer the master of the world, and culturally menaced by extinction" (Mircea Eliade, The Quest [1969], 51).

ference and transmutation of a particular absolutism from one context to another—from the overtly exclusivist hegemonic version (Christian supremacist dogmatism) to the openly pluralistic universalist one (world religions pluralism)—and at the same time makes this process of transmutation very hard to identify and nearly impossible to understand.

As the final destination of Troeltsch's train of thought may be but one indication, it is sobering to entertain the possibility that, as far as greater Europe's stakes in the future destiny of the world are concerned, there is no ideological disjuncture between the theological discourse of traditional Christendom and the world religions discourse of today's multicultural world. On the contrary, we have good reason to suspect that the discourse of world religions came into being precisely as a makeshift solution to the particular predicament that confounded European Christianity at the end of the nineteenth century, that is to say, as a covert way out of the profound conceptual difficulty confronting Europe and its imperial subject-position.

To interrupt a certain dominant current of thought in order to gain a momentary respite, so that we may think afresh and imagine anew—these are the general terms in which I have rendered my aspirations. I do realize that, should it succeed in any measure at all, the implications could be uncontainably broad. By proposing to place such a voluminous subject as the entire genealogy of the world religions discourse on the examining table—even though, I must stress, this is decidedly not the same as putting it on trial or issuing an indictment—this study seems to invite, potentially, all manner of "What, now?" and "So what?" questions. For example: If the scientific efficacy of the world religions discourse is put in doubt, what alternative method, what new strategies should be adopted in its stead in order to conduct basic research, or to teach an introductory course on various religions?

It behooves me to acknowledge the legitimacy, reasonableness, and urgency of such questions, even though I am unable to answer them, at least not here, not on this occasion. Nor do I presume to be able to imagine the full range and all possible directions from which questions of implications may arise. This being the condition at the end of this work, I will limit myself to commenting, lastly, on just one such direction. The question concerns the region of scholarship on religion with which I probably have the most affinity, insofar as I can be said to belong to this guild at all.

Today, self-consciously secularist scientists of religion tend to identify the persistence of Christian ideology as the foremost problem in the field of religious studies: not enough cleansing of the past legacy, and too much fresh infusion of religiously motivated interests. This, to be sure, may be true. But when we thus complain that some illicit religiosity—which may be by nature dogmatic and hegemonic—seems to be inhabiting academic discourse with impunity, do we understand our condition adequately? And if and when we will finally manage to round up sundry varieties of crypto-theology scurrying in the tribunal of science, will we then apprehend the right suspects? Or are we not failing to see a much larger, systemic network of discursive organization, of which the ones in custody are but low-level functionaries? Is the effort to prosecute these "theological assumptions" for illegally traversing and thereby downgrading the science of religion, then, not like an attempt to punish some unknown evil still at large by burning a host of effigies?[15]

If we are to be serious in our critical intention, the exorcism of an undead Christian absolutism would not suffice. Instead, criticism calls for something far more laborious, tedious, and difficult: a rigorous historical investigation that does not superstitiously yield to the comforting belief in the liberating power of "historical consciousness." We must attend to the black folds, the billowing, and the livid lining of the fabric of history we unfurl, the story we tell from time to time to put ourselves to sleep. This is one of the reasons historiography must always include the historical analysis of our discourse itself.

15. I am obliged to acknowledge the infelicity of appearing to cast, albeit figuratively, "theology" as a society of petty criminals. I would also concede the injustice (probably) of equating theology with dogmatic stances or Christian-hegemonic assumptions, as it sometimes happens in certain moments of secularists' self-definition of science, as we have had occasion to observe in the course of the present study. (The secularist reasoning, I surmise, seems to be that theology is predicated on profession of faith in some form, and that this bottom line entails a particularly determined system of valuation that privileges the tradition of the faith community.) I can only add that I personally do not know how today's theologians stand on these issues that troubled Troeltsch, for example, and I do not understand theology either as a field or as a vocation adequately enough to entertain any definitive views regarding its relation to the science of religion, or even more vaguely, its relation to whatever is called "study of religion" or "religious studies."

Bibliography

Adam, Robert. *The Religious World Displayed, or A View of the Four Grand Systems of Religion, Judaism, Paganism, Christianity and Mohammedanism; And of the Various Existing Denominations, Sects and Parties, in the Christian World; To Which Is Subjoined, a View of Deism and Atheism.* Edinburgh: Printed by James Ballantyne for Longman, Hurst, Rees, and Orme, 1808.

Adams, Hannah. *An Alphabetical Compendium of the Various Sects Which Have Appeared in the World from the Beginning of the Christian Era to the Present Day; With an Appendix, Containing a Brief Account of the Different Schemes of Religion Now Embraced among Mankind; The Whole Collected from the Best Authors, Ancient and Modern.* 1st ed. Boston: B. Edes and Sons, 1784. Fourth edition published as *A Dictionary of All Religions and Religious Denominations, Jewish, Heathen, Mahometan and Christian, Ancient and Modern; With an Appendix, Containing a Sketch of the Present State of the World, as to Population, Religion, Toleration, Missions, etc.*, and the Articles in which all Christian Denominations Agree, with correction and large editions (New York: James Eastburn and Co.; Boston: Cummings and Hilliard, 1817).

Albright, William Foxwell. *From the Stone Age to Christianity: Monotheism and the Historical Process.* Baltimore: Johns Hopkins University Press, 1940.

Almond, Philip C. *The British Discovery of Buddhism.* Cambridge: Cambridge University Press, 1988.

Anderson, Robert. *The Buddha of Christendom: A Book for the Present Crisis.* London: Hodder and Stoughton, 1899.

App, Urs. *Richart Wagner und der Buddhismus: Liebe—Tragik.* Zurich: Museum Rietberg, 1997.
———. "Notes and Excerpts by Schopenhauer Related to Volumes 1–9 of the *Asiatick Researches.*" *Schopenhauerjahrbuch* 79 (1998): 11–33.

Archer, John Clark. *Faiths Men Live By.* New York: Ronald Press, 1934. Second edition, revised by Carl E. Purinton, published in 1958.

Arnold, Edwin. *The Light of Asia.* London: Macmillan, 1884.

Arnold, Matthew. *Culture and Anarchy.* Edited by Samuel Lipman. New Haven: Yale University Press, 1994. Incorporates the pagination of the 1869 edition published by Smith, Elder.
———. *Literature and Dogma: An Essay towards a Better Apprehension of the Bible.* New York: Macmillan, 1883.

Asad, Talal. *Genealogies of Religion: Discipline and Reasons of Power in Christianity and Islam.* Baltimore: Johns Hopkins University Press, 1993.

Atkins, Gaius Glenn. *Procession of the Gods.* London: Constable, 1931.

Baeck, Leo. *The Essence of Judaism.* Translated by Victor Grubenwieser and Leonard Pearl. London: Macmillan, 1936. Revised translation by Irving Howe (New York: Schocken, 1948). Originally published as *Das Wesen des Judentums* (Berlin: Nathansen und Lamm, 1905).
———. "The Religion of the Hebrews." In *Religions of the World: Their Nature and Their History,* edited by Carl Clemen, 265–98. New York: Harcourt, Brace, 1931.

Barrows, John Henry, ed. *An Illustrated and Popular Story of the World's First Parliament of Religions, Held in Chicago in Connection with the Columbian Exposition of 1893*. 2 vols. Chicago: Parliament Publishing Co., 1893.

———. *Christianity, the World-Religion: Lectures Delivered in India*. Barrows Lectures, 1896–97. Madras: Christian Literature Society for India, 1897.

———. "Words of Welcome." In *The Dawn of Religious Pluralism: Voices from the World's Parliament of Religions, 1893*, edited by Richard Hughes Seager, 23–30. La Salle, IL: Open Court, 1993.

Barthélemy Saint-Hilaire, Jules. *Buddha et sa religion*. Paris: Didier, 1862.

Barton, George Aaron. *The Religions of the World*. Chicago: University of Chicago Press, 1917. Second edition published in 1919.

Bellamy, John. *The History of All Religions, Comprehending the Different Doctrines, Customs, and Order of Worship in the Churches . . . from the Beginning of Time to the Present Day; The Accomplishment of the Prophecies of Christ, Etc.* London: Longman and Co., 1812.

Bendix, Reinhard. *Max Weber: An Intellectual Portrait*. With a new introduction by Guenther Roth. Berkeley: University of California Press, 1984. Originally published in 1960 by Doubleday.

Benedict, David. *A History of All Religions, as Divided into Paganism, Mahometanism, Judaism and Christianity*. Providence: J. Miller, 1824.

Benjamin, Walter. "Karl Kraus." In *Reflections: Essays, Aphorisms, Autobiographical Writings*, edited by Peter Demetz, translated by Edmund Jephcott, 239–73. New York: Harcourt Brace Jovanovich, 1978.

Berman, Morris. *Social Change and Scientific Organization: The Royal Institution, 1799–1810*. Ithaca: Cornell University Press, 1978.

Bernal, Martin. "Black Athena Denied: The Tyranny of Germany over Greece and the Rejection of the Afroasiatic Roots of Europe: 1780–1980." *Comparative Criticism* 8 (1986): 3–69.

———. *Black Athena: The Asiatic Roots of Classical Civilization*. Vol. 1. New Brunswick: Rutgers University Press, 1987.

Berry, Thomas Sterling. *Christianity and Buddhism: A Comparison and a Contrast*. London: Society for Promoting Christian Knowledge, 1891.

Besant, Annie Wood. *Four Great Religions: Four Lectures Delivered on the Twenty-first Anniversary of the Theosophical Society at Adyar, Madras*. Chicago: Theosophical Press, 1897.

Bharti, Brahm Datt. *Max Müller, a Lifelong Masquerade: The Inside Story of a Secular Christian Missionary Who Masqueraded All His Lifetime from behind the Mask of Literature and Philology and Mortgaged his Pen, Intellect and Scholarship to Wreck Hinduism*. New Delhi: Erabooks, 1992.

Bigandet, Paul Ambroise. *The Life or Legend of Gaudama*. Rangoon: American Mission Press, 1858. Second edition published in 1866 as *The Life or Legend of Gaudama, the Buddha of the Burmese*.

Bonney, Charles Carroll. "Words of Welcome." In *The Dawn of Religious Pluralism: Voices from the World's Parliament of Religions, 1893*, edited by Richard Hughes Seager, 17–22. La Salle, IL: Open Court, 1993.

———. "Prefatory Sketch of the World's Congress Work and the World's Parliament of Religions." In *Universal Religion*, edited by Edmund Buckley, first course, 7–16. Chicago: University Association, 1897.

Bopp, Franz. *Über das Conjugationssystem der Sanskritsprache in Vergleichung mit jenem der griechischen, lateinischen, persischen und germanischen Sprache*. Frankfurt, 1816.

———. *Vergleichende Grammatik des Sanskrit, Zend, Griechischen, Lateinischen, Litthuasischen, Goth- ischen und Deutschen.* Berlin: F. Dummler, 1833.

Bosch, Lourens P. van den. *Friedrich Max Müller: A Life Devoted to the Humanities.* Numen Book Series: Studies in the History of Religions, vol. 94. Leiden: Brill, 2002.

Botting, Douglas. *Humboldt and the Cosmos.* London: Michael Joseph, 1973.

Bouquet, Alan C. *Is Christianity the Final Religion? A Candid Enquiry with the Materials for an Opinion.* London: Macmillan, 1921.

———. *The Christian Religion and Its Competitors To-Day: Being the Hulsean Lectures for 1924–25 Delivered before the University of Cambridge.* Cambridge: Cambridge University Press, 1925.

———. *Comparative Religion.* Hammondsworth: Penguin, 1942.

Braden, Charles Samuel. *Modern Tendencies in World Religions.* New York: Macmillan, 1933.

———. *The World's Religions: A Short History.* Whitmore and Smith, 1939.

Branford, Victor. *Living Religions: A Plea for the Larger Modernism.* Westminster: Leplay House Press, 1924.

Brerewood, Edward. *Enquiries Touching the Diversity of Languages, and Religions through the Chiefe Parts of the World.* Edited by Robert Brerewood. London: Printed for John Bill by W. Stansby, 1614.

Broughton, Thomas. *Bibliotheca Historico-Sacra, or An Historical Library of the Principal Matters Re- lating to Religion, Antient and Modern; Pagan, Jewish, Christian, and Mohammedan. . . .* London: Printed by R. Reily for Stephen Austen, 1737.

Brown, J. Newton, ed. *Encyclopedia of Religious Knowledge, or Dictionary . . . Containing Definitions of All Religious Terms; An Impartial Account of the Principal Christian Denominations That Have Ex- isted in the World from the Birth of Christ to the Present Day with Their Doctrines, Religious Rites and Ceremonies, as well as Those of the Jews, Mohammedans, and Heathen Nations, together with the Manners and Customs of the East.* Brattelboro, VT: Typographic Co., 1837.

Brown, Robert. *Semitic Influence in Hellenic Mythology: With Special Reference to the Recent Myth- ological Works of the Rt Hon. F. Max Müller and Mr. Andrew Lang.* Reprint ed., Clifton, NJ: Ref- erence Book, 1966. Originally published in 1898.

Browne, Lewis. *This Believing World: A Simple Account of the Great Religions of Mankind.* New York: Macmillan, 1926.

Buckley, Edmund, ed. *Universal Religion: A Course of Lessons, Historical and Scientific, on the Various Faiths of the World; Prepared for the University Association, by a Corps of Specialists in Asia, Europe and America. . . .* Chicago: University Association, 1897.

Bunsen, Christian. *Christianity and Mankind.* London: Longman, Brown, Green, and Long- mans, 1854.

Bunsen, Ernst von. *The Angel-Messiah of Buddhists, Essenes, and Christians.* London: Longmans, Green, 1880.

———. *The Hidden Wisdom of Christ and the Key of Knowledge.* 2 vols. Longmans, Green, 1865.

Burder, William. *A History of All Religions in the World: With Accounts of the Ceremonies and Customs, or the Forms of Worship Practiced by the Several Nations of the Known World, from the Earliest Records to the Present Time.* Philadelphia: Leary and Getz, 1848.

Burnouf, Émile. *La Science des religions: Sa Méthode et ses limites.* 2nd ed. Paris: Maisonneuve, 1872. Translated by Julie Liebe as *The Science of Religions,* with a preface by E. J. Rapson (London: Swan Sonnenschein, Lowrey, and Co., 1888).

————. "Le Bouddhism en Occident." *Revue de deux mondes* (Paris), July 15, 1888, 340–72.

————. *Le Vase sacré et ce qu'il contient dans l'Inde, la Perse, la Grece et dans l'Eglise Chrétienne: Avec un appendice sur le Saint-Graal.* Paris: Bibliothèque de la Haute Science, 1896.

————, ed. *Dictionnaire classique Sanscrit-Français.* With collaboration of L. Leupol. Paris: B. Duprat, 1865.

Burnouf, Eugène. *Introduction à L'histoire du buddhisme indien.* Paris: Imprimerie Royale, 1844.

Burrell, David James. *The Religions of the World.* Philadelphia: Presbyterian Board of Publication and Sabbath-School Work, 1888.

Burtt, Edwin A. *Man Seeks the Divine: A Study in the History and Comparison of Religions.* New York: Harper, 1957.

Caird, John. *The Universal Religion: A Lecture Delivered in Westminster Abbey . . . Nov. 30, 1874.* Glasgow: J. Maclehouse, 1874.

————. "Religions of India: Vedic Period; Brahmanism." In *The Faiths of the World: St. Giles' Lectures,* 1–30. New York: Scribners, 1882.

————. *The Evolution of Religion: Gifford Lectures, 1890–92.* 2 vols. Glasgow: Maclehouse, 1893.

Caird, John, et al. *Oriental Religions.* New York: J. Fitzgerald, 1882.

Calmet, Augustin. *Dictionnaire historique, critique, chronologique, géographique et littéral de la Bible: Enrichi d'un grand nombre de figures en taille-douce, qui représent les antiquitez judaïques.* Paris: Eméry père, Eméry fils, Saugrain aîné, P. Martin, 1712. First translated as *An Historical, Critical, Geographical, Chronological, and Etymological Dictionary of the Holy Bible, in Three Volumes: . . . The Whole . . . Illustrated with above One Hundred and Sixty Copper-Plates. . . . To Which Is Annexed, Bibliotheca Sacra, or a Copious Catalogue of the Best Editions and Versions of the Bible,* by Samuel D'Oyly and John Colson (London: Printed for J. J. and P. Knapton, [etc.], 1732). Later translated as *Calmet's Great Dictionary of the Holy Bible: Historical, Critical, Geographical, and Etymological . . . Revised, Corrected, and Augmented, with an Entirely New Set of Plates. . . .* 2 vols. (London: Printed for Charles Taylor, 1794–1801), and in its fourth English edition as *Calmet's Great Dictionary of the Holy Bible: Historical, Critical, Geographical, and Etymological; Wherein Are Explained the Proper Names in the Old and New Testaments; The Natural Productions, Animals, Vegetables, Minerals, Stones, Gems, &c.; The Antiquities, Habits, Buildings, and Other Curiosities of the Jews; With a Chronological History of the Bible, the Jewish Calendar, Tables of the Hebrew Coins, Weights, Measures, &c.* (London: B. J. Holdsworth, 1827).

Caroe, Gwendy M. *The Royal Institution: An Informal History.* London: John Murray, 1985.

Carpenter, J. Estlin. "Religion." In *Encyclopaedia Britannica.* 11th ed. 1910.

————. *Comparative Religions.* New York: Henry Holt, 1913.

Catoir, John T. *World Religions: Beliefs behind Today's Headlines.* New York: The Christophers, 1985. Revised edition of *The Way People Pray* (1974)

Cave, Sydney. *An Introduction to the Study of Some Living Religions of the East.* London: Duckworth, 1921.

————. *Christianity and Some Living Religions of the East.* London: Duckworth, 1929.

Champion, Selwyn Gurney. *The Eleven Religions and Their Proverbial Lore: A Comparative Study.* London: Routledge, 1944.

Chantepie de la Saussaye, Pierre Daniël. *Manual of the Science of Religion.* Translated by Beatrice S. Colyer-Fergusson. London: Longmans, 1891. Volume 1 of *Lehrbuch der Religionsgeschichte,* 2 vols. (Freiburg: J.C.B. Mohr [Paul Siebeck], 1887–89).

Chaudhuri, K. N. Asia before Europe: Economy and Civilisation of the Indian Ocean from the Rise of Islam to 1750. Cambridge: Cambridge University Press, 1990.

Chaudhuri, Nirad C. Scholar Extraordinary: The Life of Professor the Rt. Hon. Friedrich Max Müller, P.C. New York: Oxford University Press, 1974.

Chidester, David. Savage Systems: Colonialism and Comparative Religion in Southern Africa. Charlottesville: University of Virginia Press, 1996.

Clarke, James Freeman. Ten Great Religions: An Essay in Comparative Theology. Boston: Houghton, Mifflin, 1881. First edition published in 1871.

———. "Affinities of Buddhism and Christianity." North American Review 136 (May 1883): 467–78.

Clemen, Carl, ed. Religions of the World: Their Nature and Their History. New York: Harcourt, Brace, 1931. Originally published as Die Religionen der Erde: Ihre Wesen und Ihre Geschichte (München: F. Bruckmann, 1927).

Cohen, Arthur A. The Myth of the Judeo-Christian Tradition. New York: Harper and Row, 1969.

Cohon, Samuel Solomon, and Harris Franklin Rall. Christianity and Judaism Compare Notes. New York: Macmillan, 1927.

Conder, Josiah. An Analytical and Comparative View of All Religions Now Extant among Mankind: With Their Internal Diversities of Creed and Profession. London: Jackson and Walford, 1838.

Constant, Benjamin. De la religion, considérée dans sa source, ses formes et ses développements. 5 vols. Paris: Bossange [etc.], 1824–31. Reissued in one volume by Tzvetan Todorov and Etienne Hofmann (Arles: Actes Sud, 1999).

Cook, Stanley A. The Study of Religions. London: Adam and Charles Black, 1914.

Cull, Nicholas J. "Overture to an Alliance: British Propaganda at the New York World's Fair, 1939–1940." Journal of British Studies 36 (July 1997): 325–54.

Damrosch, David. What Is World Literature? Princeton: Princeton University Press, 2003.

Darmesteter, James. "Ernest Renan." In Selected Essays of James Darmesteter, edited by Morris Jastrow, Jr., translated by Helen B. Jastrow, 178–240. Boston: Houghton, Mifflin, 1895.

———. "The Prophets of Israel." In Selected Essays of James Darmesteter, edited by Morris Jastrow, Jr., translated by Helen B. Jastrow, 16–104. Boston: Houghton, Mifflin, 1895.

Darmesteter, Madame James A. [Mary F. Robinson]. The Life of Ernest Renan. 2nd ed. London: Metheuen, 1898.

Dawson, John William. Fossil Men and Their Modern Representatives. London: Hodder and Stoughton, 1880.

De Jong, J. W. A Brief History of Buddhist Studies in Europe and America. 2nd ed. Delhi: Sri Satguru Publications, 1987.

De Vries, Simon John. Bible and Theology in the Netherlands: Dutch Old Testament Criticism under Modernist and Conservative Auspices, 1850 to World War I. Wegeningen: H. Veenman, 1968.

Defoe, Daniel. Dictionarium Sacrum Seu Religiosum: A Dictionary of All Religions, Ancient and Modern, Whether Jewish, Pagan, Christian, or Mahometan. London: J. Knapton, 1704.

Despland, Michel. La Religion en Occident: Évolution des idées et du vécu. Montreal: Fides, 1979.

———. L'Emergence des sciences de la religion: La monarchie de Juillet; Un moment fondateur. Paris: Harmattan, 1999.

Dirks, Nicholas B. The Hollow Crown: Ethnohistory of an Indian Kingdom. Cambridge: Cambridge University Press, 1987.

———. "Colonialism and Culture." Introduction to *Colonialism and Culture*, edited by Nicholas B. Dirks, 1–25. Ann Arbor: University of Michigan Press, 1992.

———. "Caste of Mind." *Representations* 37 (1992): 56–78.

Dobbins, Frank S. *Error's Chains: How Forged and Broken—Complete, Graphic, and Comparative History of the Many Strange Beliefs, Superstitious Practices, Domestic Peculiarities, Sacred Writings, Systems of Philosophy, Legends and Traditions, Customs and Habits of Mankind throughout the World, Ancient and Modern*. New York: Standard Publishing House, 1883.

Drey, Johann Sebastian von. "Von der Landesreligion und der Weltreligion" (in two parts). *Tübinger Quartalschrift*, 1827, 234–74 and 391–435.

———. *Brief Introduction to the Study of Theology, with Reference to the Scientific Standpoint and the Catholic System*. Notre Dame: University of Notre Dame Press, 1994.

Droit, Roger-Pol. *The Cult of Nothingness: The Philosophers and the Buddha*. Translated by David Streight and Pamela Vohnson. Chapel Hill: University of North Carolina Press, 2003. Originally published as *Le Culte du néant: Les philosophes et le Bouddha* (Paris: Editions Seuil, 1997).

Dubuisson, Daniel. *The Western Construction of Religion: Myths, Knowledge, and Ideology*. Translated by William Sayers. Baltimore: Johns Hopkins University Press, 2003. Originally published as *L'Occident et la religion: Mythes, science et idéologie* (Paris: Éditions Complexe, 1998).

Dupuis, Charles François. *Origine de tous les cultes, ou Religion universelle*. 7 vols. Paris: H. Agasse, 1795. Republished with additional material, in ten volumes. (Paris: L. Rosier, 1835–36). An abridged version was translated as *The Origin of All Religious Worship* (New Orleans, 1872).

Durkheim, Emile. *The Elementary Forms of Religious Life*. Translated by Karen E. Fields. New York: Free Press, 1995. Originally published as *Les Formes élémentaires de la vie religieuse: Le système totémique en Australie* (Paris: F. Alcan, 1912).

Eck, Diana L. Foreword to *The Dawn of Religious Pluralism: Voices from the World's Parliament of Religions, 1893*, edited by Richard Hughes Seager, xiii–xvii. La Salle, IL: Open Court, 1993.

———. *A New Religious America: How a "Christian Country" Has Become the World's Most Religiously Diverse Nation*. New York: Harper Collins, 2001.

Eck, Diana L., and the Pluralism Project at Harvard University. *On Common Ground: World Religions in America*. 2nd ed. New York: Columbia University Press, 2000.

Eliade, Mircea. *The Quest: History and Meaning in Religion*. Chicago: University of Chicago Press, 1969.

Ellinwood, Frank Field. *Oriental Religions and Christianity: Course of Lectures Delivered on the Ely Foundation before the Students of Union Theological Seminary, New York, 1891*. 3rd ed. New York: Scribners, 1906. First edition published in 1892.

Estlin, John Prior. *The Nature and Causes of Atheism . . . To Which Are Added Remarks on a Work, Entitled, Origine de tous les cultes, ou Religion universelle, par Dupuis*. Bristol: N. Biggs, 1797.

Faber, George Stanley. *The Origin of Pagan Idolatry Ascertained from Historical Testimony and Circumstantial Evidence*. 3 vols. London: F. C. Rivington, 1816.

Fabian, Johannes. *Time and the Other: How Anthropology Makes Its Object*. New York: Columbia University Press, 1983.

Fairbairn, Andrew Martin. *Studies in the Philosophy of Religion and History*. London: W. Mullan, 1877.

———. Introduction to Louis Henry Jordan, *Comparative Religion: Its Genesis and Growth*, vii–ix. Edinburgh: T. and T. Clark, 1905.

The Faiths of the World: St. Giles' Lectures. Edinburgh: Blackwood, 1882.

Farquhar, John Nicol. *Modern Religious Movements in India*. London: Macmillan, 1915.

Finegan, Jack. *The Archaeology of World Religions: The Background of Primitivism, Zoroastrianism, Hinduism, Jainism, Buddhism, Confucianism, Taoism, Shinto, Islam, and Sikhism*. Princeton: Princeton University Press, 1952.

Finkelstein, Louis, J. Elliot Ross, and William Adams Brown. *The Religions of Democracy: Judaism, Catholicism, Protestantism in Creed and Life*. New York: Devin-Adair, 1941.

Fitzgerald, Timothy. "Hinduism and the 'World Religion' Fallacy." *Religion* 20 (1990) 101–18.

———. *The Ideology of Religious Studies*. New York: Oxford University Press, 2000.

Flint, Robert. "Christianity in Relation to Other Religions." In *The Faiths of the World*, 335–64. Edinburgh: Blackwood, 1882.

Forlong, James George Roche. *Rivers of Life, or Sources and Streams of the Faiths of Man in All Lands Showing the Evolution of Faiths from the Rudest Symbolism to the Latest Spiritual Developments*. 3 vols. London: Turnbull and Spears, 1883.

———. *Short Studies in the Science of Comparative Religions, Embracing All the Religions of Asia*. London: B. Quaritch, 1897.

———. *Faiths of Man: Encyclopedia of Religions*. Introduction by Margery Silver. London: B. Quaritch, 1906.

Foucart, George. *La Méthode comparative dans l'histoire des religions*. Paris: Alphonse Picard et Fils, 1909.

Fox, William Johnson. *The Apostle John, an Unitarian*. 1823.

———. *The Religious Ideas*. London, 1849.

Fradenburgh, J. N. *Witness from the Dust, or The Bible Illustrated from the Monuments*. Cincinnati: Cranston and Stowe; New York: Hunt and Eaton, 1885.

———. *Living Religions, or The Great Religions of the Orient: From Sacred Books and Modern Customs*. New York: Eaton and Mains, 1888.

———. *Departed Gods: The Gods of Our Forefathers*. Cincinnati: Cranston and Stowe; New York: Hunt and Eaton, 1891.

———. *Fire from Strange Altars*. New York: Eaton and Mains, [1891].

Frank, Andre Gunder. *ReOrient: Global Economy in the Asian Age*. Berkeley: University of California Press, 1998.

Frankfort, Henri, et al., eds. *The Intellectual Adventure of Ancient Man: An Essay on Speculative Thought in the Ancient Near East*. Chicago: University of Chicago Press, 1947.

Friess, Horace L., and Herbert W. Schneider. *Religion in Various Cultures*. New York: Holt, 1932.

Gaer, Joseph. *The Wisdom of the Living Religions*. New York: Dodd, Mead, 1956.

Garden, James. *Comparative Theology, or The True and Solid Grounds of Pure and Peaceable Theology . . . First Laid Down in an University Discourse, and Now Translated from the Original Latin*. Bristol: Printed for T. Cadell, 1756.

George, Kirsten, et al. "Das Bild des Islam und des Buddhismus: Eine empirische Untersuchung." *Zeitschrift für Religionswissenschaft* 4 (1996): 55–82.

Girardot, Norman J. *The Victorian Translation of China: James Legge's Oriental Pilgrimage*. Berkeley: University of California Press, 2002.

Goblet d'Alviella, Eugène. *Lectures on the Origin and Growth of the Conception of God as Illustrated by Anthropology and History*. Translated by Philip Henry Wicksteed. London: Williams and Norgate, 1892.

Goodrich, Charles A. *Religious Ceremonies and Customs, or The Forms of Worship Practiced by the Several Nations of the Known World, from the Earliest Record to the Present Time; On the Basis of the Celebrated and Splendid Work of Bernard Picart; To Which Is Added a Brief View of Minor Sects, Which Exist at the Present Day; Designed Especially for the Use of Families; Not Only as Entertaining and Instructive, but of Great Importance as a Work of Reference; Accompanied with a Large Map of the World, and Embellished with Elegant Engravings.* Engraver and original author Bernard Picart, and Jean Frédéric Bernard. Hartford: Hutchinson and Dwier, 1834.

Gordis, Robert. *The Judeo-Christian Tradition: Illusion or Reality?* New York: Judaica Press, 1965.

Gover, Yerach. "Why Be a Nebbish? A Response to Marshall Grossman" *Social Text* 22 (spring 1989): 123–29.

Grant, George Monro. *The Religions of the World in Relation to Christianity.* New York: Fleming H. Revell Co., 1898.

Grossman, Marshall. "The Violence of the Hyphen in Judeo-Christian." *Social Text* 22 (spring 1989): 115–22.

———. "Come to the Movies Yerach: Not a Response to 'Why Be a Nebbish?'" *Social Text* 23 (autumn/winter 1989): 165–66.

Halbfass, Wilhelm. *India and Europe: An Essay in Understanding.* Albany: SUNY Press, 1988.

Hanson, J. W., ed. *The World's Congress of Religions: The Addresses and Papers Delivered before the Parliament, and an Abstract of the Congresses Held in the Art Institute, Chicago, IL, USA, August 25 to October 15, 1893, under the Auspices of the World Columbian Exposition.* Chicago: Beezley, 1894.

Hardwick, Charles. *A History of the Articles of Religion: To Which Is Added a Series of Documents, from* A.D. *1536 to* A.D. *1615; Together with illustrations from Contemporary Sources.* London: Rivington, 1851.

———. *Christ and Other Masters: An Historical Inquiry into Some of the Chief Parallelisms and Contrasts between Christianity and the Religious Systems of the Ancient World; With Special Reference to Prevailing Difficulties and Objections.* 2nd ed. 2 vols. Cambridge: Macmillan, 1863.

———, ed. *A Catalogue of the Manuscripts Preserved in the Library of the University of Cambridge,* edited for the Syndics of the University Press. Vols. 1–3. Cambridge: University Press, 1856–67.

Hardy, Robert Spence. *Christianity and Buddhism Compared.* Colombo: Wesleyan Mission Press, 1874.

———. *Manual of Buddhism in Its Modern Development.* London: Partridge and Oakey, 1853.

Hare, William Loftus, ed. *Religions of the Empire: A Conference on Some Living Religions within the Empire.* New York: Macmillan, 1925.

Harnack, Adolf. *What Is Christianity?* Translated by Thomas Bailey Saunders. New York: Harper Torchbooks, 1957. Originally published as *Das Wesen des Christentums: Sechzehn Vorlesungen vor Studierenden aller Facultäten im Wintersemester 1899/1900 an der Universität Berlin gehalten* (Leipzig: J. C. Hinrichs, 1900).

Harrison, Peter. *"Religion" and the Religions in the English Enlightenment.* Cambridge: Cambridge University Press, 1990.

Hay, Stephen N. *Asian Ideas of East and West: Tagore and His Critics in Japan, China, and India.* Cambridge: Harvard University Press, 1970.

Haydon, A. Eustace, ed. *Modern Trends in World-Religions.* Haskell Foundation Institute. Chicago: University of Chicago Press, 1934.

Heckscher, William S. "Bernini's Elephant and Obelisk." Art Bulletin 29, 3 (September 1947): 155–82.

Hegel, G. W. F. The Philosophy of History. Translated by J. Sibree. New York: Dover, 1956.

————. On the Episode of the Mahābhārata Known by the Name Bhagavad-Gītā by Wilhelm von Humboldt, Berlin, 1826. Edited and translated by Herbert Herring. New Delhi: Indian Council of Philosophical Research, 1995. Originally published as "Über die unter dem Namen Bhagavad-Gita bekannte Episode des Mahabharata, von Wilhelm von Humboldt," Jahrbücher für Wissenschaftliche Kritik (1827).

Herrliberger, David. Gottesdienstliche Ceremonien, oder H. Kirchen-Gebräuche und Religions-Pflichten der Christen. Engravings by Bernard Picart. Basel: Eckenstein, 1746.

Heschel, Susannah. Abraham Geiger and the Jewish Jesus. Chicago: University of Chicago Press, 1998.

Hess, Jonathan M. Germans, Jews and the Claims of Modernity. New Haven: Yale University Press, 2002.

Hinnells, John R., ed. A New Handbook of Living Religions. Oxford: Blackwell, 1997.

Hocking, William Ernest. Living Religions and a World Faith. Hibbert Lectures. London: Allen and Unwin, 1940.

Hopfe, Lewis M. Religions of the World. Beverly Hills: Glencoe, 1976.

Hopkins, Edward Washburn. The History of Religions. New York: Macmillan, 1918.

Houghton, Walter Raleigh. Neely's History of the Parliament of Religions and Religious Congress at the World Columbian Exposition. 2 vols. Chicago: F. T. Neely, 1893.

Humboldt, Wilhelm von. "Über die unter dem Namen Bhagavad-Gītā bekannte Episode des Mahābhārata: Mit Bezug auf die Beurteilung der Schlegelschen Ausgabe in Pariser Asiatischen Journal." Proceedings of the Historical Philological Section of the Berlin Royal Academy (1827).

————. On Language: On the Diversity of Human Language Construction and Its Influence on the Mental Development of the Human Species. Edited by Michael Losonsky, translated by Peter Heath. Cambridge: Cambridge University Press, 1999.

Hume, David. The Natural History of Religion. In Writings on Religion, edited by Anthony Flew, 107–82. Chicago: Open Court, 1992. Originally published in 1757.

Hume, Robert Ernest. The World's Living Religions: An Historical Sketch. New York: Scribners, 1924.

————, ed. Treasure-House of the Living Religions: Selections from Their Sacred Scriptures. New York: Scribners, 1932.

Irwin, William A. "The Hebrews." In The Intellectual Adventure of Ancient Man: An Essay on Speculative Thought in the Ancient Near East, edited by Henri Frankfort et al., 223–360. Chicago: University of Chicago Press, 1947.

————. The Old Testament: Keystone of Human Culture. Rev. ed. London: Abelard-Schuman, 1959. First edition published in 1952.

Jacob, Margaret C. The Radical Enlightenment: Pantheists, Freemasons and Republicans. London: George Allen and Unwin, 1981.

Jacobson, Thorkild. "Mesopotamia." In The Intellectual Adventure of Ancient Man: An Essay on Speculative Thought in the Ancient Near East, edited by Henri Frankfort et al., 125–219. Chicago: University of Chicago Press, 1947.

Jacolliot, Louis. *La Bible dans l'Inde: Vie de Iezeus Christna*. Paris: Librairie Internationale, 1869.

———. *Occult Science in India and among the Ancients: With an Account of their Mystic Initiations and the History of Spiritism*. Translated by William L. Felt. London: Wm. Rider, [1919]. Originally published as *Le Spiritisme dans le monde: L'Initiation et les sciences occultes dans l'Inde et chez tous les peuples de l'antiquité* (Paris, 1875).

Jaki, Stanley L. *Lord Gifford and His Lectures: A Centenary Retrospect*. 2nd ed. Edinburgh: Scottish Academic Press, 1995.

James, Frank A. J. L. *The Common Purpose of Life: Science and Society at the Royal Institution of Great Britain*. Burlington, VT: Ashgate, 2002.

James, William. *The Varieties of Religious Experience: A Study in Human Nature; Being the Gifford Lectures on Natural Religion Delivered at Edinburgh in 1901–1902*. London: Longmans, Green, 1902.

Jastrow, Morris. *The Study of Religion*. The Contemporary Science Series, edited by Havelock Ellis. New York: Scribners, 1901.

Johnson, Samuel. *Oriental Religions and Their Relation to Universal Religion*. 3 vols. Boston: Houghton, Osgood, 1872–85.

Jordan, Louis Henry. *Comparative Religion: Its Genesis and Growth*. Edinburgh: T. and T. Clark, 1905.

———. *The Study of Religion in the Italian Universities*. London: Oxford University Press, 1909.

———. *Comparative Religion: A Survey of Its Recent Literature*. Edinburgh: Otto Schulze, 1910. Second edition, revised and augmented, published in 1920 by Humphrey Milford and Oxford University Press.

———. *Comparative Religion: Its Adjuncts and Allies*. London: Oxford University Press, 1915.

Jung, C. G. *Psychology and Religion*. New Haven: Yale University Press, 1938.

Jurji, Edward J., ed. *The Great Religions of the Modern World: Confucianism, Taoism, Hinduism, Buddhism, Shintoism, Islam, Judaism, Eastern Orthodoxy, Roman Catholicism, Protestantism*. Princeton: Princeton University Press, 1946.

Kant, Immanuel. *Critique of Pure Reason*. Translated and edited by Paul Guyer and Allen W. Wood. Cambridge: Cambridge University Press, 1998.

Kellogg, Samuel Henry. *The Light of Asia and the Light of the World*. New York: Macmillan, 1885.

———. *The Genesis and Growth of Religion*. New York: Macmillan, 1892.

———. *A Handbook of Comparative Religion*. Philadelphia: Westminster, 1899.

Kiernan, V. G. *The Lords of Human Kind: European Attitudes toward the Outside World in the Imperial Age*. London: Weidenfeld and Nicolson, 1969.

———. *European Empires from Conquest to Collapse, 1815–1960*. Leicester: Leicester University Press, 1982.

King, Richard. *Orientalism and Religion: Postcolonial Theory, India and "the Mythic East."* London: Routledge, 1999.

King, Ursula. *Indian Spirituality and Western Materialism: An Image and Its Function in the Reinterpretation of Modern Hinduism*. New Delhi: Indian Social Institute, 1985.

———. "Some Reflections on Sociological Approaches to the Study of Modern Hinduism." *Numen* 36 (1989): 72–97.

Kippenberg, Hans G. "Max Weber und die vergleichende Religionswissenschaft." *Revue internationale de philosophie* 2 (1995): 127–53.

———. *Discovering Religious History in the Modern Age*. Translated by Barbara Harshav. Princeton: Princeton University Press, 2002. Originally published as *Die Entdeckung der Religionsgeschichte: Religionswissenschaft und Moderne* (Munich: C. H. Beck, 1997).

Kirby, Richard, and Earl Brewer. *The Temples of Tomorrow: World Religions and the Future*. London: Grey Seal, 1993.

Kitagawa, Joseph M. "The History of Religions in America." In *The History of Religions: Understanding Human Experience*, 3–26. Atlanta: Scholars Press, 1987. Originally published in *The History of Religions: Essays in Methodology*, edited by Mircea Eliade and J. M. Kitagawa (Chicago: University of Chicago Press, 1959).

———. "The 1893 World's Parliament of Religions and Its Legacy." Appendix to *The History of Religions: Understanding Human Experience*, 353–68. Atlanta: Scholars Press, 1987.

———, ed. *Modern Trends in World Religions: Paul Carus Memorial Symposium*. La Salle, IL: Open Court, 1959.

Koeppen, Karl Friedrich. *Die Religion des Buddha und Ihre Entstehung*. Berlin: F. Schneider, 1857.

König, Franz, ed. *Christus und die Religionen der Erde*. 3 vols. Freiburg: Verlag Herder, 1951.

Kopf, David. *The Brahmo Samaj and the Shaping of the Modern Indian Mind*. Princeton: Princeton University Press, 1979.

Kuenen, Abraham. *National Religions and Universal Religions*. Hibbert Lectures, 1882. Translated by P. H. Wicksteed. London: Macmillan, 1882.

Küng, Hans. *Freud and the Problem of God*. New Haven: Yale University Press, 1979.

Lach, Donald F. *Asia in the Making of Europe*. 3 vols. [9 books]. Chicago: University of Chicago Press, 1965–93.

Laderman, Gary, ed. *Religions of Atlanta: Religious Diversity in Centennial Olympic City*. Atlanta: Scholars Press, 1996.

La Grasserie, Raoul de. *Des Religions comparée au point de vue sociologique*. Paris: V. Giard et F. Brier, 1899.

Lash, Nicholas. *The Beginning and the End of "Religion."* Cambridge: Cambridge University Press, 1996.

Lassen, Christian. *Indische Alterthumskunde*. 5 vols. Leipzig: Kittler [etc.], 1858–74.

Lazaron, Morris S. *Seed of Abraham: Ten Jews of the Ages*. New York: Century Co., 1930.

———. *Common Ground: A Plea for Intelligent Americanism*. New York: Liveright, [1938].

———. "Judaism, a Universal Religion." *Christian Century* 56, 35 (August 30, 1939): 1042–45.

Lees, James Cameron. "Mahommedanism." In *The Faiths of the World: St. Giles' Lectures*, 304–34. New York: Scribners, 1882.

Legge, James. Introduction to *A Record of Buddhistic Kingdoms: Being an Account by the Chinese Monk Fâ-Hien of his travels in India and Ceylon. . . . Translated and Annotated with a Corean Recension of the Chinese Text by James Legge*, 1–8. Oxford: Clarendon Press, 1886.

Leopold, Joan. *The Letter Liveth: The Life, Work and Library of August Friedrich Pott, 1802–1887*. Amsterdam: John Benjamins, 1983.

———, ed. *The Prix Volney: Contributions to Comparative Indo-European, African and Chinese Linguistics; Max Müller and Steinthal*. Dordrecht: Kluwar Academic Publishing, 1999.

Lessing, Gotthold Ephraim. *Nathan the Wise*. Translated by Bayard Quincy Morgan. In *Nathan the Wise, Minna von Barnhelm, and Other Plays and Writings*, edited by Peter Demetz, 173–275. New York: Continuum, 1994. Originally published in 1778 or 1779.

—————. "The Education of the Human Race." Translated by Henry Chadwick. In *Nathan the Wise, Minna von Barnhelm, and Other Plays and Writings*, edited by Peter Demetz, 319–34. New York: Continuum, 1994. Originally published in 1780.

Lillie, Arthur. *Buddha and Early Buddhism.* The World's Epochmakers series. London: Trübner, 1881.

—————. *The Popular Life of Buddha; Containing an Answer to the Hibbert Lectures (by T. W. Rhys Davids) of 1881.* London: Kegan Paul, 1883.

—————. *Buddhism in Christendom, or Jesus, the Essene.* London: Kegan Paul, Trench, 1887.

—————. *The Influence of Buddhism on Primitive Christianity.* London: Sonnenschein, 1893.

Lincoln, Bruce. *Theorizing Myth: Narrative, Ideology, and Scholarship.* Chicago: University of Chicago Press, 1999.

Lopez, Donald S., Jr., ed. *Curators of the Buddha: The Study of Buddhism under Colonialism.* Chicago: University of Chicago Press, 1995.

Lowell, Percival. *Occult Japan, or The Way of the Gods: An Esoteric Study of Japanese Personality and Possession.* Boston: Houghton Mifflin, 1895.

MacCulloch, John Arnott. *Comparative Theology.* Churchman's Library Series. London: Metheuen, 1902.

—————. *Religion, Its Origin and Forms.* London: J. M. Dent, 1904.

Mackay, Robert William. *The Progress of the Intellect, as Exemplified in the Religious Development of the Greeks and Hebrews.* London: J. Chapman, 1850.

Mallory, J. P. *In Search of the Indo-Europeans: Language, Archaeology and Myth.* London: Thames and Hudson, 1989. Reprint ed., 1999.

Mansel, Henry Longueville. *The Gnostic Heresies of the First and Second Centuries.* Edited by J. B. Lightfoot. London: John Murray, 1875.

Mariano, Raffaele. *Cristo e Budda, e altri iddii dell'Oriente: Studii di religione comparata.* Florence: G. Barbèra, 1900.

Marshall, P. J. *The British Discovery of Hinduism in the Eighteenth Century.* Cambridge: Cambridge University Press, 1970.

Marshall, P. J., and Glyndwr Williams. *The Great Map of Mankind: Perceptions of New Worlds in the Age of Enlightenment.* Cambridge: Harvard University Press, 1982.

Martin, Alfred Wilhelm. *Universal Religion and the Religions of the World.* Tacoma, WA: First Free Church, 1896.

Martin, Thomas. *The Royal Institution.* London: Longmans, Green, 1949.

Masuzawa, Tomoko. *In Search of Dreamtime: Quest for the Origin of Religion.* Chicago: University of Chicago Press, 1993.

—————. "Origin." In *The Guide to the Study of Religion*, edited by Willi Braun, and Russell McCutcheon, 209–24. London: Cassell, 2000.

—————. "The Production of 'Religion' and the Task of the Scholar: Russell McCutcheon among the Smiths." *Culture and Religion* 1, 1 (May 2000): 123–30.

—————. "Our Master's Voice: F. Max Müller after a Hundred Years of Solitude." *Method and Theory in the Study of Religion* 15, 4 (2003): 305–28.

Matheson, George. *The Distinctive Messages of the Old Religions.* Edinburgh: Blackwood, 1892.

Maurice, Frederick Denison. *The Religions of the World and Their Relations to Christianity, Considered in Eight Lectures Founded by the Right Hon. Robert Boyle.* London: John W. Parker, 1847.

Maw, Martin. *Visions of India: Fulfilment Theology, the Aryan Race Theory, and the Work of British Protestant Missionaries in Victorian India*. Frankfurt am Main: Peter Lang, 1990.

McCutcheon, Russell. *Manufacturing Religion: The Discourse on Sui Generis Religion and the Politics of Nostalgia*. New York: Oxford University Press, 1997.

McGuire, William. *Bollingen: An Adventure in Collecting the Past*. Princeton: Princeton University Press, 1982.

Mensching, Gustav. *Structures and Patterns of Religion*. Translated by Hans F. Klimkeit and V. Srinivasa Sarma. Delhi: Motilal Banarsidas, 1976. Originally published as *Die Religion: Erscheinungsformen, Strukturtypen und Lebensgesetze* (Munich: W. Goldmann, 1959?).

Menzies, Allan. *History of Religion: A Sketch of Primitive Religious Beliefs and Practices, and of the Origin and Character of the Great Systems*. London: John Murray, 1895.

Milner, Vincent L. *Religious Denominations of the World: Comprising a General View of the Origin, History and Condition of the Various Sects of Christians, the Jews, and Mahometans, as well as the Pagan Forms of Religion Existing in the Different Countries of the Earth; With Sketches of the Founders of Various Sects; From the Best Authorities*. Philadelphia: Bradley, Garretson, 1872. First published around 1860.

———*Paganism, Popery, and Christianity, or The blessing of an Open Bible: As Shown in the History of Christianity, from the Time of Our Savior to the Present Day*. Boston: L. P. Crown, 1855.

Mitter, Partha. *Much Maligned Monsters: History of European Reactions to Indian Art*. Oxford: Clarendon Press, 1977.

———. "Rammohun Roy and the New Language of Monotheism." *History and Anthropology* 3 (1987): 177–208.

Moffat, James Clement. *A Comparative History of Religions*. 2 vols. New York: Dodd and Mead, 1871–73.

Monier-Williams, Monier. *Indian Wisdom, or Examples of the Religious, Philosophical and Ethical Doctrines of the Hindûs; With a Brief History of the Chief Departments of Sanskrit Literature and Some Ac[c]ount of the Past and Present Condition of India, Moral and Intellectual*. London: Allen, 1875.

———. *Buddhism: In Its Connexion with Brâhmanism and Hindûism, and in Its Contrast with Christianity*. London: John Murray, 1889.

Montgomery, James A., ed. *Religions of the Past and Present: A Series of Lectures Delivered by Members of the Faculty of the University of Pennsylvania*. Philadelphia: J. B. Lippincott, 1918.

Moore, Deborah Dash. "Jewish GIs and the Creation of the Judeo-Christian Tradition." *Religion and American Culture* 8 (winter 1998): 31–53.

Moore, George Foot. *History of Religions*. 2 vols. New York: Scribners, 1913–19.

Murdoch, John. *The Religions of the World: An Illustrated Sketch*. London: Christian Literature Society for India, 1902.

Müller, Friedrich. *Grundriss der Sprachwissenschaft*. Vienna: A. Hölder, 1876–88.

Müller, F. Max. "Last Results of the Turanian Researches Respecting the Non-Iranian and Non-Semitic Languages of Asia or Europe, or the Turanian Family of Language." In Christian Bunsen, *Christianity and Mankind*, vol. 3, *Outline of the Philosophy of Universal History applied to Language and Religion*, 263–21. London: Longman, Brown, Green, and Longmans, 1854. Originally published in 1853.

———. *The Languages of the Seat of War in the East: With Survey of the Three Families of Languages, Semitic, Arian and Turanian*. 2nd ed. Williams and Norgate, 1855.

———. "Reply to Monsieur Renan's Remarks." Printed in London by Longmans, 1855. Max Müller Papers, Bodleian Library, Oxford, shelfmark MS. Eng. d.2358.

———. "Comparative Mythology." In *Chips from a German Workshop: Essays on Mythology, Traditions, and Customs*, 2:1–141. New York: Scribners, 1871. Originally published in *Oxford Essays*, April 1856.

———. *Lectures on the Science of Language, First Series, Delivered at the Royal Institution of Great Britain in April, May, and June, 1861*. First American edition (based on the second edition published in London, 1862). New York: Scribner's, 1862. Originally published in 1861; sixth edition published in 1880 by Scribners.

———. *Lectures on the Science of Language, Second Series*. New edition. New York: Scribners, 1880. Originally published in 1864.

———. *On the Stratification of Language: Sir Robert Rede's Lecture, Delivered in the Senate House before the University of Cambridge, on Friday, May 29, 1868*. London: Longmans, Green, Reader, and Dyer, 1868.

———. "Buddhism." In *Chips from a German Workshop: Essays on the Science of Religion*, 1:179–231. London: Longmans, 1869.

———. "Christ and Other Masters." In *Chips from a German Workshop: Essays on the Science of Religion*, 1:49–60. London: Longmans, 1869.

———. "Semitic Monotheism." In *Chips from a German Workshop: Essays on the Science of Religion*, 1:337–74. London: Longmans, 1869.

———. *Introduction to the Science of Religion: Four Lectures Delivered at the Royal Institution; With Two Essays, On False Analogies, and The Philosophy of Mythology*. London: Longmans, Green, 1873.

———. "Forgotten Bibles [on the Sacred Books of the East]." In *Last Essays, Second Series: Essays on the Science of Religion*, 1–35. London: Longmans, Green, 1901. Originally published in *Nineteenth Century*, 1884.

———. "Philology versus Ethnology; Letter to H. H. Risley, Esq." In *Biography of Words*, 243–51. London: Longmans, Green, 1888.

———. "Oriental Scholarship during the Present Century: Inaugural Address by the President of the International Congress of Orientalists, London, 1892." *Transactions of the International Congress of Orientalists* 1 (1892): 1–37.

———. "The Parliament of Religions, Chicago, 1893" and "Letter [April 2, 1893] to the Rev. John Henry Barrows, D.D., Chairman of the General Committee." In *Last Essays, Second Series: Essays on the Science of Religion*, 324–45. London: Longmans, Green, 1901.

———. "Mohammedanism and Christianity." In *Last Essays, Second Series: Essays on the Science of Religion*, 240–58. London: Longmans, Green, 1901. Originally published in *Nineteenth Century*, February 1894.

———. "The Alleged Sojourn of Christ in India." In *Last Essays, Second Series: Essays on the Science of Religion*, 171–209. London: Longmans, Green, 1901. Originally published in *Nineteenth Century*, October 1894.

———. "The Kutho-Daw." In *Last Essays, Second Series: Essays on the Science of Religion*, 210–30. London: Longmans, Green, 1901. Originally published in *Nineteenth Century*, September 1895.

———. *Three Lectures on the Science of Language, Delivered at the Oxford University Extension Meeting, with a Supplement "My Predecessors."* 2nd ed. Chicago: Open Court, 1895.

———. *Contributions to the Science of Mythology*. 2 vols. London: Longmans, Green, 1897.

———. *My Autobiography: A Fragment*. New York: Scribners, 1901.

————The Life and Letters of the Right Honourable Friedrich Max Müller: Edited by His Wife [Georgina Adelaide Grenfell Max Müller]. 2 vols. London: Longmans, 1902.

Nagarkar, B. B. "Spiritual Ideas of the Brahmo-Somaj." In The Dawn of Religious Pluralism: Voices from the World's Parliament of Religions, 1893, edited by Richard Hughes Seager, 433–39. La Salle, IL: Open Court, 1993.

Neufeldt, Ronald W. F. Max Müller and the Rg-Veda: A Study of Its Role in His Work and Thought. Calcutta: Minerva, 1980.

Neusner, Jacob, ed. World Religions in America. Louisville, KY: Westminster John Knox Press, 2000.

Niebuhr, Reinhold. The Self and the Dramas of History. New York: Scribners, 1955.

Noll, Richard. The Jung Cult: Origins of a Charismatic Movement. Princeton: Princeton University Press, 1994.

————. The Aryan Christ: The Secret Life of Carl Jung. New York: Random House, 1997.

Oldenberg, Hermann. Buddha: His life, His Doctrine, His Order. London: Williams and Norgate, 1882. Originally published as Buddha, sein Leben, seine Lehre, seine Gemeinde (Berlin: W. Hertz, 1881).

Olender, Maurice. The Languages of Paradise: Race, Religion, and Philology in the Nineteenth Century. Translated by Arthur Goldhammer. Cambridge: Harvard University Press, 1992. Originally published as Les Langues du Paradis: Aryens et Sémites; Un couple providentiel (Paris: Gallimard-Le Seuil, 1989).

Orelli, Conrad von. Allgemeine Religionsgeschichte. 2 vols. Bonn: A. Marcus und E. Weber, 1899.

Osburn, William. The Religions of the World, Being Historical Sketches of Ancient and Modern Heathenism; Romanism; Mohammedanism; and Christianity. London: Seeley, Ackson, and Halliday, 1857.

Otto, Rudolf. Mysticism East and West: A Comparative Analysis of The Nature of Mysticism. Translated by Bertha L. Bracey and Rechenda C. Payne. New York: Macmillan, 1932.

Pailin, David A. Attitudes to Other Religions: Comparative Religion in Seventeenth- and Eighteenth-Century Britain. Manchester: Manchester University Press, 1984.

Panikkar, K. M. Asia and Western Dominance: A Survey of the Vasco da Gama Epoch of Asian History, 1498–1945. New edition. London: George Allen and Unwin, 1959. First edition published in 1953.

Parker, Theodore. A Discourse of Matters Pertaining to Religion. Boston: C. C. Little and J. Brown, 1842.

————. Theism, Atheism, and the Popular Theology. London: Chapman, 1853.

Parsons, Talcott. "Translator's Preface." In The Protestant Ethic and the Spirit of Capitalism, by Max Weber, 9–11. London: Routledge, 1992. First published in 1930 by Harper Collins.

Parrish, Fred Louis. The Classification of Religions: Its Relation to the History of Religions. Scottdale, PA: Herald Press, 1941.

Pfleiderer, Otto. Philosophy and Development of Religion. Gifford Lectures, 1894. 2 vols. London: Blackwood, 1894.

————. The Philosophy of Religion on the Basis of Its History. Translated by Alexander Stewart and Allan Menzies. 2 vols. London: Williams and Norgate, 1886–87. Originally published as Religionsphilosophie auf geschichtlicher Grundlage (Berlin: Georg Reimer, 1878).

————. Religion and Historic Faiths. Translated by Daniel A. Huebsch. New York: B. W. Heubsch, 1907. Originally published as Religion und Religionen (Munich: J. F. Lehmann, 1906).

Picart, Bernard, engraver. *The Ceremonies and Religious Customs of the Various Nations of the Known World: Together with Historical Annotations, and Several Curious Discourses Equally Instructive and Entertaining . . . Written Originally in French, and Illustrated . . . by Mr. Bernard Picart, . . . Translated into English, by a Gentleman. . . . 7 vols.* London: Printed by William Jackson for Claude du Bosc, 1733–39. Originally published as *Histoire générale des cérémonies, moeurs, et coutumes religieuses de tous les peuples du monde, représentées en 243 figures dessinées de la main de Bernard Picard ; Avec des explications historiques, & curieuses; Par M. l'Abbé Banier . . . & par M. l'Abbé Le Mascrier* (Amsterdam: Jean Frédéric Bernard, 1723–43?), and in a later version as *Histoire des religions et des moeurs de tous les peuples du monde; Avec 600 gravures, représentant toutes les cérémonies et courtumes religieuses, dessinées et gravées par le célèbre B. Picart; Publiées en Hollande, par J.-Fr. Bernard . . . ; avec 30 planches nouvelles,* 2nd ed., 6 vols. (Paris: De l'Impr. de A. Belin [etc.], 1816–19).

Poliakov, Léon. *The Aryan Myth: A History of Racist and Nationalist Ideas in Europe.* Translated by Edmund Howard. London: Sussex University Press, 1974. Originally published as *Le Mythe aryen: Essai sur les sources du racisme et des nationalismes* (Paris: Calmann-Lévy, 1971).

Pott, August Friedrich. "M. Müller und die Kennzeichen der Sprachenverwandtschaft." *Zeitschrift der deutschen morgendländischen Gesellschaft* 9 (1855).

———. *Die Ungleichheit menschen Rassen: Hauptsachlich von sprachwissenschaftlichem Standpunkt.* Lemgo: Meyer'sche Hofbuchhandlung, 1856.

Prakash, Gyan. *Another Reason: Science and the Imagination of Modern India.* Princeton: Princeton University Press, 1999.

Pulman, Bertrand. "Aux 'Origines' de la science des religions: Lorsque le savoir prend chair(e) . . ." *Cahier Confrontations* (Paris) 14 (1985): 7–24.

Purchas, Samuel. *Purchas His Pilgrimage, or Relations of the World and the Religions Observed in Al[l] Ages and Places Discovered, from the Creation unto This Present; In Foure Parts; This First Contayneth a Theologicall Historie of Asia, Africa, and America, with the Ilands Adiacent, Declaring the Ancient Religions before the Floud, the Heathenish, Jewish, and Saracenicall in All Ages Since. . . . 3rd ed.* London: Printed by W. Stansby for H. Fetherstone, 1617. First edition published in 1613.

Rafael, Vicente. *Contracting Colonialism: Translation and Christian Conversion in Tagalog Society under Early Spanish Rule.* Ithaca: Cornell University Press, 1988.

Raffles, Thomas Samford. *The History of Java.* 2 vols. London: Black, Parbury and Allen, 1817.

Rapson, E. J. Preface to *The Science of Religion* by Émile Burnouf. London: Swan Sonnenschein, Lowrey, 1888.

Rauwenhoff, Lodewijk Willem Ernst. "Wereldgodsdiensten." *Theologisch Tijdschrift* (Leiden) 19, 1 (1885): 1–33.

Reichwein, Adolf. *China and Europe: Intellectual and Artistic Contacts in the Eighteenth Century.* Translated by J. C. Powell. London: Kegan Paul, Trench, Trübuner, 1925.

Reid, John Morrison, et al. *Doomed Religions: A Series of Essays on the Great Religions of the World. . . .* New York: Phillips and Hunt, 1884.

Reinach, Salomon. *Cultes, mythes, et religions.* 5 vols. Paris: E. Leroux, 1906–23.

———. *Orpheus: A History of Religions.* Translated by Florence Simmonds. London: William Heinemann, 1909. Originally published as *Orpheus: Histoire générale des religions* (Paris: Calmann-Lévy, 1909).

———. *A Short History of Christianity.* Translated by Florence Simmonds. London: William Heinemann, 1922.

Religious Systems of the World: A Contribution to the Study of Comparative Religion; A Collection of Addresses Delivered at South Place Institute; Now Revised, and in Some Cases Rewritten by the Authors. 2nd ed. London: Sonnenschein, 1891.

Renan, Ernest. *Histoire générale et système comparée des langues sémitiques.* Paris: Imprimerie Impériale, 1855.

————. *The Life of Jesus.* Translated by Charles Edwin Wilbour. New York: Carleton, 1864. Originally published as *La Vie de Jésus* (Paris: Michel Lévy, 1863).

————. *History of the People of Israel.* 5 vols. Translated by C. B. Pitman and D. Bingham. London: Chapman and Hall, 1888–93. Originally published as *Histoire du peuple d'Israël* (Paris: Calmann-Lévy, 1887–93).

————. *L'Avenir de la science, pensée de 1848.* Paris: Calmann-Lévy, 1890.

Réville, Albert. *Prolegomena of the History of Religions.* London: Williams and Norgate, 1884. Originally published as *Prolégomènes de l'histoire des religions,* 3rd ed. (Paris: Fischbacher, 1881).

Rhys Davids, T. W. *Lectures on the Origin and Growth of Religion as Illustrated by Some Points in the History of Indian Buddhism.* Hibbert Lectures of 1881. 2nd ed. London: Williams and Norgate, 1891.

————. *Buddhism: Being a Sketch of the Life and Teachings of Gautama, the Buddha.* London: Society for Promoting Christian Knowledge, 1899.

————. *Early Buddhism.* London: Constable, 1908.

Richards, Thomas. *The Imperial Archive: Knowledge and the Fantasy of Empire.* London: Verso, 1993.

Riddle, Joseph E. *The Natural History of Infidelity and Superstition in Contrast with Christian Faith; Eight Sermons Preached before the University of Oxford in 1852.* Bampton Lectures. London: J. W. Parker, 1852.

Ries, Julien. "Quelques aspects de la science des religions à la fin du XIXe siècle." Postface to *Christianism, église et religions: Le dossier Hyacinthe Loyson, 1827–1912,* edited by Lucienne Porter, 147–72. Louvain: Centre d'Histoire des Religions, 1982.

Rittelmeyer, Friedrich von. *Buddha oder Christus?* Tübingen: J. C. B. Mohr, 1909.

Ross, Alexander. *Pansebeia, or A View of All Religions in the World: With the Severall Church-Governments from the Creation to These Times; Also, a Discovery of All Known Heresies in All Ages and Places, and Choice Observations and Reflections throughout the Whole.* London: Printed by T. C. for John Saywell, 1653.

Roth, Guenther. Introduction to *Economy and Society: An Outline of Interpretive Sociology,* by Max Weber, 1:xxxiii–cx. Berkeley: University of California Press, 1978.

Ryan, W. Carson. *Studies in Early Graduate Education: The Johns Hopkins, Clark University, the University of Chicago.* New York: Arno Press, 1971. Originally published in 1939.

Sahae, Y. "Brahma Samaj und Arya Samaj." Ph.D. diss., University of Bonn, 1964.

Said, Edward W. *Orientalism.* New York: Pantheon Books, 1978.

Sarma, Dittakavi Subrahmanya. *Studies in the Renaissance of Hinduism.* Benares: Benares Hindu University, 1944.

Schivelbusch, Wolfgang. *Tastes of Paradise: A Social History of Spices, Stimulants, and Intoxicants.* Translated by David Jacobson. New York: Pantheon, 1992.

Schlegel, Friedrich. *On the Language and Wisdom of the Indians.* In *The Aesthetic and Miscellaneous Works of Frederick von Schlegel,* edited by E. J. Millington. London: Henry G. Bohn, 1849. Originally published as *Über die Sprache und die Weisheit der Indier: Ein Beitrag zur Begründung der Altertumskunde* (Heidelberg: Mohr und Zimmer, 1808).

Schlunk, Martin. *Die Weltreligionen und das Christentum: Eine Auseinandersetzung vom Christentum aus.* Hamburg: Agentur des Rauhen Hauses, 1923.

Schmidt, Francis. "Polytheisms: Degeneration or Progress?" *History and Anthropology* 3 (1987): 9–60.

Schrader, Otto. *Prehistoric Antiquities of the Aryan Peoples: A Manual of Comparative Philology and the Earliest Culture; Being the "Sprachvergleichung und Urgeschichte" of Dr. O. Schrader.* Edited by Frank Byron Jevons. London: C. Griffin, 1890.

Schwab, Raymond. *The Oriental Renaissance: Europe's Discovery of India and the East, 1680–1880.* Translated by Gene Patterson-Black and Victor Reinking. New York: Columbia University Press, 1984. Originally published as *La Renaissance orientale* (Paris: Payot, 1950).

Schweitzer, Albert. *Christianity and the Religions of the World.* Translated by Johanna Powers et al. London: Selly Oak Colleges Central Council Publication, 1923.

Seager, Richard Hughes. *The World's Parliament of Religions: The East/West Encounter, Chicago, 1893.* Bloomington: Indiana University Press, 1995.

———, ed. *The Dawn of Religious Pluralism: Voices from the World Parliament of Religions, 1893.* La Salle, IL: Open Court, 1993.

Senart, Émile Charles Marie. *Essai sur la légende du Buddha, son caractère et ses origines.* Paris: Imprimerie Nationale (Extrait du Journal Asiatique, 1873–75), 1875.

Sharpe, Eric J. *Comparative Religion: A History.* 2nd ed. La Salle: Open Court, 1986. First edition published in 1975 by Duckworth.

Silberman, Neil Asher. *Digging for God and Country: Exploration, Archeology, and the Secret Struggle for the Holy Land, 1799–1917.* New York: Knopf, 1982.

Silk, Mark. "Notes on the Judeo-Christian Tradition in America." *American Quarterly* 36 (1984): 65–85.

———. *Spiritual Politics: Religion and America since World War II.* New York: Simon and Schuster, 1988.

Smart, Ninian. *The Religious Experience of Mankind.* 1st ed. New York: Scribners, 1969. Revised throughout numerous editions; in Prentice-Hall's fifth edition of 1996, the title of the volume was modified to *The Religious Experience.*

Smart, Ninian, and Richard D. Hecht, eds. *Sacred Texts of the World: A Universal Anthology.* New York: Crossroad, 1982.

Smith, John. *The True Travels, Adventures, and Observations of Captaine Iohn Smith, in Europe, Asia, Affrica, and America, from Anno Domini 1593 to 1629; His Accidents and Sea-Fights in the Straights, His Service and Stratagems of Warre in Hungaria, Transilvania, Wallachia, and Moldavia, against the Turks, and Tartars; His Three Single Combats betwixt the Christian Armie and the Turkes; After How He Was Taken Prisoner by the Turks, Sold for a Slave, Sent into Tartaria; His Description of the Tartars, Their Strange Manners and Customes of Religions, Diets, Buildings, Warres, Feasts, Ceremonies, and Living, How He Slew the Basnaw of Nalbrits in Cambria, and Escaped from the Turkes and Tartars.* London: Printed by J[ohn] H[aviland] for Thomas Slater, 1630.

Smith, Jonathan Z. *Map Is Not Territory: Studies in the History of Religions.* Leiden: Brill, 1978.

———. *Imagining Religion: From Babylon to Jonestown.* Chicago: University of Chicago Press, 1982.

———. "A Matter of Class: Taxonomies of Religion." *Harvard Theological Review* 89 (1996): 387–403.

————. "Religion, Religions, Religious." In *Critical Terms for Religious Studies*, edited by Mark C. Taylor, 269–84. Chicago: University of Chicago Press, 1998.

Steigmann-Gall, Richard. *The Holy Reich: Nazi Conceptions of Christianity, 1919–1945*. Cambridge: Cambridge University Press, 2003.

Stone, Jon R., ed. *The Essential Max Müller: On Language, Mythology, and Religion*. New York: Palgrave Macmillan, 2002.

Styers, Randall. *Making Magic: Religion, Magic, and Science in the Modern World*. New York: Oxford University Press, 2003.

Tiele, C. P. *Outlines of the History of Religion to the Spread of the Universal Religions*. Translated by J. Estlin Carpenter. London: Kegan Paul, Trench, Trübner, 1877. Originally published as *Geschiedenis van den Godsdienst tot Aan de Heerschappij der Wereldgodsdiensten* (Amsterdam, 1876).

————. "Religions." In *Encyclopaedia Britannica*. 9th ed. Edinburgh: 1885.

————. *Elements of the Science of Religion*. Gifford Lectures. Edinburgh: William Blackwood, 1897–99.

Tillich. Paul. "Is There a Judeo-Christian Tradition?" *Judaism* 1, 2 (1952): 106–9.

Timpanaro, Sebastiano. "Friedrich Schlegel and the Beginnings of Indo-European Linguistics in Germany." Translated by J. Peter Maher. In Friedrich Schlegel, *Über die Sprache und die Weisheit der Indier*, vol. 1 of *Amsterdam Studies in the Theory and History of Linguistic Science*, xi–lvii. New edition. Amsterdam: John Benjamins B. V., 1977. Originally published as "Friedrich Schlegel e gli Inizi della Linguistica Indoeuropea in Germania," *Critica Storica* 9, 1 (1972): 72–105.

Tisdall, William St. Clair. *Comparative Religion*. Anglican Church Handbooks. London: Longmans, Green, 1909.

Todd, Jesse T. "Producing the Judeo-Christian Tradition at the New York World's Fair, 1939–1940." Paper presented at the Annual Meeting of the American Academy of Religion, November 1997.

Toland, John. *Nazarenus, or Jewish, Gentile, and Mahometan Christianity; Containing: The History of the Ancient Gospel of Barnabas, and the Modern Gospel of the Mahometans, Attributed to the Same Apostle . . . Also the Original Plan of Christianity Occasionally Explain'd in the History of the Nazarens . . . With the Relation of an Irish Manuscript of the Four Gospels, as Likewise a Summary of the Ancient Irish Christianity, and the Reality of the Keldees . . . against the Two Last Bishops of Worcester*. London: Printed and sold by J. Brown, etc., 1718.

Trautmann, Thomas R. *Aryans and British India*. Berkeley: University of California Press, 1997.

Troeltsch, Ernst. "Christianity and the History of Religion." In *Religion in History*, translated by James Luther Adams and Walter F. Bense, 77–86. Minneapolis: Fortress Press, 1991. Originally published in 1897.

————. *The Social Teaching of the Christian Churches*. 2 vols. Translated by Olive Wyon, with an introduction by H. Richard Niebhur. Chicago: University of Chicago Press, 1981. This translation of *Die Soziallehren der christlichen Kirchen und Gruppen* (1912; Tübingen: J. C. B. Mohr, 1919) was originally published by Allen and Unwin in 1931.

————. "The Dogmatics of the History-of-Religions School." In *Religion in History*, translated by James Luther Adams and Walter F. Bense, 87–108. Minneapolis: Fortress Press, 1991. Originally published in 1913.

————. "The Place of Christianity among the World Religions." In *Christian Thought: Its History* and Application, edited by Baron von Hügel, 3–35. London: University of London Press, 1923.

Trompf, G. W. Friedrich Max Mueller as a Theorist of Comparative Religion. Bombay: Shakuntala Publishing House, 1978.

Turner, William. The History of All Religions in the World: From the Creation Down to This Present Time; In Two Parts; The First Containing Their Theory, and the Other Relating Their Practices, Each Divided into Chapters, Which by the Several Heads, or Common Places of Divinitiy, Viz. The Object of Religious Worship, the Place, the Time, the Persons Officiating, the Manner, and the Parts of Worship, &c; With Various Instances upon Every Head; To Which Is Added, a Table of Heresies; As Also A Geographical Map, Shewing in What Countrey Each Religion Is Practised; Written in a Different Method from Anything Yet Published on This Subject. London: Printed for John Dunton, 1695.

An Universal, Historical, Geographical and Poetical Dictionary: Containing Likewise the Lives of Eminent Persons, also the History of the Pagan Gods, of the Several Sects among the Jews, Christians, Heathens and Mahometans, of General Councils and Synods, of the Establishment and Progress of Religious and Military Orders; And of Genealogies of the Most Illustrious Families/Extracted From Moreri, Bayle, Baudrand, Hoffman, Danet, and Many More of the Best and Choicest Historians, Geographers, Chronologers and Lexicographers. 2 vols. London: Printed for J. Hartley, 1703.

Van Hamel, M. "L'Enseignment de l'histoire des religions." In Maurice Vernes, L'Histoire des religions: Son esprit, sa méthode, et ses divisions, son enseignement en France et à l'etranger, 217–29. Paris: Ernest Leroux, 1887. Originally published in Revue de l'histoire des religions (Paris) 1 (1880).

Veth, Pieter Johannes. Java, geographisch, ethnologisch, historisch. 3 vols. Haarlem: De Erven F. Bohn, 1875–82.

Vernes, Maurice. L'Histoire des religions: Son esprit, sa méthode, et ses divisions, son enseignement en France et à l'etranger. Paris: Ernest Leroux, 1887.

Viswanathan, Gauri. Outside the Fold: Conversion, Modernity, and Belief. Princeton: Princeton University Press, 1998.

Vivekananda. "Hinduism." In The Dawn of Religious Pluralism: Voices from the World's Parliament of Religions, 1893, edited by Richard Hughes Seager. La Salle, IL: Open Court, 1993.

Voigt, Johannes H. Max Müller: The Man and His Ideas. Calcutta: Firma K. L. Mukhopadhyay, 1967.

Vollers, Karl. Die Weltreligionen in ihrem geschichtlichen Zusammenhange. Jena: Eugen Diederichs, 1907.

Voltaire ["Jean Soret"]. An essay on Universal History, the Manners, and Spirit of Nations, from the Reign of Charlemaign to the Age of Lewis XIV: Written in French by M. de Voltaire, Translated into English, with Additional Notes and Chronological Tables, by Mr. Nugent. 4 vols. London: Printed for J. Nourse, 1759. Revised English edition published in Edinburgh by William Creech in 1782. Originally published as Essai sur les moeurs et l'esprit des nations et sur les principaux faits de l'histoire depuis Charlemagne jusqu'à Louis XIII.

Waardenburg, J. Jacques. Classical Approaches to the Study of Religion: Aims, Methods and Theories of Research. 2 vols. The Hague: Mouton, 1973–74.

Wallerstein, Immanuel. The Modern World-System. 3 vols. New York: Academic Press, 1974–89.

Wallerstein, Immanuel, et al. Open the Social Sciences: Report of the Gulbenkian Commission on the Restructuring of the Social Sciences. Stanford: Stanford University Press, 1996.

Ward, Duren James Henderson. *How Religion Arises: A Psychological Study.* Boston: G. H. Ellis, 1888.

———. *The Classification of Religions: Different Methods, Their Advantages and Disadvantages.* Chicago: Open Court, 1909.

———. *A Receivership for Civilization: From Biblical Church with Its Primitive World and Jewish Legends to Aryan Science with Its Infinite Universe and Established Facts.* Boston: Four Seas Co., 1922.

———. *The Biography of God, as Men Have Told It from Fetishism to Monism; An Anthropological Sketch from Early Credulous Query to Latest Verified Facts.* Denver: Up the Divide Publishing, 1925.

Warren, William Fairfield. *The Religions of the World and the World-Religion.* New York: Methodist Book Concern, 1911. First published in Boston in 1892.

Wasserstrom, Steven. *Religion after Religion: Gershom Scholem, Mircea Eliade, and Henry Corbin at Eranos.* Princeton: Princeton University Press, 1999.

Weber, Albrecht. *Akademische Vorlesungen über indische Literaturgeschichte.* Berlin: Ferdinand Dümmler, 1852. Translated into French as *Histoire de la littérature indienne: Cours professé à l'Université de Berlin* (Paris: A. Durant, 1859), and into English by John Mann and Theodor Zachariae as *History of Indian Literature* (London: Trübner, 1878).

———. *Indische Skizzen: Vier bisher in Zeitschriften zerstreute Vorträge und Abhandlungen.* Berlin: Ferdinand Dümmler, 1857.

Weber, Max. *The Protestant Ethic and the Spirit of Capitalism.* Translated by Talcott Parsons. London: Routledge, 1992. This translation of "Die protestantische Ethik und der Geist des Kapitalismus," *Archiv für Sozialwissenschaft und Sozialpolitik,* 20 and 21 (1904 and 1905), was originally published in 1930 by HarperCollins.

———. "The Social Psychology of the World Religions." In *From Max Weber: Essays in Sociology,* translated by H. H. Gerth and C. Wright Mills, 267–301. New York: Oxford University Press, 1958. Originally published as "Die Wirtschaftsethik der Weltreligionen: Vergleichende religionssoziologische Versuche; Einleitung," in *Gesammelte Aftsätze zur Religionssoziologie* (Tübingen: Mohr, 1921), 1:237–68.

———. "Religious Rejections of the World and Their Directions." In *From Max Weber: Essays in Sociology,* translated by H. H. Gerth and C. Wright Mills, 323–59. New York: Oxford University Press, 1958. Originally published as "Zwischenbetrachtung: Theorie der Stufen und Richtungen religiöser Weltablehnung," in *Gesammelte Aftsätze zur Religionssoziologie* (Tübingen: Mohr, 1921), 1:536–73.

———. *The Religion of China: Confucianism and Taoism.* Translated and edited by Hans H. Gerth. New York: Free Press, 1951. Originally published as *Konfuzianismus und Taoismus,* in *Gesammelte Aftsätze zur Religionssoziologie* (Tübingen: Mohr, 1921), vol. 1.

———. *Ancient Judaism.* Translated and edited by Hans H. Gerth and Don Martindale. New York: Free Press, 1952. Originally published as *Antike Judentum,* in *Gesammelte Aftsätze zur Religionssoziologie* (Tübingen: Mohr, 1921), vol. 3.

———. *The Religion of India: The Sociology of Hinduism and Buddhism.* Translated and edited by Hans H. Gerth and Don Martindale. New York: Free Press, 1958. Originally published as *Hinduismus und Buddhismus,* in *Gesammelte Aftsätze zur Religionssoziologie* (Tübingen: Mohr, 1921), vol. 2.

———. *Economy and Society: An Outline of Interpretive Sociology.* Edited by Guenther Roth and Claus Wittich. 2 vols. Berkeley: University of California Press, 1978. Originally published as *Wirtschaft und Gesellschaft: Grundriss der verstehenden Soziologie*, 4th ed., 2 vols. (Tübingen: J. C. B. Mohr, 1956). Volume 1, chapter 6, was translated into English by Ephraim Fischoff and published separately under the title *The Sociology of Religion* (Boston: Beacon Press, 1963).

Wedgwood, Julia. *The Moral Ideal, a Historic Study*. London: Trübner, 1888.

Whitney, William Dwight. "On the So-Called Science of Religion." *Princeton Review* 57 (May 1881): 429–52.

———. *Max Müller and the Science of Language: A Criticism*. New York: D. Appleton, 1892.

Widgery, Alban G. *Living Religions and Modern Thought*. London: Williams and Norgate, 1936.

Wilson, John A. "Egypt." In *The Intellectual Adventure of Ancient Man: An Essay on Speculative Thought in the Ancient Near East*, edited by Henri Frankfort et al., 31–122. Chicago: University of Chicago Press, 1947.

Windisch, Ernst. *Geschichte der Sanskrit-Philologie und indischen Altertumskunde*. Part 1, Strassburg: Karl J. Trübner, 1917; part 2, Berlin: Vereinigung wissenschaftlicher Verleger, 1920. Reprinted in one volume, together with the extant chapters of part 3, by Walter de Gruyter in 1992.

Wolf, Eric R. *Europe and the People without History*. Berkeley: University of California Press, 1982.

Woods, James Haughton. *Practice and Science of Religion: A Study of Method in Comparative Religion*. The Paddock Lectures, 1905–1906. New York: Longmans, Green, 1906.

Wordsworth, John. *The One Religion: Truth, Holiness and Peace Desired by the Nations, and Revealed by Jesus Christ; Eight Lectures Delivered before the University of Oxford in the Year 1881, on the Foundation of John Bampton, M.A., Canon of Salisbury*. 2nd ed. London: Longmans, Green, 1893. First edition published in 1881.

Yerushalmi, Yosef Hayim. *Zakhor: Jewish History, Jewish Memory*. Seattle: University of Washington Press, 1982.

Young, Robert J. C. *Colonial Desire: Hybridity in Theory, Culture and Race*. London: Routledge, 1995

Yuyama, Akira. *Eugène Burnouf: The Background to His Research into the Lotus Sutra*. Tokyo: The International Research Institute for Advanced Buddhology, Soka University, 2000.

Zaehner, R. C. *Foolishness to the Greeks: An Inaugural Lecture Delivered before the University of Oxford on 2 November 1953*. Oxford: Clarendon, 1953.

———, ed. *The Concise Encyclopedia of Living Faiths*. New York: Hawthorn Books, 1959.

Ziolkowski, Eric J., ed. *A Museum of Faith: Histories and Legacies of the 1893 World's Parliament of Religions*. Atlanta, GA: Scholars Press, 1993.

Index

Adam, Robert, 49n, 59, 68n
Adams, Hannah (1755–31), 55n, 58–59
Albright, William, 300
Alexander the Great, 182, 191, 245, 246
Almond, Philip, 125–26, 137n
American Academy of Religion (AAR), 7n, 316–17n, 317
Anderson, Sir Robert, 140n
Anquetil-Duperron, Abraham Hyacinthe (1731–1805), 17, 151n
App, Urs, 157n, 255n
Archer, John Clark (1881–1957), 40n, 44–45, 46n
Arnold, Matthew (1822–88), 99, 173; on Émile Burnouf, 248–49, 254–55; on Hebraism and Hellenism, 147–48, 176
Asad, Talal, 6n, 20n
Atkins, Gaius Glenn (1868–1956), 297n
Augustine, Saint, 48, 52, 149n

Baeck, Leo (1873–1956), 298–300
Bampton, John, Bampton Lectures, 98–100, 103, 276
Barrows, John Henry (1847–1928): Christianity the World Religion, 23, 119; Haskell Lectureship, 269; Barrows Lectureship, 278; World's Parliament of Religions, 268–70, 273n
Barth, Karl (1886–1968), 277n, 300
Barthélemy Saint-Hilaire, Jules (1805–95), 132
Barton, George Aaron (1859–1942), 45n
Bellamy, John: on etymology of "pagan," 48n; on sacred books of China, 215n; deistic view held by, 49n
Bendix, Reinhard, 309n

Benedict, David (1779–1874): cause of idolatry, 51; classification of nations, 59
Benjamin, Walter (1892–1940), 29, 31
Berg, Joseph F. (1812–71), and Catholicism as idolatry, 68n
Berman, Morris, 210n
Bernal, Martin, 171n, 311n;
Bernard, Jean Frédéric, 63
Bernini, Gian Lorenzo, ix
Berry, Thomas Sterling, 140n
Besant, Annie (1847–1933), 75n
Bigandet, Paul (1813–94), 131–32
Blumenbach, Johann Friedrich (1752–1840), 238
Bodin, Jean (1530–96), 47n
Boehtlingk, Otto von (1815–1904), 235n
Bonney, Charles Carroll (1831–1903), 270, 272n
Bopp, Franz (1791–1867): and beginning of comparative grammar, 156, 159; as friend of Jean-Louis Burnouf, 250n; as teacher of Müller, 208; relation to W. Humboldt and A. W. Schlegel, 157–58
Bosch, Lourens P. van den, 207n
Botting, Douglas, 239n
Boyle, Robert (1627–91): Boyle Lectureship, 75–76, 79, 276
Braden, Charles Samuel (b. 1887), 38–39
Branford, Victor, 40n
Brerewood, Edward (1565?–1613): on spread of Islam, 57; classification of nations, 58–59
Brewer, Earl, 40n
Brockhaus, Hermann: as Müller's teacher, 157n
Broughton, Thomas (1704–74), 59, 103n

Brown, J. Newton (1803–68), *Encyclopedia of Religious Knowledge*, 61

Brown, Lewis, 40n

Brunner, Emil (1889–1966), 277n, 300

Buckley, Edmund, 45n

Bultmann, Rudolf (1884–1976), 277n

Bunsen, Christian Karl Josias Freiherr von (1791–1860), 157n, 172n, 211n, 234–36

Bunsen, Ernst von, 140n

Burder, William, 57n, 63n, 66–67

Burnouf, Émile (1821–1907): criticized by M. Arnold, 248–49; relation to Eugène Burnouf, 249–50, 254–55; on Aryan origin of Christianity, 250–51, 254; on Semitic character, 251–53

Burnouf, Eugène (1801–52): as teacher of Müller, 208; impression recorded by Müller, 294n; in development of Oriental philology, 125–26, 156; relation to Émile Burnouf, 249–50, 254–55; relation to Jean-Louis Burnouf, 153n, 249n

Burnouf, Jean-Louis (1775–1844), 153n, 250n

Burtt, Edwin A., 42n

Caird, John (1820–98): evangelical aim of comparative theology, 80–81; problem of pre-Christian religions, 81–83

Calmet, Augustin (1672–1757): on cause of idolatry, 50; on various meanings of the word "religion," 60; eclectic nature of his *Dictionary*, 62

Campbell, Joseph (1904–87), 279

Camper, Petrus (1722–89), 238

Caroe, Gwendy M., 210n

Carpenter, J. Estlin (1844–1927), 270

Catoir, John T., 40n

Cave, Sydney, 40–41n, 84n

Chantepie de la Saussaye, P. D. (1848–1920): on controversy over the term "world religion," 114–17; on A. Weber's view of Buddhism, 136n, 137n; on terminology "Aryan," 189n; publication of *Manual of the Science of Religion*, 108–9, 192; on the first use of the term "world religion," 114–16; and beginning of science of religion, 108–9

Chaudhuri, K. N., 181n

Chézy, Antoine-Léonard de (1773–1832): Sanskrit instruction to Bopp, 156; Sanskrit instruction to Jean-Louis and Eugène Burnouf, 250n

Chidester, David, 7n, 65n

Clarke, James Freeman (1810–88): popularity of his work, 74n; evangelical aim of comparative theology, 82; Mentioned, 120, 312, 316n; *Ten Great Religions*, 77–79; views on Buddhism, 134n, 141n; liberal (Unitarian) orientation of his work, 92, 102, 116; list of "great religions," 80n

Clemen, Carl (1865–1940): *Religions of the World*, 28, 295–99

Cohen, Arthur A., 302n

Colebrooke, Henry Thomas (1765–1837), 157

Coleridge, Samuel Taylor (1772–1834), 89

Colyer-Fergusson, Beatrice S. (née Max Müller), 109

Comte, Auguste (1798–1857), 12

Conder, Josiah (1789–1855), 65–68

Congrès International d'Histoire des Religions, 271

Constant, Benjamin (1767–1830), 293n

Conway, Moncure, 102

Cook, Stanley A. (1873–1949), 37–38

Corbin, Henry, 91n, 279

Craufurd, Quentin, 284n

Cuvier, Georges (1769–1832), 238

D'Harlez, Charles, 270

Damrosch, David, 115n

Dante Alighieri (1265–1321), 196

Darmesteter, James (1849–94): reference to contest between W. Jones and Anquetil-Duperron, 151n; on Renan's view of prophetic tradition, 191–92; study of Zend-Avesta altering Müller's view, 213n; on Renan's life, 172n

Darmesteter, Madame James (A. Mary F. Robinson [1857–1944]), 172n
Darwin, Charles (1809–82), 236, 241
Davids, T. W. Rhys (1843–1922), 132, 138–41
Davy, Sir Humphrey (1778–1829), 211
De Vries, Simon John, 108n
Defoe, Daniel (1661?–1731): classification of nations, 59–60; on cause of idolatry, 52–53; on etymology of "pagan," 48n; on Fe or Fo (Buddha), 123–24; religious problem of multiplicity, 55
Despland, Michel, 6n
Dirks, Nicholas B., 20–21, 289n
Dobbins, Frank S., 62n
Dow, Alexander (d. 1779), 151n, 284n, 286n
Drey, Johann Sebastian von (1777–1853), 114–116, 119n, 120
Dubuisson, Daniel, 7n
Duff, Alexander (1806–78), 127
Dumézil, Georges, 279
Duncker, Max, 137n
Dupuis, Charles François (1742–1809), 92, 292–93
Durkheim, Émile (1858–1917), 74n, 294n

Eck, Diana L., 6n, 267–68, 270–71
Eliade, Mircea: valorization of historical consciousness, 4n, 326; Haskell Lectures, 278; association with Bollingen Foundation, 91n, 278; religious essentialism in, 91n, 313, 314n, 316
Ellinwood, Frank Field (b. 1826): comparative theology from evangelical standpoint, 101–2; view on Buddhism in comparison to Christianity, 130n, 141–43
Estlin, John Prior, 293

Fabian, Johannes, 3n
Fairbairn, A. M. (1838–1912), 266n
Faraday, Michael (1791–1867), 211
Farquhar, John Nicol, 283n
Fessenden's Encyclopedia. See Brown, J. Newton (Encyclopedia of Religious Knowledge)
Finegan, Jack, 43–44

Finkelstein, Louis, 301n
Fitzgerald, Timonthy, 265n, 283n
Flint, Robert (1838–1910), 102
Fox, William Johnson (1786–1864), 92
Fradenburgh, J. N. (1843–1914), 84–87
Frank, Andre Gunder, 181n
Frankfort, Henri (1897–1954), 300
Frazer, James George (1854–1941), 12, 74n, 277n
Freud, Sigmund (1856–1939), 74n
Froebe-Kapteyn, Olga, 279n

Gaer, Joseph, 40n
George, Kirsten, 179n
Gerth, H. H., 304n, 305
Gifford, Adam (1820–87), 280–81
Girardot, Norman J., 207n
Gladstone William E. (1809–98), 247
Goblet d'Alviella, Eugène, Comte (1846–1925), 277
Goethe Johann Wolfgang von (1749–1832): comparative logic, 65; preference for Persia over India, 190n; coining of the term "world literature," 115n
Goodenough, Erwin (1893–1965), 279
Goodrich, Charles A. (1790–1862), 49n, 53–56, 63n
Gordis, Robert, 301n, 302n
Gover, Yerach, 303n
Grossman, Marshall, 303n

Hacker, Paul, 283n
Halbfass, Wilhelm: on early modern Indology, 150n; on articulation of Hindu identity, 283; on Hindu modernism, 286–89; quoting Schlegel, 154n
Halhed, Nathaniel Brassey (1751–1830), 17, 151n, 284n, 286n
Hamel, M. van, 108n
Hamilton, Alexander, 153, 155, 263n
Hardwick, Charles (1821–59), 86–98; on Buddhism, 127; on Hinduism, 133–34n; later devaluation of, 95–98; Mentioned, 99, 100, 292, 312, 316n

Harnack, Adolf (1851–1930), 298
Harrison, Jane (1850–1928), 74n
Harrison, Peter, 7n
Hartley, John, 62
Hartmann, Eduard von (1842–1906), 118n
Haskell, Caroline E., 269, 278
Hay, Stephen N., 290–91
Haydon, A. Eustace, 38–40, 278
Heckscher, William S., ix n
Hegel, G. W. F. (1770–1831), 118n, 189; on
   W. Humboldt's study of Bhagavad Gita,
   161n; Philosophy of History, 12, 42; views
   on India, 157, 183, 190n
Helmholtz, Hermann (1821–94), 211n
Herbert of Cherbury (1583–1648), 47n
Herrliberger, David (1697–1777), 63n
Heschel, Susannah, 177n
Hess, Jonathan M., 177n
Hinnells, John R., 40n, 46n
Hocking, William Ernest, 40n
Hodgson, Brian H. (1800–94), 125, 211n
Holwell, John Zephaniah (1711–98), 151n,
   284n, 286n
Hopfe, Lewis M., 4n
Hopkins, Johns, 269n
Humboldt, Alexander (von) (1769–1859):
   Kosmos cited as authority by Müller, 238–
   40; relation to Müller, 157n, 158n, 239n;
   scholarly assistance to W. Humboldt,
   158n, 163–64n; scientific achievements
   of, 158n
Humboldt, Wilhelm von (1767–1835), 157–
   73 passim; mentioned, 196n, 210, 219,
   300n; on superiority of inflection, 166–
   69; theory of inflection criticized by
   Müller, 222–27, 235n; valorization of
   Greek antiquity, 171
Hume, David (1711–76): notion of world history, 12, 49n; idolatry and polytheism,
   47n; monotheism as basis of universality,
   187n; Separation of confessional and scientific, 237n
Hume, Robert Ernest, 40n, 44
Hyde, Thomas (1636–1703), 17

Ingersoll, Caroline Haskell, 277n
International Association for the History of
   Religions (IAHR), 7n, 271
Irwin, William A. (1884–1967), 300

Jacob, Margaret C., 311n
Jacobsen, Thorkild (b. 1904), 300n
Jacolliot, Louis (1837–90), 246–48, 250, 253
Jaki, Stanley L., 280n
James, Frank A. J. L.. 210n
James, William (1842–1910), 277
Jastrow, Morris (1861–1921), 117–19, 255n
John Paul II (pope), 278
Jones, William (1746–94): and beginning of
   Oriental philology and "Indomania," 17,
   149–51, 153, 286n; contestation with An-
   quetil-Duperron, 151n; mentioned, 152n,
   155, 156, 263n
Jordan, Louis Henry (1855–1923): on com-
   parative theology, 72n, 103; on founding
   of science of religion, 45–46n, 107; on
   C. Hardwick, 97; on J. H. Barrows, 269;
   on private endowments and lectureships,
   276–77, 281–82; on World's Parliament of
   Religions, 265–66
Jung, C. G., 278–79, 293n

Kant, Immanuel, 188
Kellogg, Samuel Henry (1839–99), 103, 119
King, Richard, 265n, 283n, 289n
King, Ursula, 289n
Kippenberg, Hans G., 7n, 304n
Kirby, Richard, 40n
Kitagawa, Joseph M., 266n, 274
Klaproth, Julius von (1783–1835), 131–32
Koeppen, Karl Friedrich (1808–63), 132
König, Franz, 296n
Kopf, David, 284n
Kuenen, Abraham (1828–91): Hibbert Lec-
   tures, 277; mentioned, 107n, 118n, 254;
   on distinction between "world religions"
   and "national religions," 108–9, 111–12,
   208, 306; on Islam and Semitic character-
   istics, 192–204 passim, 179, 228n, 253,

324n; on universality of prophetic tradition, 193–94, 299, 323; views on Buddhism, 136n, 137n
Küng, Hans, 278

La Grasserie, Raoul de (1839–1914), 118n
Lach, Donald, 180, 181n, 311n
Laderman, Gary, 6n
Lang, Andrew (1844–1912), 277n
Lao-Tzu, 124, 133, 215, 267n
Lash, Nicholas, 317n
Lassen, Christian (1800–1876), 132n, 156, 166–67
Lazaron, Morris S. (1888–1979), 302
Lees, James Cameron (1834–1913), 82–83
Legge, James (1815–97): controversy over the number of adherents to Buddhism, 138, 140n; contribution to Sacred Books of the East, 261; mentioned, 207n
Leibniz, Gottfried Wilhelm (1646–1716), 152n
Leopold, Joan, 227n
Lessing, Gotthold Ephraim (1729–81), 12, 49–50
Lillie, Arthur (b. 1831), 140n, 245–46
Lincoln, Bruce, 6n, 265n
Loftus, William, 40n
Lopez, Donald S., 264–65n
Lowell, Percival (1855–1916), 291n
Luther, compared with Buddha, 134

MacCulloch, John Arnott (1868–1950): on monotony of primitive religions, 44; on Islam, 196–97; on Sufism, 203n; comparative theology from evangelical standpoint, 103
Mackey, Robert William (1803–82), 92
Mallory, J. P., 149n, 208n, 232n
Mansel, Henry Longueville (1820–71), 245, 245–46n
Marett, R. R. (1866–1943), 277n
Marino, Raffaele, 141n
Marshall, P. J., 181n, 284, 311n
Martin, Alfred Wilhelm, 119n

Martin, Thomas, 210n
Martineau, Harriet (1802–76), 74n
Massignion, Louis, 279
Masuzawa, Tomoko, 10n, 190n, 207n, 237n, 292n
Matheson, George (1842–1906): non-Christian religions as defunct, 79–80; absence of Islam in the account of, 82; Christianity as basis of comparativism, 85–86; mentioned, 87
Maurice, Frederick Denison (1805–72): aim of comparative theology, 82; Boyle Lectures, 75–77, 79; later evaluation of his lectures, 95–96, 99; mentioned, 74n, 120, 312, 316n; on universality of Christianity, 76–77; present at Müller's lectures on language, 211
Maw, Martin, 127n
McCutcheon, Russell, 6n
McGuire, William, 279
Mellon, Mary and Paul, Bollingen Foundation, 278–79
Mill, John Stuart (1806–73), present at Müller's lectures, 211
Mills, C. Wright, 304n, 305
Milner, Vincent: etymology of "pagan," 47–48; paganism as denial of universal deity, 47; understanding of religious difference, 58; innovation in classification of religions, 67–69
Mitter, Partha, 190n, 283, 285–86
Moffat, James Clement (1811–90), 103
Monier-Williams, Monier (1819–99): Boden Professorship, 211–12; Duff Lectures, 127–31, 138–39, 144; Indian Wisdom, referred to by Kuenen, 137n; on "true" Buddhism, 128–31, 187; on number of adherents to Buddhism, 138–39; Buddhism as death-desiring pessimism, 139, 201; Buddhism and Christianity compared, 129–30, 144
Moore, Deborah Dash, 302n
Moore, George Foot (1851–1931), 43n
Moyers, Bill, 316–17n

Müller, F. Max (1823–1900): absence of
the term "world religion" in, 303–4;
against political use of philology, 168n,
241n; classification of religions, 118n,
207, 212–21, 227–28, 255n; editing of
Sacred Books of the East, 207, 259–63; failure
to obtain Boden Professorship, 211–12;
Gifford and Hibbert Lectureships, 277;
mentioned, 151, 161, 171; on Emile
Burnouf, 248–55; on Eugène Burnouf,
125–26, 294n; on Greek monstrosity,
190n; on history of Oriental philology,
132, 150n; on Jacolliot, 247–48; on origin
of language groups, 218–21; on Pâṇini
and Hindu grammarians, 169n; on Theosophy and Esoteric Buddhism, 141–42,
143; popularity of works by, 74n; rejection
of the theory of pure inflection, 222–27;
relation to Alexander Humboldt, 157n,
158n, 238–40; relation to Christian Bunsen, 157n, 234, 236n; relation to Renan,
172; relation to Schelling, 157n; response
to Matthew Arnold regarding "E. Burnouf," 248–49, 254–55; role in founding of
science of religion, 24, 27, 107, 209–10;
solar myth theory, 292–93
— works: "The Kutho-Daw" (1895), 138n;
"The Last Results of the Turanian Researches," 26, 234–40; Lectures on the Science
of Language (1861), 221–27, 231–37; Lectures
on the Science of Language, 2nd series (1864),
230n; Lectures on the Science of Religion
(1873), 24, 65, 212–21, 247–49; The Languages of the Seat of War in the East, 26, 228–
31; Three Lectures on the Science of Religion
(1889), 237–42
Müller, Friedrich (1834–98), 208n
Müller, Georgina Grenfell Max, 157n, 212n,
234n
Müller, J. G., 46n
Musée Guimet, 292n

Nagarkar, B. B., 288n
Neusner, Jacob, 5n

Niebuhr, Reinhold (1892–1971), 277n, 300
Nietzsche, Friedrich Wilhelm (1844–1900),
190n, 301n
Nobili, Roberto de (1577–1656), 150n
Noll, Richard, 293n
North American Association for the Study of
Religion (NAASR), 7n
Novalis (1772–1801), 154

Oldenberg, Hermann (1852–1920), 132–36
passim; Hinduism as land-religion of India, 133n; on Buddha's rejection of Vedic
authority, 134–35
Olender, Maurice, 191n
Otto, Rudolf (1869–1937), 275, 278, 279n,
313, 315

Pailin, David, 317n
Palgrave, William Gifford, 197
Panikkar, Kavalam Madhava (1896–1963),
181–86
Pâṇini, 169n
Parker, Theodore (1810–60), 92
Parsons, James, 149n
Parsons, Talcott, 304n, 305n
Pfleiderer, Otto (1839–1908): Hibbert and
Gifford Lectures, 277; on Buddhism,
137n; on debate concerning national and
universal religions, 108, 179, 208; on Is-
lam and Semitic characteristics, 197–204,
253–54; on monstrosity of Indian reli-
gion, 190; on Sufism, 202–4; on univer-
sality of prophetic tradition, 299
Philo of Alexandria, 47n
Picart, Bernard (1673–1733), 63, 66–67
Poliakov, Léon: on Jones's place in the his-
tory of Oriental philology, 152n, 153n;
conflation of Müller and Renan, 242–43;
on Christian Lassen, 166
Pons, J. F., 150n
Pott, August Friedrich (1802–87), 226n,
227n
Prakash, Gyan, 283
Prichard, James Cowles (1786–1848), 238

Pulman, Bertrand, 107n
Purchas, Samuel (1577?–1626): on justifications for reviewing non-Christian religions, 51–52, 56–57, 87; eclectic interest shown in book by, 62; view of Catholicism as pagan, 100n
Purinton, Carl E., 46n

Quatremère, Étienne Marc (1782–1857), 156n

Radin, Paul (1883–1959), 279
Rafael, Vicente, 20n
Raffles, Sir Thomas Stamford (1781–1826), 196n
Ramakrishna (1836–86), 287–89
Rask, Rasmus Kristian (1787–1832), 156n
Rauwenhoff, L. W. E. (1828–89), 108, 111
Reichwein, Adolf, 311n
Reinach, Salomon (1858–1932), 293–95
Renan, Ernest (1823–92), 171–78; abandonment of Christianity, 172n, 189; Hibbert Lectures, 277; mentioned, 300n, 323; discussed by Poliakov, 242–43; on impure inflection of Semitic languages, 25, 224; on mission of Semitic race, 174–78; on Semitic characteristics, 198, 227–28n, 253–54; on universality of prophetic tradition, 191–92; valorization of ancient Greece, 173–74
Réville, Albert (1826–1906): role in founding of science of religion, 107n, 118n; founding of Revue de l'histoire des religions, 292n; Hibbert Lectures, 277; participation in World's Parliament of Religions, 270–71
Réville, Jean (1854–1908), 270
Richards, Thomas, 41n
Riddle, Joseph E. (1804–59), 103n
Ries, Julien, 108n
Rittelmeyer, Friedrich von, 141n
Roberton, William (1721–93), 284n
Rockefeller, John D. (1839–1937), 269
Roth, Guenther, 305n

Roy, Rammohun (1772?–1833), 283, 286–87, 289
Royal Institution of Great Britain, 209–11
Royce, Josiah (1855–1916), 277
Ryan, W. Carson, 269n

Said, Edward, 20
Saladin, 183
Sarma, Dittakavi Subrahmanya, 283n
Schelling, Friedrich Wilhelm Joseph von (1775–1854), 157, 217
Schivelbusch, Wolfgang, 183n
Schlegel, August Wilhelm von (1767–1845), 154, 157–58, 163–64n
Schlegel, Friedrich von (1772–1829): criticized by Müller, 222–27; influence on Indology, 156, 158; mentioned, 169, 219; on inflection and agglutination, 163–66; role in the onset of Indomania, 153–55
Schlegel, Karl August von (d. 1789), 154n
Schlötzer, Ludwig von (1735–1808), 152n
Schlunk, Martin (1874–1958), 119n
Schmidt, Francis, 47n
Scholem, Gershom (b. 1897), 91n, 279
Schopenhauer, Arthur (1788–1860), 157, 190n
Schwab, Raymond (The Oriental Renaissance), 132n, 150n, 263n; on Bopp, 156n; on Schlegel, 154–55; on the Burnoufs, 249–50; on W. Humboldt, 158n
Scrafton, Luke, 284n
Seager, Richard Hughes, 266–69
Sen, Keshub Chunder (1838–84), 283, 287–88
Senart, Émile (1847–1928), 136n
Shap Working Party on World Religions in Education, 8n
Sharpe, Eric: on comparative theology, 74n; on founding of science of religion, 46n, 107–8; comparison of F. D. Maurice and C. Hardwick, 95–98; on S. Reinach, 295; on World's Parliament of Religions, 271–73
Silberman, Neil Asher, 265n

Silk, Mark, 303n
Silvestre de Sacy, Antoine Isaac (1758–1838), 156n
Smart, Ninian (1927–2000), 5n, 296n, 297n
Smith, Huston, 316n
Smith, Captain John, 63n
Smith, Jonathan Z., 6n, 8n, 10n, 108n, 109n
Smith, William Robertson (1846–94), 74n
Snyder, Gary, 279
Society for Biblical Literature (SBL), 7n
Society for the Scientific Study of Religion (SSSR), 7n
Söderblom, Nathan (1866–1931), 277n
Spencer, Herbert, 12
Stace, Walter T., 279
Stanley, Arthur Penrhyn (1815–81), 247
Steigmann-Gall, Richard, 302n
Stirling, James Hutchison (1820–1909), 277n
Styers, Randall, 19n
Suzuki, D. T. (1870–1966), 279

Tagore, Debendranath (1817–1905), 283, 287, 290
Tagore, Rabindranath (1861–1941), 290–91
Tieck, Ludwig (1773–1853), 154
Tiele, Cornelis Petrus (1830–1902): mentioned, 192, 195, 207; Gifford Lectures, 277; on distinction between world religions and national religions, 108–114, 117–18; on terminology "Aryan," 189n; participation in World's Parliament of Religions, 270–71; role in founding of science of religion, 107–8
Timpanaro, Sebastiano, 153n 156n
Tindal, Matthew, 103n
Tisdall, William St. Clair (1859–1928), 103
Todd, Jesse T., 302n
Toland, John (1670–1722), 49–51
Trautmann, Thomas R., 150n, 151n, 263n, 284–85, 286n
Troeltsch, Ernst (1865–1923), 309–27; "Christianity and the History of Religion" (1897), 204, 310–15, 318, 319; "The Place of Christianity among the World Religions" (1923), 29, 317–24; pluralist universalism of, 288n; view on Islam, 324n; importance placed on historical consciousness, 325–26; religious essentialist position of, 313–318; equation of Christendom and Europe, and its consequences, 320–23; view on primitive religions, 323
Turner, William (1653–1701): ambiguous classification of religions by, 57n; on variety of heathens, 60n, 122–23
Tylor, Edward Burnett (1832–1917), 12, 74n, 293; Gifford Lectures, 277n

Underhill, Evelyn (1875–1941), 74n

van der Leeuw, Gerardus, 313, 315
Vernes, Maurice (1845–1923), 107–108n, 292n
Veth, Pieter Johannes (1814–95), 195
Viswanathan, Gauri, 20n
Vivekananda (1863–1902), 263–64, 283, 287, 289
Vossius, Gerardus Joannes (1577–1649), 47n

Waardenburg, J. Jacques, 7n
Wagner, Richard, 255n
Wallerstein, Immanuel, 14–16, 180, 181n
Ward, Duren J. H. (1851–1942), 242n, 254n
Warren, William Fairfield (1833–1929), 45n, 119
Wasserstrom, Steven, 91n
Watts, Alan (1915–73), 279
Weber, Albrecht (1825–1901): view of Buddhism as a revolutionary movement, 136–37; as authority on India and Buddhism, 142; on Müller and Boden Professorship, 211
Weber, Max (1864–1920): Economic Ethic of the World Religions, 28, 204, 304n; relation to Troeltsch, 309; transformation of the category "world religions," 28, 204, 303–7
Wedgwood, Julia (1833–1913), 75n
Welby, Victoria, 262n

Whitney, William Dwight (1827–94), 211n

Widgery, Alban G., 40n

Wilkins, Charles (1749–1836), 157, 286n

Williams, Glyndwr, 181n, 311n

Wilson, H. H. (1786–1860), 156, 211

Wilson, John A., 300n

Windisch, Ernst (1844–1918), 250n

Wolf, Eric R., 181n

Woods, James Haughton, 103

Wordsworth, John, Bishop of Salisbury (1843–1911): comparative theology from evangelical standpoint, 99–101, 312; on the danger of comparison without religious conviction, 99, 316n; Bampton Lectures, 98–101

World's Parliament of Religions, 23, 27, 263, 265–74

Yerushalmi, Yosef Hayim, 4n

Yuyama, Akira, 254n

Zaehner, R. C. (1913–74), 3n, 40n, 277n

Zimmer, Heinrich (1890–1943), 279

Ziolkowski, Eric J., 267n

Zoroaster (Zarathustra), 48, 78, 90, 133, 190n, 263n